INTEGRATING COMPUTER TECHNOLOGY INTO THE CLASSROOM

Integrating Computer Technology into the Classroom

▶ **Gary R. Morrison**
Wayne State University

▶ **Deborah L. Lowther**
University of Memphis

▶ **Lisa DeMeulle**
Sonoma State University

Merrill,
an imprint of Prentice Hall
Upper Saddle River, New Jersey   Columbus, Ohio

Library of Congress Cataloging-in-Publication Data

Morrison, Gary R.
  Integrating computer technology into the classroom / Gary R.
Morrison, Deborah L. Lowther, Lisa DeMeulle.
      p.   cm.
  Includes bibliographical references and index.
  ISBN 0-13-270000-X
    1. Computer-assisted instruction.   2. Computer managed
instruction.   3. Computers—Study and teaching.   4. Instructional
systems—Design.   I. Lowther, Deborah, L.   II. DeMeulle, Lisa.
III. Title.
LB1028.5.M6373   1999
371.33′4—dc21   98-18778
                                                                              CIP

Editor: Debra A. Stollenwerk
Developmental Editor: Linda Scharp McElhiney
Production Editor: Mary Harlan
Design Coordinator: Diane C. Lorenzo
Text Design and Production Coordination: Elm Street Publishing Services, Inc.
Cover art: ©SuperStock
Cover Designer: Tom Mack
Production Manager: Pamela D. Bennett
Director of Marketing: Kevin Flanagan
Marketing Manager: Suzanne Stanton
Marketing Coordinator: Krista Groshong

This book was set in Sabon by The Clarinda Company and was printed and bound by
Courier/Westford. The cover was printed by Phoenix Color Corp.

 ©1999 by Prentice-Hall, Inc.
Simon & Schuster/A Viacom Company
Upper Saddle River, New Jersey 07458

Photo credits: All photos supplied by the authors.

Printed in the United States of America

10 9 8 7 6 5 4 3 2 1

ISBN: 0-13-270000-X

Prentice-Hall International (UK) Limited, *London*
Prentice-Hall of Australia Pty. Limited, *Sydney*
Prentice-Hall of Canada, Inc., *Toronto*
Prentice-Hall Hispanoamericana, S. A., *Mexico*
Prentice-Hall of India Private Limited, *New Delhi*
Prentice-Hall of Japan, Inc., *Tokyo*
Simon & Schuster Asia Pte. Ltd., *Singapore*
Editora Prentice-Hall do Brasil, Ltda., *Rio de Janeiro*

Dedication

*This book is dedicated to our children,
Jennifer, Keegan, Kenneth, Tina, Benjy, and Nicholas.*

▲▲▲

▶ PREFACE

The introduction of computers into the K–12 classroom has been exciting, but many educators would probably agree that we have not seen the results we anticipated. Most students today are still educated the same way students were a generation or two ago. Students are no more likely to sit in front of a computer for all their instruction than they would with one of Skinner's programmed learning machines. Why has the computer not revolutionized education as some scholars predicted?

We conducted an informal survey of teachers in 1996 and found that the most commonly used software in the classroom included games, drill-and-practice, and tutorials. If we were to survey the students' parents, we would probably find that they use spreadsheets to solve problems, manipulate databases to find patterns, send e-mail for communication, create reports with a word processor, and design multimedia presentations to sell their ideas at work. Individuals in the workplace are using computers as a tool while educators generally *tend* to think of computers as an instructional delivery device—something to replace the teacher, much like Skinner's teaching machine. This is interesting because if we asked why computers are being placed in the schools, the primary reason is to prepare students for the workforce—where, as mentioned earlier, computers are used as a tool.

OUR APPROACH

This book is about students using computers as a tool to solve problems as part of the learning process. We provide a rationale and model for integrating computer technology into your curriculum by using it as a tool rather than as an instructional delivery device.

This book presents an approach to creating an integrated inquiry lesson; however, we do not propose that it is the only way to teach. Instead, it is an alternative approach that stresses the student's use of the computer to solve real-world problems while learning rather than use of the computer as a delivery system.

The type of computer you have does not matter. All your students need is access to integrated software such as ClarisWorks, MicrosoftWorks, MicrosoftOffice, or individual applications for creating spreadsheets, databases, word processing, drawings, presentations, and Internet browsing. This book is written for the teacher who has *very basic* computer skills such as using a mouse; opening, creating, and saving documents; and using menus. The software is not as important as learning how to use the tool in a productive manner to solve problems. The software you use in your classroom will most likely change, and some programs will be replaced by more powerful software in a year or two. Because you and your students will know how to use word processing, databases, spreadsheets, and the Internet, however, the brand name and version will no longer matter.

Organization of This Text

Chapter 1 presents a rationale for rethinking the use of computers in the classroom, and Chapter 2 provides a basis for using technology as a tool. The next four chapters focus on the process of integrating computer technology into the curriculum. Chapter 3 provides a model you can use with almost any teaching approach to develop an integrated lesson. Chapter 4 describes the facilitation skills a teacher needs to create an open-ended learning environment. Chapter 5 covers how to manage the classroom when using an integrated lesson, and Chapter 6 discusses how to address the diverse needs of your learners. The next four chapters present information on how to develop an integrated lesson using each of the learning tools: word processing (Chapter 7), spreadsheets (Chapter 8), databases (Chapter 9), and drawing (Chapter 10). Chapter 11 describes how to publish the results of the investigation. The world beyond the classroom is the next focus with information on how to integrate the Internet into the lesson (Chapter 12) and how to search the Internet (Chapter 13). Our emphasis in the last chapters is on how the teacher can use the computer as a productivity tool to produce classroom materials (Chapter 14) and to manage classroom information (Chapter 15).

Features

Each chapter starts with a listing of the computer skills needed in the chapter and a brief listing of the topics. The chapters conclude with *At the Classroom's Doorstep*, which includes questions a teacher might ask about the chapter and answers to those questions. The sections on learning tools, the Internet, and teacher productivity all include detailed instructions on how to use the tools. The tool chapters also include ideas for lessons, specific instructions on how to use our model to develop an integrated lesson, an example lesson plan that integrates the tool into the lesson, and *Lesson Bytes,* which are ideas for integrated lessons.

Many of the chapters include one or more Power Tips, which provide step-by-step ideas for using the software or computer and a listing of valuable resources. Each chapter also includes Fran's Diary, reflections written by a school teacher (whose real name is Fran) with more than 20 years of experience. During the past five years, she has developed a number of integrated lesson plans to use with the five computers in her classroom and has described her successes and failures with computers in her diary. We have also provided a number of URLs for accessing web sites; however, these sites often change locations or suddenly drop from cyberspace. We have tried to identify locations that are resistant to "cyber rust."

We have created a web page to provide a variety of resources for this book: www.nteq.com

Sequence

The chapters in this book can be taught sequentially from Chapter 1 through Chapter 15, or you can sequence them in a manner that best suits your needs. For example, you might want to start with Chapters 14 and 15 to illustrate how teachers can benefit from the use of computers. Another approach is to start with either Chapters 7–10 to teach the software tools or Chapters 12–13 to introduce the Internet tools. You can then focus on Chapters 1–6, which center on the NTeQ model and teacher facilitation skills so that students can work independently or in groups to develop units or lessons.

It is important to note that our goal is not to have teachers integrate computers into every lesson but to integrate computers into lessons in a meaningful manner that enhances student learning. The line between various computer platforms grows fuzzier each day. Our focus in this book is not on developing basic computer literacy skills but on developing new methods for using computers in the classrooms. We have focused on the Macintosh version of ClarisWorks, but the applications and commands you use may be different. (Apple Computer made a decision after we completed this book to change the name of ClarisWorks to AppleWorks.) However, the overall process and goal of each chapter remain the same.

ACKNOWLEDGMENTS
▲▲▲

Most of the ideas for the lesson plans in this book were conceived or suggested by our colleagues and classroom teachers whom we want to thank for sharing. We would like to offer a special thanks to the Project SMART teachers, to Lynn Morrison, and to Dr. Richard Petersen, who gave us ideas and helped us develop some of the materials. Three people deserve a special thank you. First, we want to thank Dr. Katherine Abraham, the Project SMART director, who was always willing to provide us with ideas related to the math curriculum and help us with our spreadsheet and database problems. Second, we would like to thank Dr. Tom Buggey for his contributions on adaptive technology and its importance in creating equity for all learners in Chapter 6. Third, we want to thank Fran Clark, who not only helped us refine but also tested the NTeQ model in her third grade classroom. She documented her experiences in the Fran's Diary section that appears in each chapter.

As we developed this book, several of our graduate assistants provided feedback and used the manuscript in their courses. We would like to thank Robert Plants, Posey Saunders, John Ward, and Renée Weiss for their feedback and ideas.

We also want to thank our two editors, Debbie Stollenwerk and Linda Scharp McElhiney, who supported our ideas from the beginning and provided us with numerous suggestions for developing each chapter. We would also like to thank Martha Beyerlein, the project editor, who carefully guided us through the production process. Last, we want to thank the following reviewers who provided us with valuable ideas for improving this book: Gayle V. Davidson-Shivers, University of South Alabama; Leticia Ekhaml, State University of West Georgia; Lynne M. Pachnowski, University of Akron; Nancy H. Phillips, Lynchburg College; W. Michael Reed, West Virginia University; Gregory C. Sales, University of Minnesota; Edna B. Schack, Morehead State University; Markham B. Schack, Morehead State University; Penelope Semrau, California State University–Los Angeles; Neal Strudler, University of Nevada–Las Vegas; Robert Tennyson, University of Minnesota; Mary Tipton, Kansas State University; Nancy H. Vick, Longwood College; and Barbara Watson, Eastern Michigan University.

Gary R. Morrison
Deborah L. Lowther
Lisa DeMeulle

▶ About the Authors

Gary R. Morrison received his doctorate in instructional systems technology from Indiana University in 1977. Since then, he has worked as instructional designer at the University of Mid-America, Solar Turbines International, General Electric Company's Corporate Consulting Group, and Tenneco Oil Company. As a professor at the University of Memphis, he taught courses in instructional design and served as a faculty associate in the Center of Academic Excellence. Presently, he is a professor of instructional technology at Wayne State University, where he teaches courses in instructional design and distance learning. His credits include print projects, multimedia projects, and more than 30 hours of instructional video programs, including a five-part series that was aired nationally on PBS-affiliated stations. Dr. Morrison recently served as co-director of Project SMART, which focused on how to enhance science and math instruction through innovative uses of microcomputers.

Dr. Morrison has written more than 100 papers on topics related to instructional design and computer-based instruction and has contributed to several books and instructional software packages. He is co-author of *Designing Effective Instruction* with Jerold E. Kemp and Steven M. Ross. He is the associate editor of the research section of *Educational Technology Research and Development* and past president of AECT's Research and Theory Division.

Deborah L. Lowther received her Ph.D. in educational technology from Arizona State University. Prior to completing her doctoral work, she was a seventh-grade science teacher. She is currently an assistant professor in the Department of Instruction and Curriculum Leadership at the University of Memphis. Her area of concentration is instructional design and technology. She teaches courses primarily focused toward preparing inservice teachers to integrate computer technology into their curriculum. She also teaches courses that lead to state certification in instructional computing applications. Her research is centered on factors influencing the integration of technology into various learning environments.

Over the past two years, Dr. Lowther has been very involved with technology integration from the international to the local level. Her involvement includes conference presentations, co-guest editing a special edition (Technology in the K–12 Schools) of a national journal, working with three grants focused toward technology integration, providing professional development to K–12 schools in multiple states. She is also president of AECT's Research and Theory Division.

Lisa DeMeulle received her doctorate in educational psychology with an emphasis in teaching and learning from the University of California, Santa Barbara, in 1993. She was assistant professor of instruction and curriculum at the University of Memphis and is currently associate professor of educational technology at Sonoma State University. She teaches courses in action research, integrating the Internet into the curriculum, web publishing and multimedia presentations, and curriculum design and evaluation. In the last several years, Dr. DeMeulle has developed expertise in the integration of Internet technology into the curriculum. Her research in the area of using Internet technology for action research by teachers has appeared in journals such as *Teaching Education* and in the text *Reconceptualizing Practice: Self-Study in Teacher Education* published by Falmer Press. She was a co-author of Project SMART (Science and Math Radically Raised Through Technology), a three-year Eisenhower grant, which emphasized teacher professional development in technology integration. At the University of Memphis, she served two years as a university liaison with a professional development school, and she facilitated the Elementary Education Program. She was recognized for her work by the Association of Teacher Educators in 1995 when she received their Distinguished Research Award, and she was also an invited research fellow at the Center for Advanced Study in the Behavioral Sciences Summer Institute.

► Contents

CHAPTER 1

Rethinking Computers and Instruction

▶ Introduction

The United States has a history of introducing technology into the schools to solve educational problems (see Figure 1-1). Shortly after the launch of Sputnik in 1957, Congress passed the National Defense Education Act to improve science and math achievement in public schools. One aspect of this plan was to place an overhead projector in most if not all of the K–12 classrooms. In the 1960s we saw the introduction of both programmed instruction and educational television in the classroom. In the early 1980s we finally found some of the first microcomputers in the classroom. In the 1990s we are seeing state and federal initiatives to place more computer technology in the P–12 classrooms, the hope being that technology will again solve our educational problems. Although Bork (1987) predicted that microcomputers would revolutionize our schools, we have yet to see any major gains attributed to the infusion of this latest technology into the classroom. One reason the revolution has yet to start may be due to our conceptions of how we should use technology versus how we are using it.

▶ Key Topics

Conceptions of Technology
    The Use of Computers in Schools
    The Use of Computers in Business
Educational Reform and Technology
    Constructivism
    Open-Ended Learning Environments
    Learning Context
    Collaborative Learning
Starting the Revolution

Figure 1-1   Incoming Technology

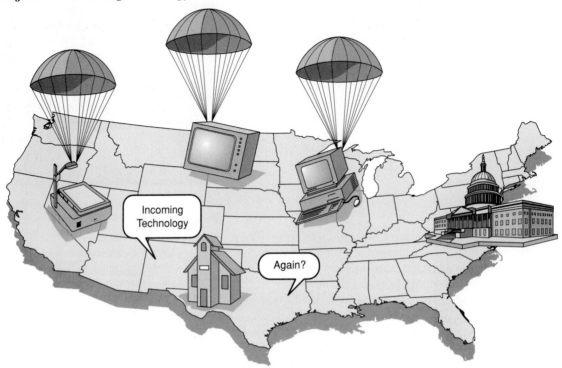

CONCEPTIONS OF TECHNOLOGY

▲▲▲

If you were to survey teachers on what type of software they use, what do you think they would say they use most often? Your results would probably reflect recent surveys (Becker, 1991) indicating computers were used most often for drill-and-practice, tutorials, and educational games. Let's examine these three types of software.

THE USE OF COMPUTERS IN SCHOOLS

Drill-and-practice software was quite common and readily available in the 1970s and 1980s and often mimicked flash cards. The computer would display a stimulus such as a math problem or foreign vocabulary word and the student would select an answer. The computer would provide some type of response ranging from a simple line of text indicating the correctness of the answer to eye-catching graphics and sounds. Sometimes, the displays for an incorrect answer were more intriguing than for a correct answer which lead students to purposefully select incorrect answers! Drill-and-practice software is not used to teach new information; rather, it reinforces existing knowledge, such as multiplication facts. While drill-and-practice software is an efficient way to achieve rote learning objectives, current educational trends question the value of rote learning promoted by this type of software.

Tutorials are another form of popular instructional software. These, however, attempt to teach the learner new information. Strategies used with tutorial software can range from a simple implementation of programmed instruction to a highly sophisticated application that allows for branching and adaptation to individual differences (see Figure 1-2). (Ross and Morrison, 1988) Some of the more advanced tutorials represent the more sophisticated approaches to individualizing instruction. For example, we can adapt the instruction to include personalized information (e.g., name, friend's or teacher's name) about the student to create a concrete problem (see Figure 1-2). Tutorials are still useful for introduction of new content and remediation; however, they typically do not provide a sophisticated context for exploration and experimentation.

Figure 1-2   Examples of Branching and Adaptive Software

Lesson 3

Converting Fractions
to Decimals

You may select from 2 to 10 practice examples.
Recommended Level: 7 Examples
Enter your selection (2-10):

You answered 12. It appears that you have
subtracted 3 from 15.

The problem is 15/3.

The / symbol is the division symbol.

Divide 15 by 3 and enter the answer. _____

Branching Example

Jamie had entered a contract with Mr. Keegan
to finish her work on time. She has earned 6
hours of free time from Mr. Keegan to paint.
She divides her free time into sessions of
3/4 hours. How many sessions will Jamie have
to paint?

Adaptive example from Ross & Anand (1987).

Educational games are often based on a drill-and-practice approach and usually provide an interesting theme such as solving a math problem to save the earth from an alien attack. Games are often a variation of drill-and-practice software, sometimes adding a time variable. Students must complete a task within a set amount of time to prevent a catastrophic event (such as an alien destroying the computer screen). The reward structures of the game may involve more graphic and sound displays than a typical drill-and-practice application. Students may also be able to achieve various levels of proficiency (e.g., first mate, co-pilot, pilot, etc.) to reflect their performance rather than a reporting of the number of correct items. Like drill-and-practice software, educational games often promote rote learning.

Technology has typically been viewed by educators as a means to *deliver* instruction to students. Lumsdaine (1964) characterized this view as Technology Type I that stresses the importance of teaching aids. This view assumes the technology of the *machine* is intimately associated with the technology of *teaching* (Davies, 1973). The overhead projectors placed in the classroom after the launch of Sputnik were seen as amplifying the teacher's message by projecting it on a screen. Similarly, educational television during the 1960s was seen as amplifying and extending the message of the master teacher.

In contrast to the overhead projector and television, we would classify computer-based instruction as Technology Type II that emphasizes *software* designed through the application of scientific principles. Lumsdaine (1964) provided programmed instruction as an example of this type of technology because it applied learning principles (e.g., shaping and reinforcement) to the design of the materials. Technology Type II *replaced* the teacher as opposed to amplifying the teacher's message.

Both types of technology emphasized the *delivery* of instruction using technology. This view of technology is best expressed by Thomas Edison who championed the motion picture by stating that anything a teacher could teach could be taught by film (Heinich, Molenda, Russell, & Smaldino, 1996).

THE USE OF COMPUTERS IN BUSINESS

We have seen that schools use computers to deliver instruction through games, drill-and-practice, and tutorial software. If we were to conduct a survey of the students' parents who use computers at work, we would most likely find that parents use computers differently. Computers are used as a *tool* to solve problems in the workplace. Professionals use applications such as spreadsheets, databases, word processing and graphics programs, desktop publishing tools, e-mail, and the Internet (Inks, 1997). The use and conceptualization of computers as tools in the workplace stands in stark contrast to an educator's view of computers as instructional delivery mechanisms.

Although we can find isolated examples of successful computer utilization in education, we have not seen the revolution in learning as predicted by Bork (1987). If we consider the effect of computers on our work culture, then we see a revolution that has affected everything from tracking an overnight Federal Express package via a telephone keypad as a computer interface, to the design of new computers with other computers, to creating corporate financial models to predict revenue. Could we start a revolution in education as predicted by Bork if we changed our conception of computers from a delivery mechanism to a tool?

EDUCATIONAL REFORM AND TECHNOLOGY
▲▲▲

Since the turn of the century, schools in the United States have operated on a factory model—their aim was to create obedient and competent workers for the many factories and industries that were a part of the industrial revolution. Thus, like factory workers, students sat individually in rows, completing their individual tasks, memorizing their work, and learning not to question but rather to obey authority. As the century continued, industry changed. Specialized workers with communication skills who could work as part of a team, think independently, and question the status quo were needed. Schools, however, have remained essentially unchanged since the early 1900s. Soon after the publication of *A Nation at Risk* (National Commission on Excellence in Education, 1983), educators, politicians, parents, and citizens began to look critically at the educational process which resulted in the current educational reform movement. These various reforms have taken many paths, but a consistent theme was to break from the more traditional factory models of education. One criticism of both the past and current reform movements is the lack of a relationship between educational reform and educational technology (Means, 1994). Educational reform and technology have developed innovative approaches to teaching. Restructuring in the schools, however, has often failed to consider the use of technology when designing new programs. Similarly, the technologists have often failed to consider the redesign of the school when implementing technology.

One reason for the lack of technology integration into the restructured schools may be attributed to both the way technology is used and the types of technology available. As previously mentioned, technology has typically been used to *deliver* instruction in the classroom. The most common type of software used in the classroom is drill-and-practice, which is based on a behavioral approach to teaching and emphasizes rote memorization (Becker, 1991). Both the approach to using technology and the software used are often inconsistent with the current reform approaches and current views of instruction. Today's educational reform is based on a constructivist approach (emphasizing student-centered learning in an open-ended environment) and is not usually supported by the traditional use of computer technology. Thus, it is not surprising that the reform movement has not successfully integrated the use of technology in the classroom.

Technology and a constructivist approach to education do not, however, need to be at odds with one another. If we change our view of computers from merely a means to deliver instruction to one of a tool to solve problems, then the reform movement can influence the use of technology, and technology can influence the reform of education.

Constructivism

Before considering how we might use technology as a tool, let's examine three basic premises of a constructivist learning environment. First, constructivism emphasizes understanding one's world rather than mimicking (i.e., rote memory) the content. Understanding is a result of the learner reshaping and transforming information (Gardner, 1991). Understanding one's world requires the student to actively process and manipulate information. Second, students will strive to reduce discrepancies between what they know and what they observe. Savery and Duffy (1995) refer to this phenomena as *puzzlement*. This cognitive dissonance between what the student knows and what is observed is a motivating factor for seeking resolution difference by developing a new understanding (Brooks & Brooks, 1993). Third, one's knowledge is refined through negotiations with others and evaluation of individual understandings (Savery & Duffy, 1995). Students use other students to test their understandings and examine the understandings of others. This collection of understandings provides a means for an individual to evaluate and understand propositions, which when grouped together are called *knowledge*. Collaborative groups allow a student to learn the views of others in order to challenge and test the viability of his or her own views. The constructivist teacher's main goal is to understand what and how students think.

In the following sections, we will examine the three components of a constructivist learning environment that form the basis of our approach to integrating computers into the curriculum. These three components are open-ended learning environments, learning context, and collaborative learning.

Open-Ended Learning Environments

One characteristic of a constructivist teaching approach is the use of open-ended learning environments. These environments often require students to solve a problem which exposes them to new information. As a result, students gain new understandings by reshaping and transforming their knowledge. Let's examine inquiry learning, guided design, and problem-based learning as ways of creating an open-ended learning environment.

Inquiry Learning.
The new social studies movement of the 1960s used a discovery approach to teaching students conceptual knowledge about the social sciences (Hertzberg, 1981). Teachers created inquiry units that required students to seek information in order to discover concepts and principles. As part of this process, students discovered new concepts (e.g., classifications) and relationships (e.g., principles) between the concepts. Although the instruction in an inquiry unit was carefully structured (Woolever & Scott, 1988), the units were student-centered and they encouraged students to ask questions and find the answers.

Guided Design.
Guided design was created to improve the teaching of engineering courses, but it has enjoyed success in many other disciplines (Wales & Stager, 1977). This teaching approach helped students gain knowledge and develop decision-making skills and values. Students typically worked in small groups on projects

Students discussing the best way to collect data.

using an approach similar to the scientific method to solve unstructured problems. Initially, each group received background information on the problem which could range from a single paragraph to rather elaborate packages of data. Once students identified the problem, they received a feedback sheet describing an expert's identification of the problem. There was no one right answer and students were encouraged to determine if they were following the process rather than evaluating the correctness of their answer. Information for the next step was also included with the feedback materials. This process of feedback and information guided the students' problem-solving process.

PROBLEM-BASED LEARNING. Another teaching methodology from the 1960s was problem-based learning that started in medical schools (Albanese & Mitchell, 1993). Problem-based learning (PBL) strategies have recently caught the attention of P–12 educators (Barrows & Kelson, 1996; Savery & Duffy, 1995) as a strategy consistent with a constructivist approach. PBL models the problem-solving approach experts use to solve real-world problems (Barrows & Kelson, 1996).

Barrows (1985) describes this approach as follows: Students are provided with the problem first, before they begin studying the material. Students must then think about what they know individually and collectively and what they need to learn to solve the problem. By determining what they need to know, the students develop knowledge structures based on problem-solving approaches rather than traditional subject matter approaches as presented in textbooks.

Like the inquiry approach, PBL is based on the use of the scientific method for gathering information, generating hypotheses, manipulating the data, testing hypotheses, and identifying a solution. Problems are designed to entice the learner into acquiring the knowledge and skills of a domain of knowledge (Barrows & Kelson, 1996). Students are motivated to learn new information they can use to solve problems. This approach fosters self-directed learning based on intrinsic rewards, such as finding a solution rather than an extrinsic reward, such as a score on a test.

FEATURES OF OPEN-ENDED LEARNING ENVIRONMENTS. The open-ended learning environments described focus on the learner by allowing the learner to make decisions about what information is needed and what approach should be taken to solve a problem. These environments stand in contrast to traditional instruction where content is selected and transmitted through lectures and assigned readings in textbooks. Each of these open-ended methods can also vary in the amount of structure and direction the teacher can provide (Albanese & Mitchell, 1993; Land & Hannafin, 1997). Direction from the teacher can range from providing specific tutoring or resources to coaching individual students on how to identify needed information.

Open-ended learning environments also require the teacher to adopt new approaches. The primary mode of teaching switches from one of lecturing to one of facilitating student investigation. Teachers work as facilitators and tutors to help students understand the material and to provide the necessary scaffolding. The emphasis is on the student developing an understanding of the material through direct contact with information, data collection, and data manipulation. Students then generate and test hypotheses and determine the best solution.

Selecting content for an open-ended learning unit is a process of negotiation involving input from students and knowledge of the curriculum frameworks. Teachers must consider standards imposed by the schools and recommended by their professional societies (e.g., National Council of Teachers of Mathematics) when designing the units. Similarly, students should have input based on their interests. The final objectives for the unit evolve from discussions between the teacher and students on how to address the needs expressed by society and the interests of the students.

Inquiry learning, guided design, and problem-based learning all use a problem-solving approach to acquire knowledge. Inquiry learning and guided design provide a more structured approach and thus are less student-centered than PBL. The PBL approach places more responsibility on the learner for solving the problem and acquiring the knowledge the *individual* needs to solve the problem. As a result, students using the PBL approach are more likely to have a better understanding of the problem and solution than students in an inquiry learning environment.

LEARNING CONTEXT

Traditional textbooks and instruction separate learning from the context. The effectiveness and appropriateness of this practice is now questioned by researchers (Brown, Collins, & Duguid, 1989). For example, a common time-distance math problem might appear as "It is 932 miles between Philadelphia and St. Louis. A car leaves Philadelphia at 8:00 A.M. headed west and is traveling at 65 miles per hour. A second car leaves St. Louis at 8:00 A.M. and is headed east traveling at 57 miles per hour. What time will they meet?" A logical answer is never, because the car from Philadelphia is headed to Chicago and the car from St. Louis is headed to Nashville! The "author" of this fictional problem (and others like it) intended both cars to take the same route and for the student to calculate when they would meet. Consider, however, a student who lives in Memphis or Houston and the probability that they have either traveled the route from St. Louis to Philadelphia, or if they have visited the two cities. For most students, the names of the two cities are just names or maybe names associated with a big McDonald's-type arch and the Liberty Bell.

A more appropriate problem and teaching example is one that provides a context the student can understand. Ross and his associates (Anand & Ross, 1987; Ross & Anand, 1987; Ross, McCormick, & Krisak, 1986) have found that providing a meaningful context for teaching significantly improves student achievement. In one study, each student's name, birthday, favorite candy, and friends' names were substituted into a word problem that required the student to determine how to divide a candy bar between four individuals. These substitutions provided a concrete context for the student to use in solving the problem. Brown et al. (1993) refer to this type of instructional context as *authentic learning*. When the knowledge is placed in a meaningful context for the learner, it is referred to as *situated cognition* (Brown et al.).

An appropriate context is a crucial factor for learning. When the knowledge the student needs to learn is placed within a meaningful context, the students can understand and construct a meaningful semantic network. As a result, students are better able to apply the knowledge in real-life situations (Kotovsky, Hayes, & Simon, 1984; Lajoie & Lesgold, 1988). Using our original word problem, students may have difficulty relating to the cities stated in the problem. However, if the problem uses cities with which the students are familiar, then the students can concentrate on solving the problem rather then trying to assign meaning to the two cities.

The Cognition and Technology Group at Vanderbilt (CTGV) has further refined the situated cognition construct and has developed example materials using anchored instruction (CTGV, 1990, 1991, 1992). They used video programs as anchors to provide a macrocontext for the learner. These macrocontexts provided a story scenario for a problem. For example, one video context to teach a time-distance problem created a situation where the characters had to rescue an injured eagle and transport the eagle to a veterinarian.

COLLABORATIVE LEARNING

Teachers and students today are required now more than ever to collaborate in their work. As reform movements push teachers toward site-based management, team planning, peer coaching, and community partnerships, we can no longer accept the notion of teacher as an isolated decision maker. Our evolving society requires citizens to have specialized skills. Employees must be able to work as part of a team, support a larger vision, and communicate and work effectively with others.

With an open environment, students collaboratively decide how to solve problems.

Thus, teachers are not only modeling collaboration in their own work, but they are also required to use instructional processes that facilitate collaboration and the development of social skills among their students.

THE SOCIAL NATURE OF LEARNING.   The social impact on learning has been discussed for centuries by scholars such as Aristotle, Dewey (1916), and Vygotsky (1978). While constructivists emphasize the self construction of meaning, it would be a misconception to believe that whatever an individual thinks is "the truth." Rather than prescribing to this form of relativism, constructivists support the notion of the self construction of meaning within a *social* context. As people attempt to find the meaning in an experience or encounter, they reflect on their beliefs, values, and concepts that all arise from a common and shared understanding within their culture. For example, a teacher who encounters an angry parent experiences her own emotions, feelings, and attitudes about the experience, but the labels she uses to make meaning of the experience, such as "anger," "misunderstanding," "reconciliation," are labels that have been socially constructed and are commonly understood by a larger culture. Her individual experience is thus mediated by larger social forces.

COOPERATION VERSUS TRADITIONAL GROUPWORK.   How can teachers effectively capitalize on the social nature of learning? Many educators are now taught to integrate small group learning into their pedagogy. However, as more teachers move toward the use of group learning such as dyads, triads, and cooperative learning, it is important to distinguish among features of teaching that promote coopera-

Table 1-1 Cooperative versus Traditional Groups

Cooperative Groups	Traditional Learning Groups
Heterogeneous	Homogeneous
Social skills emphasized	Social skills assumed
Task and group maintenance emphasized	Only task emphasized
Teacher observes and facilitates	Teacher ignores group functioning
Shared leadership and responsibility	One leader and self-responsibility
Interdependent	No interdependence

Adapted from Johnson & Johnson, 1984.

tion and the development of social skills and features of traditional groupwork (Table 1-1).

One of the main aims of cooperative learning is the promotion of social skills in conjunction with the academic task at hand (Johnson & Johnson, 1984). Rather than placing students in groups and expecting them to perform expertly as a team, students need to learn how to work as a team. In cooperative learning, teachers have students focus on social skills such as active listening, taking turns, and accepting responsibility for self and other group nemeses as a part of the instructional process. This focus is usually accomplished through processing—group discussion at the end a specific time period when the group talks about its social functioning (Johnson & Johnson, 1990; Joyce & Weil, 1996). For example, if a science teacher has required groups of students to complete a multimedia report, she might structure or scaffold the lesson in this way:

1. Groups decide report topics   →   process group functioning
2. Choose information sources   →   process group functioning
   and collect data
3. Collect information, create report,   →   process group functioning
   and present

The need for the development of group social skills is also necessary when integrating technology as a tool. A collaborative group is doomed for failure when given a task without appropriate teacher support to develop the necessary social and technical skills needed to complete the assignment. We have often seen group members passively sit while others work at the computer. Had the teacher required these groups to divide responsibilities and accept responsibility for one another, this type of problem might have been overcome. The use of technology in group work also provides the opportunity for students to educate one another. For example, if a student is unfamiliar with web browsers, the teacher might decide to assign that student the responsibility for locating web sites on a given topic with the support of a knowledgeable student sitting by his side as they work. The learners are empowered as they acquire new skills, and the student serving as coach becomes empowered through the opportunity to educate others.

Let us introduce Fran. Fran is an experienced elementary teacher who was one of the first in her district to have computers in her classroom. She was also the first teacher to use the model we describe in this textbook. In each chapter, Fran has provided us with an entry from her diary that describes her successes and failures while integrating computer technology into her classroom.

Fran's Diary

I have had a great deal of interest in computers for many years. Before training was available in my school, I took evening and summer computer classes at a local technical college where I learned word processing and desktop publishing. I became very excited about the possibilities of using a computer in the classroom, and was very interested in using the computer for creative writing applications. I talked my husband into letting me take his old computer and printer to school, and I used them to set up a creative writing center in my classroom. It was very successful and my students loved it! My only frustration was that I had twenty-five students and only one computer. It took a long time to complete projects and I sometimes felt that I was neglecting the other areas of the curriculum.

At the end of the year, I received four more computers. One of my student's mother was a bank executive, and through her help, the bank donated four very old computers to my classroom. All that these computers could be used for was word processing, as I did not have any other software. But I was excited! I was able to expand my creative writing program, and what took a week to accomplish could now be accomplished in a day.

Unfortunately, I was transferred to a new school the next year and I was not able to take the computers with me. At my new school, the school system was choosing teachers to become *technology teachers,* and I was chosen to be the technology teacher for my grade level. This selection meant that I would be given one computer and a printer for use in my classroom. I had a week of basic computer skills training during that summer. I received my computer when school began. I felt very fortunate as I now had two computers; a very old IBM and a brand new Macintosh. I continued to use them mainly for creative writing, but was able to use them in other curriculum areas as I now had access to all of the MECC software programs appropriate to my grade level. I used the computers for centers and rewards, but I felt that I should be doing something more with the computers.

That fall, the school system chose two technology teachers from each school to become Twenty-First Century teachers, and I was chosen to be in the first group. The state had funded money to put computers and technology into the classroom. As a Twenty-First Century teacher, I would now have a teaching station with an AV/CD-ROM Macintosh, large screen TV, color printer, and laser disc player computer; five student computer stations, a color printer; and access to a color scanner, video camera, and digital camera. Needless to say, I was thrilled and a little bit overwhelmed, as I had limited experience with these new peripherals.

I received another week of basic computer training before I received my computers. The training, however, did not focus on how to implement this technology into the curriculum. We had already received training on how to use the software applications! I was given the hardware, the software, and instructions on how to use the hardware, and then sent back to my classroom to figure out what to do with all of this. I was very frustrated. I felt that I had been forgotten and that it was going to be my responsibility to figure out how to use these computers. I spent many hours before and after school learning how to use the equipment, and I read everything that I could read about computers in the classroom.

I was getting my master's degree at this time and I devoted much of my study to trying to learn how to implement computer technology into the curriculum. During that summer, I heard about the NTeQ model and felt that this was what I had been looking for. Having a very brief introduction to the model from Dr. Morrison, I decided that this was the way that I should use the computers in my classroom. I told him that I was going to try it for one year and if I couldn't make it work, I was going to quit teaching.

I started the school year with a new plan. I was going to integrate technology into my classroom using a problem-based approach. At the parent orientation meeting, I told my students' parents that my classroom would be different from the other grade level classrooms because we would be doing a lot of our work on the computer. I also had to shut my door and ignore what was going on in the other classrooms. I could not do it *their* way anymore, and they could not do it my way. I jumped in and started developing thematic units based on the literature book and tried to use the computers as much as possible. It was not easy. I spent a lot of time preparing lesson plans and developing activities. I had good days and bad days. It was quite an adjustment for me and my students.

By the middle of the year, things had settled in and the students really liked coming to school. In fact, I probably had the best overall attendance in the school and my students' parents scheduled their children's doctor/dentist appointments during lunch so they wouldn't miss anything! At times, I felt like a symphony conductor—everyone was doing something different. I just hoped that all the parts would come together at the end when we took

Continued

our achievement tests. In my heart, I felt that my students had learned more than any other class that I had ever had . . . not only content, but also technology and interpersonal skills. We took our achievement tests that spring and as a class they did very well. In fact, their reading comprehension scores were very high.

At the end of the year I had them write letters to me to tell me how they felt about the school year. They all mentioned that they had learned a lot and had fun learning. One of the girls summed it up nicely. She wrote, "You are the best teacher there is! You taught us so much and we taught you a little bit. The computers are very helpful. Who could work without a computer? I know that the computer is a tool. Everyone does!" Did I go back the next year? You bet!

Starting the Revolution
▲▲▲

▶ *You say you want a revolution*
Well, you know
We all want to change the world . . .
"Revolution" by Lennon and McCartney

It has been over ten years since Bork (1987) made his prediction that computers would revolutionize the way students learn. We have yet to see computers have any major impact. Perhaps the revolution is ready to start now that we have a better understanding of how to use computers in the classroom for the following reasons:

1. After experimenting with computers in the classroom for some 20 years, we now know what does and does not work.
2. We are approaching the critical mass of computers in the classroom.
3. Teachers, administrators, politicians, and parents are ready for a new approach to using computers.
4. Current teaching practices emphasize using realistic contexts for learning.

First, after experimenting with computers in the classroom for some 20 years, we now know what works and what does not work. Using computers as a delivery device has not produced the results we expected. We predict that if we integrate computers into the curriculum as a tool for solving real-world problems, we will start a revolution that can affect how students learn. This shift in thinking about computers as a tool instead of a delivery mechanism is consistent with the use of computers outside of the classroom. Our focus will shift from the skill of just using a computer (e.g., keyboarding) to one of knowing not only how and when to use a computer, but how to use the computer to solve a problem. More importantly, the tool-using approach is consistent with the current constructivist approach in education. During the past 20 years, the primary mechanism driving the computer delivery approach has been a behavioral perspective which has often taken a passive approach to learning. Using computers as tools can help teachers create a student-centered learning environment. Students create an understanding of the world that will lead to the development of knowledge.

Second, we are approaching the critical mass of computers in the classroom. Today we see more computers in classrooms as opposed to only in computer labs. To use a computer lab, teachers have to schedule the lab in advance and move the class between rooms (Pruett, Morrison, Dietrich, & Smith, 1993). These labs are not always available and might require scheduling several weeks in advance. This lack of easy access makes it difficult to plan a lesson integrating computers. In addition, the focus is on computer literacy and computer-based instruction (Lowther, Bassoppo-Moyo, & Morrison, 1998). As a result, computer labs encourage the use of computers as delivery mechanisms. Placing computers in the classroom, where they are readily available throughout the school day, allows students to use them as a tool. Consider the effect of a school that *only* allowed students to use a pencil and paper in the school cafeteria. In addition, only one class could use the cafeteria at a time. Teachers would probably have a difficult time trying to use paper and pencils in their lesson plans. A typical trip to the "cafeteria writing lab" might result in nothing more than drawing some pictures or copying some letters or words. When students are allowed to use pencil and paper in the classroom at any time, they can use them as tools. Similarly, when computers are readily available in the classroom, teachers can take a different approach to integrating them into a lesson.

Third, teachers, administrators, politicians, and parents are ready for a new approach to using computers. Schools, states, and the federal government have invested a great deal of money in hardware and software without seeing revolutionary changes in student learning. Changing our approach from one of a delivery mechanism to one of computers as tools allows for better integration of computers into the curriculum and the development of real-life skills and knowledge. There is currently little economic need for a student who has progressed to the sixth level of destroying alien ships. There is, however, a need for a student who knows when and how to use a computer to solve problems.

Fourth, current teaching practices emphasize using realistic contexts for learning. Using computers as tools provides both support and a means of extending this practice. Students can apply solutions used in the real world to analyze and manipulate real-world problems. Today's microcomputers and Internet access allow teachers and students to extend problems and search for answers beyond the classroom, community, state, and nation.

Our focus in the following chapters is to illustrate how to combine an open-ended learning environment with using computers as a tool to create a new approach to integrating computers in the classroom.

At the Classroom's Doorstep

▲▲▲
Questions Teachers Ask

Must I use a problem-based learning approach in my classroom to use computers as a tool? No, you do not need to use a problem-based learning approach. We have found that integrating computers as a tool works best in an open-ended environment. The most common approaches to creating this type of learning environment is some form of problem-based learning, inquiry, or guided design. The approach presented in this text is flexible and will allow teachers to adapt it to their own teaching style.

Can I still use tutorials and drill-and-practice software? Yes, there is a place for computer-based instruction (CBI) if it is used appropriately. CBI is most useful when it supports the scaffolding the students need to solve a problem. Thus, you need to carefully select applications that support your objectives for the unit.

Won't I have to spend a great deal of time to develop these units of instruction? It does take some time and effort to develop an integrated computer lesson. Many times you can adapt a unit you are currently using, or you might work with a group of teachers in the same grade level or closely grouped grades. The payback in developing one of these units comes from using it more than one time. It will take less effort to implement the unit each time you use it. Starting with the second use, you should be able to focus on minor modifications to strengthen the lesson.

References
▲▲▲

Albanese, M. A. & Mitchell, S. (1993). Problem-based learning: A review of the literature on its outcomes and implementation issues. *Academic Medicine, 68*, 52–81.

Anand, P., & Ross, S. M. (1987). Using computer-assisted instruction to personalize math learning materials for elementary school children. *Journal of Educational Psychology, 79*, 72–77.

Barrows, H. S. (1985). *How to design a problem-based curriculum for the preclinical years.* New York: Springer Publishing Company.

Barrows, H. S. & Kelson, A. M. (1996). Problem-based learning: A total approach to education. Unpublished monograph. Springfield, IL: Southern Illinois School of Medicine.

Becker, H. J. (1991). How computers are used in United States schools: Basic data from the 1989 I.E.A. computers in education survey. *Journal of Educational Computing Research, 7*, 385–406.

Bork, A. (1987). *Learning with personal computers.* New York: Harper & Row, Publishers.

Brooks, J. G. & Brooks, M. G. (1993). *In search of understanding: The case for constructivist classrooms.* Alexandria, VA: Association for Supervision and Curriculum Development.

Brown, A. L., Ash, D., Rutherford, M., Nakagawa, K., Gordon, A., & Campione, J. C. (1993). Distributed expertise in the classroom. In G. Salomon (Ed.), *Distributed Cognition,* (pp. 47–87). New York: Cambridge University Press.

Brown, J. S., Collins, A., & Duguid, P. (1989). Situated cognition and the culture of learning. *Educational Researcher, 18*, 32–42.

Cognition and Technology Group at Vanderbilt (1990). Anchored instruction and its relationship to situated cognition. *Educational Researcher, 19*, 2–10.

Cognition and Technology Group at Vanderbilt (1991). Technology and the design of generative learning environments. *Educational Technology, 31*, 34–40.

Cognition and Technology Group at Vanderbilt (1992). The Jasper series an example of anchored instruction: Theory, program description, and assessment data. *Educational Psychologist, 27,* 291–315.

Davies, I. K. (1973). *Competency based learning: Technology, management, and design.* New York: McGraw-Hill Book Company.

Dewey, J. (1916). *Democracy and education.* New York: Macmillan.

Gardner, H. (1991). *The unschooled mind: How children think and how schools should teach.* New York: Basic Books.

Heinich, R., Molenda, M., Russell, J. D., & Smaldino, S. E. (1996). *Instructional media and technologies for learning.* Columbus, OH: Merrill.

Hertzberg, H. (1981). *Social Studies Reform, 1880–1980* (A Project SPAN Report). Boulder, CO: Social Science Education Consortium.

Inks, S. A. (1997). *Understanding the factors affecting salesperson acceptance of sales force automation implementation: An investigation of sales force change.* Unpublished doctoral dissertation, University of Memphis, Memphis.

Johnson, D. W. & Johnson, R. T. (1984). *The new circles of learning.* Englewood Cliffs, NJ: Prentice Hall.

Joyce, B. R. & Weil, M. (1996). *Models of teaching.* Needham Heights, MA: Simon & Schuster.

Kotovsky, K., Hayes, J. R., & Simon, H. A. (1984). Why are some problems hard? Evidence from Tower of Hanoi. *Cognitive Psychology, 17,* 248–294.

Lajoie, S. P., & Lesgold, A. (1988). Conceptual transfer in simple insight problems. *Memory & Cognition, 16,* 36–44.

Land, S. M. & Hannafin, M. J. (1997). Patterns of understanding with open-ended learning environments: A qualitative study. *Educational Technology Research & Development, 45,* 47–73.

Lowther, D. L., Bassoppo-Moyo, T., & Morrison, G. R. (1998). Moving from computer literate to technological competent: The next educational reform. *Computers and Human Behavior, 14,* 93–109.

Lumsdaine, A. A. (1964). Educational technology: Issues and problems. In P. C. Lange (Ed.), *Programmed instruction: the sixty-sixth yearbook of the National Society for the Study of Education.* Chicago: National Society for the Study of Education.

Means, B. (1994). Introduction: Using technology to advance educational goals. In B. Means (Ed.), *Technology and educational reform* (pp. 1–21). San Francisco: Josey-Bass Inc., Publishers.

National Commission on Excellence in Education (1983). *A nation at risk: The imperative for educational reform.* Washington, D.C.: Decision Resources Corporation.

Pruett, P. L, Morrison, G. R., Dietrich, A. P., & Smith, L. J. (1993). Integration of the microcomputer into the mathematics classroom. *Computers and Human Behavior, 9,* 17–26.

Ross, S. M. & Anand, P. (1987). Computer-based strategy for personalizing verbal problems in teaching mathematics. *Educational Communication and Technology Journal, 35,* 151–162.

Ross, S. M., McCormick, D., & Krisak, N. (1986). Adapting the thematic context of mathematical problems to student interests: Individual versus group-based strategies. *Journal of Educational Research, 79,* 245–252.

Ross, S. M. & Morrison, G. R. (1988). Adapting instruction to learner performance and background variables. In D. Jonassen (Ed.), *Instructional Designs for Microcomputer Courseware.* (pp. 227–245). Hillsdale, NJ: Lawrence Erlbaum Associates, Publishers.

Savery, J. R. & Duffy, T. M. (1995). Problem-based learning: An instructional model and its constructivist framework. *Educational Technology, 45,* 31–38.

Vygotsky, L. (1978). *Mind in society.* Cambridge, MA: Harvard University Press.

Wales, C. E. & Stager, R. A. (1977). *Guided design.* Morgantown, WV: West Virginia University.

Woolever, R. & Scott, K. P. (1988). *Active learning in social studies: promoting cognitive and social growth.* Glenview, IL: Scott, Foresman and Company.

CHAPTER 2

iNtegrating Technology for inQuiry: The NTeQ Model

▶ Introduction

The primary purpose of this book is to provide teachers with the knowledge and skills they need to successfully integrate the use of computers into their curriculum. As seen in Chapter 1, successful integration involves having students use the computer as a tool rather than a delivery system for drill-and-practice of basic skills. When the computer is integrated as a tool, students apply the same skills used in the workplace to analyze and manipulate information. By using the computer in this manner, students not only learn lesson objectives but also develop real-life knowledge and skills. This type of integration supports the current teaching practices which emphasize an open-ended learning environment that uses realistic contexts for learning. The iNtegrating Technology for inQuiry (NTeQ, pronounced "in-tech") model provides a framework for creating this type of environment.

The NTeQ model approaches the creation of the open-ended learning environment by examining the roles of the teacher, the student, the computer, the lesson, and the environment itself. The first section of this chapter is a scenario of the NTeQ model being implemented in a classroom. The remaining sections provide a detailed description of the model's components.

▶ Key Topics

NTeQ in the Classroom
NTeQ Philosophy
   NTeQ and the Teacher
   NTeQ and the Student
   NTeQ and the Computer
   NTeQ and the Lesson
   NTeQ and the Multidimensional
     Environment

NTeQ in the Classroom

▲▲▲

Perhaps one of the best ways to introduce you to the iNtegrating Technology for inQuiry (NTeQ) model is to take you into a sixth-grade classroom that is beginning a math lesson using the NTeQ model. The scenario will be followed by a discussion of the various components of the model.

Mr. Carter begins today's math lesson by placing the following problem on the large-screen monitor. "You have been given $50 to buy a some groceries for your family. You have to buy everything that is on the grocery list from one store that has an advertisement in today's paper. To help save money, you can buy store brands, and you can use three special coupons for each store: two for one, 15% off the regular price, and save 75¢ when you buy two. You may want to shop carefully, because you get to keep any money that is left over." He tells the students that they will be working in groups of three to find the most economical store. The group that has the lowest grocery bill will receive 15 bonus points for the class field trip.

Mr. Carter uses a Know/Want/Learned (KWL) chart to find out what the students know about the problem, and what they want to learn. This helps him guide the students' thinking as they begin to define the problem. Following is a chart with possible student responses.

What Do We Know?	What Do We Want to Know?	What Have We Learned?
We have $50.	How much can we save?	
We can use the three special coupons.	Which store will have the best prices?	
We can buy store brands.	How do we set up the spreadsheet?	
We must stay in one store.	What is the best way to use the coupons?	
We get to keep any leftover money.		
We can only use information in today's paper.		

After the first two columns of the KWL chart are filled in, Mr. Carter divides the class into groups of three students and assigns each group to a computer. His class has five computers for 30 students, so he assigns one computer to two

Figure 2-1   Computer Groups and Schedule

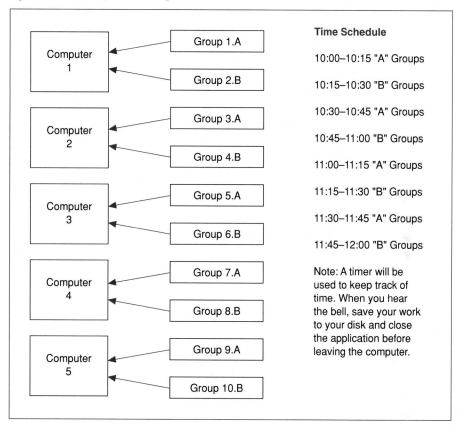

groups. For this lesson, he has created a 15-minute rotating schedule (see Figure 2-1).

A member of each group then gets the following materials from the resource table: today's newspaper, several grocery list recording sheets, special coupons, Think Sheet 1, and a computer disk with the spreadsheet template (grocery list is added, but students need to add the correct formulas). Mr. Carter then asks each group to spend five minutes browsing through the resources to get an idea of how the results might turn out. After five minutes, he has each individual student answer the questions on Think Sheet 1:

- What will be the easiest part of this assignment?
- What will be the most difficult part of this assignment?
- How much money do you think your group will save?

Each group then creates a "Define and Assign" sheet to determine which tasks need to be completed and who will complete them. A sample sheet is seen here:

GROUP 7 DEFINE	GLORIA, ROBERT, RENÉE ASSIGN
Locate grocery stores ads	everyone
Complete price list for each store	divide evenly
Enter data in spreadsheet	each student enters his/her list
Determine formulas	everyone
Add formulas to spreadsheet	Gloria
Experiment with coupon savings	everyone
Word process draft of report	Robert
Edit report	Renée
Word process final report	Gloria

After the assignments are made, each group begins to complete the tasks. Mr. Carter circulates among the groups to see how each one is progressing. He asks questions to guide their actions and thinking. For example, What would happen if you purchased two of the smaller items rather than the large size? Why did you decide to use your 15% off coupon to buy your milk rather than eggs? Is there anything else your group could do to make your time at the computer more efficient? Is there a simpler way to write your spreadsheet formula?

As each group finishes their report, they add their results to a class list that contains the group number, store with best prices, and amount of money spent. When all groups have added their data, Mr. Carter gives each student Think Sheet 2 with these items to address individually:

Look at your answers on Think Sheet 1 to answer these questions.

- Was the easiest task as easy as you thought it would be?

  ☐ Yes   ☐ No

  Please explain your answer.

- Was the most difficult task as difficult as you thought it would be?

  ☐ Yes   ☐ No

  Please explain your answer.

- What is the difference between the amount of money you predicted your group would save and the amount that was actually saved?

- What was the most surprising thing about the class results?

The students are then placed into five groups, based on computer assignments. In these groups, the students review Think Sheet responses and decide which ones they would like to share with the class and who will report the findings. Mr. Carter facilitates the final presentations by encouraging students to make comments and ask questions of each other. Mr. Carter also participates by asking probing questions. For example, How would the results change if store brands were not used? What would happen if you could go to more than one store? The discussion ends with, What would you change about this lesson? The final aspect of the lesson is for the students to answer the last column of the KWL chart to verify what they have learned.

This scenario demonstrates how the NTeQ model can be applied in a classroom. This chapter provides the basic philosophy underlying the NTeQ model and examines each of the model's major components: the teacher, the student, the computer, the lesson, and the multidimensional environment.

NTeQ Philosophy

Five basic components comprise the NTeQ philosophy: the teacher, the student, the computer, the lesson and the multidimensional environment. When the NTeQ model is successfully implemented:

- the teacher is technologically competent and assumes the roles of designer, manager, and facilitator (Lowther, Bassoppo-Moyo, & Morrison, in press).
- the student actively engages in the learning process, assumes the role of a researcher, and becomes technologically competent.
- the computer is used as a tool, as it is in the workplace, to enhance learning through the use of real-world data and problems.
- the lesson is student-centered, problem-based, and authentic, and technology is an integral component.
- the environment incorporates multiple, resource-rich activities.

NTeQ and the Teacher

As computers become increasingly available to students, teachers obviously need to know how to use the computers. As a result, teachers attend workshops and seminars to learn the basics of how a computer works. Many times this training includes the history of computers, computer terminology, and how to use basic programs such as word processing, Internet browsers, and e-mail. It is assumed that if teachers learn how to use these common applications or become computer literate, then they will be able to integrate technology into their lessons. Yet many teachers who have attended the basic literacy sessions often let the computers sit idly at the back of the classroom, or have students use them for simple drill-and-practice or educational games (Durham, Morrison, & Ross, 1995).

Fran's Diary
▲▲▲

When I first got my computers I used them mainly for word processing activities. I felt very secure and comfortable using the word processing application. My students wrote paragraphs, reports, and books. They always enjoyed these activities and, for the most part, I was satisfied with their final products. As I learned more of the applications, I was able to begin using the computer as a tool for me. I began to make the connection that if the computer could be a tool for me, it could also be a learning tool for my students. Unfortunately, I didn't know how to help my students learn to use the computer as a tool. I didn't know how to integrate this technology into the curriculum.

As I learned new applications, my comfort level expanded and I tried a few very simple spreadsheet and database activities. The students loved them. Although these activities were motivating, I wasn't sure that they were actually helping my students learn. I wasn't satisfied. I knew that I needed to know more.

We propose that teachers need to go beyond computer literacy to become technologically competent. Several things need to happen for this to occur.

- Teachers need to experience using the computer as a tool to learn new information.
- Teachers need to understand the relationship between basic computer functions and student learning.
- Teachers need to use their knowledge of student learning and technology to design, manage, and facilitate a student-centered, multidimensional learning environment.

Teachers need to experience using the computer as a tool to learn new information. Most people have spent the majority of their academic lives in a traditional classroom. In this setting, the teacher typically lectured while the students listened and sometimes took notes. Classroom activities included answering questions at the back of the book or on a worksheet, copying diagrams from books, drawing pictures, writing stories, doing science activities, and taking quizzes. So, when we ask teachers to assume the new role of a facilitator and to create lessons that integrate the use of technology as a tool, they have little if any prior experience to draw upon. Therefore, it is imperative for teachers to experience learning activities similar to those of their students. This simulation of a student activity will not only let the teachers experience the benefits of using technology to enhance learning, but it will also let them encounter some of the frustrations that tend to arise when computers are used.

For example, we begin one of our graduate classes by having the teachers assume the role of third grade students for a lesson named, What shape are you? (adapted from "Are you a square?", 1986). The purpose of the lesson is to teach metric system measuring skills, to practice estimations, and to collect and analyze data. The lesson involves teachers estimating their height and arm span in centimeters, then using meter sticks to measure the actual height and arm span of their group members. This information is used to determine their shape (square: height = arm span; rectangle: height > arm span; far-reaching rectangle: arm span > height). The teachers enter the estimated and actual height and arm span measurements into a class database. (They are taught how to create this simple database during this lesson.) After the data are entered, the teachers use the Sort feature of the database to answer questions similar to the following: What shape is most common in girls? Who had the best estimate of their height? Arm span? Who was the tallest rectangle? After this experience, the class was able to generate numerous examples of how they could integrate databases as a tool in their lesson plans.

Teachers need to understand the relationship between basic computer functions and student learning.
Teachers typically learn how to use basic computer applications such as creating a test with word processing, a spreadsheet grade book, or a database with student names, addresses, test scores, and favorite snack food. However, they do not learn how to analyze the actual computer functions to determine how these functions can help students learn.

An analysis of a database will reveal that it can sort, match, find, and group sets of information. The next logical step, then, is to determine how students can use sorting, matching, finding, and grouping sets of information to achieve one or more lesson objectives. For example, in a traditional lesson studying endangered species, students might learn which animals are endangered, where they live, what they eat, and why they are endangered by reading, completing worksheets, and writing a report on an animal of their choice. If teachers realize that students can place the endangered species information into a database, the students can then discover some of the common elements or patterns that exist. Students could manipulate the data in numerous ways, such as by sorting where the animals live or what they eat or why they are endangered. As students work with the data, patterns begin to emerge, giving rise to new questions and new ways to look at the data. Students can also identify other information to add to the database. By having the students use a database to examine the information rather than fill in blanks on a worksheet or answer questions from the back of a book, they not only learn the information, but they manipulate the data (e.g., sort or match records) to solve problems or discover new information.

Teachers need to use their knowledge of student learning and technology to design, facilitate, and manage a student-centered, multidimensional learning environment.
Once teachers understand the basic computer functions, they can combine this understanding with what they know about how students learn to create an environment that integrates technology to enhance learning. Generating the *design* is the first step (see Chapter 3). When the teacher assumes the role of a de-

signer, each aspect of the lesson has to be considered and carefully arranged to support and foster meaningful student learning.

As the teacher designs the lesson, she will need to specify the objectives, match the objectives to computer functions, and identify a problem the students will be solving (e.g., "What Shape are You?" or "Given $50 to buy a list of groceries, how much money can your group save?"). She will also need to determine how the students will manipulate the information or data, and how they will present their results. The teacher must carefully plan what the students need to do before they go to the computer, what they will do at the computer, and what they will do with the computer-generated materials. In addition, teachers must plan noncomputer activities that support the achievement of the lesson objectives. All of the classroom activities need to support the students' acquisition of the learning outcomes. Check the activities by asking the following question for each one: "What are the students going to learn from completing this activity?" By asking this question, busy work that is related to the lesson topic, but not meaningful, will be avoided.

The next step in creating the learning environment involves the teacher assuming the role of a *facilitator* (see Chapter 4). In a traditional classroom, the teacher provides the students with what they are to learn, typically with a lecture. The facilitator process is different because a facilitator does not tell the students the information they need to learn but rather provides a resource-rich environment through which she guides the students into learning. In this environment, the students work collaboratively to learn or "solve a problem." The teacher as facilitator keeps a close watch on the progress of each group and asks directed questions to stimulate student thinking and decision making. For example, Mr. Carter asked, "Why did you decide to use your 15% off coupon to buy milk rather than eggs?" or "Is there a simpler way to write your spreadsheet formula?"

Facilitation also involves teachers modeling different processes for the students. This modeling can include both physical processes, such as how to create fields in a database, and cognitive processes, such as describing each step the teacher might take to solve a problem. For example, the teacher might say the following to a group of students who were having trouble beginning an assignment. "If I were given this same problem, I would probably start by writing down all of the key parts of the problem. Next, I would list all of the resources that were available. After that, I would just brainstorm and write down all of the solutions I could think of, even if they were unreasonable. Once I had the list, I would start evaluating each one to find the best solutions."

Facilitation also assures students receive the necessary scaffolding or remediation to proceed with the lesson (Vygotsky, 1978). For students to complete the grocery list lesson, they need to already know how to add and subtract numbers and how to calculate percentages. If, however, there are a few students who need some calculation practice, the teacher must make sure that they receive the information and practice they need to go on with the lesson. This practice could take the form of computer-based instruction where a specific module helps students calculate percentages or practice sheets that provide step-by-step guidance, one-on-one tutoring, or direct instruction.

The last step to creating the environment is *management* (see Chapter 5). This aspect not only involves planning, but also the actual management of a classroom that now has several computers. The lesson plan depicts what the students need to do before they go to the computer, what they do at the computer, and what they do after finishing with the computer. However, the lesson plan does not designate how or when they will rotate to and from the computers. As you can see from Mr. Carter's lesson plan, this rotation process can be rather involved, and it takes practice for the students to learn. As the management plan is developed, it is again important to keep it as instructionally sound as possible by keeping student learning as the primary focus. It is also important to address equity issues to assure that *all* students participate in computer activities. For example, if students are working in pairs at the computer, they should rotate who is using the keyboard on a regular basis (e.g., every ten minutes).

Another way to plan for managing a technology-based lesson is for the teacher to actually use the software to create a product similar to what the students will produce during the lesson. This activity not only gives him the expertise to handle student problems as they arise, it also ensures that the lesson can be completed. The management plan also needs to include procedures for addressing two technology-related issues: lack of student computer skills and technical problems. The use of job aides (simple instruction sheets posted in the computer area) can help, and teachers can employ the assistance of the students who are "computer experts." It won't take long before the teacher learns how to solve some of the common computer glitches that seem to occur on a regular basis (e.g., how to reboot a computer, check cable connections, install software, and locate files that have been saved to the wrong places).

With the NTeQ model, teachers themselves gain technological competence. They create a learning environment where students use technology to enhance their learning in a way similar to what they will use in the workforce.

NTeQ and the Student

When examining the role of students in relation to the NTeQ model, we find the students are impacted in three important ways:

- the student is actively engaged in the learning process.
- the student assumes the role of a researcher.
- the student becomes technologically competent.

The student is actively engaged in the learning process. Students involved in a lesson based on the NTeQ model spend very little time, if any at all, sitting quietly at their desks while they take notes on the teacher's lecture. They also very rarely, if ever, answer the chapter questions in their history or science books. The students instead, are very involved in a learning environment that has small groups of students collaboratively solving problems using real-life resources. This approach is seen in the scenario of Mr. Carter's class presented earlier in this chapter. If he were not using the NTeQ model, he could have used word problems to teach his stu-

A small group of students using the computer as a tool.

dents about working within a budget. For example, "Mrs. Smith has $50 and needs to buy the items on her grocery list. She wants to save as much money as possible. Should Mrs. Smith go to Grocery Store A or Grocery Store B?" He also could have given his students a worksheet with percent problems such as: If Sally bought a pair of $35 shoes that had a 15% discount, how much would she save? Students working individually, answering word or math problems on a work sheet does not reflect a real-life setting. The learning environment created by Mr. Carter, however, had the students actively engaged in a simulation of what actually happens when grocery shopping. The students used actual advertisements from the newspaper and had the option of using coupons to enhance their savings. Students also worked in collaborative groups, in this case simulating what might happen in a family or with roommates. This type of active engagement and discussion with peers reinforces what is being learned by giving students the opportunity to apply their knowledge.

The student assumes the role of a researcher. The inquiry approach taken with the NTeQ model places students in the role of researchers. The students are not merely given the information they have to learn, but instead they are given situations they must investigate. During the investigation, or problem-solving process, the students work collaboratively to solve the problem which leads to learning the appropriate concepts and principles. In order for the students to solve the situation or problem, they must use the techniques of a researcher, or the scientific method: identify the problem, formulate a hypothesis, collect and analyze data, and draw conclusions. The students in Mr. Carter's class completed all of these steps, as the following shows:

Identify the problem	Determine which store has the best prices (with the use of three discount coupons) for a particular list of groceries.
Formulate a hypothesis	Save-A-Lot will have the best prices
Collect data	Record prices from advertisements
Analyze data	Use computer to calculate totals and best places to use the discount coupons
Draw conclusions	Piggly Wiggly (with the use of three discount coupons) had the best prices

The student becomes technologically competent. When students are given the opportunity to learn in an environment that is based on the NTeQ model, they will begin to become technologically competent. Technological competence means the student:

- is a capable user of the basic computer applications often found in the workplace, such as word processing, database, spreadsheet, draw, Internet browser, e-mail, and presentation.
- understands the capabilities of each type of computer application and when and where it is appropriate to use each one.

This technological competence will enable students to not only attain more from their K–12 and post-secondary education, but it will benefit them throughout their future careers.

NTeQ and the Computer

The role of the computer in the NTeQ model is somewhat different because it is seen from two different vantage points: the computer is not the point of emphasis, yet it is a critical component. The computer is not what the students learn about. For example, there is no emphasis on learning the history of computers, the electronic functions of a computer, or a glossary of computer terms. For example, we have several business colleagues who know very little about how computers operate or even common computer terminology. Yet, they use computers all day long to solve complex financial problems for major corporations.

We view the computer as a learning tool, similar to a calculator. When calculators were introduced into the classroom, students were not expected to learn the history of calculators, or how the electronic circuitry enabled the calculator to function. Instead, students were shown the basics of how a calculator could assist them in solving math problems. The computer should be viewed in the same manner. It is a tool that can help students look at information in new and different ways.

The computer is used as an extension of what the students are able to do for themselves because computer functions closely align with students' abilities. The computer, however, is more efficient in performing these functions (see Appendix A for a list of computer functions aligned to learning tasks). Students, then, can place a greater emphasis on discovering new ideas than on sorting and classifying data.

For example, students in Mr. Carter's class could have done the grocery lesson without a computer, but it would have taken a tremendous amount of time for the students to experiment with differently priced items or where to use the discount coupons. With the use of a spreadsheet, the students can quickly and accurately experiment with the information to reach the best solution. The students studying the endangered species could have placed their information on note cards rather than in a database. When looking at various sets of data (e.g., all the reptiles who eat plants and live in Europe), though, it would take more time for students to gather this information from note cards. With the database, it could be done within a few minutes. Students are then free to focus on the why, what, and where questions which can help them discover relevant principles.

Because the NTeQ model closely aligns what the students are learning to the functions of a computer, the computer becomes an integral part of the lesson. The students must use the computer to answer the questions in an efficient and effective manner. After students have used computers in this manner, *they* begin to ask the teacher if they can use the computer. They start to realize that the information they are learning is more meaningful if they can categorize it and place it into a database. Students may express an interest in composing their reports with a word processor because they can import bar graphs to support their results, or clip art to add meaning to what they have written. In other words, each student begins to recognize that the computer is an integral part of his or her learning process.

NTeQ and the Lesson

The NTeQ lesson is composed of ten major components (see Figure 2-2). The components fit together to create lessons that are student-centered, problem-based, authentic, and dependent upon the integration of technology.

The lessons are designed to keep the students actively involved in the learning process. With the students playing a greater role in the classroom, the teacher assumes the role of facilitator and guide. The lessons are also formulated around

Figure 2-2   NTeQ Lesson Plan Model

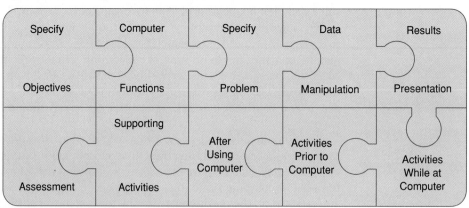

problems that are embedded in a context that is meaningful and authentic for the students. This context is created by incorporating the use of real resources that the students gather themselves. For example, the students use real newspaper advertisements for the grocery problem, they use their actual height and arm measurements for the "What shape are you?" lesson, and they use information they collected from the Internet for the endangered species lesson. This data gathering and/or manipulation makes the information something that is real and more meaningful than the information lifted from their textbook. Students can relate to the material because they are involved in the collection process, i.e., deciding what to collect, finding the information, and determining what part of the information is relevant. Plus, they have a reason for collecting and analyzing the information—they need to solve the problem. Thus, the lessons are student-centered, problem-based, and authentic. But as the name, iNtegrating Technology for inQuiry implies, the NTeQ model focuses on the integration of technology, so the lessons are also dependent on the integration of technology.

The NTeQ model is not intended for use with every lesson taught. It takes a careful analysis of what the students are going to learn to determine if technology can be integrated. The technologically competent teacher determines if there is alignment between what the students are learning and the functions of a computer. If it is determined that the students will benefit from using the computer to manage, manipulate, or retrieve the information, then the model can be applied.

NTeQ and the Multidimensional Environment

When the NTeQ model is implemented, the classroom environment becomes multidimensional, or one which incorporates multiple, resource-rich activities. There are two primary aspects to creating the multidimensional environment: the activities and the rotation schedule. When planning, the teacher needs to consider if the *activities:*

- are closely aligned to the lesson objectives.
- meet the needs of diverse learners: tactile, visual, auditory, etc. (see Chapter 6).
- use multiple "real-life" resources, including those collected by the students.
- are interdisciplinary when possible, i.e., math, science, and social studies are included in one lesson.
- are clearly defined—a task list can be used to guide student work (see Figure 2-3).

The next consideration for planning the multidimensional activities is the *rotation schedule,* or how students will work through the various activities. Several things to consider when planning the schedule include the following.

- Efficient use of existing resources. For example, if your class has one computer with Internet access, your lessons should not depend on students needing a lot of Internet resources. Or if your class has five computers equipped with ClarisWorks, your activities can consistently integrate the use of databases, spreadsheets, word processing, draw, and presentations.

Figure 2-3   Task List for Spreadsheet Work

Fill Your Cart for Less

**Saving $$
at the Grocery Store
Task List for the Spreadsheet Work**

Element

1. Grocery List Recording Sheet is accurate.

2. Spreadsheet data for each store is accurate.

3. Each store has formulas for:
   Three coupons
   - 2 for 1
   - 15% off
   - Save 75¢ when you buy 2
   Total Amount Spent

4. The coupons were tested with a variety of grocery items to determine where they could save the most money.

5. A graph was created to show the final amount of money spent at each store.

- Student groups. It is important to use a variety of student groupings during a lesson. Mr. Carter's lesson involved whole-class discussion sessions, small group work to choose the store advertisements and formulas, and some independent work supported by group work, e.g., writing the final report—Robert wrote the first draft, Reneé edited the draft, then Gloria completed the final report. It is often helpful to have student pairs or small groups work together at the computer, because students can share in the problem-solving process. This strategy was seen in Mr. Carter's class, when the students were grouped at the computer to determine the best places to use the coupons.

- Rotating student groups. There are two primary ways to rotate student groups in a multidimensional environment: group rotation and independent rotation.

When NTeQ is implemented, students are engaged in a variety of activities.

With the group rotation, all group members rotate through each activity together. Or all five members go to the observation station to collect data on snails, then all five go to the computers at the same time. With the independent rotation, each group is assigned a computer, and they go to the different activities as needed, as was seen in Mr. Carter's class.

It takes time and practice to learn how to plan and implement multidimensional activities. It is helpful to keep a notebook handy to jot down ideas for how the activities can be improved the next time. It is also important to remember that glitches will always occur, especially when you are using technology, so keep some contingency plans available. Remember to smile and let the students know that this is "real life."

In conclusion, the NTeQ model provides teachers with a means for integrating technology into their curriculum in a meaningful manner. It proposes the creation of a learning environment that places the teacher in a supporting role that fosters relevant and lasting student learning.

At The Classroom's Doorstep
▲▲▲
Questions Teachers Ask

Most of my students do not know anything about the computer. How am I suppose to teach them the content as well as computer skills? One good thing about computers is that you do not need to know very much to begin working with them. There are just two basic things the students need to know before they begin using the computer: how to use the mouse and how to use the keyboard. Following are the first things they need to learn about each one:

- mouse basics
  - point and click,
  - drag and select/highlight,
  - double click
- keyboard basics
  - shift key for capital letters or symbols on top of keys
  - space bar for spaces
  - delete/backspace key to remove errors
  - return/enter key when requested

You can demonstrate these basics to the whole class as they take notes; then students can be rotated through the computers to practice. Job aids, or step-by step instructions, can also be used. Once students can use the mouse and keyboard, they can begin to use the simplest aspects of various applications. For example, to have your students use word processing for the first time, begin by having the application open on each computer. Send pairs of students to the computer to enter information that they have previously written on paper. For young students, begin with a list of three to five words, maybe spelling words. Older students can begin by entering from one sentence to a small paragraph.

Students can begin using databases by entering information into fields that the teacher has created. All they need to know is how to type information into the fields, and how to use the tab key to move to the next field. For example, if they are creating a database of cities in their state, the fields could include: city name, population, square miles, mayor, etc. Again, students need to have this information recorded on paper before they go to the computer.

When students use a spreadsheet for the first time, begin with a very small set of numbers that can easily be charted (see Figure 2-4). Again, the teacher can have a template with the column and row names in place so the students need only to add the numbers. The teacher can also include any formulas. However, it is important for the teacher to guide the students through the underlying calculations by having them identify what needs to be done. After the numbers are added, the students highlight the cells with information in them, then select Create Chart from the Options menu. A bar graph is automatically created. Figure 2-4 displays a sample spreadsheet and bar graph created by Mindy Morris for a fifth grade unit on monarch butterflies. Students collect the information during a study of monarch butterflies, then enter it into the spreadsheet. The spreadsheet results are used to answer the question "Is chrysalis size related to wingspan length?"

Figure 2-4   Simple Spreadsheet and Chart

	A	B	C	D	E
1		Difference in inches	Circumference of Chrysalis in inches	Length of Wingspan in inches	
2	Chrysalis #1	1.5	1.75	3.25	
3	Chrysalis #2	2.25	1.25	3.5	
4	Chrysalis #3	1.75	2.25	4	
5	Chrysalis #4	1.75	2.5	4.25	
6	Chrysalis #5	2	1.5	3.5	

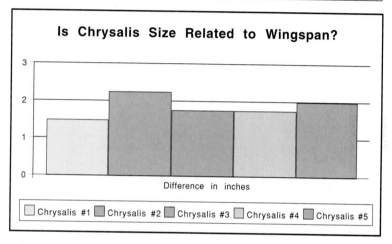

I only have one computer in my classroom. What can I do? If the one computer is fairly out of date, you may be able to use it only for word processing or scaffolding/remediation purposes. If the computer is connected to the Internet, has a CD-ROM drive, and has some type of an integrated software package such as Apple-Works, ClarisWorks or Microsoft Works, you can do quite a bit. The first consideration is that technology will have to play a smaller role in your lessons due to limited computer access by the students. In that case, the following suggestions may help.

- Create a class database where each group of students is responsible for entering a certain number of records and for generating a specific report that reflects one type of sorting or matching of records.
- Each student group conducts one aspect of an Internet search, e.g., collect the information on one city, or collect the information on one endangered animal.
- Groups turn in one computer-generated report reflecting the work of all members rather than a set of individual reports.
- Students work on a document over a period of several days by saving the work to a disk.
- Students should be very prepared before they go to the computer.

- Templates for student products can be placed on the computer, e.g., have a database with the fields already created, a word-processing document with a table set up, or a spreadsheet with the columns and rows labeled.

REFERENCES
▲▲▲

Are you a square? (1986) Hardhatting in a GeoWorld. AIMES Educational Foundation, Fresno, CA.

Durham, P., Morrison, G. R., & Ross, S. M. (1995). Technology training of 21st century classroom teachers. *Tennessee Educational Leadership, 22*(1), 41–45.

Lowther, D. L., Bassoppo-Moyo, T., & Morrison, G. R. (in press). Moving from computer literate to technological competent: The next educational reform. *Computers and Human Behavior.*

Vygotsky, L. (1978). *Mind in Society.* Cambridge: Harvard University Press.

CHAPTER 3
Teacher as Designer

▶ Introduction

Creating an integrated computer lesson using the NTeQ model (see Chapter 2) requires careful planning and design of the lesson. Actually, any use of computer software for instruction requires planning. Unfortunately, we have observed many teachers who use the computer only for drill-and-practice, tutorial, games, and simulations with little or no planning. This practice has lead to rather disappointing results when using computer-based instruction in the classroom. In this chapter, we explain the process for designing an integrated computer lesson. An integrated computer lesson is one in which the students use the computer to organize and manipulate data or information to solve problems while learning new content and skills.

▶ Computer Skills Used in This Chapter

Familiarity with
   database
   spreadsheet
   word processor
   graphics

▶ Key Topics

Designing an Integrated Lesson
   Specifying Objectives
   Matching Objectives to Computer Functions
   Specifying a Problem
   Planning the Data Manipulation
   Planning the Results Presentation
   Planning the Activities While Using the
      Computer
   Planning the Activities Prior to Using the
      Computer
   Planning the Activities After Using the
      Computer
   Planning the Supporting Activities
   Planning the Assessment

Designing an Integrated Lesson

▲▲▲

An integrated computer lesson can vary in length from an hour, to a whole day, to one period a day for a week, or for several weeks. The length of the lesson depends on the complexity of the problem, the content you intend to cover during the lesson, and the capabilities of your students. As you design a lesson that integrates the use of computers, you need to consider the following two factors. First is the attention span of your students. How long in minutes, hours, or days can your students stay focused and interested in solving a problem? For example, a lesson for third graders might last two to five days, whereas a high school geography lesson might last two or three weeks or longer.

Second, you should not expect to teach all of your objectives at the computer. Students should use other resources (e.g., books and videotapes) and other instructional activities (e.g., group and individual work). Historically, educators have viewed the computer as an all-inclusive teaching machine that a student could learn *from* throughout the school day. Our approach views the computer as a *tool* rather than as a teacher. It is used by the students to solve problems rather than receive instruction. Thus, each individual student does not need full-time access to a computer as was needed with the computer-as-teacher model.

When students use a computer to help solve a problem, their motivation and engagement can increase. The initial motivation may come because using the computer is something new or novel (Clark, 1983). With time, however, the motivation stems from the computer being a useful tool. Students are motivated to use the computer because the job gets done more easily and quickly than without it, just as we use a microwave oven because it is more efficient and quicker than a traditional oven.

The NTeQ model consists of 10 steps (see Figure 3-1) for *planning* an integrated computer lesson. Although you can complete the steps in any sequence, we have found that starting with objectives and working in a clockwise sequence is the most efficient. As you gain experience and expertise in developing integrated lessons, you will find that you may complete the steps in various sequences based on your ideas. This model is for *planning* your lessons. The sequence in which the lesson occurs in your classroom will be much different; this sequence is discussed further in Chapter 5. Let's examine the process for designing an integrated lesson that uses the computer as a tool.

Specifying Objectives

The lesson planning starts with the specification of your objectives (see Figure 3-2). These objectives should cover *all* the instruction for the unit or lesson, not just the information related to the computer component. A lesson can also cross disciplines either in your own classroom or as part of a team teaching project. For example, you might collect the data in a geography or a science class, analyze the data in a math class, and prepare the report or presentation in an English class. The objectives for the lesson should be inclusive of all the content.

Two popular methods for writing instructional objectives are the behavioral (e.g., Mager type) and cognitive approaches. Objectives specify what the learner

Figure 3-1 NTeQ Model

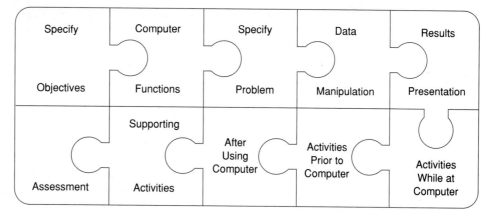

can do when he or she finishes the instruction. The following section describes the application of each type of objective and how to write each.

BEHAVIORAL OBJECTIVES.

Mager (1984) popularized the use of behavioral objectives in instruction. These objectives are useful when you can identify specific behaviors you want the student to demonstrate. For example, calculating an average, identifying a sonnet, or arranging a list alphabetically are specific behaviors. With each of these behaviors, you can devise a simple test item such as "Determine the average of the following numbers . . ." to find out if the student has mastered the content. A Mager style objective has three parts—the action verb and related content, the criteria, and the conditions. For example, "*Given* a right triangle, the student will *correctly calculate* the length of the hypotenuse." The following paragraph explains each part.

Figure 3-2 Specifying Objectives

Problems need to be interesting and relevant to the students.

Action verbs, the first part, describe a behavior you can observe (e.g., "Draw a triangle") or that you can observe results of the behavior (e.g., "Calculate the average"). The content part describes the subject matter the student will use or act on. Thus, triangle is the content-related part and calculate is the action verb described in the previous example. The second component of the behavioral objective is the criteria or performance standard. This standard describes *how well* the learner must perform. These standards can specify how much (e.g., 8 out of 10 or 100% correct), how accurate (e.g., within a quarter of an inch), or how fast (e.g., in 5 minutes or less). The third component describes the conditions of the performance. For example, if you want the students to calculate the average population of a five-county region, can they use a calculator or spreadsheet on the test? Other conditions can specify resources the student can or cannot use, such as a book or chart. Table 3-1 illustrates several behavioral style objectives.

COGNITIVE OBJECTIVES. An alternative approach to behavioral objectives are cognitive objectives (Gronlund, 1985, 1995). Cognitive objectives are used to describe student learning that cannot easily be specified in a single sentence. Objectives that cover such topics as interpreting a graph, searching the Internet for information, working effectively in a group, or writing an essay or report are not easily reduced and explained in a single behavioral objective. Cognitive objectives provide you with a means to specify a number of behaviors that can describe the achievement of the objective.

Cognitive objectives consist of two parts. The first part is a general instructional objective that is stated in broad terms (Kemp et al. 1998). Examples include:

Table 3-1 Behavioral Objectives

- Given a table with the population and area of the 50 states, the student will use a database to determine the highest and the lowest population densities.
- The student will use a spreadsheet to solve five time-distance problems with 100% accuracy.
- Using the draw module of ClarisWorks, the student will accurately draw a map showing the location of the fire exits and extinguishers in the west wing of the school.
- Given another student's essay, the student will correct all spelling errors with 100% accuracy using a word processor and spell checker.

Selects information using Yahoo.

Interprets a chart of classroom cookie sales.

Explains the meaning of story.

The second part of the cognitive objective includes one or more statements describing specific performances that indicate mastery of the objective. The following examples illustrate specific behaviors that indicate mastery of the general statements.

Selects information using Yahoo.

Finds a specific article related to the problem.

Compiles a list of web sites related to the problem.

Identifies productive search terms.

Interprets a chart of classroom cookie sales.

Identifies the student with the most sales.

Compares this year's sales with the sales during the past three years.

Identifies the students who sold more than the class average.

Explains the meaning of story.

Summarizes the plot.

Identifies the characters.

Explains the meanings of the characters' actions.

Cognitive objectives are useful for describing higher level learning tasks that allow for more than one approach to mastery. Behaviors such as apply, interpret, solve, or evaluate suggest that there is *more* than one solution to a problem. In the example involving the interpretation of the graph, there are a number of questions a student could answer to demonstrate the ability to interpret a graph. In contrast, a behavioral objective might simply focus on a specific behavior. "Given a graph, the student will correctly identify the bar that shows the maximum sales." Although the objective indicates the student will need to learn to interpret a graph, it is a very specific interpretation. In contrast, the cognitive objective allows for greater flexibility without the specifics, which places a greater emphasis on teacher interpretation and implementation of the instruction.

As you write your objectives, remember to focus on what the *student* will do (e.g., demonstrate a skill or knowledge) as a result of the instruction rather than what the *teacher* will do. For example, many teachers and instructors mistakenly use objectives to write descriptions of what will happen during the instruction by using such phrasing as "to teach the learner how to calculate an average." This type of statement is an activity (Kemp, et al., 1998). A simple test for an objective is to ask yourself if the objective specifies what the learner will demonstrate after the instruction. Both cognitive and behavioral objectives focus on the outcomes or product of the learning process. This product is what the learner can demonstrate, not the instructional activities themselves.

Matching Objectives to Computer Functions

To create a successful integrated computer lesson, you must find a match between your objective(s) and one or more computer functions (see Figure 3-3). Computer functions are tasks that computer software can assist with or perform. For example, spreadsheet software can *convert* fractions to decimals and decimals to percentages. A database can *match* or *select* specific items while a spreadsheet can *calculate* the area of rectangle when the student enters the length and width. Draw and paint software are used to *create diagrams and maps* while spreadsheet software can *plot* and *chart* data. A table of learning tasks (e.g., objectives) and related computer functions are in Appendix A.

Now that you have defined your objectives, you need to determine if there is a match between an objective and a computer function. Some objectives such as calculate, draw, graph, and sort are easy to match with a spreadsheet, drawing, or database application. Objectives describing such behaviors as plan, discriminate, evaluate, combine, infer, predict, interpret, judge, and evaluate require careful plan-

Figure 3-3   Matching Objectives and Computer Functions

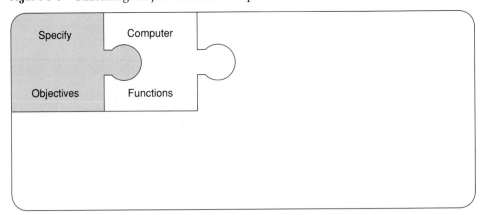

ning and thinking to match the process with a computer function. For example, an objective requiring the student to evaluate a story or some data might use a spreadsheet or database to aid the analysis, a chart to evaluate the data, and a word processor to generate the report that explains the evaluation.

One approach to finding an appropriate match between your objectives and computer functions is to analyze how you would achieve the objective if you were the student. What processes would you need to perform to master the objective? For example, would you need to collect data, perform a calculation, and then graph it? Once you have identified the process or processes required to master the objective, you can select one or more computer functions for the student to use as part of the learning process. In this example, you might use a spreadsheet or database to help collect or organize the data, a spreadsheet to calculate the means and highest and lowest values, and a spreadsheet to chart the results. An objective might require only one computer function such as calculate, draw, or sort; or it might involve a number of functions to arrive at the solution.

SPECIFYING A PROBLEM

The next step in the design of the integrated lesson is specifying a problem the students will investigate and solve as part of the instructional process (see Figure 3-4). This problem helps students develop the thinking skills and gain the knowledge specified in the objectives. There are three aspects to specifying the problem—identifying the nature of the problem, collecting the data, and using the data to solve the problem. These aspects of specifying the problem are examined in the following paragraphs.

NATURE OF THE PROBLEM. Problems in an integrated lesson are realistic, based on real-world events, issues, or phenomena. The problems need to come from students' world so that they can relate to them in a meaningful manner. By using a realistic problem, the students can more readily manipulate the data

Figure 3-4   Specifying the Problem

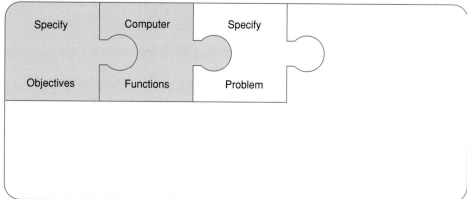

needed to solve the problem and interpret the results in terms of the original situation (Hancock, Kaput, & Goldsmith, 1992). As the problem is being developed, it is important to make it as relevant as possible to the students by keeping the problem "real-world" (Bransford, Sherwood, Hasselbring, Kinzer, & Williams, 1990).

Using realistic problems requires you, the teacher, to take an additional step in the lesson-planning process. For example, we can recall the teaching of frequency distributions in one of our advanced high school math classes. The problem was more than likely presented without any context or concrete data—it was simply a calculation we were supposed to complete with no purpose. Little did we realize then that this calculation is a central part of doing research! Today, if we were to teach this topic, we could easily present it as a problem in a realistic context for our students. We could construct a problem where they survey how much their fellow students make an hour or week at work, how many CDs they own, the number of hours of television they watch during the week, or the amount of time they spend on the telephone on a school night. They could then construct a frequency distribution to determine the average, the mode, and the median. Of course, as a teacher you might have to deal with the parents of the students who place the greatest restrictions on television or telephone time! Presenting a realistic problem to which the students can relate increases both their chances of comprehending the content and their motivation.

When you define your problem, it is important to address the following four questions (Moursund, 1996).

- Do the students clearly understand the *given* problem?
- Do they know what the *goal* is?
- Do they know what *resources* are available to solve the problem?
- Do they have *ownership* of the problem?

There are several ways to assure that students have a clear understanding of the problem they are solving. One way is to write the problem statement on the board or large screen monitor. This can be a problem statement the teacher has developed, or one that is generated by the teacher and students during class discussion. The teacher can also put the problem on a handout that has sections entitled: Given, Goals, and Resources.

You can establish the goal in several ways: You can lead the whole class in a discussion that identifies the goal, cooperative groups can define the goal, or you can provide the goal as a separate part of the handout. If students define the goal of the problem they are solving, it will more than likely not be a statement of the learning objectives. Yet as they achieve the goals of the problem, they will also be achieving the learning objectives. Through teacher facilitation skills, the students are able to "discover" the content or skills defined in the learning objective through a problem-based approach (Bruner, 1960; Collins & Stevens, 1983; Grambs & Starr, 1976; Mayer, 1987).

When possible, involve students in identifying the resources needed to solve the problem. Provide multiple sources so that students have some flexibility in reaching solutions to the problem. For example, students might use CD-ROM encyclopedias, the Internet, books, magazines, field trips, visits from experts, and survey or experimental data collected by the students.

Student ownership of the problem is very important. Student ownership is easier to achieve in a student-centered learning environment rather than in a traditional setting. The more involved students are in various aspects of solving the problem, such as identifying the goal, deciding what resources are needed, and determining how to configure the database, the more ownership they will feel. Ownership is also increased if the problem is relevant to the students. This relevancy is enhanced by having students generate their own data when possible, or having them use real data collected from a survey, an experiment, the Internet, newspapers, or television. Another means of achieving ownership is by letting students define the initial problem. Present a rough idea of what you want to accomplish, then let them develop a clear problem. For example, you might tell the students, "Our school is doing a school-wide thematic unit on Native Americans. One of our learning objectives for this year is for you to identify different kinds of Native American art from the 1800s. If we had to create a display of this artwork, how could we approach this project?" The teacher can facilitate the discussion to guide the students in reaching a problem similar to the one he defined. However, since this problem is created by the students, they will have more ownership and more involvement in reaching a solution.

Specifying a problem for the student typically begins by translating a problem or topic in the textbook or curriculum into a realistic problem as illustrated with the frequency distribution problem. You might also let your students participate in the development of the problem by asking them to suggest ideas or problems. They can provide a number of rich contexts that you can use to embed the problem.

PROBLEM DATA.
To solve a problem the students must have access to the appropriate data or information. There are three sources of data you can use for the lesson.

1. You can provide the students with the data. This approach is used when the instructional time is limited, the students have no feasible way of obtaining the data, or students lack the necessary search skills (e.g., Internet search). For example, you might be teaching a geography unit that compares the type of crops grown in different countries with the students looking for relationships between the weather and crops. Searching for the raw data is not a focus of this unit, so you might provide students with the necessary information so that they can focus on manipulating the data and discovering relationships.

2. Students can generate their own data through experiments or observations. They can generate data through a laboratory experiment (e.g., chemistry, physics, or biology), a survey, an interview, or by observation such as the number of students wearing seat belts as they arrive at school. A sixth grade class, for example, could measure the height of a sampling of boys and girls in several grade levels as they study the relationship between physical growth, age, and gender.

3. Students can search for data in a library, on CD-ROMs, or on the Internet (see Chapters 12 and 13). Computers create many opportunities for finding both useful and not so useful data. Student searches for data should not be limited to just computer-based searches, but should include print materials and other materials from the library as appropriate. For example, an economics class studying organized labor might search the Internet for historical events in the labor movement, and then search the local newspaper for information on strikes or other organized labor activity in their community.

As you plan the lesson, you will need to decide if students should gather the data or you should provide them with it. If the process of gathering the data is part of the instruction such as in a lab experiment or a survey, then the students need to collect the data. However, when the emphasis of the lesson is primarily on manipulating the data (e.g., calculations or probing the database), you may decide that it is a more efficient use of classroom time to provide the students with a template and the data, or even the finished database. You will need to determine the importance and value of the students collecting and entering data as opposed to using an existing data file. The tradeoff is one of instructional time and how it is used.

COLLECTING DATA. If the students will be collecting the data, you will need to determine the type and amount of data they will need to collect. If the students are conducting a survey or an interview, how many individuals must each student survey? If they are collecting data from an experiment, how many observations does each student or group need to complete? You can also involve the students in this decision as part of the problem-solving process. If you need consistency in the data between students or groups, the class can create a data collection form to record their results.

USING EXISTING DATA. When students will use a data set created by you or by others, you need to consider the following. First, are the data in a format (either on paper or on disk) that the students can use? If the data are not in an appropriate format, can you change them so they are useful to the student? Second, are students allowed to modify, delete, or add data? Third, if the students are entering the data, must each one enter all the data or can they divide the work among groups and then merge the files? Fourth, where will the students save their data? Will they use their own disk(s), the hard drive, or the server? Careful consideration is needed to protect students from losing their data and becoming frustrated with the process.

We encourage teachers to try a test run of the data at this stage of the planning cycle. You can conduct this test with random data to make sure your recording form and file template (e.g., database, spreadsheet, etc.) are designed correctly. This simple test run can save you time and embarrassment if there is a problem.

PLANNING THE DATA MANIPULATION

The fourth step in designing an integrated lesson is to plan how the learners will manipulate data (see Figure 3-5). This decision is directly related to the computer functions and your objectives. Once the students have the data entered into a com-

Figure 3-5   Data Manipulation

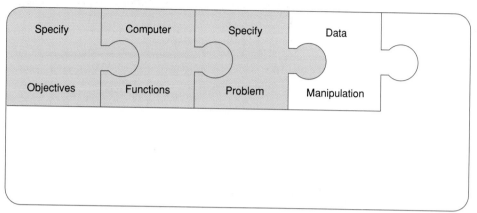

puter file such as a spreadsheet or database, what will they do with it? Similarly, how much instruction or guidance must you provide the students concerning the manipulation?

PROVIDING INSTRUCTIONS. If your students are advanced in the use of the required application such as a spreadsheet or database, they may be quite capable of simply answering the questions either you or they have posed. Less advanced students may need step-by-step instructions on how to enter a formula or matching and searching criteria (see Figure 3-6). Another alternative is to teach all the students how to do the data manipulation and then provide assistance on an individual basis. We have observed both good and bad examples of both approaches. One excellent approach was by a teacher who modeled the steps on a large monitor as the students created their own lists of steps. At the other extreme was a teacher who let four students at a time complete the process as she and the other students observed and commented. The students sitting at their desks could not see the individual monitors and there was little if any motivation to focus their attention on what the teacher was doing.

THINK SHEET. Simply entering a formula, sorting data, creating a graph, or creating a drawing is rather mechanical. Students can complete the steps to solve the problem, but fail to process or reflect on the results. A *Think Sheet* provides guidance to help students organize their thinking and to probe the implications of the data manipulations. It helps them determine what to do once they have sorted the data, performed the calculations, or created a chart. Think Sheets can include generic information such as which is the largest, which is smallest, what is the most common, and what is the least common. Specific lesson think sheets can include probing questions asking the student about implications, interpretations, generalizations, and predictions using the data. Figure 3-7 illustrates a sample think sheet.

There are three broad categories of strategies (Jonassen, 1985) that you can use in your Think Sheets to encourage students to actively process the information.

Figure 3-6   Sample Spreadsheet Calculation Instructions

	A	B	C
	Cookie Sales	Students	Total
1			
2	50	3	94
3	47	2	
4	45	1	
5	38	3	
6	34	1	
7	31	1	
8	23	7	
9	20	4	
10	15	2	

C2   × ✓   =A3*B3

Calculating the number of packages sold.

1. Click in cell C2.

2. Enter the following into entry bar.

    =A3*B3

3. Press return and you will see the results of your calculation.

4. Now, you can create a formula to calculate the number of packages sold for each of the remaining rows.

1. **Integration strategies.** These strategies help students transform the information so that it is easily learned. One integration strategy is having the students paraphrase the information; that is, they read the information and then write it in their own words. Another strategy is to develop questions and new examples. For example, a student might create an electronic test board displaying questions and answers that causes a light to glow when the correct answer is selected. Students could also create "study" sheets for other groups.

2. **Organizational strategies.** Students can use these strategies to group information into similar and dissimilar groupings. For example, they can create a database of food and complete fields regarding fat, protein, and vitamin content of each item. They could then group the food according to different levels of a characteristic such as high protein or low-fat content.

Figure 3-7   Sample Think Sheet

LOCAL WEATHER THINK SHEET

Now that you have collected weather data for three weeks, think of these questions as you examine your database.

1. Does anything happen to the relative humidity as the temperature changes?

2. Look at the types of cloud formations that were present each day when you collected your weather data. Can you find any information in your database that might explain the changes that occurred (more humidity, lower barometric pressure, etc.)?

3. Use the information in your database to write "Weather Rules." For example, "When the temperature rises, the barometric pressure (rises, falls, or stays the same)."

4. Use the patterns you discover in your data to predict what would happen to the variables in your database if the temperature dropped by 20 degrees.

5. Using a weather map from the newspaper or from a web site, find a location that had the same weather as your area, one that was colder, and one that was warmer. What factors (e.g., atmospheric and geographical) affected the weather in each location?

---

3. **Elaboration strategies.** This strategy requires students to embellish the ideas presented in the instruction. Student activities can range from creating a drawing or diagram to writing activities. For example, students completing a science lesson on the geological development of their area might create a drawing depicting how their area might look in 200 years. Or, as a writing activity, they might create a bill and list the steps describing how it would become law. They might also list possible arguments others might offer for and against the bill's passage.

During this planning phase, develop a Think Sheet to guide the students' thinking. This sheet should include questions or other strategies that focus student's attention on the processes you expect them to develop (e.g., interpret a chart, make a prediction, etc.) that are specified in your objectives. Students can also create their own Think Sheet or modify yours as part of the instruction. Involving the students in the development of a Think Sheet will help them observe your critical thinking skills and provide them with extra motivation to think about their results.

PLANNING THE RESULTS PRESENTATION

The next step of planning the integrated lesson is presentation of the results (see Figure 3-8). What type of product will the students produce to illustrate they have achieved the objectives? While these reports can take a variety of formats (see Chapter 11), there are four basic ways of presenting the results.

Figure 3-8   Results Presentation

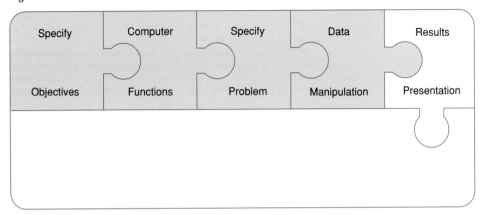

1. Each student or group of students can prepare a written report using either a word processor or paper and pencil. Using desktop publishing techniques, the students can prepare books or newsletters and distribute their products to other students, students in lower grade classes, parents, or possibly a government agency such as the city council.

2. Students can prepare a poster or bulletin board display of their results. This type of presentation can take a variety of formats, from interactive displays to timelines, and can include both computer-generated and non-computer-generated student products.

3. Students can publish their results on a web page (see Chapter 11). This format is similar to a written report, but is presented in a different format. The emphasis, however, should be on presenting the results, not learning HTML (Hyper Text Markup Language) or how to create a web page.

4. Students can make a presentation to other students and/or to parents. Students can present their findings in a scientific format using an electronic slide show. Or the presentation might take the format of a lesson (e.g., a HyperStudio stack) to teach other students.

Publishing the results encourages students to analyze their findings in a critical manner and to draw appropriate conclusions because their work will be viewed by others. This analysis was started with Think Sheets as students analyzed their data. The presentation component allows students to interpret their results and apply their findings to a solution.

As you plan the results presentation, you need to develop your criteria for what the students need to include. For example, you might include a basic outline for a report similar to that used in scientific journals. A report of a survey the students have completed might use the outline in Figure 3-9. You can create similar outlines and criteria for web pages, posters, and presentations. The criteria will help you assess the results presentation as well as let students know your expectations.

Figure 3-9 Sample Instructions for a Report

Format for Survey Reports on
Students Who Wear Seatbelts
  I. **Background information**
      A. Why you did the survey.
      B. Recent state law requiring seatbelts.
      C. Statement of the problem.
  II. **Method**
      A. Who was surveyed?
      B. How were they selected?
      C. Describe the survey instrument.
  III. **Results**
      A. What did you find?
  IV. **Discussion**
      A. What do your findings mean?
      B. What are your conclusions?

This step of the planning process requires careful thought to avoid problems such as computer access if *all* the students are required to prepare a written report. Students are easily frustrated if they have completed all the steps but cannot complete the final step because of the limited number of computers in the classroom. Thus, a paper and pencil report supplemented with database reports or a spreadsheet chart may be a more efficient use of instructional time than requiring each individual to use word processing for the report.

Fran's Diary
▲▲▲

When I plan a literature-based thematic unit, I always look through my district's curriculum frameworks and classroom literature and language text books. I use these frameworks to help me define my instructional goals for the unit and review my textbooks for ideas in the content areas. After I had reviewed my textbooks, I decided that the students needed to learn how to use an index and table of contents to find information. I also determined that they needed to learn how to read for specific information and to summarize in writing what they had read. With these instructional goals in mind, I went to our school library and began searching for literature related to the theme, owls. I

Continued

looked for books that would be of high interest and age appropriate to my students. I checked out a variety of books. I chose two books on owls as the basis for this unit. As I read these books, I began to formulate how I would use them to meet my instructional goals, and I made a list of activities.

The next day I asked my students to create knowledge charts about owls. On one side of their paper, they listed everything that they already knew about owls, and on the other side, those things that they would like to learn about owls. The class then discussed what they wanted to learn about owls. We made a list of questions about owls that they would like to have answered. We ended up with 34 excellent questions!

I recorded their questions and took them home with me that night. I used my list of instructional goals and activities and the students' questions to help me write the instructional objectives for this unit. After I had written the objectives, I checked my objectives against the list of state mandated objectives. I wanted to make sure that I had included as many of these objectives as possible in this unit.

Then, I created a thematic activity web. I used the activity list and the students' questions to help me choose the activities for this unit. I tried to include a variety of activities that would cross all curriculum areas. I also tried to include the use of the computer in as many of the activities as possible. I wanted the students to use the computer in real-life situations and as a tool to help them accomplish their instructional goals.

I got on the Internet and found some excellent owl resources that the students could access. I also brought in several different CD-ROM encyclopedias. The students used both the computer materials and books checked out from the school and public libraries to obtain information about owls. They then used this information to create an owl database, to write informative paragraphs about owls, and to create an owl multimedia report.

The final assessment for this unit was a group multimedia report about a topic related to owls. Considering student interest expressed in the questions, the topics for these reports were: (1) unusual owls, (2) feathers and flight, (3) special owl features, (4) owl habitats, (5) owl diet, and (6) owl babies. Each group was responsible for a topic. They searched for information on that topic using printed materials, the Internet, and the CD-ROM encyclopedias. The students kept individual notes and combined this information with other group members to create a group HyperStudio multimedia report. These reports were shared with other students in the classroom.

The next step is to plan the specific activities you will use in the classroom. There are two reasons for these activities. First, not all objectives are best taught with a computer. Second, many classrooms have only a limited number of computers; therefore, a number of activities are used to achieve the objectives. We can hardly expect each student in a class of 27 to have extensive computer time when there are only four computers in the classroom. To address these two issues, the integrated lesson uses multidimensional activities. Activities are grouped into four time frames: prior to using the computer, at the computer, after the computer, and supporting activities used anytime (the management of the classroom is discussed in Chapter 5). Notice, however, that planning the *activities at the computer* is done before planning the *activities prior to the computer*. We have reversed these steps because you must know what your students will do while they are using the computer *before* you can determine what they must do prior to using the computer. Many of the data collection, data manipulation, and report presentation aspects of the lesson are included as part of these multidimensional activities. The following section describes each type of activity.

Planning the Activities While Using the Computer

Now that you have identified your objective and the problem the students will be solving and know how the students will use the computer to manipulate the data, the next step is to determine what the students will do while they are working with the computers (see Figure 3-10). There are two factors to consider when planning the computer activities. First, identify the activities the students will engage in while using the computer. How will the students obtain information to find an answer or to solve the problem? If students are searching for information, will they search a CD, the Internet, a database on the hard drive, or all three? If students are using a database or spreadsheet, will they use a template you have created or make their own? Depending on your objectives, you might want the students to use your template and concentrate on entering and manipulating the data to find an answer. For other lessons, the emphasis might be on finding the correct solution by creating the correct formula. If students are doing a report or drawing, can they use clip art or must they do original artwork? Similarly, do they need to show a graph of the results in their report? Students will need clear and precise instructions of what they are to do while working at the computer.

Figure 3-10   While Using the Computer

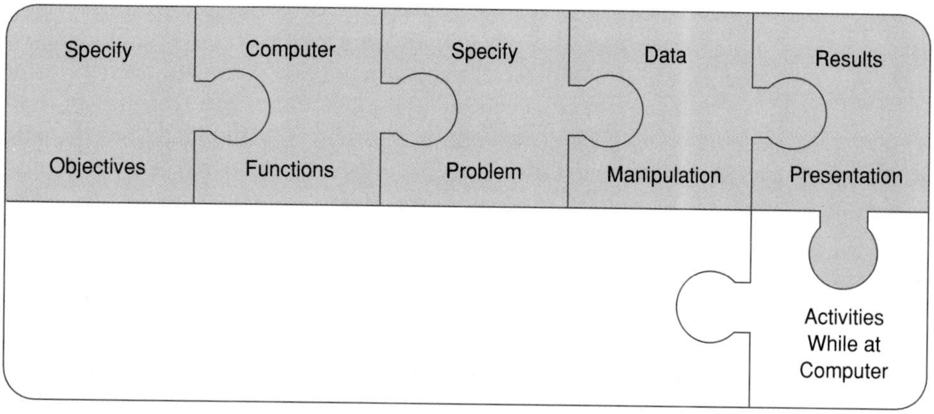

Students collecting data prior to going to the computers.

Second, will the students work individually or in groups? If you are using groups at the computer, assist students with identifying and assigning students to the different roles, assuring that students have the opportunity to rotate through the different roles. When working in a group, one student can read the data, another can enter the data, and a third can check the accuracy of the entry. Defining the roles prior to going to the computer can help you develop a rotation schedule so that students have a variety of experiences.

PLANNING THE ACTIVITIES PRIOR TO USING THE COMPUTER

Once you have determined the activities the students will engage in while at the computer and whether the students will work individually or in groups, then you can focus on the activities they *must* complete prior to using the computer. If you have limited access to computers either due to time limitations or lack of computers in your classroom, it is essential to plan activities the students need to complete *prior* to using the computer (see Figure 3-11). For example, if the students are entering data from an experiment or survey into a spreadsheet, they can collect the data and organize it before they start to use the computer. Similarly, if they are writing a report they can create their outline and gather their materials before their computer time. Students who are searching a CD-ROM encyclopedia or the Internet need to plan their search by identifying the key words before they start using the computer. With proper planning, students can have efficient and productive use of their computer time.

Figure 3-11   Activities Prior to Computer

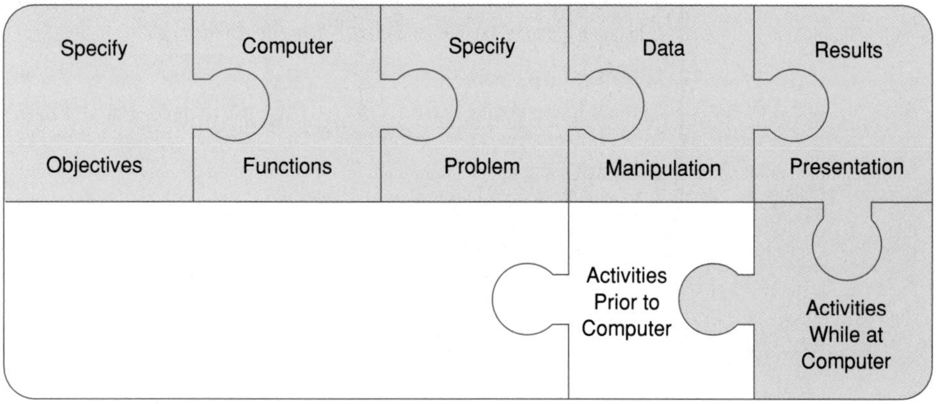

In the previous planning steps you identified one or more ways students would use the computer and manipulate information. Think through each of these steps and identify what the student needs *to complete before* using the computer. You may find it easier to complete the steps and make notes as to what you did to complete the steps. This listing of information and steps to complete before using the computer is part of your lesson plan that you can communicate to the students with a handout, through a lecture, or with a poster or on the blackboard. For some students, a checklist with space for notes or blanks is helpful for organizing their thoughts and data (see Figure 3-12).

PLANNING THE ACTIVITIES AFTER USING THE COMPUTER

If students are using the computer to solve problems, then their learning and work do not end with their computer time (see Figure 3-13). While working at the computer, they have produced some results. Activities after the computer should focus on exploring the results of the computer activity. If the students have analyzed the results of an experiment or study, they should focus on interpreting or explaining the results. Students who have searched for information can read, paraphrase, compare and contrast, and interpret the articles in a written report.

The purpose of this activity is to use the information generated from using the computer as a tool. You might find a Think Sheet helpful for guiding the students' analysis and interpretation. This handout can include either generic questions such as "What is the writer's perspective in this news story?" or specific questions "Using the graph you created, what happened to barometric pressure as temperature increased?" Think Sheets can also include directions as to how the student should read an article or story, including steps for what they should do (e.g., paraphrase or summarizing the content) after they finish reading the material.

Figure 3-12   Checklist for Work Prior to the Computer

Getting Ready to Do a Search on the Internet

What is your topic? _____
List at least three terms you can use to search for information on this topic:

_____

_____

_____

_____

_____

List at least two other terms that mean the same as some of the above:

_____

_____

What are you searching for?
☐ Articles
☐ Pictures
☐ Movies
☐ Sound
☐ Software

☐ Other: _____

Figure 3-13   Activities After Using the Computer

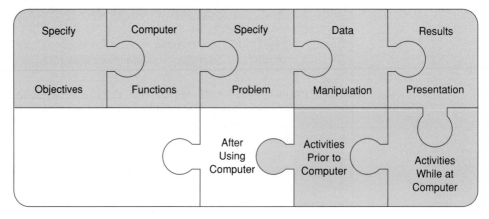

Planning the Supporting Activities

An integrated computer lesson incorporates a variety of instructional activities. Some require the use of a computer while others rely on other forms of instruction (see Figure 3-14). After you have designed the activities that are directly related to the computer activities, you will need to focus on the supporting activities that also help students achieve the objectives.

Lesson Related Supporting Activities.

The objectives for the lesson should cover a variety of skills and topics. Some require the use of a computer while others require different student engagement activities such as experimentation, practice, and gathering information via multiple resources (reading, videotapes, teacher and other content experts). Students engage in these activities as part of the instruction for the total lesson. It is often helpful to have a variety of activities that are not dependent upon completing the computer activities so that students can work on them at *any time*. We observed one classroom where the students were using the computer to research a topic and build a database. The supporting activities included research and reading in a number of books, creating a poster, developing a presentation for the class, and writing test items over the topic. Students were engaged in these activities as they waited their turn to do additional research on the Internet and build their database.

Multiple Lesson Supporting Activities.

Another approach to designing supporting activities is to provide multiple units for the students. If you only teach only one subject, such as math, science, or social studies, then you may want to develop several units students can work on at a time. You do not, however, need to use a computer for each of the units. If you are teaching a geography class, for example, you might have the students working on units on reading maps, weather, and

Figure 3-14   Supporting Activities

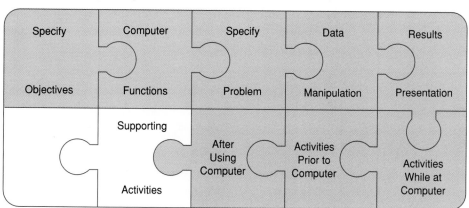

influences of technology on people and towns. Similarly, a math teacher might have students working on addition of fractions, fraction strips, converting fractions to decimals, and doing fraction additions with a calculator. These units are independent and are not sequential; thus, students can work on them at any time. All of the units provide instruction leading to the achievement of the objectives, although the objectives may be for different units of instruction.

CROSS CONTENT AREA SUPPORTING.
An integrated computer lesson is an excellent approach to use across content areas. Such activities require a team-teaching approach if the students are not in a self-contained classroom. For example, students might collect data in science class or sociology class, make the calculations in a math class, and prepare the results presentation in an English class. Using this approach, students can work on various tasks related to the project in the different classes with the goal of completing the project in a timely manner.

The supporting activities are often the most difficult to develop. These activities should provide instruction related to an objective(s) as opposed to "busy" work. If you are having difficulty identifying supporting activities, reconsider your objectives. You may need to broaden their scope or add additional objectives.

PLANNING THE ASSESSMENT

The final step of the NTeQ model is the development of your assessment strategies (see Figure 3-15). In the 1990s, educators are moving away from traditional forms of assessment such as multiple choice tests, and toward more authentic forms of assessment such as portfolios, performance assessment, presentations, and experiments (Marcoulides & Heck, 1994). Assessment of an integrated computer lesson will typically require more than a paper-and-pencil test. We might use a traditional multiple choice and short answer test to assess the students' understanding of the concepts and principles. Then, we might develop a rubric to

Figure 3-15   Evaluation

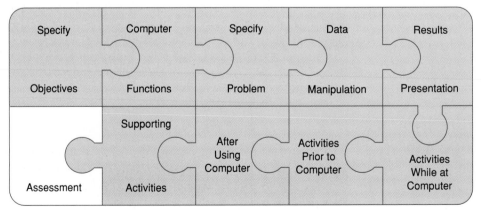

assess student portfolios documenting their searches, the completion of the Think Sheets, and their presentation. We might also include an assessment of the group and individual work behaviors based on both a journal we kept and students own personal journals.

Rubrics provide a means of rating student productivity on content standards according to predetermined performance standards. Content standards define the subject knowledge and skills students should reflect. Performance standards indicate to what level a student presentation meets the content standard (Gandal, 1995).

At the Classroom's Doorstep
▲▲▲
Questions Teachers Ask

Why should I create an integrated computer lesson rather than use some of the existing computer-based instructional (CBI) software? We do not see the use of integrated computer lessons and CBI as an either/or question. Decide instead which approach will best help your students achieve the objectives. You may decide that the CBI can help provide the scaffolding (see Chapter 2) necessary to solve the problem you present in the integrated lesson. The integrated lesson allows you to create unique problem-based units that are highly relevant for your students. You can custom tailor problems to meet your curriculum standards while providing a local context to which the students can relate. Providing this type of real-world, local context increases the meaningfulness of the instruction. Students see a problem that is concrete and is easily understandable. The integrated lesson also helps construct a multidimensional learning environment incorporating a variety of instructional strategies rather than *just* focusing on the computer. As a result, "book" learning has as much importance as "computer" learning in the minds of the students.

I will never be able to create enough units for next year. Is there any reason to adopt this approach? The first year of any new approach is the most difficult. We would not expect any teacher to develop enough materials in a year to cover every lesson of instruction for every class. Teachers that we have observed start with a few units the first year and add additional new units each year. There are also units that you can adapt and modify available from teachers on the Internet. Teachers are also able to adapt some of their existing units to an integrated lesson by rethinking the problem and objectives.

NTeQ Model
▲▲▲

The NTeQ model provides a general framework for creating an integrated computer lesson using a multidimensional learning environment (see Figure 3-16). The general sequence is to complete the process in a clockwise manner; however, with experience you may want to rearrange the steps.

Figure 3-16   NTeQ Model

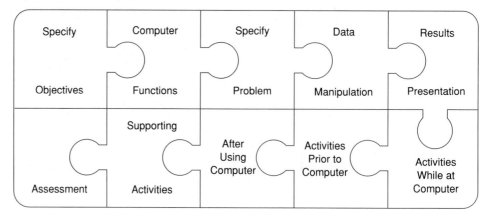

REFERENCES
▲▲▲

Bransford, J. D., Sherwood, R. D., Hasselbring, T. S., Kinzer, C. K., & Williams, S. M. (1990). Anchored instruction: Why we need it and how technology can help. In D. Nix & R. J. Spiro (Eds.), *Cognition, education, and multimedia: Exploring ideas in high technology* (pp. 115–142). Hillsdale, NJ: Erlbaum.

Bruner, J. S. (1960). *The process of education.* Cambridge, MA: Harvard University Press.

Clark, R. E. (1983). Reconsidering research on learning from media. *Review of Educational Research, 53,* 445–459.

Collins, A. & Stevens, A. L. (1983). A cognitive theory of inquiry teaching. In C. M. Reigeluth (Ed.), *Instructional design theories and models: An overview of their status.* Hillsdale, NY: Macmillan.

Danielson, C. (1997). *A collection of performance tasks and rubrics: Middle school mathematics.* Larchmont, NY: Eye on Education.

Gandal, M. (1995). Not all standards are created equal. *Educational Leadership,* March, 16–21.

Grambs, L. H. & Starr, I. S. (1976). *Modern methods in secondary education* (5th ed.). Forth Worth, TX: Holt, Rinehart and Winston.

Gronlund, N. E. (1985). *Stating behavioral objectives for classroom instruction.* New York: Macmillan.

Gronlund, N. E. (1995). *How to write and use instructional objectives* (5th ed.). New York: Prentice Hall.

Hancock, C., Kaput, J. J., & Goldsmith, L. T. (1992). Authentic inquiry with data: Critical barriers to classroom interpretation. *Educational Psychologist, 27,* 337–364.

Jonassen, D. H. (1985). Integrating learning strategies into courseware to facilitate deeper processig. In D. Jonassen (Ed.), *Instructional Designs for Micro-computer Courseware.* (pp. 151–181). Hillsdale, NJ: Lawrence Erlbaum Associates, Publishers.

Kemp, J. E., Morrison, G. R., and Ross, S. M. (1998). *Designing Effective Instruction* (2nd ed.). New York: Merrill.

Mager, R. F. (1984). *Preparing instructional objectives* (2nd ed.). Belmont, CA: Pitman.

Marcoulides, G. A. & Heck, R. H. (1994). The changing role of educational assessment in the 1990s. *Education and Urban Society, 26*(4), 332–337.

Mayer, R. (1987). *Educational psychology: A cognitive approach.* Boston, MA: Little Brown and Co.

Moursund, D. (1996). *Increasing your expertise as a problem solver: Some roles of computers* (2nd ed.). Eugene, OR: International Society for Technology in Education.

CHAPTER 4
Teacher as Facilitator

► Introduction

Many teachers like to consider themselves facilitators of learning, but what exactly does it mean to be a facilitator? Facilitation is the act of making learning easier (Freiberg, 1996). Facilitation involves guiding students through the learning process by being both directive and nondirective at the same time. A good facilitator uses active listening, reflection, explanations, and questioning, and provides resources to push students forward in meaningful inquiry.

Constructivist perspectives have forced us to reexamine the role of teacher (Murphy, 1995). Traditionally, a teacher's job has been to "fill" the minds of students with deposits of "true" knowledge (Friere, 1971). Students were expected to regurgitate specific information back at appropriate intervals. This approach to education may have served its purpose during the Industrial Revolution when many people were hired to work passively in factories or to return to the farm. However, the complex nature of today's society requires citizens who can conceptualize ideas, work as part of a collaborative team, problem solve, and take action. In today's world, the teacher must go beyond knowledge transmission. A teacher must engage and empower students and educate for insight.

In this chapter, we take an in-depth look at several key strategies used in the facilitation process: negotiating the curriculum, group learning, and questioning strategies.

► Key Topics

Negotiating the Curriculum
   Four Stages of Negotiating the Curriculum
   Negotiating the Curriculum and NTeQ
Group Learning
   Classroom Environment
   Creating a Culture of Collaboration
   Establishing Groups
   Principles of Cooperative Learning
Questioning Strategies
   Higher and Lower Level Questions
   Convergent and Divergent Questions
   Techniques of Questioning

Negotiating the Curriculum

▲▲▲ As experienced teachers know, negotiating the curriculum is much like negotiating a boat up a river. The river has set boundaries. The captain of the boat must take the river boundaries, the type of ship, and the passengers into consideration when negotiating a way up the river to the final destination.

The extent and manner in which a teacher negotiates her curriculum directly influences the facilitation process. For learning to be meaningful to students, they must have some amount of *ownership* in the curriculum (Cook, 1992). Students are motivated when their desires, needs, and wants are fulfilled through the curriculum. They are willing to strive for excellence in ways that completing a worksheet could never promote. This aspect of negotiation is critical in inquiry learning. However, many teachers are hesitant to engage in curriculum negotiation. Some teachers view it as a handing over responsibility to the students. Is there a way to provide students ownership by negotiating curriculum, yet at the same time assist the teacher in meeting mandated objectives and goals?

Four Stages of Negotiating the Curriculum

Jon Cook (1992) states that natural learning occurs in three phases: engagement, exploration, and reflection. He builds on this natural learning tendency by offering a four-step process for negotiating the curriculum with students:

1. What do we know already?
2. What do we want, and need, to find out?
3. How will we go about finding out?
4. How will we know, and show, what we found out when we are finished?

What Do We Know Already? What Do We Want, and Need, to Find Out?

The first two questions go hand in hand and are the starting point in negotiating the curriculum. As students discuss what they know about a given topic, they automatically begin to uncover what they don't know or would like to know more about. The intent of this initial questioning is to engage students in the learning process up front, pique their interest and curiosity, develop some initial ownership in the learning, get a sense of direction, and explore initial hypotheses (Cook, 1992).

Negotiating the curriculum can come at the beginning of a course, unit, or lesson. When using the NTeQ planning model for inquiry learning, projects usually last one to several weeks. For example, one goal of a unit might be "Demonstrate use of the metric system as a form of mathematical measurement." Rather than ask the students "What do you know about the metric system?" begin by first finding out what students know about measurement in general. After some initial brainstorming has occurred, you can introduce the concept of the metric system, and then further probe their understandings, needs, and wants.

One effective technique is to brainstorm in small groups and then have students share their answers with the entire class. The teacher facilitates the discussion by making sure students stay focused on the initial provided topic and by recording students' answers to the questions on butcher paper. It's important to keep a visual and written record of the class discussion, and the record should be posted on the wall until the unit is completed. This record shows students their thinking is valuable and important, and that they "own" their own learning. If there is any type of an imposed curriculum (e.g., syllabus, objectives, requirements), let students know this up front, and they can negotiate from there. Because many students are used to passive learning, many are often initially uncomfortable negotiating the curriculum. Providing boundaries and limitations will assist these students.

The extent to which a teacher uses this information to shape the curriculum is her choice. For teachers new to negotiation, use student ideas as you make your decisions about the types of activities and results presentation students will engage in. Then show them how your plan took their interests into consideration. As you gain experience with negotiation, you will feel more comfortable letting students take more control of the learning. As long as your objectives are being met, learn to *trust* that students are motivated to learn and will make appropriate choices when given the opportunity.

After working with your students on the previous two questions, you should be ready to decide the following:

- things that all students should answer or do.
- things that each group should consider or do.
- things of individual interest or concern.

After these two questions have been developed to their fullest potential, it's time to move to the next step.

How Will We Go About Finding Out?
You and your students are now ready to discuss strategies for how best to answer what they want or need to know. These strategies might include experiments, writing a report, interviewing people, reading books, or looking on the Internet. Again, have students first discuss ideas in small groups, and then move to whole class discussion. It is important to move between small groups and whole class discussion so that each person voices his or her opinion but each student must also create class consensus about the work under consideration. See Chapter 13 for more help on determining information needs and steps for locating required information.

Showing and Sharing Our Learning.
Evaluation at the end of a lesson or unit should be negotiated and made clear before any work has begun. By making the final evaluation procedure explicit up front, students can work toward a goal—they know who their final audience is and what form the results presentation should take. Although some teachers might see this as a form of "teaching to the test," we are trying to exemplify the real world for our students. When we adults work, we must know at the beginning what form the results need to take.

There are many ways students might present results, including written reports, multimedia presentations, hypercard stacks, poster presentations, demonstrations, dramas, or discussion and debate sessions. Criteria for evaluation can be negotiated with students as well. For example, if they are completing a multimedia presentation, you might agree as a class to grade based on specific information included in the report, a certain number of slides, visual presentation, and an introduction and conclusion. See Chapter 3 for more information on presenting results.

Fran's Diary

▲▲▲

What I liked most about using the NTeQ model in my classroom was that I became a facilitator of learning. As a facilitator, I was able to let my students help me determine how and some of what they would learn in my classroom.

At the beginning of a thematic unit on trains, I asked my students to fold a piece of paper into fourths. I then asked them to write the following headings on their papers: (1) "What I Know About Trains," (2) "What I Want to Know About Trains," (3) "Where Can I Find Information About Trains," and (4) "Who Would I Like to Work With." My students' responses to "What I Know About Trains" reflected a diversity of knowledge about trains. They wrote about freight trains, passenger trains, subways, monorails, model trains, and famous trains. I noticed a pattern in their responses to "What I Want To Know About Trains." Many of them were interested in learning about passenger trains, particularly eating and sleeping on trains. Because of their interest in passenger trains, I arranged a field trip to the Historic Train Display. Here my students were able to go into different types of passenger train cars and experience first hand what it was like to be a passenger on a train. I also used these responses to develop a series of class projects. These projects encompassed everything from train history time lines to student created train safety cartoons.

My students' responses to "Where Can I Find Information About Trains" were very interesting. Their responses went beyond the usual library books, CD-ROM encyclopedias, and Internet resources. One student wrote that she had a grandmother who lived near the Casey Jones Village in Jackson, Tennessee, and that her grandmother could send the class some things from there. Another student wrote that he had an aunt who worked for Norfolk and southern Railroad and that she could send the class some information about the railroad. Another student wrote that his dad had a model train and that his dad could set it up in our classroom. Some students wrote that they could get information about trains from the mayor. They knew that he had a model train that went around his office. They even mentioned watching a current TV program about a train station. Many suggested taking a field trip to a train station.

As for their responses to "Who Would I Like to Work With," they all picked a friend to be their partner. I asked them to write a paragraph to tell me why I should let them work with that person. Most students wrote that they should work together because they liked each other, got along well together, and could help each other.

At the end of the train unit I asked my students to fold another piece of paper into fourths and put the following headings on it: (1) "What I Learned About Trains," (2) "What I Learned About the Computer," (3) "What I Learned About Getting Along With Others," and (4) "Project Review." They wrote about what they had learned about trains. Their new knowledge came from taking a field trip to the Historic Train Display, listening to guest speakers invited into the classroom, watching train videos, reading library books, and using CD-ROM encyclopedias and the Internet to search for information.

They wrote about some of the things that they had learned to do on the computer. They wrote about how to use the Internet to find information and graphics, how to use word processing to write a business letter, how to use the drawing and painting applications to make labels and illustrations for displays, and how to use the HyperStudio program to create multimedia presentations. They wrote about what they had learned about getting along with each other. They wrote about sharing ideas and supplies, doing their best, staying on task, being a responsible partner, and compromising to solve differences.

One student summed up the feelings of her classmates when she wrote, "I liked this project. It was really fun. The project helped me too. It taught me about trains." For a class review, they all gave this project a "Thumbs Up."

Negotiating the Curriculum and NTeQ

How does a teacher combine negotiating the curriculum as a part of the NTeQ planning model (see Figure 4-1)? Although it may at first appear complex, it is a natural and fluid process to use curriculum negotiation as part of the NTeQ model. Although the main objectives may be mandated by curricular frameworks, students can develop additional objectives they wish to achieve as part of the lesson. Based on these combined objectives, teachers and students can work together to examine computer functions, specify problems, plan data manipulation, and determine results presentation. For teachers unfamiliar with curriculum negotiation, start slowly. Choose one piece of the model to negotiate. For example, let students determine the format their results presentation will take. Your comfort level with negotiating the curriculum will build over time as you begin to see the powerful and meaningful learning that begins to take place in your classroom.

Figure 4-1   NTeQ Planning Model

Specify	Computer	Specify	Data	Results
Objectives	Functions	Problem	Manipulation	Presentation

	Supporting			
		After Using Computer	Activities Prior to Computer	Activities While at Computer
Assessment	Activities			

GROUP LEARNING

▲▲▲

While inquiry learning doesn't necessarily require students to work in groups, learning to function as an effective group member is a necessary skill for all students to master. The complexity of our modern society and increases in informational technology require individuals who are effective at interpersonal communication and understand the dynamics of group interaction. A strong facilitator assists his students by guiding groups in an effective and efficient manner, knowing when to intervene and when to leave the group alone.

In the previous section on negotiating the curriculum, we offered some examples of how teachers might alternate between group and whole class instruction. In this section, we offer more specific information on facilitating group learning in the classroom by considering the classroom environment, creating a culture of collaboration, considering group size and assignment, and using basic principles of cooperative learning.

CLASSROOM ENVIRONMENT

The set-up of your classroom environment will affect the nature of your learning groups (Freiberg & Driscoll, 1996). For groups to work effectively over time, there must be space and time for groups to meet. Some teachers solve this dilemma by grouping students' desks into teams of three or four students. Other teachers create specific places in the classroom where groups can meet. To figure out what arrangement will work best for you, consider the following ideas.

- How will you structure time for group work? Will all groups meet at the same time, with you moving from group to group? Or will groups of students rotate among different learning centers? Or will students work individually, and break into a group when you are ready to work with them? There are a variety of ways you and your groups can interact in the classroom. Experiment with several approaches (see Chapter 5).

- Make group work space conducive to learning. Be sure that students can sit near one another and are able to make eye contact with all other members in the group. Consider creating at least one "comfortable" group meeting place using pillows, cushions, etc.
- Consider how time restrictions will impact group work. High school students are able to work longer and more independently in groups than elementary age students. Will you designate certain days or periods as "group time," or will you have a more laissez-faire approach?
- What type of access do you have to computer technology? If students have to go to the library to use the Internet, and they can only go once a week, this will severely limit the group's ability to use that tool. Conversely, if you have a computer work station in your classroom, groups can take turns rotating during the day to accomplish their assignments.

CREATING A CULTURE OF COLLABORATION

Teaching students to work effectively in groups is a process of establishing group norms. By establishing and supporting group norms, in effect you are saying, "In this classroom, we work in this way for these reasons." Students are taught that collaboration is normal, expected, and valued. Following are some group norms that teachers should establish.

- Every team member is important.
- We work as a team and as individuals to accomplish our goals.

Student collaboration is encouraged in an NTeQ classroom.

- Diversity in opinions is important. We respect the right to be different, but we must work toward consensus.
- Instead of blaming or criticizing, we seek solutions to our problems.
- We structure our work according to individual needs.
- We help those who request it.

ESTABLISHING GROUPS

To create effective groups, teachers need to consider the size of the groups and how students will be assigned to them. For teachers and/or students new to group work, begin by using pairs. Working in dyads ensures that each student participates. Students develop basic interpersonal communication skills and teachers begin to feel comfortable having students "talk" in the classroom. Pairing is also effective when using technology. Students teach and learn from one another when sitting at the keyboard. Most inquiry projects function effectively with groups of three or four students. This size allows for expression of individual opinions, and yet is large enough to share the workload involved in inquiry projects. Although groups of five or more are useful in certain situations, we do not generally recommend them for inquiry groups. Groups this size can become difficult to manage, and some students are more likely to sit back while others do the work.

In terms of assigning students to groups, teachers have one of two choices—either assign students or let students assign themselves. We have used both approaches with varying effectiveness. In terms of ownership, students are naturally more motivated when they can choose their own group members. However, this can often lead to problems in group dynamics. Two "best friends" may tend to dominate group interaction, two or more "problem" students in the same group may impact group effectiveness and morale, or students may not be exposed to diverse opinions or skill levels when like minds choose to work together consistently over time. In these cases, it may be appropriate for the teacher to assign students to groups. When one of the authors, Lisa DeMeulle, was a second grade teacher, she often began the year by letting students choose their own work groups based on the understanding that some reassignments may be necessary to help support a collaborative work environment. Most students created effective working groups; however, there were times when Lisa felt it was necessary to reconfigure groups. She always discussed the reassignments privately with students so they wouldn't feel demoralized by the reassignment.

PRINCIPLES OF COOPERATIVE LEARNING

Cooperative learning has been touted as a highly effective structure for group learning. To distinguish cooperative learning from group learning in general, Johnson and Johnson (1991) describe the basic principles of cooperative learning.

1. **Positive interdependence.** Assignments are arranged so students become responsible to and for one another. One meaningful way of accomplishing this is to divide tasks and information collecting that is to be used by the whole group in compiling the results presentation.

2. **Face-to-face positive interaction.** Students support group members through "friendly" critique, praise, encouragement, and motivation. Teachers can support these interactions by directly teaching social skills (see Point 4).

3. **Individual accountability and responsibility.** Although students may be working as a team, individuals are still required to be personally responsible for their own work. This can be achieved by assessing individual contributions, and by asking students for peer evaluation during and at the completion of the inquiry project.

4. **Social skills aren't assumed.** In cooperative learning, teachers spend time teaching and reinforcing social skills. This is often the most neglected, yet most critical aspect of cooperative learning. Many teachers are often resentful that students don't take turns listening, support one another, problem solve, or stay on task. We can't assume that our students, at any age level, have developed these skills and must take time to reinforce them through group work.

5. **Group processing.** Processing is the time devoted to reflection on group functioning. This can occur during group work and/or at the completion of an assignment. Processing is the means by which group norms and social skills are reinforced. *Group processing is the key to creating a culture of collaboration in the classroom.*

SOCIAL SKILLS AND PROCESSING. Based both on research (Cohen, 1994) and our own personal experience, the time used to develop social skills through direct instruction ensures that group work will be productive. To highlight what social skills need to be taught, Johnson, Johnson & Holubec (1994) outline four levels of cooperative skills:

1. **Forming skills.** These include skills such as transitioning into groups quickly and quietly, using soft voices, taking turns, using group members' names, making eye contact, and respecting all opinions.

2. **Functioning skills.** These include group management skills such as restating the purpose of the assignment, keeping track of time limits, expressing support and praise for other members, clarifying, paraphrasing, and sharing feelings and humor.

3. **Formulating skills.** These include skills necessary for critical thinking and processing of the material being learned such as summarizing, seeking accuracy, elaborating to other material and ideas, seeking alternative means of processing information (drawing flow charts, visuals, etc.), and explaining the reasoning process.

4. **Fermenting skills.** These include reconceptualization skills such as criticizing ideas, not people, integrating various ideas into a new perspective, asking probing questions that lead to a deeper understanding, problem solving several alternative explanations or solutions, and justifying a solution.

Introduce one skill at a time. Let students know that along with an academic objective, you also have a social objective for the lesson. Another way to think about it is that every group lesson should include a task and a social skill. Introduce the task and the social skill at the beginning of the lesson. Let students know why the skill is important in the real world—this step is critical. Start with forming skills when new groups are initiated. Add additional skills each time groups work together.

At the completion of the group work (usually at the end of the period or the end of the week), allow time for the group to process its effectiveness with given social skills. In groups of three or four, 10–15 minutes is usually sufficient for processing. As groups become more efficient at processing, less time will be required. Encourage honesty and risk-taking during processing. Have students share in their group, one by one, how they felt the group performed on a given skill. Following is a scenario of what skill instruction and group processing might look like in a sixth grade classroom.

> Mr. Johnson is forming new groups for a social studies inquiry project. Students are already sitting in groups of four. Mr. Johnson begins by saying, "As you work in your groups today, I want you to focus on taking turns speaking. Be sure that everyone has a chance to share his/her opinion. If one person is speaking too much, the group should feel free to encourage others to participate. It's important in team efforts that the discussion includes everybody's opinions. This is how we become aware of the world around us, and how we get new ideas and learn." After the groups begin working on their task, Mr. Johnson monitors each group. He drops by and listens to the conversations. In one group he asks, "Has everyone had a chance to share their ideas?" In another, he notices that one student is overly quiet and withdrawn. At an appropriate interval in the conversation he draws this student in by asking, "Michael, what do you think about what's just been said?" After the groups have had a chance to work together, and then discuss their results in a whole class discussion, Mr. Johnson asks each group to spend 10 minutes processing. "Processing is a time for each group member to reflect on how their group functioned today. Today I asked you to focus on taking turns. One by one, go around the group and share how well you think your group achieved this task. In addition, share what you would like to see the next time your group works together. I encourage you to be honest with one another as that is how you will learn to work together and trust one another. Remember, no put downs."

Notice that Mr. Johnson is facilitating the groups—he directs and guides them to achieve both the academic task and the social skill he has assigned for the day. He keeps his dual objectives in mind and supports students so they can achieve these objectives effectively.

QUESTIONING STRATEGIES
▲▲▲

Questioning is the second most dominant instructional strategy (lecture is first) in upper elementary and high school teaching (Gall, 1984). Though second in usage, it can be easily argued that questioning is the most important teaching strategy. Research has shown that increased questioning increases student involvement and achievement (Pratton & Hales, 1986). All questions, however, are not alike.

Appropriate questioning strategies can facilitate the use of critical thinking skills.

A teacher can ask a question that leaves the student in a passive role, simply providing the stimulated response. A different type of question can engage a student to conceptualize ideas in new ways by articulating thought processes and opinions. It has been demonstrated that this type of questioning can actually create "neural branching," a literal strengthening of the brain (Cardellichio & Field, 1997). Most teachers want to engage their students in higher level thinking, yet their questioning strategies sometimes don't reflect this desire. Many teachers ask closed-response questions aimed at factual recall or at getting the "right" answer. Indeed, research has repeatedly shown that as little as 10–20 percent of questioning is aimed at higher level thinking (Dillon, 1988; Gall, 1984; Wragg, 1993).

As facilitators of learning, most teachers need new ways of engaging their students with questioning techniques aimed at higher level thinking. Because most of us were not taught this way, the process doesn't come naturally. Skilled questioning involves several things at once (Eggen & Kauchak, 1994): remembering the goals of the lesson, monitoring verbal and nonverbal behaviors, maintaining the flow of the lesson, and thinking about the next question. Today's teachers must be conscious of the way they question. With constant reflection and awareness, we and others (Rowe, 1986; Kerman, 1979) believe most teachers can develop the skills necessary to achieve higher level questioning.

We discuss three styles of questioning that help promote higher level thinking. These include higher level (analytical) vs. lower level (factual) questioning and convergent (one answer) vs. divergent (several possible answers) questioning. Finally, we examine techniques of effective questioning.

Figure 4-2   Example Questions Using Bloom's Taxonomy

CATEGORY	EXAMPLE QUESTIONS
Knowledge	Who were the major leaders in the civil rights movement? Who wrote *Uncle Tom's Cabin*?
Comprehension	Given the present rate of growth in Internet web pages, what will be the number of sites available in the year 2001? Where is an example of a simile in the poem?
Application	How has the ruling in *Brown* vs. *the Board of Education* affected schooling in this country? Let's measure the square footage of this room. How should we proceed?
Analysis	What are the facts and opinions in today's assigned reading? Why is this quote such a powerful way to begin this article?
Synthesis	What are the key findings of our study that we should communicate to the greater community? How can we work with our city to promote recycling in the schools?
Evaluation	What were the successes and failures of the women's movement in the 1960s? What are the weaknesses inherent in the Big Bang theory?

HIGHER AND LOWER LEVEL QUESTIONS

Most teachers are familiar with Bloom's Taxonomy (Bloom, Englehart, Furst, Hill & Krathwohl, 1956). The six levels of educational objectives they provide has been widely used as a model for developing sequential questions. In Figure 4-2, questioning can start at the recall or knowledge level and proceed up through synthesis and evaluation.

Although the use of Bloom's Taxonomy as a questioning framework is not very practical for most teachers given its complexity, it does illustrate several important ideas. First, an information base can be established at the beginning of a lesson by asking knowledge and comprehension questions. Once this common foundation is laid, it is easier to proceed to the higher levels of analysis, synthesis, and evaluation. In fact, inquiry projects lend themselves quite well to Bloom's Taxonomy.

CONVERGENT AND DIVERGENT QUESTIONS

Labeling questions as convergent and divergent is another way to think about levels of questioning. Convergent questions are closed-ended; the teacher is seeking one right response. Examples of convergent questions include "When was Martin Luther King, Jr., assassinated?" and "Who authored *Sula*?" Divergent questions

Figure 4-3   Comparing Convergent and Divergent Questions

CONVERGENT QUESTION	DIVERGENT QUESTION
Who were the disciples of Christ?	What roles did Christ's disciples play?
When was the first airplane built?	How did mass production of the airplane change transportation in America?
What is the area of a square 4′6″ × 2′?	Figure the area of a square 4′6″ × 2′. Show your procedures.
Who wrote *Little House on the Prairie*?	What aspects of *Little House on the Prairie* appear fictional? What's your rationale?

are open-ended and have a range of answers that are considered acceptable. However, not every answer to a divergent question is correct. Divergent questions are often those at the upper levels of Bloom's Taxonomy. Figure 4-3 illustrates the way a teacher can change a convergent question to a divergent question.

TECHNIQUES OF QUESTIONING

In addition to the types of questions a teacher can ask, there are proven effective ways and techniques of questioning students. The first technique is *redirecting*. When redirecting, the teacher asks several students to respond to a question without answering the responses or acknowledging the responses as right or wrong. The question is simply redirected to another student. This technique is often used to build broader participation in the class and to engage those students who are hesitant to get involved.

A second and valuable questioning technique is *wait time*. Research has shown that teachers usually wait only one second for students to answer questions (Rowe, 1978). By waiting three to five seconds before calling on an individual, more students respond, and confidence, speculative thinking, and questions from students all increase (Rowe, 1978).

A third technique used in the successful questioning process is *active listening*. A good active listener doesn't interrupt the speaker to provide correct information. Active listening involves waiting until the speaker is finished and restating the main ideas heard. At this point, a teacher can then intervene with more information, or redirect the question to another student.

A fourth technique used in questioning is *reinforcement*, which is praise or positive comment following an acceptable response. Responses such as "Intriguing idea!," "Great," or "Now you're thinking!" can be a powerful technique for encouraging students to participate. However, overuse of praise could have negative results. Students who don't get praised begin wondering if their answers are inadequate and become hesitant to participate further. Or if praise is offered too early in the answer, the student may not be motivated to elaborate on their thinking.

A fifth questioning technique is the use of *prompting*. A prompt is any question or directive the teacher makes after receiving an incorrect or incomplete answer. Some commonly used prompts include "Can you explain your thinking?" "Ann, do you agree or disagree with Sam? Why?" or "Are you saying (restate their answer)? So how do you account for (whatever was left out of the answer)?" The point in using prompts is to avoid making a student's answer "wrong." Instead, think of the prompt as a way to help the student understand the fallacy or misconception of their thinking without damaging their willingness to participate further in class discussions.

A final questioning technique involves *modeling*. A teacher can model her thought processes with students by "thinking aloud" (Collins, Brown & Newman, 1990) as she works through a given problem. For instance, when negotiating the curriculum, a teacher might assist students by asking them questions that will move them from one stage (What do we want to know?) to the next (How will we find out?).

> Mrs. J.: I see that you are interested in knowing more about space exploration, especially forms of space travel as they exist now and as they exist in fiction. I'm wondering what might be some effective ways to get answers to your questions?
> Tom: We could look on the CD-ROM.
> Brett: I have science fiction books at home that I could bring to class.
> Glorius: We could look up NASA on the Internet.
> Mrs. J.: Those are some interesting ideas. It sounds like you have some good investigative work to accomplish. How could each group delegate tasks for finding out information so everyone can be involved without being overwhelmed?

This sharing of mental processes in the form of questions helps the students to focus on the content as well as the processes used as part of the inquiry. Students begin to learn how to generate questions for themselves, and this is a critical component of higher-level cognitive ability (Scardamalia & Bereiter, 1985).

At the Classroom's Doorstep
▲▲▲

Questions Teachers Ask

What's an easy way to begin negotiating the curriculum while still covering objectives I'm required to teach? Let students know the objectives that have to be covered in the unit. You can then negotiate the manner in which those objectives will be covered.

At my school, a noisy classroom indicates a teacher who has lost control. How do I explain the group noise to my principal and co-workers? You must first reframe your own thinking. Examine the nature of the "noise." Is it due to children being off-task and goofing around, or is it the result of students truly engaged in a social learning process? Help your colleagues understand the value of social learning—children need opportunities to express their opinions, verbally explore their thinking with others, and brainstorm various ways of problem solving. This type of learning cannot take place when students sit quietly in rows completing worksheets. Once you believe in the value of social learning, and can articulate that value to others, you'll be on your way to converting other teachers to join the bandwagon. Good luck!

I want to ask higher level questions, but when I get involved in a discussion, they often slip from my mind. What can I do? Take 5–10 minutes before each lesson to develop some higher level questions based on the objectives for the lesson. Keep these on a 3 × 5 card. When you begin the discussion, refer to the 3 × 5 card. The extra 5–10 minutes you take to prepare can mean a world of difference in the understandings your students develop during the lesson.

REFERENCES

Bloom, B. S., Englehart, M. D., Furst, E. J., Hill, W. H., & Krathwohl, D. R. (Eds.) (1956). *Taxonomy of educational objectives: The classification of education goals. Handbook I: Cognitive domain.* New York: David McKay.

Cardellichio, T., & Field, W. (1997). Seven strategies that encourage neural branching. *Educational Leadership, (54)* 6, 33–37.

Cohen, E. G. (1994). Restructuring the classroom: conditions for productive small groups. *Review of Educational Research, 64*(1), 1–35.

Collins, A., Brown, J. S., & Newman, S. E. (1990). Cognitive apprenticeship: Teaching the crafts of reading, writing, and mathematics. In L. Resnick (Ed.), *Knowing, learning, and instruction: Essays in honor of Robert Glaser* (pp. 453–494). Hillsdale, NJ: Erlbaum.

Cook, J. (1992). Negotiating the curriculum: Programming for learning. In Boomer, G., Lester, N., Onore, C., & Cook, J. (Eds.). *Negotiating the curriculum: Educating for the 21st century.* London: Falmer Press.

Dillon, J. T. (1988). *Questioning and teaching.* New York: Teachers College Press.

Eggen, P., & Kauchak, D. (1994). *Educational psychology: Classroom connections.* (2nd ed.). Columbus, OH: Merrill.

Freiberg, H. J., & Driscoll, A. (1996). *Universal teaching strategies.* Needham Heights, MA: Allyn & Bacon.

Friere, P. (1971). *Pedagogy of the oppressed.* New York: Seaview.

Gall, M. (1984). Synthesis of research on teacher's questioning. *Educational Leadership, 42,* 40–47.

Johnson, D. W., & Johnson, R. T. (1991). *Learning together and alone.* Englewood Cliffs, NJ: Prentice Hall.

Johnson, D. W., Johnson, R. T., & Holubec E. J. (1994). *The new circles of learning.* Alexandria, VA: ASCD.

Kerman, S. (1979). Teacher expectations and student achievement. *Phi Delta Kappan, 60*(10), 70–72.

Murphy, J. (1995). Changing role of the teacher. In O'Hair & Odell (Eds.). *Educating teachers for leadership and change,* (pp. 311–333). Thousand Oaks, CA: Corwin Press, Inc.

Pratton, J., & Hales, L. W. (1986). The effects of active participation on student learning. *Journal of Educational Research, 74*(4), 210–215.

Rowe, M. B. (1978). *Teaching science as continuous inquiry.* New York: McGraw-Hill.

Rowe, M. B. (1986). Wait time: Slowing down may be a way of speeding up. *Journal of Teacher Education,* Jan/Feb, 43–50.

Scardamalia, M., & Bereiter, C. (1985). Fostering the development of self-regulation in children's knowledge processing. In S. F. Chipman, J. W. Segal, & R. Glaser (Eds.). *Thinking and learning skills: Vol. 2. Research and open questions* (pp. 563–577). Hillsdale, NJ: Erlbaum.

Slavin, R. E. (1993). Ability grouping in the middle grades: Achievement effects and alternatives. *Elementary School Journal, 93*(5), 535–552.

Wragg, E. C. (1993). *Primary teaching skills.* London: Routledge.

CHAPTER 5
Managing the Classroom

▶ Introduction

One's first view of a student-centered classroom can appear as anarchy to an administrator, mass hysteria to a fellow teacher, or a total loss of faith in our educational system by a parent who is used to traditional seat work. What the outside observer often fails to notice is the underlying planning, management, and organization that is guiding each students' endeavor. Granted, our first view of a student-centered classroom did not exactly match our expectations. The teacher, however, was the calmest teacher we have ever seen, even though her students were talking, moving about the room freely, and even in the hallway. After a few minutes of explanation, we began to see the implementation of her planning. Her room was probably managed better than the "quiet" rooms down the hall. Changing to a student-centered learning environment requires careful management of the classroom environment, but the benefits and rewards are well worth the effort.

In this chapter, we will discuss how to create and manage a classroom environment for using the computer as a tool for learning. We will also introduce the three stages that teachers go through while learning how to manage the integration of computers into the curriculum. Next we give some practical guidance for managing the multidimensional environment, such as rotation of students to the computers, managing the students while they are working on the computers, and managing the resources that accompany the use of technology. This is followed with information on how to manage students using the Internet.

▶ Key Topics

Classroom Management
   Classroom Environment
   Changes Over Time
Managing the Multidimensional Environment
   Managing the Rotation
   Managing Student Activities
Managing the Resources
   Student Disks
   Software and CD-ROMs
   Printing Supplies
   Desktop Management
   Computer Care
Managing the Internet
   Supervision and Guidance
   Acceptable Use Policies
   Filters

CLASSROOM MANAGEMENT

▲▲▲

The addition of computers to a classroom brings another dimension to the role of the teacher: that of a manager. When a teacher uses the NTeQ model, he is responsible for managing a multidimensional environment that integrates technology. If you examine this multidimensional environment during a lesson, it is almost impossible to separate the instructional aspects from the managerial aspects of the classroom (Weade & Evertson, 1991). Computers can be introduced without dramatically changing the instruction, but they cannot be introduced without making immediate shifts in classroom management processes (Sandholtz, Ringstaff, & Dwyer, 1990). In addition, Sandholtz, Ringstaff, and Dwyer (1990) indicate that "instructional innovation is not likely to occur until teachers have achieved a significant level of mastery over management issues" (p. 2). They also suggest the following points.

- Classroom management is not a skill that is mastered once and for all. As classroom contexts change, so do the classroom management issues.
- Educational change takes time. Teachers tend to focus on the increased workload and drawbacks associated with the innovation before the benefits of change emerge and the innovation takes hold.

Managing a classroom that uses an innovative approach (such as the NTeQ model) involves much more than just keeping the students quiet, in their seats, and working. To effectively manage a classroom that is integrating computers in a

In a well-managed classroom, students learn in whole-group activities as well as small-group activities.

meaningful way, the teacher must create an environment that is conducive to learning. In this environment, she must manage the movement of students to and from various activities, manage them while they are engaged in the activities, and manage the extra resources that are used in these activities. If Internet access is available, the teacher must also manage student use of these web-based resources. All of these managerial responsibilities may seem overwhelming at first, but with careful planning and time they become another everyday routine.

Fran's Diary

I had been in the public school classroom for 20 years when I received my computers. I had seen a lot of innovations come and go. I felt like technology was going to be around for a long time and that it was time for me to become more technically competent. When I got the computers, I felt excited, but also overwhelmed. How was I ever going to learn how to use the equipment and remember how to create a spreadsheet or a database? There was so much to learn! I spent many hours just learning how to operate the equipment and how to use the basic computer applications. By the end of that first year, I had become comfortable with the computer and had discovered that it was going to be a useful tool for me. I could see how it was making my job easier.

When school started the next year, I was ready for a change. I had mastered the computer, so to speak, and I wanted my students to master it too. I began to look at education from a more constructivist point of view and wanted my classroom to become child-centered. One of the first things I learned was my role as a teacher had to change. I had to become a facilitator of learning, not a director. Once I accepted that role, I began to look at how I had been teaching and realized that I was going to have to make some significant changes in how I approached learning and classroom management. I had many frustrations that year as I began to make those changes! It took me more time to plan my lessons. I had peers question what I was doing. I had to develop alternative assessments. I had to learn that a noisy classroom was OK. I had to let go and allow my students to have some input into what and how they were going to learn. There were days when I questioned what I had gotten myself into. Sometimes, I wondered if my students were really learning.

We were working on thematic unit projects about trains. The students had been paired up and were working on different topics related to trains. Some were working at desks, some were working at the computers, and some were working on the floor. The room was noisy because the students were talking as they worked together on their projects. There was a lot of movement to and

Continued

from the computers. I was on the floor helping some students work on a model of a freight train. I was so engrossed in what they were doing, that I did not realize a supervisor from Central Office had come into the room until she was standing over me. She had come to visit. She said she'd only be able to stay for a few minutes, and that she would just walk around the room to see what was going on. She told me to continue what I was doing. So, I got back on the floor and continued helping. I wondered what she was thinking as the room was noisy and no one was at their own seat working!

I continued to watch her as I worked with other groups and I noticed that she was moving from group to group talking to the students about their projects and what they had learned. Her "few minutes" visit turned into the rest of the afternoon. I apologized for the noise level and what appeared to be "organized" chaos. I thought that she might be disappointed because I was not "teaching" a lesson. She wasn't disappointed. Instead, she thanked me for letting her spend the afternoon with my students. She told me that I needed to remember that learning is not always going to be neat and tidy! She said that noise and "organized" chaos were sometimes part of an effective learning environment. She said she could tell that my students were learning and that was what was really important.

CLASSROOM ENVIRONMENT

The NTeQ model emphasizes an environment that is student-centered. The students are actively engaged in the learning process and assume the roles of researchers. To engage students in this manner, the teacher must work with the students to create an atmosphere or culture that fosters and supports a high level of student involvement, not only with the information they are learning, but also with each other. Ryba and Anderson (1993) provide six guidelines that students can follow to help create what they call a "computer learning culture":

1. helping one another solve problems
2. openly sharing information and ideas
3. reinforcing each other for making progress
4. [effectively] working in physically close proximity to one another
5. collectively supporting anyone who has a personal "crisis"
6. extending their effective working relationships beyond the computer environment (p. 5)

Another important aspect of managing a classroom environment that promotes student learning is to establish classroom rules and routines early in the school year. Mayeski (1997) suggests three general guidelines to consider when establishing classroom rules.

1. Make only a few rules—neither you nor the students will remember a long list.

2. Select rules because they establish an orderly environment and contribute to successful learning . . . gum chewing probably does not impede learning.

3. Make the rules as unambiguous as possible. They should be stated behaviorally. For example, "keep your hands and feet to yourself" is clearer than "no fighting" (p. 2).

Since the NTeQ model is based on a student-centered classroom, it is important to involve students in the formation of classroom rules and routines to give them a sense of ownership and responsibility for their learning environment (Mayeski, 1997).

Changes Over Time

When teachers are faced with a new innovation, such as computers in their classroom, they evolve through three stages: survival, mastery, and impact (Hall & Loucks, 1979). In the survival stage, teacher concerns are directed toward their own knowledge and skills. They often do not know enough about the computers to anticipate problems; therefore, they have to react to problems. After time and experience, the teachers move into the mastery stage where they plan for possible problems in advance. After teachers have established a comfortable routine, they can move into the impact stage where they focus more on the impact the computers have on student learning. In this stage, the teachers begin to modify and improve the way computers are used.

These stages were seen in a study of how teachers in Apple Classrooms of Tomorrow (ACOT) managed their classrooms (Sandholtz, Ringstaff, and Dwyer, 1990). The study revealed four areas related to managing a classroom with computers: student misbehavior and attitudes, physical environment, technical problems, and classroom dynamics. During the survival stage, teachers struggled with students copying work from other student's disks (since the teacher could not tell who did the work by examining the handwriting) or with students experimenting to see if magnets really do erase disks. Teachers also found that some students enjoyed the computers so much that they were quite reluctant to leave the computer area or complete handwritten assignments. Teachers at this stage were faced with classrooms that were now overcrowded with computer hardware and equipment that was sometimes difficult to use because of improper lighting, glare from windows, or bad weather conditions. Along with the introduction of computers came the technical problems that were associated with using computers: software and equipment failures, bad disks, and printing problems. A final concern of some teachers at the survival stage was that they were often faced with students who knew more than they did about technology.

The study found that by the second year, teachers moved into the mastery stage. In this stage, the teachers' knowledge and skills had increased so they could better plan for and anticipate technology-related problems. They handled student misbehavior by restricting computer access, and they found ways to reorganize their classrooms to provide more open space and utilize the best lighting. Contingency plans were developed to handle bad weather and equipment failures. Procedures were developed to handle printing problems, and the teachers became more comfortable using their students' expertise.

After teachers mastered the management challenges presented in a technology-rich classroom, they moved to the impact stage. In this stage, they used computers to assist them with their instructional and maintenance tasks (Chapter 14 and Chapter 15), as well as to modify and improve their management techniques.

The teachers in the Apple Classrooms of Tomorrow were like pioneers when it came to integrating computers into their curricula. Teachers can now learn from the ACOT experiences and from the experiences of other teachers who have successfully integrated technology into their curriculum. Teachers from over 200 schools in 18 states participated in the ACOT study. These teachers indicated that local and peer-to-peer resources were the most valuable for technology-related issues (Casson, Bauman, Fisher, Sumpter, & Tornatzky, 1997). Therefore, as you begin to integrate technology into your curriculum, it is important that you find other teachers in your school or in your district that have experience and are willing to assist you. Perhaps these resources will make your survival stage shorter and easier.

Managing the Multidimensional Environment
▲▲▲

The following sections provide practical guidelines and advice on how to manage a multidimensional environment. This environment has students engaged in computer use as well as other activities such as researching for information from books and magazines, collecting data from observations, sketching storyboards for a multimedia presentation (Chapter 11), gathering information from a videotape, or conducting an experiment. As you can see, this type of environment is student centered, very active, and requires careful planning and cooperation from the students. Plans are needed for moving students to and from the various activities, for managing the students while they are at the computers, and also for managing the extra resources required by the technology.

Managing the Rotation

There are several factors to consider when planning student rotation through multiple activities. Your plan will vary according to computer access. For example, will your students use computers in the classroom, in the lab, or in both places? If you have computers in your classroom, then you need to consider how the students will rotate through the available computers. Both of these considerations are discussed in this section.

Working with What You Have. As you develop your NTeQ lessons, it is important to build them around the resources that you have available. The types of computer access can be categorized into three typical groups:

- *Single Use:* one to two computers per classroom
- *Small Group:* three to six computers per class
- *Computer Lab:* room of computers with one to two students per computer

The amount and type of materials that teachers manage changes when computers are added to the classroom.

Single use. If you only have one computer in your classroom, lessons should require only minimal computer access for each student. Activities for a one-computer classroom could include the following.

- Student groups collecting and entering data for designated sections of a class database, for example:
  - one state from each region
  - five presidents
  - endangered species from one country
  - examples of a particular shape (squares or rectangles)
- Each student creates one page of a classroom stack:
  - an original poem in a class book of spring poems
  - a definition and example in a "Correct Grammar" stack
  - a brief biographical sketch of a famous scientist
- Student groups enter their data into a class spreadsheet:
  - each group collects and enters different weather data
  - each group conducts the same experiment then enters their data for comparison (e.g., how high do ping pong balls bounce when dropped from different heights, or the number of people wearing seat belts at different times of day)
  - Each student or pair of students adds a paragraph to an original class story.

McClelland (1996) and Wiebe (1993) suggest that cooperative learning is very successful when you are limited to one or two computers. McClelland emphasizes the importance of establishing student roles for computer use, and ensuring that the roles are rotated to provide equal access to all students.

Small group. When a teacher has access to three to six computers in his classroom, student use of technology can be routinely included in the lessons. Students can be involved in the same types of activities listed for the one-computer classroom; however, the projects would be group projects rather than class projects. Even in a setting with more computers, though, cooperative learning is still effective for student learning at the computer (Willing & Girard, 1990). The layout of the classroom will need to accommodate from two to three chairs at each computer.

Computer labs. Computer use can also be routinely included in lessons if teachers regularly have access to a lab. The number of computers in the lab may require that students work together, or each student may work at an individual computer. It is important to encourage students to share ideas and provide assistance to one another in a lab setting to ensure that the "computer-learning culture" is maintained.

Managing the Move.
Once you know where your students will use the computers, you need a plan for how to move students to and from the computers. Since moving to a computer lab involves taking the whole class, we will focus on rotation schedules for classroom computers. As mentioned in Chapter 2, you can plan lessons around two primary types: group rotation or independent rotation.

Group rotation. With group rotation, small groups of students stay together as they move from one lesson activity center to another (Figure 5-1). To manage this type of rotation, the teacher needs to determine approximately how long the activity at each station or center will take. If possible, each center should take about the same amount of time for completion. This scheduling helps students rotate through the centers at regular intervals.

Another consideration is to have more than one center for activities that take longer. For example, if students are collecting information about several different categories from a variety of travel brochures, the research activity may take longer than setting up the database and entering the collected information. In this case, you may want to set up two research centers so students can spend twice as long on this activity. One center could be for researching historical sites and the other could be for researching weather patterns. The rotation can be managed by having students move through the stations in a clockwise or other predetermined pattern. You can use a kitchen timer to alert students when it is time to move. If the timer is set for two minutes before they need to move, the students will have time to finish the task at hand and to straighten the area. When group rotations are used, the student-to-computer ratio is often one to one, which ensures equal computer access. But again, just as was mentioned for the lab, you need to encourage students to work as a team.

Figure 5-1   Classroom Layout for Group Rotation

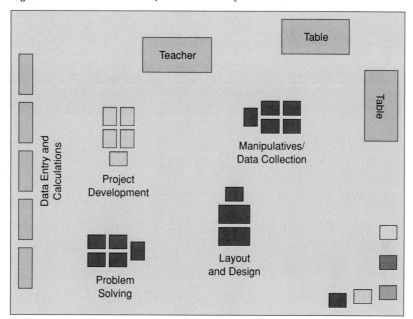

Independent rotation. The second type of rotation, independent rotation (see Figure 5-2), still has students in small cooperative groups, but the groups do not rotate to each activity in an established pattern. Rather, in this setup, students can access all the resources needed to solve the problem designated in the lesson, thus allowing the students to use the resources on an as-needed basis. With independent rotation, each group is assigned a computer. (Sometimes, though, more than one group has to be assigned to a computer, as was seen in Mr. Carter's class in Chapter 2.) If more than one group is assigned to a computer, you will need to establish a schedule for computer use. The teacher can create a schedule (see Figure 2-1 in Chapter 2), or the student groups who are sharing the computer can establish their own schedule. It is probably wise to have the teacher create the first schedules so students can experience well-planned routines. After students have been involved with several integration lessons, they will be better able to plan their own rotation schedules. In either situation, however, computer tasks must be divided equally among the group members.

Managing Student Activities

Once students are using the computers, the teacher must manage three primary types of student activities: assisting students who need help with computer skills, dealing with any technical problems, and keeping students on task. Management suggestions for these activities are described in the following paragraphs.

Figure 5-2 Classroom Layout for Independent Rotation

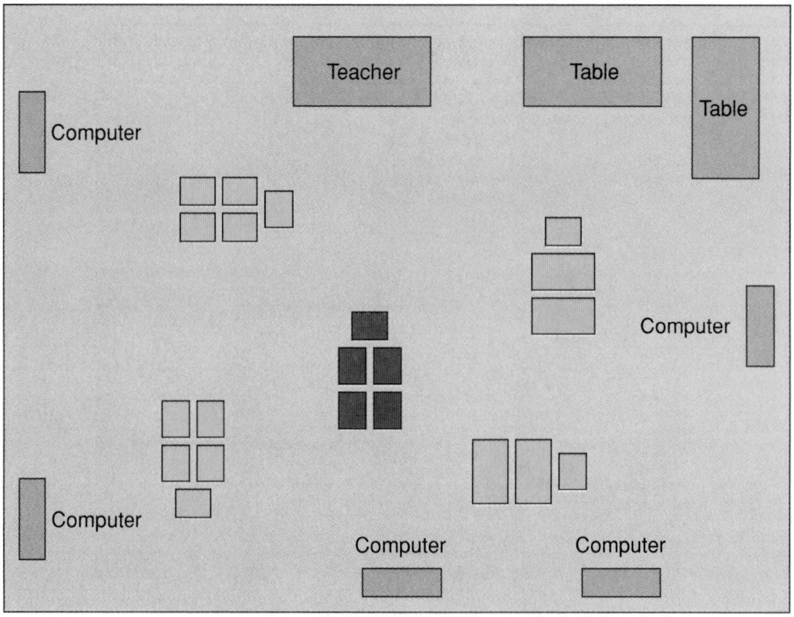

ASSISTING STUDENTS WITH COMPUTER SKILLS.
When computers are added to a classroom, many teachers are faced with not only teaching subject-matter content, but also with teaching computer skills. There are several ways to help students acquire and use new computer skills. We will discuss four of those methods.

- teacher modeling/demonstration
- peer-modeling and assistance
- technology posters or job-aids
- student handouts

Teacher modeling/demonstration. Students can learn new computer skills by observing the teacher as she models the desired task (Churchward, 1997). Monica Campbell teaches her fifth grade students new computer skills by first modeling the skill with the aid of a large monitor. She has her students take notes and ask questions during the demonstration. Student groups then rotate to the computers to practice what they have learned.

Peer-modeling and assistance. Another method involves training a corps of students to help their peers learn new computer skills and assist students that are experiencing problems (Sandholtz et al., 1990). When students at the computers need help, they can raise their hand, or they can use another system for alerting the teacher or student assistant. One method uses a paper cup marker. With this system, a paper cup is placed on each monitor. If the paper cup is upside down, the students are OK; if it is turned upright, the student needs assistance. This type of

Figure 5-3 Technology Poster

How to save your work on a disk.

1. Insert disk into disk drive.

2. Select **Save** as from **File** menu

3. Click on **Desktop**.

4. Select your disk, and click on **Open**.

5. Enter the name of your file in the box.

6. Click on **Save**.

system, or another type of "marker" system, avoids students waving their arms and causing distractions to get attention.

Technology posters or job-aids. Students can also learn computer skills by using technology posters or job-aids of frequently used tasks. Technology posters consist of very brief step-by-step instructions for common computer tasks such as saving to a disk, opening an application, or printing a document. The posters are displayed by the computers so students can easily refer to them when needed (see Figure 5-3). Job-aids also provide easy, step-by-step instructions for commonly used computer functions and applications. They typically include more information than a poster can display, however, and are often kept in folders, notebooks, or on note cards. The job-aids are not put on display because they are created for tasks that are not completed everyday. For example, job-aids might be made for creating a simple database, a simple spreadsheet, or mail merge documents.

Student handouts. You can also assist with computer skills by including step-by-step instructions with the handouts used for a lesson. This method automatically integrates the content with the technology guidelines. Many times the teacher can create one handout that serves several purposes. The handout can include the problem statement, general instructions for the lesson, step-by-step guidelines for using the computer as a tool to solve the problem, and the Think Sheet questions (Chapter 3). Mary Kemp, a middle school teacher, uses the following student handout for a lesson she created on vertebrates (see Figure 5-4).

Assisting with Technical Problems.

The most frequent complaints of teachers in the ACOT classrooms were those related to technical problems (Sandholtz et al., 1990). The teachers indicated that their curriculum "got bogged down and students fell behind in their work" when the computers malfunctioned (p. 4).

Figure 5-4   Lesson Handout with Technology Guidelines

Vertebrate Unit

Problem Statement
Do all vertebrates lay eggs? If not, which groups do not? Are there any exceptions?

Directions:
To answer these questions, you will go to the computer station assigned to your group and use the vertebrate database compiled by the class. Follow the directions below and work cooperatively with your group to sort the data by different fields, analyze the data to answer some questions, and complete a word processing document (using the format previously taught in class) that answers the questions. You will have the entire class period to complete the assignment. Turn the word processing document, along with the printouts of your database sorts, into the basket by the end of the class. If you finish early, return to your table and work on your plan for your group's multimedia presentation.

Step-by-Step:
1. Open the vertebrate database and select **Layout 2** under **Layout** on the menu bar.
2. Select **Sort** under **Organize** on the menu bar.
3. Select **Vertebrate Group** under the **Field List**, and click the **Move** button to move it to the **Sort Order** box. Click the **Ascending Order** button and then click **OK**. Print your sorted list.
4. Following the directions above, select the fields listed below from the **Field List**, one at a time, and **Move** them to the **Sort Order** box. Be sure to **Move** the previous field from the **Sort Order** box before clicking **OK**. Print each sorted list before choosing the next field.
   Sort by the following fields and print your sorted lists:
   • Body Temperature
   • Body Covering
   • Method of Fertilization
   • Method of Birth
5. Review your sorted lists and work together to answer the questions listed below.
6. Use word processing to answer the questions. Be sure to type each question and then a short paragraph answering it.

Think Sheet Questions:
I.   Do all vertebrates lay eggs? If not, which groups do not? Are there any exceptions?
II. What is the main body covering for each vertebrate group? Compare body temperature to body covering. How would you explain the major differences in body covering for cold-blooded versus warm-blooded vertebrates?
III. Compare body temperature to method of fertilization. Which groups are alike? Which group is different from the others?
IV. Compare method of fertilization to method of birth. What is the main difference between vertebrates with external fertilization versus those with internal fertilization? How do you explain this?
V.   What are the major subgroups for each vertebrate group?

Figure 5-5   Restarting a Macintosh Computer

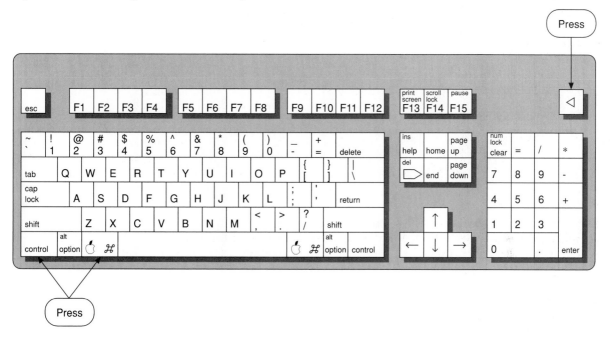

Teachers who participated in the Southern Technology Council study reported similar concerns (Casson et al., 1997). These concerns may have stemmed from school districts employing only one to three computer technicians for all the schools within their districts. When computer technicians are not available for teachers, they must then rely on some of the following methods for support (Casson et al., 1997, Sandholtz et al., 1990).

- advice from other "expert" teachers in the same building, on a listserv, or a web site
- advice from "expert" students
- troubleshooting handbooks or hotlines
- adult volunteers (parents, college staff, business or government employees) willing to assist teachers and students with technological concerns
- attending seminars and workshops to learn technical troubleshooting

As teachers spend more time with computers, they become more adept at solving common technical problems. Here are some troubleshooting tips that may be helpful.

- To restart the computer when it is "locked up," press **Control**, **Command**, and the **Startup** keys simultaneously (Figure 5-5).
- To close an application when it is "locked up," press **Control**, **Command**, and the **Escape** keys simultaneously (Figure 5-6).

Figure 5-6   Closing a "Locked Up" Application

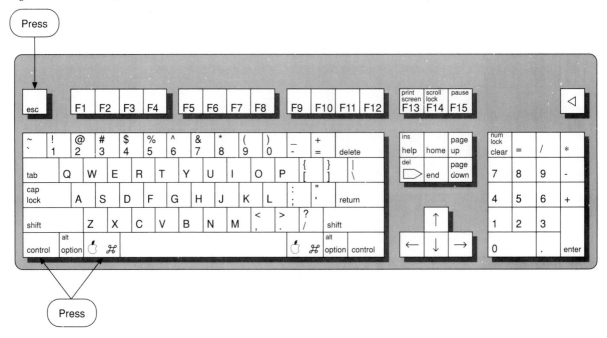

- To remove a floppy disk that will not come out with menu commands, insert the end of a paper clip into the hole by the disk drive and gently push to eject the disk (Figure 5-7).

KEEPING STUDENTS ON TASK.   Keeping students on task is often more challenging when students are working at computers. Computers are equipped with many fascinating features that beckon to inquisitive student minds. There are intriguing screen

---

Power Tip ▲▲▲   *Listservs*

There are many listservs that help computer users solve problems with computers and specific software. We created a listserv to help teachers who have technical problems with software and computers. During the past two years, a number of computer experts have joined the listserv to provide answers and suggestions to technical problems. You can join the listserv by sending an e-mail to maiser@coe.memphis.edu and including the following words in the body of the message: SUBSCRIBE TEACHTECH.

You will receive an e-mail confirmation with instructions on using the listserv within an hour or two. Be sure to save the message as it includes important information.

Figure 5-7   Manually Ejecting a Disk

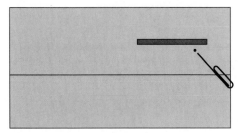

savers that can be modified, games to be played, and, of course, little mischievous pranks to be pulled. Students quickly learn that they can easily change the names of folders, (for example "Susie" to "Skinny Susie") or they can hide a student's file in an obscure folder somewhere on the hard drive. However, many of these student diversions occur because the required computer tasks are not relevant, interesting, or challenging. The following guidelines will help to keep students on task:

- implement the NTeQ model:
    - present students with interesting problems that use real-world information and data that they themselves collect
    - use collaborative learning groups
    - involve students in decision making
- monitor student activities (Churchward, 1997):
    - pass through an area about two minutes after students have started a new assignment. This delay allows the teacher to determine if the students understand what is required.
    - provide individual assistance to students as it is needed
    - make general announcements only if several students are experiencing the same problem
    - make it a habit to check the Internet sites the students have visited while conducting a search (e.g., **Go** option on Netscape's menu). More information on managing the Internet is seen in a following section.
- involve students in establishing class rules for using the computer. These rules could include:
    - only use the computer for the assigned lesson, unless special permission is obtained. Special permission might be given for students who have completed their assignments and want to create a customized screen saver, conduct an Internet search for an upcoming vacation, check on their favorite football team, or find the admission requirements for a college.
    - never open or alter another student's computer files, or any computer files other than your own

Managing the Resources
▲▲▲

Computers require more "stuff" to make them work than other learning tools, such as calculators or VCRs. Computers often need floppy disks, software, CD-ROMs, and a printer. Besides the computer needing more resources, the desktop of the computers also needs to be managed, and the computer itself needs to be maintained. This section provides some practical guidelines for managing these components.

Student Disks

Each student should have at least one high density floppy disk. If they are going to create multimedia projects, such as HyperStudio stacks, they will need more than one disk. Encourage students to purchase disks from a well-known company to avoid disk failures that result in the loss of student work. It is often best to keep the student disks in a centralized location rather than have the students keep track of their own disks. In a self-contained class, the teacher can have one disk storage box that holds the labeled student disks in alphabetical order by the student's last name. In a departmentalized setting, the teacher can have one disk storage box for each period. The disk storage boxes should be kept in a dry location without temperature extremes or direct sunlight. It is also important to keep the disks away from magnetic fields such as TVs, computer monitors, or speakers.

Software and CD-ROMs

Computers need software applications to be useful. Many computers come equipped with applications already loaded on the hard drive; however, most people want to enhance their computers by adding new applications. This new software normally comes with a user's guide and a CD-ROM or floppy disks containing the actual application. The CD-ROM or floppy disks are used to load the application on the hard drive. After the installation, the teacher needs to find a safe location to store the CD-ROM or disks and the user's manual. The manuals need to be kept in a place that is easily accessible for quick reference. The disks or CD-ROMs can be stored in a box marked as "Master Software Disks." There are strict copyright laws regarding software applications; therefore, it is very important to always have the original software for all applications on each computer.

Printing Supplies

When students complete their assignments on a computer or do an Internet or CD-ROM search for information, they have to use a printer to see a paper copy of their work. For printers to function, they need paper and some form of cartridge, both of which can get costly if a monitoring system is not used. The cost of printer cartridges can be reduced by purchasing recycled ones, or refilling them with ink when using an ink jet printer.

The amount of printing can be minimized when students create documents with one of the ClarisWorks applications, such as word processing, database, spreadsheet, or draw. Teach students to do the majority of their editing on the computer. Student printing can be reduced to only one or two copies of each paper when stu-

Figure 5-8   Print Preview

Based on a unit by Mary Kemp.

dents learn to edit on the screen. When students are conducting searches from the Internet or a CD-ROM, have them use the Preview function of the Print dialog box to determine how many pages the document contains (see Figure 5-8). They can then print only the pages they actually need.

DESKTOP MANAGEMENT

There are multiple ways to format the desktop of a computer. Following are some guidelines for managing the desktop of a classroom computer.

It is helpful to designate one folder for student work. This folder can be titled "Student Folder." Folders within the "Student Folder" can be arranged either by student's last name (see Figure 5-9), or by subject area, with student work by last name within each subject area folder (see Figure 5-10).

Power Tip ▲▲▲   *Text Editor*

If your students are quite competent in using a computer, they can use a text editor with their web browser to preview information. For example, we use Simple Text which is a free text editor for the Macintosh. When we find something on a web page that is of interest, we copy it to Simple Text, then we cut out the text that we do not want. We can then manage the number of pages sent to the printer.

Figure 5-9   Student Folder by Student Last Name

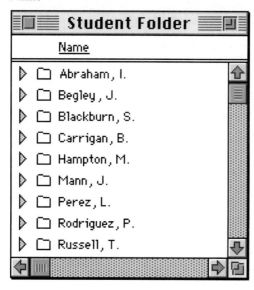

Establish a specific name for the students to use for each assignment to make it easier to locate their work. For example, the file name can include the initial for the subject area, date, and student initials. The file name for a math paper completed on February 11 by Tina Lawrence would be: M.2/11.TL. To help students remember how to label their files, a poster with labeling keys could be displayed in the computer area.

COMPUTER CARE

Not only do the computer resources and computer desktops need to be managed, but the computers themselves need to be maintained and managed. Some simple guidelines for computer management are listed here.

Power Tip ▲▲▲   *Computer Maintenance*

Computers are kind of like cars and children—they need maintenance on a regular basis. Unfortunately, most teachers do not have the time to perform this needed maintenance and they may even lack the expertise. Have you considered the other resources available? For example, you might find that many parents in your school have a great deal of computer expertise.

You can form a parents group that might meet at the school one evening a month to do computer maintenance. Often, this simple routine maintenance that takes only a few minutes can prevent major problems. Similarly, some parents might be willing to donate time to more serious repairs or complicated tasks.

Figure 5-10   Student Folder by Subject Area

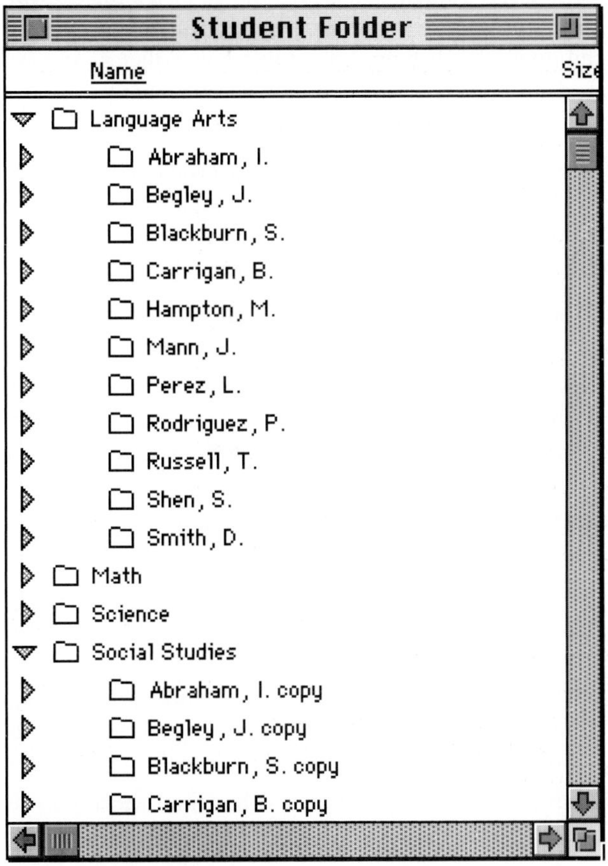

- Do not allow any food, drinks, or gum in the computer area.
- Avoid touching the computer monitor with fingers.
- Cover computers and keyboards, if possible.
- Use screen savers to protect the monitor.
- Secure cords and cables away from traffic.
- Clean the mouse tracking balls with alcohol on a regular basis.
- Use a virus protection software.

MANAGING THE INTERNET
▲▲▲

Many teachers and parents are greatly concerned about student access to the Internet. Due to the unrestricted nature of the medium, it is easy to locate web sites, newsgroups, and listservs that are sexual or violent in nature. While Congress considers regulating Internet usage from time to time, it's still a very open market with all types of information available to anyone. Rather than taking a "ban the book" approach to the Internet, most school districts have developed a variety of approaches to assist students in using the Internet for appropriate educational purposes. These approaches include offering teachers support on supervision and guidance techniques, developing Acceptable Use Policies, and using Internet filters.

SUPERVISION AND GUIDANCE

When integrating Internet technology into the curriculum, a teacher's work doesn't stop with the design process. Internet usage in the schools requires supervision and guidance, and students must be educated as to appropriate uses with the medium. Some basic first steps for teachers to take might include:

1. Discuss the Acceptable Use Policy (see following section) with your students. Have everyone sign the document, and have parents sign as well.

2. Discuss safety issues for on-line communication. Students must know that in no case should they ever give out personal information such as a telephone number, address, or school location without the teacher's permission.

3. If students would like to meet someone that they've met on-line, make sure they obtain permission from parents, and that they meet in a public place and bring a parent with them.

4. Have students inform you immediately if they access something that makes them feel uncomfortable or "not right."

5. Set limits for on-line usage. Will students be assigned specific time slots? Can they access it during free time, library time, or before and after school? How long will they be allowed to stay on-line?

6. If students wish to visit sites other than those you've bookmarked or those that support the lesson, they must first get your permission.

For more information on safety, supervision, and guidance issues, check the following sites

A Parent's Guide to Supervising a Child's Online and Internet Experience
http://www.cais.net/cannon/memos/parents.htm

Yahooligans Rules for Online Safety
http://www.yahooligans.com/docs/safety

ACCEPTABLE USE POLICIES

Acceptable Use Policies (AUP) are documents indicating to all concerned parties (parents, teachers, and students) the appropriate uses of Internet technology, as well as consequences for students when the AUP is violated. These documents are usually signed early in the school year by both students and parents. Figure 5-11 shows one example of an AUP.

Many school districts now have standard AUPs that they require of all students. If your school is in the process of developing an AUP, check the following resources for examples of AUPs, as well as issues to consider in the process:

Figure 5-11   Acceptable Use Policy

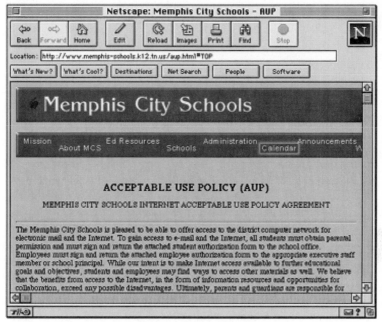

Courtesy of Memphis City Schools.

Armadillo	http://chico.rice.edu/armadillo/acceptable.html
AskEric	http://ericir.syr.edu:70/11/Guides/Agreements
Memphis City Schools	http://www.memphis-schools.k12.tn.us/aup.html

FILTERS

Filters are software programs that block access to certain Internet features. Blocking features can be based on time of day, subject of site, etc. Although many filters can be downloaded for free, registration with the software provider will provide automatic updates to sites automatically blocked by the computer. Don't rely too strong on filters in the classroom, however. Their blocking capabilities are limited at best, and older students have a particular talent for searching out inappropriate material that may be hidden under a title name that isn't blocked.

For information on where to download Internet filters, see the following.

Cyber Patrol	http://www.cyberpatrol.com
Net Nanny	http://www.netnanny.com/netnanny/
Net Shepherd	http://shepherd.net/
Safesurf	http://www.safesurf.com/
Surfwatch	http://www.surfwatch.com/

At The Classroom's Doorstep
▲▲▲
Questions Teachers Ask

It sounds good to have a corps of students who are trained as computer assistants, but how do we get these students trained? Students can become knowledgeable about computers in several different ways. A group of students can receive training when the teachers are trained. Some teachers offer mini-lessons before or after school or at lunch. If a school has a computer lab that is staffed with a computer teacher, this teacher may offer specialized training to future student technology assistants. Business or university personnel can also volunteer to train students in basic computer troubleshooting or operations.

Managing computers in my classroom sounds expensive. Are there some ways to save money? Teachers can save money on disk storage boxes by creatively using inexpensive plastic bins. Note cards can be used to create alphabetical dividers for the disks. Money can be saved on paper by printing on both sides of paper that has not been wrinkled or damaged. Businesses often will give classroom teachers paper from discarded reports, letterhead that has changed, or other documents that are no longer used. The recycled paper can be used for draft copies of student work.

How do I find "good" floppy disks? We wish we had a good answer for this question as we have many stacks of bad disks. One class project is to track the number of bad disks and the reliability of others. Once you find a reliable brand, stick with it as long as it works. Floppy disks seem to have a limited lifetime based on use. Some users state that you should never use a floppy disk for more than 100 save operations. A good defense is to have a good disk utility that you can use to recover files on a damaged disk. Once a student has a problem with a floppy disk, copy the files to another floppy and discard the bad disk. We have found it is better to be safe than sorry when dealing with disks.

References
▲▲▲

Casson, L., Bauman, J., Fisher, E., Sumpter, J., & Tornatzky, L. G. (1997). Making technology happen: Best practices and policies from exemplary K–12 Schools. Report. Southern Technology Council, Southern Growth Policies Board.

Churchward, B. (1997, September 11). The honor level system: Discipline by design: 11 techniques for better classroom discipline. [On-line]. Available: http://members.aol.com/churchward/hls/techniques.html.

Hall, G. E. & Loucks, S. (1979). Teacher concerns as a basis for facilitating and personalizing staff development. In A. Lieberman and L. Miller (Eds.). *Staff development: New demands , new realities, new perspectives.* New York: Teachers Press.

Mayeski , F. (1997, May 6). The metamorphosis of classroom management. [On-line]. Available: http://www.mcrel.org/products/noteworthy/franm.html.

McClelland, S. (1996, March 20). The one computer classroom. [On-line]. Available: http://www.indep.k12.mo.us/THS/lesley/mcclelland/one%20computer.html.

Ryba, K. & Anderson, B. (1993). *Learning with computers: Effective teaching strategies.* Eugene, OR: International Society for Technology in Education.

Sandholtz, J. H., Ringstaff, C., & Dwyer, D. (1990). Teaching in high tech environments: Classroom management revisited, first–fourth year findings.

Apple Classrooms of Tomorrow Research Report Number 10. [On-line]. Available: http://www.research.apple.com/Research/proj/acot/full/acotRpt10full.html.

Weade, R. & Evertson, C. M. (1991). The construction of lessons in effective and less effective classrooms. In U. Casanova, D.C. Berliner, P. Placier, & L. Weiner (Eds.). *Classroom management: Readings in educational research* (pp. 136–159). Washington, DC: National Education Association.

Wiebe, J. (1993). *Computer tools and problem solving in mathematics*. Wilsonville, OR: Franklin, Beedle & Associates Inc.

Willing, K. R. & Girard, S. (1990). *Learning together: Computer-integrated classrooms*. Markham, Ontario: Pembroke Publishers Limited.

CHAPTER 6

Addressing the Needs of Diverse Learners*

▶ Introduction

Public education in the United States has a rich history of attempting to adapt instruction to the individual learner (Park, 1996). In the early 1900s educators attempted to adapt instruction to the individual through self-pacing with the Burke plan, Dalton plan, and Winnetka plan (Reiser, 1987). In the early 1960s Keller's personalized system of instruction (Keller & Sherman, 1982) and Postlethwait's audio-tutorial system (Postlethwait et al., 1972) personalized the instruction for each individual. Another popular approach was Bloom's mastery learning. Students achieved content mastery by having *sufficient time* to master the content (Block, 1980). Other approaches have focused on the different aptitudes of students. For example, Kolb (1984, 1985) developed an inventory to adapt instruction to different student aptitudes; however, there is not sufficient empirical evidence to support the value of adapting instruction to these learning styles (Park, 1996). Our focus in this chapter is on how to adapt the instructional environment to support learning for all students. We will investigate ways to structure the social and physical environment to enhance student achievement, as well as look at the needs of multicultural learners and students with special needs.

▶ Computer Skills Used In This Chapter
Web browser

▶ Key Topics
Adapting the Learning Environment
  Student Learning Variables
  Determining Student Learning Preferences
  Changing the Learning Environment
Adapting to the Needs of the Multicultural Classroom
Assistive Technology for Learners with Special Needs
  Computer Access for Persons with Disabilities
  Adapting the Computer for Persons with Sensory Impairments
  Adapting the Computer for Persons with Motor Impairments
  Other Environmental Considerations for Persons with Disabilities

*Dr. Tom Buggey of the University of Memphis contributed the section on assistive technology.

ADAPTING THE LEARNING ENVIRONMENT
▲▲▲

One problem with attempting to address the various learning styles in a classroom is the need for *multiple* forms of instruction for each different learning style. Unfortunately, most textbooks and other classroom materials are only available in a generic, one-approach-fits-all learning style. While this approach might be easy, it places an extra burden on the teacher that is not always practical. A more viable approach is one of adapting of the learning environment to various learning preferences. Let's examine the variables you can change in a learning environment, how to determine a student's learning preferences, and then consider ways of adapting the learning environment.

STUDENT LEARNING VARIABLES

Dunn & Dunn (1978) identified four major groupings of variables related to student preferences for learning. As a teacher, you can often change the variables to enhance the learning environment. We will examine each of these groupings—environmental, emotional, sociological, and physical as they apply to the classroom.

ENVIRONMENTAL.
The classroom environment includes sound, light, temperature, and design elements. Have you ever compared the way you work at home versus the way you worked in a classroom as a grade school student? If your classroom was like most of ours, it was quiet. At home, however, we often have some music or the television as background noise while we work. One environmental variable you can manipulate is the availability of sound (e.g., music and class discussions) for students. Remember, though, the range of preferences is from complete quiet to some noise. The second environmental variable is the amount of light provided in the work areas. Some students might prefer to work in a softer light provided by an incandescent bulb while others might prefer the brighter light of a high intensity bulb. Temperature is the third environmental variable and is probably the one you will have the least control over—it will either be too hot or too cold! The fourth environmental variable is the design of the classroom. Preferences for design range from a very informal layout (e.g., a rug and bean bags) to a very formal layout with desks and chairs in perfect rows and students exhibiting good posture.

EMOTIONAL.
This variable refers to persistence, motivation, and structure—elements you can manipulate through instructional assignments. Persistence refers to an individual's ability to stay focused on a task to completion. Persistence varies from student to student and even between some subjects for a given student. Those with low persistence in a given subject may give up in frustration and not complete the task. Responsibility is the ability to work without teacher or adult supervision on a given task until it is completed. Last, structure refers to the number of options you can give a student. For example, some students are capable of selecting and working on a number of assignments while other students cannot make a decision when given different options.

SOCIOLOGICAL. This group of elements describes how students like to work with others. For example, some students only want to work by themselves and resent working on a team or with another student. Others want to work with the teacher or an adult while other students prefer to work with their peers.

PHYSICAL. This grouping includes a variety of ways students perceive information and the modes they prefer for learning. Dunn & Dunn (1978) describe perceptual strengths as the way students like to learn. Although students might have a preference such as reading instead of listening to a lecture, there is little evidence to suggest that students learn *only* in the preferred mode. A second variable in this category is intake, which refers to eating or drinking while studying or working. Some of us prefer to drink coffee or a soft drink and nibble on crackers while working. Time of day for studying or working is the third variable in this category. As a college student, you probably expressed your learning preference by attempting to select classes that met at your best learning times. That is, if you were a night person, then you probably tried to avoid the early morning classes. The last variable in this grouping is mobility, which refers to a student's preference to move about or sit in one location while studying. For example, some of us prefer to walk around the block or around the room when we are trying to find a solution to a problem.

Many of the elements in these four groupings are under your control as the teacher. You can make changes and create different zones or areas in your classroom to meet the needs of the students. Before you can make these changes, however, you must determine your students' preferences.

DETERMINING STUDENT LEARNING PREFERENCES

Park (1996) suggests that there is a lack of empirical evidence supporting the use of learning styles for enhancing instruction. There is, however, considerable research on the Dunn & Dunn inventory (Dunn & Dunn, 1978; Dunn, 1990, 1995) which supports that changing the environment to match learner preferences results in enhanced motivation and learning. This inventory provides ways of changing the learning environment, a more viable solution for a classroom teacher than designing alternative forms of instruction to adapt to various learning styles. The following is a brief discussion of the Dunn and Dunn inventory and two similar web-based inventories.

DUNN & DUNN'S LEARNING STYLE INVENTORY. One of the more thoroughly researched inventories was developed by Dunn and Dunn (1978). The Learning Styles Inventory (Lisa) is designed for use in grades 3–12 and takes approximately 30 minutes to complete. Sample items include "I concentrate best when I feel cool," "It's hard for me to sit in one place for a long time," and "I can ignore most sound when I study." An analysis of the student's response produces a profile of how the student prefers to learn. Dunn and Dunn also suggest an observation instrument (see Figure 6-1) a teacher can use and then verify by administering the inventory.

Figure 6-1   Learner Preferences Observation Instrument

LEARNING STYLE PREFERENCES

Student _____

ENVIRONMENTAL PREFERENCES

Sound		Yes	No
	Easily distracted by noise		
	Background music appears to bother		
Light			
	Avoids bright light		
	Prefers subdued light		
Temperature			
	Shows preference for cool temperatures		
	Shows preference for warm temperatures		
Design			
	Prefers a neat work area		
	Works well in a messy area		

EMOTIONAL

Motivation		Yes	No
	Follows directions		
	Eager to learn		
Persistence			
	Works on task until complete		
	Gives up when frustrated		
	Easily distracted		

Figure 6-1   Continued

		Yes	No
Responsibility			
	Works without supervision		
	Distractible		
Structure			
	Can choose between options		
	Unable to focus on one choice		

SOCIOLOGICAL

		Yes	No
Group work			
	Enjoys working in a group		
	Prefers to work individually		
	Prefers to work with peers		
	Prefers to work with adults		

PHYSICAL

		Yes	No
Perceptual Strengths			
	Prefers to read for information		
	Prefers to listen to others provide information		
	Prefers to learn from pictures		
	Prefers to learn tactually		
	Prefers to learn from experience		
	Prefers to learn from a combination of senses		

continued

Figure 6-1   Continued

		Yes	No
Intake			
	Prefers to eat and/or drink while learning		
Time			
	Prefers/does best early morning		
	Prefers/does best late morning		
	Prefers/does best early afternoon		
	Prefers/does best late afternoon		
	No time preference		
Mobility			
	Prefers differing sitting arrangements		
	Prefers to move about		

COMMENTS:

(Adapted from Dunn & Dunn, 1978)

WEB-BASED INVENTORIES. A search of the World Wide Web produced several learning profile inventories that students can take on-line. One site, www.fln.vcu.edu/Intensive/LearningStrategies.html, provides examples of several inventories. One of the inventories, www.fln.vcu.edu/Intensive/chronotope.html, is based on the work of Rita Dunn. A similar inventory is available at www.howtolearn.com/personal.html. Although these inventories have several questions and constructs similar to Dunn and Dunn's LSI, no statistical information regarding the development and validity of the inventory were provided.

Decisions concerning the structuring of your classroom environment should be based on data from a variety of sources. Once you decide to offer background music, different lighting, or food, you should monitor the effect of this change on student behavior and learning and make appropriate adjustments as needed.

CHANGING THE LEARNING ENVIRONMENT

Once you have determined student preferences for learning, the next step is to create a learning environment that supports the activities in the NTeQ lesson. We presented two basic classroom designs in Chapter 5 for rooms with 4–6 computers. The following paragraphs suggest some additional designs to support learning in an open-ended environment with an integrated technology lesson.

ENVIRONMENTAL CHANGES. The various activities in an open-ended lesson can generate a higher level of noise and activity than a typical classroom. If you have students who are easily distracted by noise, you can create a quiet area in the room that uses a screen(s) to block some of the sound. Another option is provide headphones and appropriate music for those who want to isolate themselves from the classroom sounds. Screens and window coverings can also be used to create areas with subdued or incandescent lighting for students who do not prefer bright lighting. Computer screens are usually most legible when away from bright lights. For example, you may need to block out bright lights that are directly overhead and arrange them so students do not face a window when working at the computers. Temperature is one environmental variable that is difficult to control. Careful planning to place areas either close to or away from heating and air conditioning units may produce some variations in temperature. Students can also bring sweaters or sweatshirts for use when it is cold. You can also designate formal and informal areas in the room to accommodate different styles (see Figure 6-2). Informal areas might include a carpet, pillows, or other comfortable chairs.

EMOTIONAL. You can create different learning environments by how you assign and manage the various NTeQ lesson activities. For unmotivated students and those with low persistence, you can create smaller tasks that will gain their interest. For example, you may need to break the data analysis process into several small steps to keep some students on-task. You can also offer various levels of guidance to those students who have not developed a high level of responsibility for completing their work. The emotional variables will draw heavily on your skills as a facilitator (see Chapter 4).

SOCIOLOGICAL. To address the various sociological learning preferences of your students, you may want to arrange your classroom environment to support a variety of learning activities. For example, Figure 6-2 shows areas for small group work, individual work, group tutoring, and a meeting area where students can work with an adult such as a parent or expert from the community. As you rearrange your

Figure 6-2   Redesigning the Environment

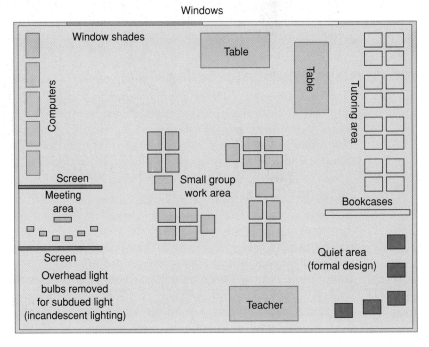

classroom, consider the noise and activity level of each area and try to separate the noisier areas from the quiet areas. You can also involve the students in the redesign and let them both help plan and help with the rearrangement. A week or so after you implement the design, you may need to consider additional changes to enhance the environment.

PHYSICAL. You may have already addressed the room environment for students' preference for intake and mobility as you designed it for the other variables. Intake and mobility may require some management rules to prevent accidents (e.g., no food and drink at the computers) and to keep "mobile" students from disrupting students working in other areas. The time variable presents more of a problem for most classrooms. Using the NTeQ model, however, you have some freedom to structure work periods by allowing students to work on different projects and different aspects of a project to meet their time preference.

Redesigning your classroom environment can enhance student activities when working on an NTeQ lesson. Using learning centers grouped by type of activity to allow for various learning preferences can also enhance motivation and achievement. For example, you can create work areas for computer preparation work which might include both small group work areas and individual research areas. You can also create small group, individual, and tutoring areas for after using the computer and supporting activities.

Fran's Diary

▲▲▲

One of the first things I noticed when I began using computers in my classroom was a higher noise and activity level. Some of the students would write in their journals that the room was really noisy or that they had a hard time concentrating because of the noise. I also noticed that my ADHD students were easily distracted by the sight and sound of the computers and the movement of other students from one activity to another. I realized that my room was going to need a major design change to support learning in a technology classroom with six computers and the NTeQ model.

The first thing that I did was move the desks into "table groups" of four desks. This created areas for collaborative small group work. I obtained some extra desks and chairs from the janitor and put these against a wall. These desks were for those students who preferred to work alone. Putting the desks into groups freed up some much needed space in the classroom.

The next thing I did was create a place for those students who needed some quiet time. I rescued a large refrigerator box from an appliance store and used it to create a miniature castle with windows, turrets, and a drawbridge! I put a piece of carpeting and some large pillows in it for the students. I put the castle in the corner of the room away from the computers and the learning centers. The castle soon became a favorite place for the students to go to read or to just sit quietly and think.

I needed some other areas in the classroom for small group work. I used my reading table for one of these areas. I also needed an area where the students could work on group projects (such as building a model) that take an extended amount of time. My teacher's desk became this area. I cleaned off the top of my desk and put my things on a shelf behind the desk. The students could work here, and leave their project undisturbed until it was completed.

I still needed an area for the leaning center activities. I had used the reading table and my desk, and the janitor would not give me anymore desks and chairs! So, I brought my old picnic table and benches from home and painted them. I also painted some pieces of pegboard and made dividers to divide the picnic table top into six learning centers. This became the learning center area and also a quiet place where my ADHD students could work when the noise and movement bothered them.

Redesigning my classroom provided the means for me to address the individual differences and learning styles found within my classroom. I was also able to create a child-centered learning environment that enhanced student motivation and achievement.

Adapting to the Needs of the Multicultural Classroom

▲▲▲

The necessity of being sensitive to the needs of multicultural learners is greater than any time in our country's history. Minority populations now account for 26 percent of the population, and a greater percentage of our students come from non-English speaking families and families living in poverty (Center for Popular Economics, 1994). Teachers, therefore, must be prepared to deal with the needs of these students. In today's world, it is no longer ethical for teachers to assume that generic teaching strategies reach all students, when in reality they may promote seclusion and discrimination (Kurth-Schai, 1991). In this section, we examine the needs of children in poverty and language minority populations, and offer suggestions for attending to the needs of multicultural learners.

Needs of Children in Poverty. Haberman (1994) makes the case that any schooling that begins with an assumption that children are deficient in some way because they aren't reflective of the established norm is "miseducative and leads to more negative than positive achievements" (p. 3). He suggests instead that teachers learn to recognize signs of four prevalent issues he has identified among poor children. These issues include lacking trust, suffering violence and abuse, living under bureaucracies, and "being done to."

Many children in poverty grow up with adults they cannot trust. These children include latchkey children, abused children, children without an extended family immediately available, or children whose parents are substance abusers. This lack of trust carries over into the school environment where students can be fearful and suspicious of adults. Students learn strategies of self-protection and survive by avoiding adults. "Being done to" is the plight of those who live in poverty and learn to deal with authoritarian bureaucracies. To survive and overcome feelings of manipulation, those who live in poverty learn to manipulate the system to their advantage. Satisfaction is derived from having control over others or learning to comply with others to fill needs. Haberman (1994) asks, "Does the school seek to change what these children bring to school or does the school deepen and enhance these themes?" (p. 7).

Thus, a role for the teacher of children who live in poverty is to assist students in developing trust of others, including school personnel, as well as offer alternative forms of interaction and communication strategies. This development of trust is promoted with the use of technology. For example, students can use word processing or e-mail to develop an ongoing communication with an author they might be studying, or with students from another school. A high school teacher of social studies might encourage her students to meet with the local chamber of commerce to develop a web site for the city. As a part of math instruction, a teacher could bring in a small business owner who needs assistance developing a spreadsheet. In each of these examples, students are connected in positive ways with adult members of the community. Students begin to see themselves as part of a larger community and can reconceptualize their ideas about adults.

NEEDS OF LANGUAGE MINORITY POPULATIONS. Schools use multiple strategies to meet the needs of language minority populations. These strategies include English as a second language (ESL), bilingual education, and sheltered English. Each of these strategies offers support in the native language while students are acquiring English. Submersion, or immersion, of non-English speaking students directly into the English language classroom has had negative effects (Campbell, 1996). Students learn that English is the preferred language, avoid their own language, and quickly develop negative attitudes about their native cultures. How can teachers address these needs to support English acquisition when using or through the use of technology? As a teacher, you can use language buddies and build on the students' native languages. Let's examine these two approaches.

First, teachers can assign "language buddies" to new students (Campbell, 1996). These buddies are viewed as assisting the *teacher* by working alongside the new non-English speaking student in the first few weeks of school. This pairing is particularly helpful when working with technology. The buddy is able to demonstrate and then support the various use of technology tools. Non-English speaking students can experience almost immediate success with a spreadsheet or other math-related computer tools that don't require an extensive knowledge of English. Using language buddies, non-English speaking students are empowered by successfully completing assignments.

Second, teachers might consider how to build on and use the languages students bring to the classroom as a way of celebrating all cultures. Classes can correspond with students from other countries, engage in inquiry projects via the Internet, share stories or weather information over e-mail, participate in foreign language newsgroups, or create multimedia reports about life in other countries. The main point is that the non-English speakers are seen as an asset to every classroom and every teacher's curriculum.

ASSISTIVE TECHNOLOGY FOR LEARNERS WITH SPECIAL NEEDS

While classroom modifications can be made to benefit students who have differing learning styles, can the same be said for students with more significant impairments such as cerebral palsy or Down Syndrome or those who are visually or hearing impaired? The answer to this question is a definite yes. Over the past 30 years, the field of assistive technology has evolved to the point that almost all students with motor or sensory impairments can access computers (thus, math and reading literacy), obtain a voice if needed, and participate in normal classroom activities. Students with significant cognitive disabilities can also develop their skills to their maximum potential through the use of assistive technology.

Students in preservice training programs must become more familiar with these advances in assistive technologies because more and more students with disabilities are included in regular classrooms. According to the Individuals with Disabilities Act (IDEA) Amendments of 1997, a regular educator must be part of the multidisciplinary team which determines placement and services for all students who qualify for special education. This teacher is also responsible for identifying any needs that regular educators might have in order to adapt or accommodate instruction for this student in regular education (Turnbull, Rainbolt, & Buchele-Ash, 1997). Obviously, the traditional roles of special and regular educators which have been established over the past 35 years are rapidly changing. The two fields are merging, and it is no longer practical to allocate skills necessary for adapting instruction for special needs students to the special educator alone.

The range of assistive devices in terms of price and technology is enormous. For example, children with cerebral palsy who are nonverbal can make choices or answer questions by having an eye-gaze board placed between themselves and the instructor. An eye-gaze board can be made by placing pictures or words on a clear acetate or vinyl plate. The teacher can determine the response by following the eye movements of the student. The same students can be fitted with advanced computer systems that allow them full access to all computer functions and also supply them with a voice. We will address these items in more detail later in this chapter, but it should be clear that the price for these various technologies can run from virtually nothing to thousands of dollars. Likewise, the level of applied technology can range from simple adaptations of existing print materials to something resembling the bridge of the Starship Enterprise. (Do not panic. These advanced systems are quite consumer friendly.)

Before we continue our discussion of the types of technology available for particular disabilities we should define some terms. The term "assistive technology" refers to any device or method which makes the environment more accessible to a person with a disability (e.g., a ramp, Braille lettering on an elevator, glasses, a hearing aid). Similarly, "assistive computing" is a method which incorporates any method or device which makes the computer more accessible for a user with a disability. In the area of assistive communication there are two essential terms, "augmentative" and "alternative" communication. Augmentative communication refers to a communication system that enhances a person's ability to communicate, while an alternative communication system serves as the individual's primary communication method. For example, some hearing-impaired persons use American Sign Language (ASL) to enhance their oral communication. This is an example of augmentative communication. Others in the deaf community either cannot, or have chosen not to, use oral communication and rely on ASL exclusively. In this situation ASL becomes an alternate communication system. In professional jargon, augmentative and alternate communication are often referred to collectively as AAC. A comprehensive list of AAC manufacturers is presented at the end of this chapter.

COMPUTER ACCESS FOR PERSONS WITH DISABILITIES

Students with disabilities typically need access to a personal computer or network workstation for the same reasons as students without disabilities. (The one exception to this is for persons who use the computer as their primary method of oral communication—alternative communication.) However, adaptations and even alternatives to standard computer hardware and software are often necessary to make the computer accessible to the user with a disability (Wilson, Kotlas, & Martin, 1994). The standard personal computer system including disk drive, input devices, and monitor can present barriers to persons with sensory or physical disabilities. Some common access problems are described in the following paragraphs.

INPUT DEVICES. The standard QWERTY (top row of letters on the keyboard) keyboard used on virtually every personal computer is often inaccessible to people with impaired mobility or fine motor control and may present problems to those with visual impairments. Users with a motoric problem such as cerebral palsy may not have the strength required to press the keys or may not be able to compensate for the compactness or touch sensitivity of the keys on a standard keyboard. Use of the mouse presents similar problems for those with motoric disabilities (with the additional complication of clicking and dragging with sustained pressure) and also for those with vision impairments who may find it impossible to track the cursor on the monitor.

DISK DRIVE. Manipulation of disks or CDs is impossible for some users due to lack of strength or dexterity. In addition, those with impaired mobility or vision may not have access to the on-off switch which is often located at the rear of the computer.

MONITOR AND SCREEN. Screen displays are obviously not accessible to persons who are blind and may not be accessible to those with low vision without magnification or text-to-speech conversion. Screen displays are usually accessible to the person with motoric disabilities and to hearing-impaired persons if audible error messages or "beeps" are modified to text or visual signals (Wilson, Kotlas, & Martin, 1994).

ADAPTING THE COMPUTER FOR PERSONS WITH SENSORY IMPAIRMENTS

Computer access for persons with visual impairments may require either speech input, screen magnification, or Braille input with text-to-speech translation. The person who is blind is usually limited to Braille or speech input with text-to-speech translation.

Fitting the most appropriate modifications to meet the user's need is usually carried out at an assistive device center or by a technician employed by the schools and is a critical factor in ensuring ease of consumer use. The technologies available to disabled computer users who are blind or have low vision are extensive and must be individualized to meet personal needs. The choice of the appropriate technology depends on a number of factors including the cause of the visual loss, the degree of acuity loss, and the range of peripheral vision (Wilson, Kotlas, & Martin, 1994).

A popular adaptation for persons who are blind or have visual impairments is a text-to-speech translation system. These screen reading programs usually consist of two parts: a software program and a speech synthesizer. Most Macintosh computers come installed with the Simple Text program, which is a simple word processing program that provides text-to-speech translation. Newer versions of ClarisWorks (Version 4.0) and Microsoft Word (Version 6.0) also come with this feature. There are also scripts for some Macintosh applications (e.g., Claris Emailer) that will translate the text to speech. These new applications come with a variety of synthesized voices including male-female, child-adult that permits users to personalize or vary their output. Apple also offers a freeware application called Plain Talk which offers voice-to-text input in addition to text-to-speech translation. The PlainTalk Software components are available for free download on the Web at http://www.speech.apple.com/ptk. IBM produces several text-to-speech translators including ScreenReader/2 and ScreenReader/DOS (call the IBM Independence Series Information Center, 1–800–426–4832, for more information; TDD 1–800–426–4833 or access Special Needs Systems for IBM at http://www.austin.ibm.com/sns/index.html. Another standard Macintosh feature designed to facilitate computer access for persons with visual impairments is CloseView. An illustration of the screen configuration possible with CloseView is presented in Figure 6-3. This program can enlarge print size by up to eight times. There is a similar program for IBM which is available commercially for about $500 called Screen Magnifier/2 v1.2 OS/2. The magnification programs can also transfer text to white print on black background which eases reading and reduces eye strain for some users.

Persons who have hearing impairments or are deaf usually adapt most easily to using the computer, since the standard medium of exchange between user and com-

Figure 6-3   Improving Screen Legibility with CloseView

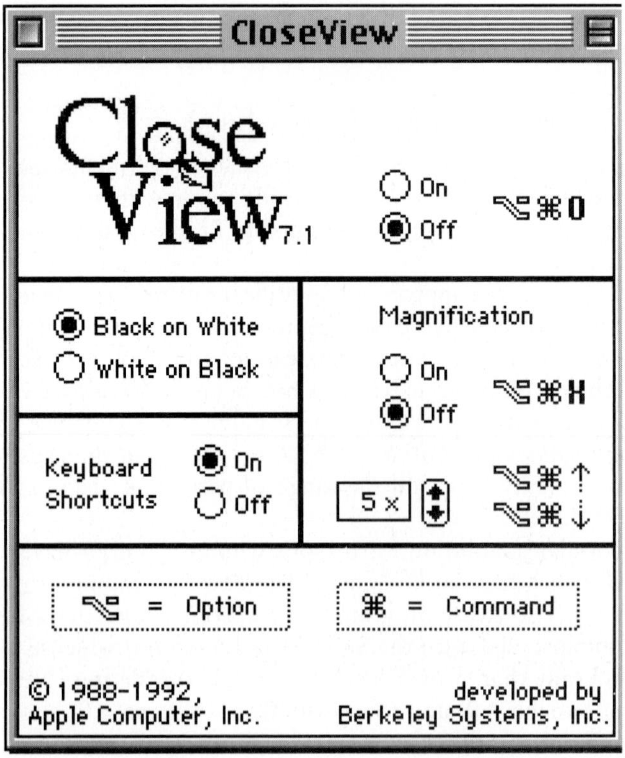

puter is visual. Often only minor modifications, such as an alternative to the audible warning beep, are needed for these individuals.

Adapting the Computer for Persons with Motoric Impairments

As with persons with vision impairments, the adaptations necessary for persons with motoric disorders will be determined only after careful professional evaluation. Assistive technology has evolved to the point that any electrical device can be accessed by a person with physical disabilities if they have only the slightest of voluntary muscle control. Evaluators will determine a student's best remaining motor function to incorporate access to the computer or other devices. Switches can be designed for use with a toe or even eyebrow movements, giving complete access to any electrical device or appliance.

Computer keyboards can be modified for persons with less severe physical impairments, such as gross motor control over arm and finger movement, but lack of adequate fine motor skills. Again, Macintosh computers have led the way in this regard by outfitting all their computers with a program called Easy Access. This software permits someone to program the amount of time a key needs to be held down before it registers. This type of program is often used in conjunction with a "keyguard." The keyguard is an overlay for the keyboard with holes over individual keys. The keyguard helps direct the fingers to the keys, while the Easy Access program inhibits or prohibits the repetitive production of a letter when pressure is applied on the key over time. A similar program, AccessDOS

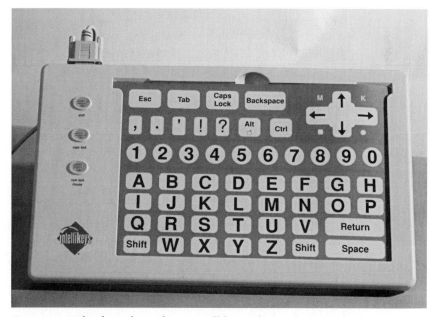

Easy-to-use keyboards such as Intellikeys shown here, make computers accessible to a wider range of learners.

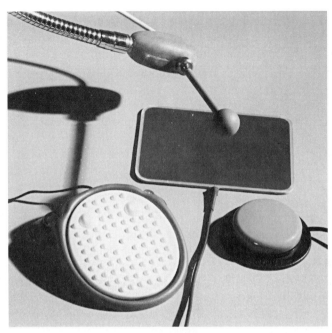

A variety of input devices enable learners with diverse needs to use the computer as a learning tool.

v1.2, is available for Intel-based computers and can be downloaded free from http://www.austin.ibm.com/sns/index.html. Intellitools, Inc., a leader in adaptive computer hardware and software, has developed an ingenious method to use with their line of products. This method involves an overlay of clear plastic bubbles that fit over their adapted keyboard, Intellikeys. The bubbles respond to direct pressure, but protect other keys from being depressed.

If the person's physical disability is such that use of the conventional keyboard with modifications is not an option there are alternative keyboards, ability switches, headpointers, and joysticks. These methods may be used in many variations and combinations based on the abilities and needs of the user. Whatever the method, the computer treats the input from these methods as if it had been received through the standard keyboard.

Alternative keyboards come in many styles and with a range of programmable functions and methods of input. These modified keyboards consist of a series of touch sensitive membrane switches arranged for easy use. Most alternative keyboard designs provide the option to program the complexity of the display. Overlays allow for a gradual progression of skill development. Thus, the learner can begin with simple yes-no responses (the entire right and left sides of the keyboard are dedicated to one of these responses) and can progress to the standard QWERTY keyboard arrangement. The level of complexity is related only to users' cognitive abilities. Adaptations can be made to compensate for almost any degree of physical ability. Popular interface units include Ke:nx (pronounced "connects") and Key Largo for both Macintosh and Windows put out by Don Johnston, Inc., and the Expanded Keyboard Emulator or DADA Entry Keyboard Emulator for IBM and compatibles. The Intellikeys keyboard produced by Intellitools is favored by many educators and therapists because of its user friendliness and the extensive line of software produced specifically for it. Each of the software packages includes overlays for the Intellikeys designed specifically for that program. Intellikeys is both Windows and Apple compatible, and information about their line of products can be accessed at http://www.intellitools.com. It should be noted that the prices of these adapted keyboards have been falling. Intellikeys and Key Largo retail for approximately $450 and $300, respectively. Fifteen years ago a comparable system would have cost several thousand dollars. Likewise, voice recognition systems have also dropped from several thousand to several hundred dollars over the past five years.

Any of these adapted keyboards can be accessed directly through touch or by means of a switch. Adaptations for touch activation include head pointers, which are attached to firm headbands, and touch-sensitive screens such as TouchWindow produced by Edmark, Inc. Touch-sensitive screens can be attached directly to the computer monitor or can be removed and placed on a board or table in front of the student. The touch-sensitive membrane functions as a mouse so that finger or pointer movements activate the cursor function.

Switches provide direct access to screen displays without the need for a keyboard. Switches come in a variety of shapes and sizes and can be mounted in almost any position relative to the user. A simple pressure-sensitive switch can be mounted on a wheelchair adjacent to the user's head, near his or her toe, near the elbow, or anywhere else where the person has some degree of voluntary movement. Toggle switches can also be mounted on adjustable arms attached to clamps to allow for a range of positioning possibilities. A switch interface unit (often built into modified keyboards) acts as the link between the switch and the computer. Any electrical device can be activated by these types of switches; thus, toys, tape recorders, CD players, and other educational or recreational devices are now accessible to persons with even the most severe physical disabilities. A common switch adapted for persons with upper spinal cord injuries involves sip-and-puff technology. This switch allows full access to devices by merely inhaling and exhaling.

Operating a computer or other device with a switch usually involves a process referred to as *scanning*. When scanning with a switch, the user pushes (or puffs on) the switch once to activate the process. The cursor then scrolls down rows of characters. When the desired row is reached, the user activates the switch again and the cursor scans across the columns until the desired character is reached. One more press of the switch registers that character or response with the computer. The scanning process can take an extensive amount of time, especially with word processing. To help compensate for this time, several "intelligent" word prediction programs have been developed such as Co:Writer by Don Johnston, Inc. Using standard grammatical frequency data, these programs will automatically produce the most common word beginning with the letter chosen by the user. For example, the letter "T" produced at the beginning of a sentence will produce the word "the" on the screen. The user then chooses "the," thus reducing the number of keyboard activations from three to two for this word. For longer words the time saving is more dramatic. The program also "remembers" the grammatical style of the user so that word prediction improves the more the user works with the program.

Many other forms of assistive computing and AAC devices are available. Some are designed specifically for an individual. The presence of these technologies in the classroom may benefit more than just the student with disabilities. Imagine having a student in a cooperative learning group who has his or her own portable computer for collecting and recording data. There are some lower tech communication devices that have windows or slots for pictures connected to mini-tape recorders. The student with disabilities scans the windows to the desired picture and then activates the message. The messages or responses on these devices can be changed frequently and as easily as any tape recorder, providing a very versatile tool for including students in discussions and activities. Students without disabilities can supply the voice for these responses. Imagine the values education potential of being able to provide a voice for someone incapable of producing oral language.

Other Environmental Considerations for Persons with Disabilities

The term *accessibility* is frequently used in the context of providing equal opportunity to enter into an environment. For educational purposes, the term is more encompassing. Accessibility in educational contexts includes adaptations necessary to ensure successful goal attainment by students with disabilities. This adaptation may require changes in the communication methods (using methods discussed earlier) as well as the physical arrangements. Programs that cater to individual needs will be easy to adapt for children with sensory or physical disabilities. In these programs, modifications to meet the needs of individuals are part of the presentation of daily activities. Programs that are geared for more general "one-size-fits-all" instruction will need more adaptation to accommodate children with disabilities.

Physical Disability Adaptations.
As a rule, environmental adaptations to accommodate a student should be kept to a minimum. In other words, adaptations should be as unobtrusive as possible to minimize pointing out the "differences" in the student with the disability (Buggey, 1998). The adaptations needed will depend on the type and severity of the disability. Students with severe physical disabilities will need additional space for maneuvering and therapy, and may require a range of adaptive equipment to facilitate therapy and to aid in accessing aspects of the school program. Equipment often used in this context includes wedges, wheelchairs, prone standers, sidelyers, posture chairs, and support bars. Teachers must work closely with physical and occupational therapists and parents to ensure that individual needs for successful participation are met. For example, the purpose of a wedge is to give the lower trunk and torso support so that head, arms, and hands are free to manipulate objects. A child using a wedge may freely participate in ac-

tivities such as reading, art, and science labs. Sidelyers and prone standers serve the same purpose for persons with a variety of physical disabilities. Teachers should ensure that the environment is barrier-free by ensuring access to, from, and within the classroom is available to all students.

COMMUNICATION ADAPTATIONS.

Adaptations to the communication environment may require adopting augmentative or alternative communication material. This type of adaptation may include a range of materials and methods such as signing, communication boards, and picture-symbol cards, as well as high tech devices previously discussed. It may be necessary to modify bulletin boards and other classroom materials to accommodate these alternative forms of communication. The use of Braille, signs, or symbols with the related printed word on materials may help all class members learn the techniques. This, then, improves accessibility of nonverbal children by providing a universal method of classroom communication (Buggey, 1998).

The advent and subsequent development of assistive devices in the area of mobility, computer access, and communication has eradicated barriers that have existed for persons with disabilities for centuries. Previously, the path to literacy for a person with cerebral palsy may have been blocked by the inability to turn a page or enter a neighborhood school. This lack of access should no longer be the case. The ability to speak and to access knowledge is now possible for almost all individuals with cognitive, physical, and sensory impairments. We must use these technologies to ensure that persons with disabilities have equal opportunities for participation in our classrooms and communities.

AT THE CLASSROOM'S DOORSTEP
▲▲▲
QUESTIONS TEACHERS ASK

How can I redesign my classroom on my limited budget? If you need carpeting, chairs, lamps, etc., you can ask parents for donations. Your class might also participate in a fundraiser and make arrangements to purchase a small scrap of carpeting from a carpet store. Screens can consist of bookcases or file cabinets to block light or sound. Students can also construct screens from paper loops, yarn, and other materials to define various areas. Aluminum foil makes an inexpensive light block when taped to a window with masking or duct tape. You can also involve the students and encourage them to generate ideas to help solve the problems.

Is there a way to adapt at least some of my instruction to individual learners? Yes, you can create a variety of instructional materials. For example, you can make an audiotape of a story or chapter the students must read. Students who prefer to listen can follow the tape with their book. You can also provide a variety of resources such as CD-ROMs, picture books, and hands-on learning experiences for students. If you work on only a few projects at a time, over the years you can develop a variety of alternative delivery strategies.

RESOURCES
▲▲▲

AAC Manufacturer List

Ability Research, Inc.
P.O. Box 1721
Minnetonka, MN 55345
(612) 939–0121
ability@skypoint.com
http://www.skypoint.com/~ability/

AbleNet, Inc.
1081 10th Avenue, S.E.
Minneapolis, MN 55414
(800) 322–0956

ADAMLAB
33500 Van Born Road
Wayne, MI 48184–2497
(313) 467–1415
http://www.wcresa.k12.us/adlab/

Adaptivation, Inc.
224 S.E. 16th Street, Suite 2
Ames, IA 50010
(800)723–2783
adaptaac@aol.com
http://users.aol.com/adaptaac

Assistive Technology, Inc.
850 Boylston Street
Chestnut Hill, MA 02167
(800)–793–9227
http://www.assistivetech.com

Attainment Company, Inc.
P.O. Box 930160
Verona, WI 53593–0160
(800) 327–4269

Aurora Systems, Inc.
2647 Kingsway
Vancouver, BC V5R–5H4 Canada
(800) 361–8255
aurora@cyberstore.ca
http://www.scbc.org/hinet/business/
CoProf/Aurora/aurora.html

Boden Rehab AB
Industrivägen 12
961 68 Boden
Tel:+46 921 18769
Fax:+46 921 50479
info@bodenrehab.se
http://www.bodenrehab.se

Box-Talk Sales Office
Box 1180
Litchfield, CT 06759
http://www.box-talk.com/

Canon USA, Inc.
1 Canon Plaza
Lake Success, NY 11042
(800) 828–4040 or
(516) 488–6700
http://www.usa.canon.com/
commaids/cc7p.html

Common Cents Systems
P.O. Box 110514
Nashville, TN 37222
(615) 834–7666

Communication Devices, Inc.
2433 Government Way, Suite A
Coeur d' Alene, ID 83814
(208) 765–1259

Companion Products International
P.O. Box G
Milford, PA 18337–0208
(800) 258–6423 or
(717) 686–4713

Consultants for Communication
Technology
508 Bellevue Terrace
Pittsburgh, PA 15202
(412) 761–6062
70272.1034@compuserve.com

Crestwood Company
6625 N. Sidney Place
Milwaukee, WI 53209
(414) 352–5678
Crestcomm@aol.com

D. C. & D., Inc.
42 Skinner Road
East Windsor, CT 06016
(860) 623–7364

Don Johnston Incorporated
1000 N. Rand Road-Bldg. 115
(P.O. Box 639)
Wauconda, IL 60084
(800) 999–4660
djde@aol.com
http://www.donjohnston.com

Frame Technologies
W681 Pearl St.
Oneida, WI 54155
(920) 869–2979
http://www.frame-tech.com

Franklin Electronic Publishers, Inc.
One Franklin Plaza
Burlington, NJ 08016
(609) 386–2500

GMR LABS, Inc.
1030 E. El Camino Real #308
Sunnyvale, CA 94087–3759
(800) 234–8288
roark@gmrlabs.com

Great Talking Box Company
2211 B Fortune Drive
San Jose, CA 95131
(408) 456–0133
102375.3351@compuserve.com
http://ourworld.compuserve.com/
homepages/gtb

Griffin Laboratories
27636 Ynez Road, Suite L7199
Temecula, CA 92591
(800) 330–5969

Gus Communications, Inc.
1006 Loantree Court
Bellingham, WA 98226
(360) 715–8580
gus@gusinc.com
http://www.gusinc.com

Innocomp
26210 Emery Road, Suite 302
Warrensville Hts., OH 44128
(800) 382–8622
Innocomp@aol.com
http://www.sayitall.com

IntelliTools, Inc.
55 Leveroni Court, Suite 9
Novato, CA 94949
(800) 899–6687
intellitoo@aol.com
http://www.intellitools.com

Klein & Melgert
't Holland 24
6921 AD Duiven
Postbus 166
6920 AD Duiven The Netherlands
Tel: +31 316 268021
Fax: +31 316 281160.
http://www.kmdev.com

LC Technologies, Inc.
9455 Silver King Court
Fairfax, VA 22031
(800) 733–5284
info@lctinc.com
http://www.lctinc.com

LingraphiCARE America
3600 West Bayshore Road, Suite 202
Palo Alto, CA 94303
(800) 332–4913
steele@cdr.stanford.edu
http://members.aol.com/tolfa1/

Luminaud, Inc.
8688 Tyler Boulevard
Mentor, OH 44060
(800) 255–3408

Magic Laboratories, Inc.
1733 Woodside Road, Suite 315
Redwood City, CA 94061
(415) 368–9498
gordonhc@aol.com

Mayer-Johnson Company
P.O. Box 1579
Solana Beach, CA 92075
(619) 550–0084
Mayerj@aol.com

Med Labs, Inc.
28 Vereda Cordillera
Goleta, CA 93117
(800) 968–2486

Microsystems Software, Inc.
600 Worcester Road
Framingham, MA 01701
(508) 879–9000
Hware@microsys.com
http://www.handiware.com

Park Surgical Company, Inc.
5001 New Utrecht Avenue
Brooklyn, NY 11219
(800) 633–7878

Prentke Romich Company
1022 Heyl Road
Wooster, OH 44691
(800) 262–1984
info@prentrom.com
http://dialup.oar.net/~Pprco/index.html

Romet, Inc. (manufacturer)/
EZ Speech (distributor)
P.O. Box 31
Chester, VA 23831
(800) 758–8255

Sentient Systems Technology, Inc.
2100 Wharton Street, Suite 630
Pittsburgh, PA 15203
(800) 344–1778
sstsales@sentient-sys.com
http://www.sentient-sys.com

Siemens Hearing Instruments, Inc.
16 E. Piper Lane, Suite 128
Prospect Heights, IL 60070
(800) 333–9083
http://www.siemens-hearing.com

Stanton Magnetics, Inc.
101 Sunnyside Boulevard
Plainview, NY 11803
(516) 349–0235

TASH, Inc.
Unit 1, 91 Station Street
Ajax, ON L1S 3H2 Canada
(800) 463–5685
tashcan@aol.com

Toys for Special Children
385 Warburton Avenue
Hastings-on-Hudson, NY 10706
(800) 832–8697

UltraVoice
19 E. Central Avenue
Paoli, PA 19301
(800) 721–4848
http://www.ultravoice.com

UNI Manufacturing Co.
(Manufacturer)
Dean Rosecrans (distributor)
P.O. Box 607
Ontario, OR 97914
(800) 438–7757
rosecran@cyberhighway.net

Williams Sound Corporation
10399 West 70th Street
Eden Prairie, MN 55344–3459
(800) 328-6190

Words Plus, Inc.
40015 Sierra Highway,
Bldg. B-145
Palmdale, CA 93550
(800) 869–8521
http://www.words-plus.com

Zygo Industries, Inc. (Distributor)
Toby Churchill Ltd (manufacturer)
P.O. Box 1008
Portland, OR 97207
(800) 234–6006

References
▲▲▲

Block, J. H. (1980). Promising excellence through mastery learning. *Theory and Practice, 19*, 66–74.

Buggey, T. (1998). Arranging preschool environments. In S. Graves & R. Gargiulo (Eds.). *Early Childhood Special Education*. St. Paul, MN: West Publishing.

Campbell, D. E (1996). *Choosing democracy: A practical guide to multicultural education.* New York: Prentice Hall.

Center for Popular Economics. (1994). *Field guide to U.S. economy, 1985–1995.* Amherst, MA: Author.

Dunn, R. (1990). Grouping students for instruction: Effects of learning style on achievement and attitudes. *Journal of Social Psychology, 130,* 485–494.

Dunn, R. (1995). A meta-analytic validation of the Dunn and Dunn model of learning-style preferences. *Journal of Educational Research, 88,* 353–362.

Dunn, R. & Dunn, K. (1978). *Teaching students through their individual learning styles: A practical approach.* Reston, VA: Reston Publishing Company, Inc.

Haberman, M. (1994). Contexts: Overview and framework. In O'Hair and Odell (Eds.). *Diversity and Teaching: Teacher Education Yearbook One,* (pp. 1–8). New York: Harcourt Brace Jovanovich College Publishers.

Keller, F. S. & Sherman, J. G. (1982). *The PSI handbook: Essays on personalized instruction.* Lawrence, KS: International Society for Individualized Instruction.

Kolb, D. (1984). *Experiential learning: Experience as the source of learning and development.*Englewood Cliffs, NJ: Prentice-Hall.

Kolb, D. (1985). *Self-scoring inventory and interpretive booklet.* Boston: McBer.

Kurth-Schai, R. (1991). The peril and promise of childhood: Ethical implications for tomorrow's teachers. *Journal of Teacher Education, 42*(3), 196–204.

Park, O. K. (1996). Adaptive instructional systems. In D. J. Jonassen (Ed.). *Handbook of research for educational communications and technology.* New York: Macmillan Library Reference USA.

Postlethwait, S. N, Novak, J., & Murray, H. (1972). *The audio-tutorial approach to learning.* Minneapolis, MN: Burgess.

Reiser, R. A. (1987). Instructional technology: A history. In R. Gagné, (Ed.). *Instructional technology: foundations.* Hillsdale, NJ: Erlbaum.

Turnbull, R., Rainbolt, K., & Buchele-Ash, A. (1997). *Individuals with disabilities education act: Digest and significance of 1997 amendments* [on-line]. Available at http://www.lsi.ukans.edu/beach/html/idea_update1.htm#A.

Wilson, L., Kotlas, C., & Martin, M. (1994). *Assistive technology for the disabled.* Institute for Academic Technology. (Information Resource Guides Series #IRG-20).

CHAPTER 7
Word Processing

▶ Introduction

Do you remember when you were in grade school and you wrote your first "friendly letter"? Your teacher emphasized that the draft copy was to be done in pencil, so you could erase your mistakes and write in corrections. When you were given approval to make the final copy, you took out a nice, clean sheet of white notebook paper and a new ball point pen. Using your best handwriting to copy the letter, you had the date, address, greeting, and first paragraph looking great when Bobby "accidentally" bumped your arm. Your pen slashed across the letter, ruining it. After yelling at Bobby, you pulled out another clean sheet of notebook paper and began again. This time, things went quite well (although you kept an eye out for wandering students). The writing went a little faster; because you had most of the letter memorized, you did not have to look at your draft copy as much. The letter looked great!

Then your teacher reminded you to proofread your letter before turning it in. You thought it was a waste of time, but you did it anyway. To your dismay, you realized you had left out a complete sentence, so the last paragraph did not make any sense. You reluctantly pulled out yet another clean sheet of notebook paper. All of the elation was gone. In fact, writing had become something that you did not like anymore.

Until recently, this scenario was reenacted time and again as students labored over assignments. Some teachers tried to alleviate the tediousness of rewriting by requiring fewer revisions or by accepting final products that did not represent a student's best work. But now, enter word processing! Word processing allows students to spend more

▶ Computer Skills Used in This Chapter

Entering text and numerical information
Formatting font
Copying, cutting, and pasting
Setting the margins and tabs
Printing
Saving work

▶ Key Topics

Using Word Processing in the Classroom
Ease of Use
Refinement of Work
Creativity and Personalization of Work
Equity in Final Products
Workforce Tool

Examining Word Processing
Basic Components
Editing
Formatting
Inserting
Tools

Designing an Integrated Lesson
Specifying the Instructional Objective
Matching Objective to Computer Functions
Specifying a Problem
Manipulating Data
Presenting Results
Multidimensional Activities

time engaged in meaningful learning activities because it is very easy for them to modify and refine their written work. This chapter examines the many ways that students can use word processing in the classroom. It begins with an overview of the basic word processing functions and how these can be used by students. A detailed description of how to create lesson plans that integrate the use of word processing follows.

Using Word Processing in the Classroom
▲▲▲

Word processing is the most common type of software application used by students at school (Becker, 1991; Sheingold and Hadley, 1990). Students of all ages should be using word processing applications. The following section highlights the reasons why.

Ease of Use

Word processing provides students with an easier way to complete their work. Instead of using a pencil or pen, students write their papers by simply typing in the text and numerical information using the keyboard. As the information is being entered, it is simultaneously displayed on the computer monitor so students can continuously check or "monitor" their work. Initially, it takes extra time for students to learn some of the basic word processing functions, but by starting with simple tasks and providing time for practice, the basics can even be mastered by those in primary grades. Then, by middle or high school, students can focus on actually composing their papers at the keyboard.

WORD PROCESSING BASICS
- Entering words by matching letters on the keyboard with the words entered.
- Using the **delete** or **backspace** key to erase mistakes.
- Pressing **return** at the end of a paragraph.
- Holding down the shift key to get a capital letter or the characters displayed above the number and punctuation keys.
- Using the space bar between words.
- Using the mouse to insert the cursor, highlight text, or select menu items such as **Save** or **Print**.

Refinement of Work

Word processing allows students to go beyond the tediousness of handwriting a paper over and over again. Students can become more involved in critical thinking activities by using the energy previously dedicated to legible handwriting. With word processing students can:

- think about what their words really mean.
- use the on-line thesaurus to find better, more descriptive words.
- easily elaborate on what has been written.

- reorganize material.
- refine what has been said by assessing the relevance of the content and deleting any unimportant information.

When students use a word processor for their assignments, they are better able to actively engage in the learning process and to think critically. Thus, the students reinforce their learning and continue to build their knowledge and skills (McDaniel, McInerney, & Armstrong, 1994).

FRAN'S DIARY
▲▲▲

Of all the computer applications, I use word processing the most in my classroom. The students use the computer for all of their writing activities, everything from creating lists to writing paragraphs and reports. I have discovered that if my students have any prior computer experience, it will be with this application. Although many students have experience, they still need to be taught some basic keyboarding skills. I teach keyboarding skills during the first six weeks of school. The students catch on quickly and tend to develop some word processing speed.

I guess what I really like about the word processing application is that it can be easily incorporated into other curriculum areas. I am able to create one word processing activity that can combine several curriculum areas and learning objectives. For example, the students created books on exercise for the culminating activity of a thematic unit. The book writing activity incorporated different types of exercises from the health curriculum, sequencing and identifying the parts of a book from the reading curriculum, identifying and using action verbs from the language arts curriculum, and creating a flow chart from the social studies curriculum.

Before the students began writing these books, they looked at examples of fiction and nonfiction books, and compared and contrasted the elements of fiction and nonfiction writing. They created computer-generated Venn diagrams to compare and contrast the parts of a fiction and nonfiction book.

I put the students into heterogeneous groups of four to work on this project. They brainstormed to make a list of exercises that they knew. Each student picked one exercise from our class list and created a flow chart to list the steps to follow when doing this exercise. The students then exchanged flow charts and tried to do the exercises based on the flow chart. The student that created the flow chart was not allowed to talk. It was a great learning experience for the students. They realized that their directions had to be very specific and that the steps to follow must be in sequential order.

Continued

At this point, the students were ready to begin writing their exercise books. As a class, they helped me develop the rubric that would be used to assess their exercise books. They decided that each book had to have an illustrated cover, a title page, a copyright page, a table of contents, and ten exercise pages with illustrations.

It was interesting to watch them work. I did not have to interfere. There was very little arguing about who was going to do what. They seemed to split up the tasks so that each student would be responsible for two exercise pages and an additional page. While working on their rough drafts, they always worked with a partner. One partner would write the directions, and the other would demonstrate the exercise. They would make changes to their exercise page based on this demonstration. They would also exchange pages among themselves for an informal peer review.

By the time their rough drafts were completed, there was little that needed to be corrected. They took turns word processing and usually worked in pairs. While one pair word processed, the other pair worked on the book cover or illustrations. Before the books were bound, they exchanged books among groups and tried out each other's exercises. If something was unclear about an exercise, a note was made on the editing sheet. The students also checked for spelling and grammatical errors. The groups made corrections to their books based on this feedback. The use of the word processing application made this task easy and quick.

Their books were fantastic! Each book was different. The students were proud of their accomplishments and their final products. These books were placed in the classroom library and were used quite often that year. On many days when the students couldn't go outside due to the weather conditions, they would get out an exercise book and do the exercises in the classroom!

CREATIVITY AND PERSONALIZATION OF WORK

Most word processing applications have many different types of fonts available for students to use when creating their work with the computer. Students can choose different fonts or change the appearance of some words by making them bold or italic or by underlining them (see Figure 7-1).

Color can be added if students have access to a color printer or if the teacher will assess the work from a computer. Students can also personalize their work by including borders or drawings which they have created or imported from clip art collections or from the Internet. Students can also add customized graphs and charts or use a layout that resembles a newspaper or magazine article (see Figure 7-2).

These choices help students personalize their work and demonstrate their creativity. The computer allows the students to immediately see how their work looks

Figure 7-1   Sample Text Styles

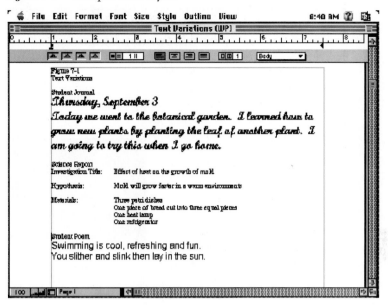

when displayed in a variety of fonts and colors. When they achieve the desired effect, they can print a copy. If student time at the computers is limited, students can print their word processed material and draw their own illustrations on printed pages. If students do not have access to a color printer, they can add clip art and then color it after it is printed.

EQUITY IN FINAL PRODUCTS

When school work is produced with a word processor, all students have an equal opportunity to create professional-looking documents. This decreases student embarrassment over poor handwriting or biased teacher grading based on poor appearance. Word processing allows students to concentrate more on what they say rather than what it looks like. All students can create a document that is legible and attractive.

Another benefit is that teachers can easily read student work, thus making the grading process more equitable. Because teachers no longer have to "guess" about what a student is trying to write, the actual learning can be assessed. However, if students can choose to use word processing or to write their papers by hand, you must use caution when grading the two types of papers. Roblyer (1997) indicates that teachers, unknowingly, tend to have higher standards for word processed papers. One reason is that word processed papers take up much less room on a page than a handwritten paper, thus appearing shorter. Rather than giving page lengths for assignments, consider giving word counts, such as a 500-word essay.

Figure 7-2   Columns and Graphics

Monarch Butterflies: The Metamorphosis
by
John Q. Student

Stages of Metamorphosis

There are four stages of metamorphosis for a Monarch Butterfly.

1. A Monarch Butterfly lays eggs.

2. A caterpillar hatches from the egg.

3. The caterpillar forms a chrysalis.

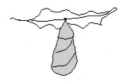

4. The monarch hatches from the chrysalis

Created by Mindy Morris

From the Butterfly's View Point

Hi! I am Shaina -the Butterfly.

I am in search of a milkweed to lay my eggs on. We butterflies only lay our eggs on milkweed leaves because we can eat the leaves and get our nourishment. Great!! I spot a milkweed!! The eggs will hatch in a few days and out will pop my children. Oh, they won't look like me, they will be long, skinny, and furry. You guessed it, a caterpillar! Isn't nature amazing!! The caterpillar will eat the milkweed to grow and shed its skin four times. This is called molting. After a few weeks, it will spin a sticky thread around itself. The thread will harden around the caterpillar, like a hard shell. This is called a chrysalis. Inside the chrysalis, the caterpillar is changing into a butterfly. The chrysalis is very beautiful (if I say so myself!). About 7 days after the chrysalis stage, the skin of the chrsalis splits and out pops a monarch butterfly. Its wings are soft and mushy and it takes some short flights before it is strong enough to fly away. Think about me, Shaina butterfly, everytime you see a monarch and all the stages that I went through to get here. Once again, isn't nature amazing!!!

Based on a unit by Mindy Morris.

WORKFORCE TOOL

One of the primary reasons students attend school is to prepare them to become productive citizens in the workforce. Word processing is a common skill needed by many employees in numerous occupations. Some applications include entering names and addresses into a computer at an auto repair shop, creating letters to people with overdue bills, writing newspaper and magazine articles, writing instruction manuals for audio equipment or new cars, or writing legal notes for a trial. Therefore, learning word processing in school will not only immediately benefit students with their school work, but it will better prepare them for their future careers.

EXAMINING WORD PROCESSING

▲▲▲

Word processing applications such as Microsoft Word, Microsoft Works, Claris-Works, or WordPerfect allow the computer user to create documents with the computer. The following section discusses the basic components of word processing, three of the major functions (editing, formatting, and inserting), and some of the tools. If you know how to use word processing, you may skip this section and move forward to Designing an Integrated Lesson on page 138.

BASIC COMPONENTS

Word processing involves using a keyboard to enter the information into the computer. The information is displayed on the computer monitor as it is being entered. Most keyboards are arranged in a way very similar to typewriters, although many are extended to include a ten-key number pad, function (F), and directional keys to add more functionality to the computer (see Figure 7-3).

Figure 7-3   Keyboard

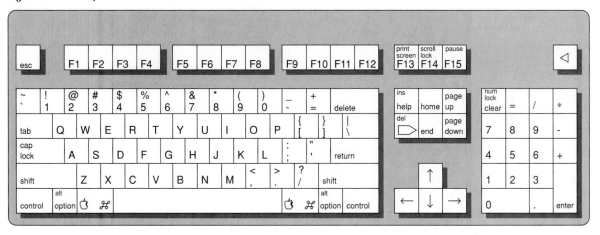

Many of the keyboard functions used with word processing are similar to those used with a typewriter. The following list contains items that are used for both word processing and typing.

- Words are entered by pressing corresponding letter keys.
- Spaces between words are created with the space bar.
- Capital letters are created by holding down the shift key as the letter is entered, or all caps can be obtained by pressing down the caps lock key.
- Characters displayed above the number and punctuation keys are entered by holding down the shift key while pressing the desired key.

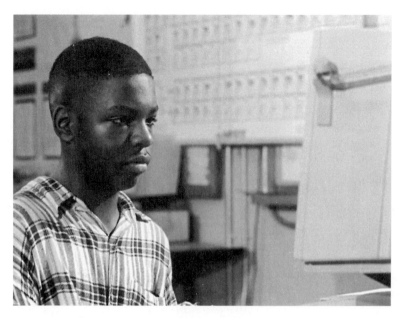

Student using word processing to enter his report.

- Indents and tabs are created by pressing the tab key.
- The return key is used to move to the next line.
- Letters or characters can be deleted by using the backspace or delete key.

The similarities between using a word processing application and a typewriter basically stop with this list, because word processing provides many functions and features that go beyond the capability of a typewriter. The next few sections present some of those functions, such as being able to edit and format existing documents and to insert page numbers, dates, charts, graphs, and clip art. Once the basics have been mastered, new and exciting things can be added. Yet, even these basic functions make the word processor an excellent tool for students to use to expand their own "information processing" capabilities.

EDITING

One of the most important functions of a word processing application is the ability to edit and change what has been entered. Most word processing applications have **Edit** as a choice on the menu. Edits can be accomplished in several ways. Table 7-1 provides guidelines for some of the basic editing procedures.

FORMATTING

There are four types of formatting discussed in this section: document, font, paragraphs, and tabs.

Table 7-1 Editing Functions

What You Want to Do	Actions Needed
DELETE a word, sentence, or paragraph	• Highlight (double-click or drag through with the mouse) the word, sentence, or paragraph. • After highlighting, press **delete** or **backspace**.
REWRITE a word, sentence, or paragraph	Option 1 • Highlight the word, sentence, or paragraph. After highlighting, press delete, then enter the new word, sentence, or paragraph. Option 2 • After highlighting, enter the new information while area is still highlighted.
ADD a word, sentence, or paragraph	• Use mouse to position cursor at the point where you want the new information to be added. Click mouse to insert the cursor at that point. • When cursor is in place, enter the new word, sentence, or paragraph.
MOVE a word, sentence, or paragraph to a new position in the document	Option 1 • Highlight the word, sentence, or paragraph. • Select **Cut** from the **Edit** menu. • After selection is cut, use mouse to move cursor to the place you want to insert the cut information. • Select **Paste** from the **Edit** menu. Option 2 • Highlight the word, sentence, or paragraph. • Use the **Command** and **X** keys (⌘X) to cut the selection. • After selection is cut, use mouse to move cursor to the place you want to insert the cut information. • Use the **Command** and **V** keys (⌘V) to paste the selection.
COPY a word, sentence, or paragraph to place in a new position in the document	Option 1 • Highlight the word, sentence, or paragraph. • Select **Copy** from the **Edit** menu. • After selection is copied, use mouse to move cursor to the place you want to insert the copied information. • Select **Paste** from the **Edit** menu. Option 2 • Highlight the word, sentence, or paragraph. • Use the **Command** and **C** keys (⌘C) to copy the selection. • After selection is copied, use mouse to move cursor to the place you want to insert the copied information. • Use the **Command** and **V** keys (⌘V) to paste the selection.

DOCUMENT. The primary function of document formatting is setting the width of the margins. Margin width is determined for the top, bottom, and left and right sides of the document (see Figure 7-4). When determining the width of your margins, consider which page layout (vertical or horizontal format) will be used (see Figure 7-5).

Figure 7-4   Document Layout

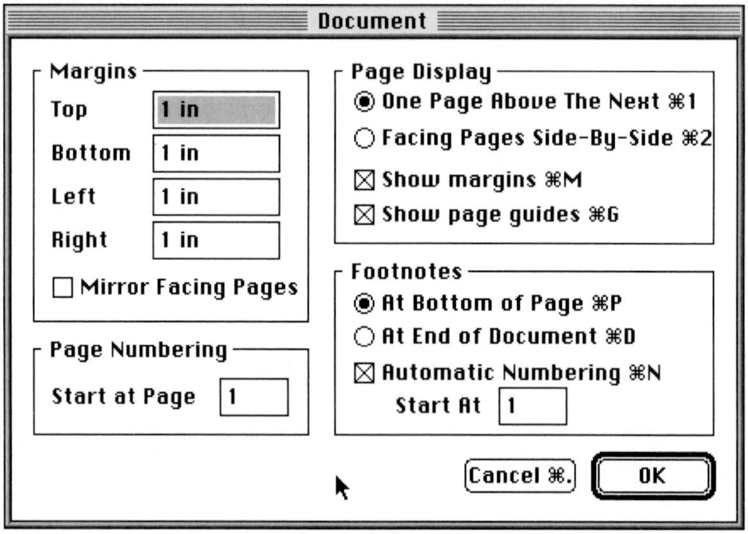

Figure 7-5   Page Layout

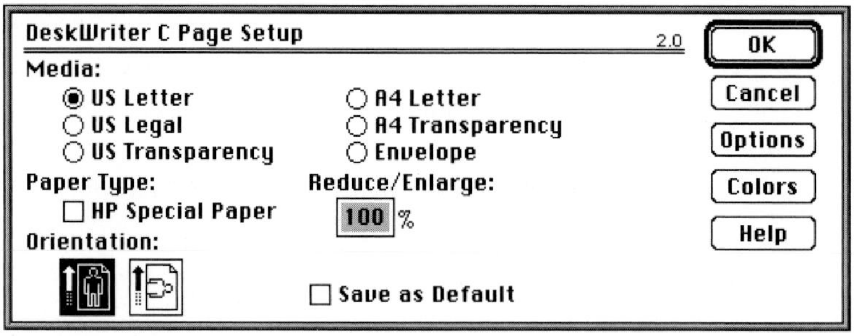

FONTS. Fonts and their appearance can be formatted by selecting the **Font, Size,** and **Style** of your choice from appropriate menu(s). Text that has already been entered can also be changed by highlighting the text you want to change, then selecting the desired font, size, and/or style. A sample of the various font choices can be seen in Figure 7-6.

Figure 7-6 Text Variations

Size	12 point	14 point	20 point	36 point
	Text	Text	Text	Text
Type	Times	Old English	Swing	Helvetica
	Text	Text	Text	Text
Style	Plain	Bold	Italics	Outline
	Text	**Text**	*Text*	Text

PARAGRAPHS. Two of the most common types of formatting variations for paragraphs are line spacing and alignment. Three types of line spacing typically are found in most word processing applications: single, one and one-half, and double space. Many applications also allow the user to customize the amount of space by specifying the specific distance between the lines. Sample line spacing can be seen here.

Single Spacing

This is a sample paragraph to illustrate the difference between single, 1.5, and double line spacing. This paragraph is formatted with single spacing.

1.5 Spacing

This is a sample paragraph to illustrate the difference between single, 1.5, and double line spacing. This paragraph is formatted with 1.5 spacing.

Double Spacing

This is a sample paragraph to illustrate the difference between single, 1.5, and double

line spacing. This paragraph is formatted with double spacing.

There are four ways to align paragraphs within a document: left, right, center, and justified. Careful use of these different types of alignment can create interesting special effects in a document. Examples of the four types of alignment are presented here.

Left Alignment

The content in this paragraph is left aligned. It is one of four sample paragraphs provided to illustrate the differences between left, center, right, and justified alignment. Notice how the left side of the paragraph is aligned together.

Right Alignment

The content in this paragraph is right aligned. It is one of four sample paragraphs provided as an illustration of the differences between left, center, right, and justified alignment. Notice how the right side of the paragraph is evenly aligned.

Center Alignment

The content in this paragraph is center aligned. It is one of four sample paragraphs provided as an illustration of the differences between left, center, right, and justified alignment. Notice that neither the left nor right margins are evenly aligned.

Justified Alignment

The content in this paragraph has justified alignment. It is one of four sample paragraphs provided as an illustration of the differences between left, center, right, and justified alignment. In this paragraph both the left and right margins are evenly aligned.

TABS. Tabs are useful for more than just indenting the typical half-inch at the beginning of each paragraph. They can also be used to create organized lists of material. Tabs, like paragraphs, can be aligned to the left, right, or center. Tab formatting dialogue boxes can be accessed in two ways: select **Tabs** from the **Format** menu or double click on the tab marker found on the ruler. These menus allow you to set the desired alignment and position of the tabs. Tabs can also be repositioned by using the mouse to "drag" them to a new position on the ruler. Following is a list that has been formatted with tabs. Notice that the words are center aligned.

Nouns	Verbs	Adjectives
chair	sit	old
car	run	fast
baby	cry	little

When you are creating a list of numbered or bulleted items, such as test questions or a list of common elements, the list looks much better and is easier to read if the numbers or bullets are separated from the text. The key to creating a list like this is Hanging Indents. Figure 7-7 shows the difference between a list that has a hanging indent and one without a hanging indent.

Power Tip ▲▲▲　　　　　　　　　　　　　*Hanging Indents*

Here are the steps for using Hanging Indents:

1. Insert cursor where you want the hanging indent list to begin.

2. Use mouse to drag the ruler markers to the desired positions (refer to the ruler in the top example of Figure 7-7.)

3. Type your information. When the questions or information are longer than one line, the second line of information will automatically be indented to the position you designated.

4. Note: You may need to adjust the position of the markers to acheive the correct amount of indenting.

Figure 7-7   Hanging Indents

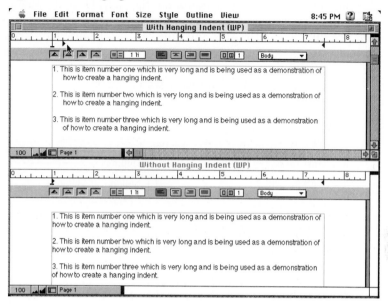

INSERTING

Most word processing applications provide a means for adding or inserting a variety of things such as page breaks, headers and footers, and graphics.

PAGE BREAKS.   Word processing applications automatically add page breaks. However, there are times that the text would be more meaningful, or the appearance more appealing, if the page break occurred earlier than what is set by the predefined margin. The preset margins can be overridden and a page break can be inserted at the desired location. To insert a page break, place the cursor at the line where you would like a new page to begin, then choose **Insert Page Break** from the **Format** menu.

HEADERS AND FOOTERS.   Headers and footers normally contain page numbers and the title and/or author of the paper. When you insert a header or footer, it automatically appears on every page of your document. The header is at the top of the paper, and as you can guess, the footer is at the bottom of the paper. If you look at the page you are now reading, you will find the chapter title and the page number at the top of the page. This information is the header. Obviously, the page number changes with each page, but the chapter information stays the same for each chapter. This information could just as easily be placed at the bottom of the page in a footer. To create a header or footer, select **Insert Header** or **Insert Footer** from the **Format** menu. The document will automatically shift to show the cursor inserted at the top of the page for the header, or at the bottom of the page for a footer. At this point you can select the alignment. If the document is to be printed on one side only, a header is often placed at the right side of the margin. Footers, on the other hand, are often centered at the bottom of the page. Once the alignment is selected, the information is entered. If you want to include page numbers, select Insert Page # from the **Edit** menu. The date and time can also be inserted, if desired. Most word processing applications provide a way to omit the header or footer from the first page (i.e., title page) of your document. This is accomplished by selecting **Title Page** from Section under the **Format** menu (see Figure 7-8).

Figure 7-8   Title Page

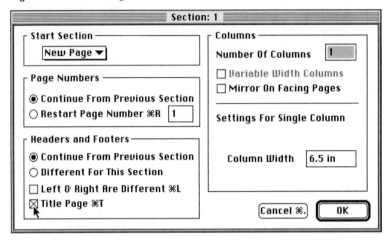

INSERTING GRAPHICS.   Inserting graphics is one of the most exciting features of word processing because it enhances student creativity and personalization. There are two primary ways to insert graphics into a document. The first one involves selecting **Insert** from the **File** menu, then selecting the item of your choice from a CD-ROM, a disk, or a file with graphics you have saved from the Internet (see Figure 7- 9). Chapter 11 gives some additional options.

Figure 7-9   Insert Graphic

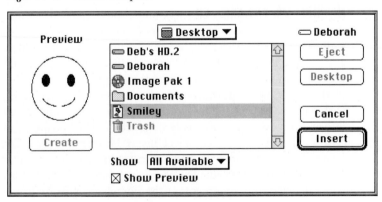

The second way to insert a graphic is to copy an object from another document or a clip art collection and then paste it into your word processing document. The object could be a picture the student has created with a draw program (see Chapter 10), a chart created in a spreadsheet (see Chapter 8), a database report (see Chapter 9), a graphic copied from the Internet (see Chapter 12), or a border taken from a clip art CD-ROM. The process is detailed here.

COPYING AND INSERTING GRAPHICS

1. Select graphic to be placed in word processing document by:
   – clicking on it with the mouse ("handles" appear at the corners)

   or

   – using the "lasso" tool to select the item.
2. Copy the graphic item by selecting **Copy** from the **Edit** menu (⌘C).
3. Open your word processing document and place the cursor in the place you want the graphic inserted. (Note that you may need to close the application from which you copied your graphic item.)
4. Paste your graphic item by selecting **Paste** from the **Edit** menu (⌘V).

TOOLS

Word processing applications provide students with different "tools" to help them create their documents. In most applications there is a spelling tool and a thesaurus. Activating the spelling tool checks spelling in the entire document or in selected sections of text. When misspelled or unrecognized words (e.g., proper names) are identified, the student is presented with the word in question and a list of suggested word replacements (see Figure 7-10). The students are required to assess the word in question and select one of the following options; replace the word with one of the suggested words, ignore or skip the word, or add it to a customized dictionary if it is a word that will be frequently used, such as the student's own name.

Figure 7-10   Spell Check

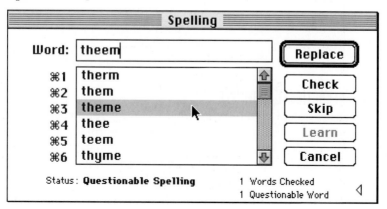

The other tool is a thesaurus. Using the mouse, students select a word they would like to replace with a synonym. The thesaurus dialogue box provides the students with a list of synonyms associated with the selected word (see Figure 7-11).

Figure 7-11   Thesaurus

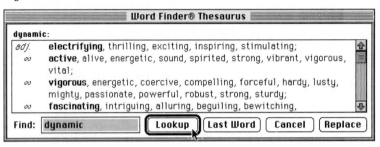

DESIGNING AN INTEGRATED LESSON

The basic components of a lesson integrating the use of computer technology were presented in Chapter 3. Figure 7-12 reiterates the components of the inNtegrating Technology for inQuiry (NTeQ) lesson. This section will discuss how to determine if word processing should be integrated into a lesson, and how to integrate word processing when it is appropriate.

Figure 7-12   NTeQ Lesson

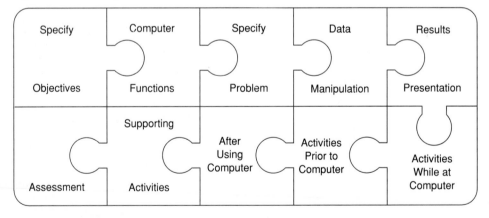

SPECIFYING THE INSTRUCTIONAL OBJECTIVE

Instructional objectives are what you want your students to know and do after they finish the lesson. These objectives are normally linked to the local curriculum guides and local, state, and/or national standards. Once you have identified the objective(s) for your lesson, you can then determine if the use of word processing will help students with the learning process.

Matching the Objective to Computer Functions

The objective can be matched to various computer functions by comparing the learning tasks required by the objective with the functions of the computer, in this case, word processing. It is important to emphasize the "action" portion of the objective when aligning it with the computer. For example, if the objective is for students to *compare and contrast* the roles and responsibilities of a mayor and a governor, you would examine the "compare and contrast" part of the objective to see if it matches computer functions rather than examining the content portion of the objective. The content, "roles and responsibilities of a mayor and a governor," could be any kind of content that would be compared and contrasted, for example, multiplication and division, French and Spanish pronouns, or Mars and Venus. Table 7-2 presents some sample student learning tasks and related word processing functions.

Specifying a Problem

When you have specified the lesson objectives and determined that the use of a word processor can be integrated effectively, the next step involves creating a problem for the students to solve. When possible, involve students in the problem development to help generate interest and personal investment in the lesson, and to keep the problem meaningful for them (Hancock, Kaput, & Goldsmith, 1992). As you guide the students through the problem identification process, keep the instructional objective in mind, because the stated outcome should be achieved as students proceed through the problem-solving process. The problem does not have

Table 7-2 Functions of Word Processing Related to Learning Tasks

Learning Task	Word Processing Function
Alter, Change, Modify	Modify a paragraph by changing all the adjectives to different adjectives.
Arrange	Arrange a scrambled list of procedures in sequential order.
Assemble, Produce	Produce a report describing the findings of a study or experiment.
Assess	Assess the differences between the first and second draft of a paper.
Collaborate, Cooperate, Contribute	Collaboratively write a poem.
Combine	Combine sections of a report that were written independently by different students.
Describe, Outline, Paraphrase	Describe, outline, or paraphrase the Declaration of Independence.
List	Create a list of brainstormed ideas.

Table 7-3 Objectives and Related Problems to Solve

OBJECTIVE	PROBLEM TO SOLVE
Students will classify items as liquid, solid, or gas.	What do you have more of in your refrigerator—liquids or solids?
Students will list key events of the Civil Rights Movement.	In honor of Martin Luther King Day, our class has been asked to create booklets for the library. Each booklet is to focus on three key events in the Civil Rights Movement. Problem: What are the important events of the Civil Rights Movement?
Students will solve a multiplication problem that involves two three-digit numbers.	Students in another classroom are having difficulty with multiplying two three-digit numbers. Which group can create the best "how to" sheet to help these students?

to be elaborate, but it needs to be interesting enough to keep students engaged as they work toward reaching a solution. Table 7-3 contains some example objectives and related problems that would involve the use of word processing to solve the problem.

MANIPULATING DATA

Once the problem has been specified, you can then plan strategies for how to manipulate data or process the information. When students are using word processing, they can be involved in all three types of generative strategies (see Chapter 3) that require active processing of information: integration, organization, and elaboration. For integration, students can manipulate the information by paraphrasing it into their own words. For example, students could rewrite the Preamble of the United States Constitution. The organizational strategy can be accomplished by having students generate an outline, or list the main ideas from a reading. You can also have students process or manipulate the information they are to learn by elaboration. Students could write a different ending to a story or historical event. For example, what would the United States be like today if Abraham Lincoln had been shot in the leg and not killed? All of these strategies take the information or data that you want your students to learn and have them manipulate it in a meaningful way.

PRESENTING RESULTS

Another consideration in planning your lesson is how students will present their results or solutions to the problems they are solving (see Chapter 11). Since this chapter focuses on word processing, the presentation of results will include some form of word processed material. This could be a traditional report including a description of the problem, the hypothesis, procedures, results, and conclusion. These reports can be enhanced by including charts (Chapter 8), database reports (Chapter 9), graphics (Chapter 10), or information from the Internet (Chapter 12). Students may also create a book or a display or write notes that are the basis for an oral presentation. Each of these methods requires the students to interpret their results and determine how to share the findings with others. In other words, students are engaged in "making meaning."

MULTIDIMENSIONAL ACTIVITIES

When you plan multidimensional activities, you not only plan what the students will do, but also how they will be grouped and what resources they will need. Again, when possible, involve students in as much of the planning process as is appropriate for the lesson. As each of these decisions is made, it is important to keep student learning as the primary motivator. As mentioned in Chapter 3, student learning is enhanced with the use of generative learning strategies. So, as you plan each activity, remember that students need to be actively engaged in processing the information (Jonassen, 1988). This information processing is enhanced when student groups work toward a common goal in a collaborative arrangement (Jonassen, 1994). For example, students working on the Civil Rights lesson are placed into groups of three, each group having to produce one booklet. In this type of setting, the students must discuss each decision and reach common solutions to problems, thus reinforcing the content.

When deciding which resources are needed for your activities, keep in mind that students can learn a great deal from finding their own resources. After the "problem" has been defined, students can determine which resources would be needed to solve the problem. For example, the students who are creating Civil Rights Movement booklets can brainstorm ideas about where to obtain the most up-to-date, accurate, and appropriate information. Their list would probably include the library, an Internet search, CD-ROM encyclopedias, and maybe some interviews. As they examine each of these resources, they actively process the information and determine if it will help solve their problem. Sometimes, students need to conduct experiments or investigations to collect the information they need to solve a problem. Again, the more students can be involved in hands-on activities, the more they will learn.

We will now look at planning the multidimensional activities. Begin by planning what the students will do while using the word processor. For some lessons, you may want to create a sample student product to make sure your directions are clear, that the planned resources are suitable, and that the time allotted is adequate. This sample can then be used as a model for the students. After planning what the students will do at the computer, you decide what they need to do before they go to the computer and after they finish their computer work. And lastly, you plan the supporting activities.

PLANNING: ACTIVITIES WHILE USING THE COMPUTER. As you plan the word processing activities that students will do at the computer, keep the lesson objective and problem statement in mind. Reexamine the functions of word processing and determine which ones can be used effectively to help your students achieve the objective. For example, if the lesson objective is for students to classify items as liquid,

solid, or gas, the students could use word processing to create information sheets describing the three states of matter. For this lesson, students will be using the computers two or three times. During the first visit, students will word process a student-generated description of each state. For the second visit, the students will enter their examples of each state of matter. A third visit will be required if the students are going to add clip art to their lists of examples.

In planning the resources for this activity, students would need word processing software, student disks, clip art (if used), and a printer. The students will need a minimum of two sessions at the computer, one to write the descriptions, and one to add to the list of examples and, if used, clip art.

Another example of a lesson that would use word processing to assist students in achieving the instructional objective is the one previously mentioned about listing key events of the Civil Rights Movement. The problem for this lesson is for students to determine three important events of the Civil Rights Movement. After these events are identified, the students are to create three memorial booklets (see Chapter 11 for more details on creating booklets) for the library. Students could use word processing for several portions of this lesson. The first visit to the computer could involve each student team planning how to identify the key events and how the booklets will be formatted. The next visit would be used to write an outline of the booklet content. Several computer sessions would then be used to write the content drafts. Each draft would be edited by the team and then the revised copy could be entered into the computer—remembering that team members should rotate the computer tasks. The final copy can have graphics added and be printed with a color printer, if available.

Students writing drafts of their paper before they go to the computer.

PLANNING: ACTIVITIES PRIOR TO USING THE COMPUTER. After you have identified the types of word processing activities your students will do at the computer, you need to plan the activities that will prepare them for the computer work. This preparation can involve from one to several activities. These activities can include brainstorming sessions to clarify the problem they will be solving or to list information sources needed to reach the solution. Once the information sources are obtained, students can take handwritten notes on relevant information. These notes will be the basis for a draft outline of the final product, which is normally written by hand and then entered into the computer.

The lesson on states of matter involves two trips to the computer. Following is a sequential list of activities that shows the rotation of students through the activities.

1. The first part of this lesson involves students working in pairs to create their own descriptions of solids, liquids, and gases. This activity requires students to do some research. You might have the final descriptions include citations from three references. Students could use their science textbook, the dictionary, and another resource book or the definitions given by an adult. They could copy these definitions on a sheet of paper to use as a reference when writing a draft of their own description. They would then use this draft to create the final descriptions on the computer.

2. The second activity is directly related to solving the problem "Does your refrigerator contain more solids or more liquids?" A class discussion will clarify why gases are not included. For their homework assignment, students should list the items in their refrigerator and classify them as liquid or solid.

3. When students return to school with a classification list of the items in their refrigerators, student pairs can review each other's lists and discuss if some items need to be reclassified. They then can combine their lists and add them to the appropriate description sheet.

4. The final activity before going to the computer will be for students to decide what kinds of illustrations should be added. For example, they could draw their own illustration of a glass of milk on the liquid page, or use a clip art picture of a drink.

It may be helpful to create a matrix to plan which activities students need to complete before they go to the computer and what they do at the computer. Following is an example for the lesson on the Civil Rights Movement (Table 7-4). This lesson requires the students to visit the computer several times.

PLANNING: ACTIVITIES AFTER USING THE COMPUTER. It is a common classroom practice to finish lessons similar to the "States of Matter" and the "Civil Rights Movement" by simply having students turn in their completed work (i.e., the descriptions of liquids, solids, and gases, and the Civil Rights Movement booklets) to the

Table 7-4 Planning Activities Prior to Computer and At the Computer

PRIOR TO COMPUTER (TEAMS OF THREE STUDENTS WORKING TOGETHER)	AT THE COMPUTER (TEAMS OF THREE STUDENTS WORKING TOGETHER)
Brainstorm ideas: • Plan of action for the project. • Format for the booklet. • Review various resources containing information about the three key Civil Rights Movement events selected by the team. • Take notes on items that may be included in the content. • Create a handwritten draft outline of the booklet.	Create a proposed plan of action for determining how to identify the key events and how the booklets will be formatted. Enter outline of the booklet content.
As a team: • Write first draft of the booklet content by hand. • After draft is entered in the computer and printed, the team engages in "read and discuss" sessions to revise and edit the content until it meets the criteria established in the plan of action.	Enter and revise the content drafts.
Team reviews clip art books to select appropriate color graphics to be added to the final document.	Create final copy that has graphics added. Print with a color printer.

teacher. The teacher grades each assignment and gives it back to the group, who quickly looks at the grade and teacher comments, then files the work in a portfolio, the desk, or the trash can.

An alternative to this approach is to engage the students in some kind of culminating activity after they have completed the computer assignments. As mentioned in Chapter 3, a *Think Sheet* can be used as part of this activity. The Think Sheets can have questions that guide critical thinking about the information the students worked with, or questions that have them predict what might happen if circumstances were different. Think Sheets also create links across disciplines. For example, the science lesson on states of matter could include math by having students calculate the percentage of foods that were liquid, or the average number of solid food items for each group. Or, you could move to social studies by having students find out if there would be any difference in the types of foods found in the refrigerator of a child in France or Kenya. Figure 7-13 provides a sample *Think Sheet* for the states of matter lesson.

After students finish their computer work, a whole-class discussion can be focused around the solutions the students found to the "problem" that was intro-

Figure 7-13   Think Sheet for States of Matter

The States of Matter
THINK SHEET

Answer the following questions in the space provided.
1. Which items in your refrigerator were the hardest to classify as either a liquid or a solid? Please explain why they were hard to classify.

2. Did you find any gases in your refrigerator? If your answer is no, please explain why.

3. What percent of the items in your refrigerator were solid?

4. For your group, what was the average number of liquid items found in the refrigerator?

5. Do you think a child living in Kenya would have a similar amount of liquids and solids in his or her refrigerator? How could you find out?

duced at the beginning of the lesson. For the lesson on the Civil Rights Movement, each group could be asked to explain why they chose the three key events selected for their booklets. The Think Sheet for this assignment could have students address the following items.

1. What was the most startling fact or idea you learned?

2. How does Civil Rights Movement impact what is happening today?

3. What still needs to be done?

Student journals are another way students can reflect on what has been learned. Before students write entries in their journals, you can facilitate a summary and review session with the whole class. During the session, you can clarify any misconceptions and also reemphasize the key objectives and why it is important for the students to have the identified knowledge and skills.

PLANNING: SUPPORTING ACTIVITIES.   Students need to be engaged in a variety of activities which are all directly related to the intended outcome. As you plan lessons that integrate student use of computers (in this case, word processing), remember that the computer is just one of several tools that help students achieve the objectives. The supporting activities discussed in this section are not intended to replace computer-related activities, but are to be used in conjunction with planned computer activities. The three types of supporting activities that will be discussed are listed here.

1. Review of Prior Learning
2. Required Research/Reading
3. Enrichment Activities

Review of prior learning.   There are several different ways to have your students review previously learned knowledge and skills associated with the identified objectives for the planned lesson. You can facilitate a large group discussion beginning with an individual activity that has students list three things they remember about a topic related to the lesson. For example, you may want students to recall what they know about historical events that may have influenced the Civil Rights Movement. You would then begin the lesson by having each student write three events they think are related to the topic. These student items can be used to create a what do you *Know,* what do you *Want* to learn, and what have you *Learned* (KWL) chart (see Chapter 2).

Students could also be asked to read a selection that describes previously studied historical events that impacted the Civil Rights movement, or they could take an open-book quiz over the same material. Please remember, though, that students do not automatically make the connections between what they have already learned and the new information; therefore, you may need to help them understand how the current topic aligns with a past lesson.

Required research/reading.   This portion of the lesson requires students to interact with the information needed to achieve the objectives for the lesson. This interaction can take the form of hands-on experiments, interviews, watching videotapes, or reading newspapers and magazines. Students need to have clearly defined goals before beginning their research or reading activities. An excellent activity for the "States of Matter" lesson is a hands-on experiment with different materials. Each student can be asked to bring 10 items from home. Small groups could then engage in an investigation of the different properties of each item. The teacher guides the investigations to assure the properties of matter are discovered.

The Civil Rights Movement lesson would require a great deal of reading and research to determine the three events the students think are the most important. The student groups decide, with teacher guidance, which resources are needed. A typical student-generated list of resources might include: library books such as biographies or historical accounts and periodicals such as news magazines, government documents, interviews, and Internet searches.

Enrichment activity. An enrichment activity for the Civil Rights Movement lesson could be based on the following National History Standard which emphasized historical thinking: Consult multiple sources reflecting differing interpretations of a historic event or individual. Student groups could choose one key event and investigate different accounts of the event. For example, the students could compare the *New York Times,* the *Chicago Tribune,* and the Montgomery, Alabama, newspaper coverage of the 1955 bus boycott launched in Montgomery, Alabama, after an African-American woman, Rosa Parks, was arrested for refusing to give up her seat to a white person.

Again, the two key factors to remember when planning the supporting activities are to always align them with the identified instructional objectives and incorporate as many generative learning strategies (see Chapter 3) as possible.

At The Classroom's Doorstep
▲▲▲
Questions Teachers Ask

If my students use the spell check tool in word processing, won't their ability to spell on their own be limited? Let's imagine that your class has just completed a unit on Egypt. For one of your culminating activities, your students are required to write, with pen and paper, a paragraph describing an Egyptian pyramid. The completed papers are turned in to you for grading. You begin reading each paper and circle the misspelled words as they are encountered. You also write in the correct spelling above each word. For other assignments, you require the students to look up the misspelled words in the dictionary and turn in a list of correctly spelled words. Both of these methods require extra time on your part, but more importantly, the students receive delayed feedback. When students run a spell check on their papers, they receive immediate feedback on questionable words. In most cases, the spell checker will suggest more than one word, so students must still think about their error and select the correct spelling. They are also better able to see possible patterns of misspelling, and how to correct them. Proofreading, however, is still necessary because spell checkers only identify misspelled words, not words out of context. For example, the spell check will not catch the misspelling of "pen" in the following example, "The author used a quill *pin* to write the letter."

I did not learn how to type until high school. How can my elementary students deal with using a keyboard? Teachers can approach keyboarding by either providing some form of instruction or allowing students to develop their own approach. When students use their own approaches to enter information with a word processor, it takes about twice as long as when they write a paper by hand (Peacock, 1993; Wetzel, 1990). However, the students who word processed their papers tended to write longer papers that were slightly higher quality than those written in pencil (Peacock, 1993).

NTeQ Lesson Plan
▲▲▲

Figure 7-14   NTeQ Word Processing Lesson

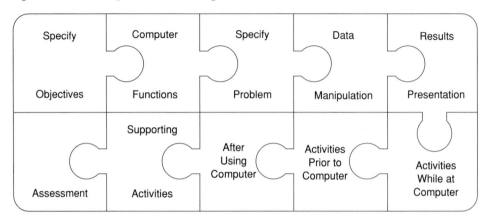

Lesson Title: Remembering The Civil Rights Movement
▲▲▲

Subject Area: Social Studies   Grade Level: 6–8

LEARNING OBJECTIVE
By the end of this lesson, the students will list and describe key events of the Civil Rights Movement.

COMPUTER FUNCTIONS
Word processing will be used to list and describe the key events of the Civil Rights Movement.

SPECIFY PROBLEM
In honor of Martin Luther King Day, our class has been asked to create memorial booklets for the library. Each booklet is to focus on three key events in the Civil Rights Movement. What are three important events of the Civil Rights Movement?

DATA MANIPULATION
Word processing will be used to edit and revise the information to be included in the final booklets.

RESULTS PRESENTATION
The final product will be the memorial booklets which will be word processed documents with graphics.

MULTIDIMENSIONAL ACTIVITIES

Divide students into teams of three and have them follow the guidelines listed below:

ACTIVITIES PRIOR TO COMPUTER
- Create a draft plan of action that includes:
  - where to obtain the best resources
  - how to choose three key events
  - how to format the booklets
- Create a list of search terms for the Internet and CD-ROM encyclopedia.
- Generate a list of questions for e-mail interview.
- Collect resources from library and classroom.
- Review collected resources containing information about the Civil Rights Movement.
- Select three key events for the booklet.
- Take notes on items that may be included in the content.
- Create a draft copy of the outline to be word processed.
- As a team, write first draft on paper. Then engage in "read and discuss" sessions with each printout to revise and edit the content.
- Team reviews clip art books to select appropriate color graphics.

ACTIVITIES WHILE AT COMPUTER
- Enter the draft plan of action.
- Conduct Internet and CD-ROM encyclopedia search.
- Use e-mail to correspond with either a Civil Rights expert or participant.
- Enter outline of the booklet content.
- Enter and revise the content drafts.
- Create final copy that has graphics added.
- Print final copy on a color printer.

AFTER USING COMPUTER
- Answer the Think Sheet questions:
  1. What was the most startling fact or idea you learned?
  2. How does Civil Rights Movement impact what is happening today?
  3. What still needs to be done?
- Teacher facilitates a summary and review session with the whole class by discussing the Think Sheet responses. During the discussion, clarify any misconceptions that arise and reemphasize the key learning objectives and why it is important for the students to have an understanding of the Civil Rights Movement.

SUPPORTING ACTIVITIES

- Play "Can you Guess?" Create a set of note cards that lists the name of a Civil Rights Movement event or person on one side and descriptive details on the other side. Selected students randomly draw a card. Other students try to identify the person or event by asking questions that can only be answered with a yes or no reply. The student who correctly guesses the answer draws the next card.
- View videotapes of events related to the Civil Rights Movement.

EVALUATION

- Create a rubric with items similar to the following for assessing the memorial booklets:
  - the three events selected by the students represent key occurrences.
  - each event is presented with clarity.
  - appropriate graphics are included.
  - booklet is formatted in an appealing manner.
  - work is free of errors.

LESSON BYTES FOR WORD PROCESSING
▲▲▲
The following list contains activity suggestions for student use of word processing.

REWRITE:

▲ the ending to a fiction or nonfiction story.

▲ a story so it is personalized by including the student's name, home town, friends names, hobbies, and favorite sports.

▲ word problems by changing the names or places, then exchange with a fellow student.

CREATE DESCRIPTIONS FOR HOW-TO:

▲ multiply two three-digit numbers.

▲ operate a balance beam scale.

▲ write a persuasive paragraph.

▲ draw a balanced illustration.

▲ read a map legend.

▲ analyze a chemical solution.

CREATE ONE-PARAGRAPH DESCRIPTION OF:

▲ a painting.

▲ a rock.

▲ a formula.

▲ the Constitution of the United States.

▲ a tornado.

▲ a snail.

▲ a battle.

▲ an author.

▲ a geometric shape.

GENERATE EXAMPLES AND NONEXAMPLES FOR:

▲ punctuation rules.

▲ grammar rules.

▲ chemical formulas.

▲ animal and plant classifications.

GENERATE COMPARE AND CONTRAST CHARTS FOR:

▲ democrats and republicans.

▲ solids and liquids.

▲ east and west coasts of the U.S.

▲ animal cells and plant cells.

▲ Spain and Mexico.

RESOURCES
▲▲▲

Word Processing Tutorials

Fields, N., Wetzel, K., & Painter, S. (1997). *Microsoft Works 4.0 for the Macintosh—A workbook for educators.* ISTE Publications, Eugene, OR, ISBN 1-56484-126-X.

Rathje, L., Heyerly, J., & Schenck, B. (1996). *ClarisWorks for students* (4th ed.). HRS Publications, Eugene, OR, ISBN 0-9644314-3-2

Wiebe, J. H., Moreton, J. M., & Slovacek, S. P. (1996). *Works for Windows for educators.* Franklin, Beedle & Associates, Wilsonville, OR, ISBN 0-938661-74-4.

Yoder, S. & Moursand, D. (1995). *Introduction to ClarisWorks 4.0—A tool for personal productivity* (Mac or Windows). ISTE Publications, Eugene, OR, ISBN 1-56484-086-7.

Word Processing in the Classroom

Ryba, K. & Anderson, B. (1993). *Learning with computers: Effective teaching strategies.* ISTE Publications, Eugene, OR, ISBN 0-924667-64-8.

Smith, I., Yoder, S., & Thomas, R. (1997). *Classroom activities with ClarisWorks 4.0.* ISTE Publications, Eugene, OR, ISBN 1-56484-099-9.

REFERENCES
▲▲▲

Becker, H. J. (1991). How computers are used in United States schools: Basic data from the 1989 I.E.A. computers in education survey. *Journal of Educational Computing Research, 7*(4), 385–406.

Hancock, C., Kaput, J. J., & Goldsmith, L. T. (1992). Authentic inquiry with data: Critical barriers to classroom interpretation. *Educational Psychologist, 27,* 337–364.

Jonassen, D. H. (1994). Thinking technology: Toward a constructivist design model. *Educational Technology, 34*(4), 34–37.

Jonassen, D. H. (1988). Integrating learning strategies into courseware to facilitate deeper processing. In D. H. Jonassen (Ed.), *Instructional design for microcomputer courseware.* Hillsdale, NJ: Erlbaum.

McDaniel, E., McInerney, W. & Armstrong, P. (1994). Computers and school reform. *Educational Technology, Research and Development, 41*(1), 73–78.

Peacock, G. (1993). Word-Processors and Collaborative Writing. In J. Beynon & H. Mackay (Eds.), *Computers into classrooms: More questions than answers* (pp. 92–97). Washington, DC: The Falmer Press.

Roblyer, M. D. (1997). Technology and the oops! effect: Finding a bias against word processing. *Learning and Leading with Technology, (24)* 7, 14–16.

Sheingold, K., & Hadley, M. (1990). *Accomplished teachers: Integrating computers into classroom practice.* New York: Center for Technology in Education, Bank Street College of Education.

Wetzel, K. (1990). Keyboarding. In S. Franklin (Ed.), *The best of the writing notebook* (pp. 46–48). Eugene, OR: The Writing Notebook.

CHAPTER 8
Spreadsheets as a Learning Tool

▶ Introduction

Much of the early success of both mainframe and personal computers is attributed to the ability of these machines to manipulate numbers quickly. Early personal computers such as the Apple II and the IBM PC allowed people to change numbers quickly and easily on a spreadsheet to portray a variety of scenarios. Thus, it became easier to determine the effects of giving everyone in a company a 3 percent raise, or having the company absorb a 5 percent increase in medical insurance. Over the past few years, educators have recognized that spreadsheets are powerful instructional tools with applications beyond accounting. Spreadsheets can be used to solve time and distance problems or predict the weather based on wind data. In this chapter, we will explore how students can enhance learning by using a spreadsheet to manipulate and analyze data.

▶ Computer Skills Used in This Chapter

Entering data into a spreadsheet cell
Using formulas in a spreadsheet
Copying and pasting

▶ Key Topics

Spreadsheets in the Classroom
  Using Spreadsheets for Learning
  Spreadsheets as Tools
Examining the Spreadsheet
  Basic Components
  Entering Information
  Creating Calculations
  Creating Charts
Designing an Integrated Lesson with a Spreadsheet
  Matching the Objective to Computer Functions
  Identifying the Problem
  Data Manipulation
  Results Presentation
  Multidimensional Activities

SPREADSHEETS IN THE CLASSROOM
▲▲▲

Even for the expert user, spreadsheets can be an enigma. How many teachers have used one of the green-ruled work sheets we associate with accountants? Many teachers avoid spreadsheet applications on the premise that they have no need to work accounting problems. In the following section we will describe examples of how students can use spreadsheets as an instructional tool.

USING SPREADSHEETS FOR LEARNING

Spreadsheets are useful for more than accounting. Spreadsheets are a useful tool for creating simulations, analyzing data, and exploring number concepts and mathematical relationships. The following paragraphs explain some of these applications of spreadsheets in the classroom.

CREATING SIMULATIONS. Simulation software often conjures up images of expensive, complex software that is beyond the budget of many public schools. Teachers can create a simulation that demonstrates manipulation of one or more variables using a spreadsheet. These simulations are much simpler than a microworld; however, they do allow the student to manipulate a variable and see the resulting numerical change or change in a graph.

Did you study the solar system and gravity in one (or more!) of your science classes? A common illustration depicted a man on Earth weighing 160 pounds and the same person on our Earth's moon and other planets with the different weights. To a student who weighs only 60 pounds, the thought of weighing more than twice as much might be difficult to imagine. So, the instructional task simply involved memorizing on which planet a person weighed the most and on which he or she weighed the least. Using a spreadsheet, however, a teacher can create realistic examples and problems to help students understand and apply the concept of gravity.

For example, when students enter the classroom, they can weigh themselves and then enter their weights in a spreadsheet (see Figure 8-1). Formulas in the spreadsheet then calculate the students' weight on the moon and other planets. Similarly, they can enter the weight of other objects such as a bag of sugar, a pair of boots, or a bicycle. Students can then use the graph function to determine where they or an object would weigh the most and the least in the solar system. In a math class, students could calculate how much a bag of sugar would cost on each planet based on a price per pound. Advanced students could use these weights to determine how much force a space shuttle would need to leave a planet's gravitational field. Using a spreadsheet, they can make adjustments in their supplies and personnel to achieve the desired load. Another use of spreadsheets is having students observe change over a period of time by graphing the results of mathematical models they have constructed of a real-world problem (Walsh, 1996). Students can change different variables in the model to observe the effect on change.

Figure 8-1   Using a Spreadsheet for a Gravitation Simulation

	A	B	C	D	E	F	G	H
1	Object		Weight in pounds					
2		Earth	Moon	Venus	Mars	Jupiter	Saturn	
3	You	67	11.18	60.3	25.46	156.78	77.72	
4	Sugar	10	1.67	9	3.8	23.4	11.6	
5	Bicycle	32	5.344	28.8	12.16	74.88	37.12	
6								
7								
8								
9								
10								
11								
12								
13								
14								
15								
16								
17								
18								
19								
20								
21								

CREATING DISCOVERY SPREADSHEETS. You can also create a spreadsheet simulation that allows students to manipulate variables and discover rules and laws. A chemistry teacher could design a spreadsheet to simulate the results of an experiment. For example, students could recreate the discovery of Charles' Law—a fixed quantity of gas at a constant pressure will increase linearly with temperature. Students enter various temperatures and the spreadsheet calculates the corresponding volume. After entering the data, the student can create a graph and then determine the relationship between temperature and volume (see Figure 8-2). This type of spreadsheet can also be used to teach students how to make predictions based on the rules or laws they have discovered. For example, they can use atmospheric data to predict the weather (Niess, 1992), or predict the results of an election based on demographic and historical voting data (North Carolina State Department of Public Instruction, 1992). Mercer (1993) describes a project where students determined the probability of winning the largest bingo prize with a spreadsheet.

EXPLORING MATH CONCEPTS AND RULES. Another example of spreadsheet use is to let students explore mathematical relationships. Either the student or teacher can create a spreadsheet to both calculate and plot the relationship between an unknown (x) and its coefficient and constants. As students change the values, the equation is solved for x, and the relationships between the coefficient, constants, and x are displayed in a graph that is automatically updated with each change (see Figure 8-3). Spreadsheets are useful for teaching math concepts such as surface area and volume problems (Verderber, 1992) and polynomial problems (Timmons, 1991). Teachers can also use spreadsheets to teach math concepts in classes such as economics (Adams & Kroch, 1989; Smith & Smith, 1988).

Figure 8-2   Using a Spreadsheet for Charles' Law Simulation

	A	B	C	D	E	F
1	Enter 4 different temperatures of increasing value in the highlight cells					
2						
3		Volume (l)	Temperature (k)			
4		0	0			
5		7.5	150			
6		10	200			
7		15	300			
8		22.5	450			
9						
10						
11						
12						
13						
14						
15						
16						
17						
18						
19						
20						
21						
22						
23						
24						
25						
26						

Adapted from a unit by Katherine Abraham. Used with permission.

Figure 8-3   Solving Linear Equations

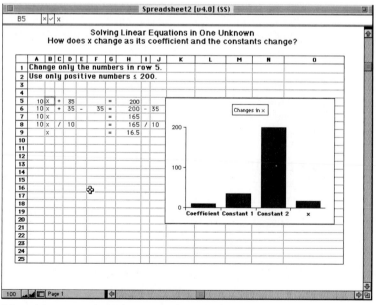

Adapted from a unit by Katherine Abraham. Used with permission.

Fran's Diary

▲▲▲

The spreadsheet was the one application that I did not use in the early years of my computing experiences. I associated the spreadsheet with numbers, and math was not one of my favorite subjects in school! I did not use the spreadsheet application until I had to develop a lesson plan that incorporated a spreadsheet. I soon discovered, much to my amazement, that the spreadsheet could be a useful tool. I learned that it could be used for creating simulations, analyzing data, and exploring number concepts and mathematical relationships.

I decided that I would give the spreadsheet a try. For my first spreadsheet lesson, I adapted the AIMS M&Ms lesson to include the use of a spreadsheet. The students sorted and counted M&Ms by color. Instead of the students entering this data on a mimeograph sheet as we had done in the past, they entered it into a spreadsheet. I was able to teach them how to enter their data into a spreadsheet and how to calculate the total number of M&Ms in a bag by entering a simple addition formula. They even created a bar graph from this data. They loved this lesson, as it was totally hands-on!

This experience gave me the confidence that I needed. I extended this lesson the next day by having the students analyze the percentage of each color in a bag. My students did not have the math skills to determine percentage, but this lack of skill did not stop us. I entered a formula in their spreadsheets that would determine the percentage of each color for them. The students made another bar graph showing the percentage of each color of M&Ms in their snack size bags. They could visually analyze this numerical data! The students wondered if the percentages of each color would be similar in other sized packages of M&Ms and made some predictions.

I was able to extend this lesson again. I purchased various size bags of M&Ms. The students sorted and counted these M&Ms by color. The students entered this data in another spreadsheet and repeated the process that was followed with the snack size bags. I entered this new data into a master spreadsheet that included the percentages of color for each size bag and created a bar graph. The students were easily able to analyze the percentages of each color in different size packages. They were surprised to discover the percentages of color were not consistent across the bag size. This led to another question. Would this also be true of the other M&M candies such as M&M peanuts? This led to more spreadsheets, more graphs, more analyzing, and more candy. But they were learning and using those higher order thinking skills!

They discovered that the percentages of colors were still not consistent across different size bags. This finding led to the next question. Was this

Continued

result due to something in the M&M manufacturing process? We discussed what might cause this to happen. I got on the Internet and found the web site for M&Ms. The students were able to take a virtual tour of the factory to see how these candies were made. We discussed what we saw and if there was anything in the process that could explain why the percentages of colors were not consistent. With a little bit of questioning, they soon discovered that the bags were filled according to weight, not percentage of each color, and that the M&M colors are already mixed in huge containers before they are poured into the bags.

You can probably guess what the next question was. Would this also be true of other candies such as Skittles? We did not pursue this one in class, but we did come back to it later when we did a group science fair project. What started out as an hour lesson turned into a week's lesson! They entered data into a spreadsheet. They performed calculations. They created and interpreted graphs. They solved a problem. They learned a lot!

SOLVING PROBLEMS. Our last example requires students to use a spreadsheet to solve a specific problem. For example, the class has collected $47.83 for a party. They have decided that they want to serve candy at the party. The problem, then, is what type of candy can they purchase so that they get the most for their money? The class can list all the various types of candy they might purchase and enter these items in a spreadsheet (see Figure 8-4). After completing their list, individuals check the weight and prices of the various items. The price and weight are then entered into the spreadsheet, and the price per ounce is calculated. Students can create a chart from the data to identify the most expensive and least expensive candies. For advanced students, you might ask them to determine a mix of "good" and "average" tasting candy based on the price per ounce. A more complex problem is one of planning a pizza party that requires the students to calculate the area of different cheese pizzas and then determine the price per square inch.

Figure 8-4   Entering Candy Prices

	A	B	C	D
1	Candy	Price/Ounce	Weight (oz)	Price
2	Hershey Bar	$0.29	1.55	0.45
3	Hershey Bar Cookie & Mint	$0.29	1.55	0.45
4	Hershey Bar w/Almond	$0.31	1.45	0.45
5	Mamba	$0.17	2.65	0.45

Candy ss (SS)

016

SPREADSHEETS AS TOOLS

Spreadsheets are excellent tools for students to use for problem solving, inquiry, and discovery learning. In each of the previous examples students manipulated data to find an answer. They changed the data and constructed new charts and graphs, or sorted the data to identify patterns. These opportunities to explore numerical relationships provide a laboratory for problem solving and inquiry. Learners discover through active learning as opposed to passively reading a text or listening to a lecture. Students can also try various options and obtain an answer as quickly as they can press the Return key. This immediacy of response provides more motivation to explore different possibilities. Spreadsheets can remove the burden of completing tedious calculations and allow the learner to focus on analyzing the patterns and results. This use of the spreadsheet as a tool not only enhances learning, it improves the likelihood of the learner transferring the use of the tool to other situations (Salomon, 1993).

EXAMINING THE SPREADSHEET

▲▲▲

For those of us who use computers primarily for word processing or creating drawings, the spreadsheet may seem foreign. Spreadsheets are very powerful tools, and an examination of all the features is beyond the scope of this book. However, we will examine the basic features so that you can explore and use the features of a spreadsheet. Let's begin by examining the basic components. We are using ClarisWorks, but most spreadsheets are very similar in operation and functions.

Teacher discussing possible ways to set up a spreadsheet.

Basic Components

A spreadsheet consists of a number of cells that form a grid (see Figure 8-5). The letters across the top of the spreadsheet are labels for each column of cells. The numbers down the left side of the spreadsheet are labels for each row of cells. We can reference a cell with the column label and the row label (e.g., A5, B10, C1). Each cell holds information such as numbers, dates, name, or titles. When you click on a cell, it becomes active and is highlighted with a border. Cell A1 is the active cell in Figure 8-5. Note that the reference for the active cell is displayed in the upper left corner (e.g., A1 in Figure 8-5). The contents of the active cell are displayed in the Entry bar.

Figure 8-5   Components of a Spreadsheet

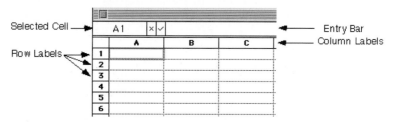

Entering Information

The following three steps illustrate how to enter data into a cell or edit existing data.

1. Click in the cell where you want to place the information or the cell you wish to edit. The cell becomes the active cell and any contents of the cell are displayed in the Entry bar.

2. Type the information into the cell. The information is displayed in the entry bar. Use the delete key, highlight text with the mouse, or use the left and right arrow keys to delete and navigate through the entry. Most spreadsheets will allow you to enter numbers, letters, or combinations of letters and numbers into the cells.

3. Once the information is entered, you must accept it. The simplest way to accept the information is to press the Return key. You can also click the checkmark (✔) to the left of the Entry bar (see Figure 8-5). If you decide to leave the cell as is rather than accept the change, then click the **X**, press **Escape,** or click in another cell.

After entering the data, you can format your spreadsheet to make it easier to read.

Changing Cell Width.   A new spreadsheet sets all the columns to the same width and height. If a cell contains a name or multiple words, however, the column may be too narrow for all the characters. For example, the default column width in

ClarisWorks is 72 points (1 inch), which will display about 12 letters or numbers. You can change the width of an individual column or group of columns. To adjust the width of only one column, move the cursor over the dividing line in the column heading (see Figure 8-6). The cursor will change to a vertical line with arrows on each side. Click and drag to resize the column. To change the width of several columns to the same size, move the cursor to the column heading of the first column, then click and drag across the other columns to select them. In ClarisWorks, select the **Column Width** item from the **Format** menu. You can then enter the new column width for the selected columns (see Figure 8-7). Row height is also changed by dragging the dividing line or with the **Row Height** menu item.

Figure 8-6   Changing the Width
of a Single Column

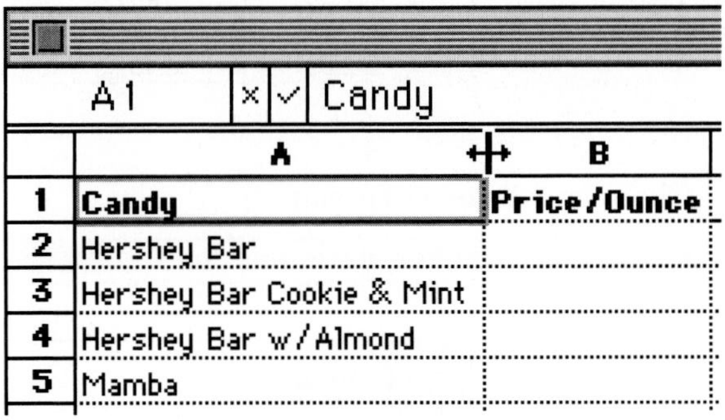

Figure 8-7   Changing the Width
of Multiple Columns

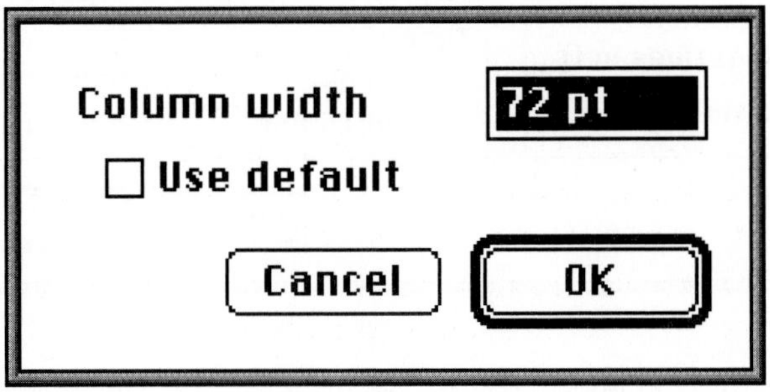

A cell filled with "########" is a sign that you need to increase the column width to display all of the data in the cell.

CHANGING NUMBER FORMATS.   Our candy prices spreadsheet (see Figure 8-8) has two columns with numbers, one for the weight and one for the price. The numbers in the two columns look exactly the same, however. We need a way to distinguish the price column from the weight column. Spreadsheets provide several ways to format numbers, dates, and time (see Figure 8-9). To format the price column as a currency, we start by selecting cell C2 and dragging to cell C5. Then, in Claris-Works, we select **Number** from the **Format** menu. Next, we click **Currency** and set the precision to two decimal places. The spreadsheet will automatically format any number in the selected cells as currency (e.g., $1.45 or $0.45).

Figure 8-8   Changing the Format of Numbers

■		Candy Prices (SS)		
C2	×✓ 0.45			
	A	**B**	**C**	**D**
1	Candy	Weight (oz)	Price	Price/Ounce
2	Hershey Bar	1.55	0.45	
3	Hershey Bar Cookie & Mint	1.55	0.45	
4	Hershey Bar w/Almond	1.45	0.45	
5	Mamba	2.65	0.45	

Figure 8-9   Choosing a Number Format

Format Number, Date, and Time	
Number	**Date**
⦿ General	○ 11/29/94
○ Currency	○ Nov 29, 1994
○ Percent	○ November 29, 1994
○ Scientific	○ Tue, Nov 29, 1994
○ Fixed	○ Tuesday, November 29, 1994
☐ Commas	**Time**
☐ Negatives in ()	○ 5:20 PM ○ 17:20
Precision 2	○ 5:20:15 PM ○ 17:20:15
	(Cancel) (OK)

The various number formats are illustrated in Figure 8-10. The first row illustrates how the number is displayed when **General** is selected. The remaining rows illustrate the other numerical formats for the same number when the precision is set to 2 (see Figure 8-9).

We can also change the formatting of a cell or cells using many of the features you have used in a word processor. For example, we can change the font, font size, and style (e.g., bold, italics, etc.) of individual cells or the whole document. We can also change the alignment of individual columns to left, center, or right. Finally, we can add borders to selected cells to set them off from other information.

Figure 8-10   Displaying Number Formats

	A	B
1	General	2.89391167445
2	Currency	$2.89
3	Percent	289.39%
4	Scientific	2.89e+0
5	Fixed	2.89

CREATING CALCULATIONS

The power of a spreadsheet is in the capability of manipulating data. For example, we can add, divide, subtract, and multiply numbers or columns. The spreadsheet can also determine the largest, smallest, range, sum, and average of a column or row. Spreadsheets include a number of functions that perform both common (e.g., average) and not so common (e.g., internal rate of return and standard deviation) functions. You can also create your own formulas using the addition (+), subtraction (–), multiplication (*), and division (/) symbols.

Let's examine how to calculate the price per ounce in column D and the average weight of the items in our Candy Prices spreadsheet. We will start with the price per ounce for the first candy item by clicking in cell D2. The formula involves dividing the price of each item by the weight, or dividing column C (the price cell) by column B (the weight cell).

1. Start by entering an equal sign (=) to tell the spreadsheet that we are entering a calculation.

2. Enter the formula, which is C2/B2. That is, divide the contents of cell C2 by the contents of cell B2 which is the price divided by the weight. The spreadsheet will display the results of our formula in the cell D2 (see Figure 8-11).

Figure 8-11   Entering a Calculation

	Candy Prices (SS)			
D2 ✕ ✓ =C2/B2				
	A	B	C	D
1	Candy	Weight (oz)	Price	Price/Ounce
2	Hershey Bar	1.55	$0.45	$0.29
3	Hershey Bar Cookie & Mint	1.55	$0.45	
4	Hershey Bar w/Almond	1.45	$0.45	
5	Mamba	2.65	$0.45	
6				

3. When the spreadsheet substitutes the values in the cells for the formula, =C2/B2, the mathematical calculation is $0.45 divided by 1.55.

We could repeat the entry of this calculation for each row, but that would take time and allow for possible mistakes. A quicker and more accurate method is to use the **Fill** option of the spreadsheet to copy the correct formula into the remaining cells. We can select the cells from D2 to D5 in our Candy Prices spreadsheet, and then select **Fill Down** from the **Calculate** menu in ClarisWorks. The spreadsheet will automatically copy the calculation and change the reference cells (e.g., B2 and C2) for each row. You can also complete calculations for entries placed in a row by selecting **Fill Right.**

Sometimes it is easier to use a function from the spreadsheet rather than entering a formula. For example, we could add all the weights together and divide by 4 to obtain the average weight of the candy. A simpler method is to use the **Average** function.

1. Select Cell B7 for the average weight.

2. Next, select **Paste Function** from ClarisWork's **Edit** menu (see Figure 8-12).

Figure 8-12   Using Functions in a Spreadsheet

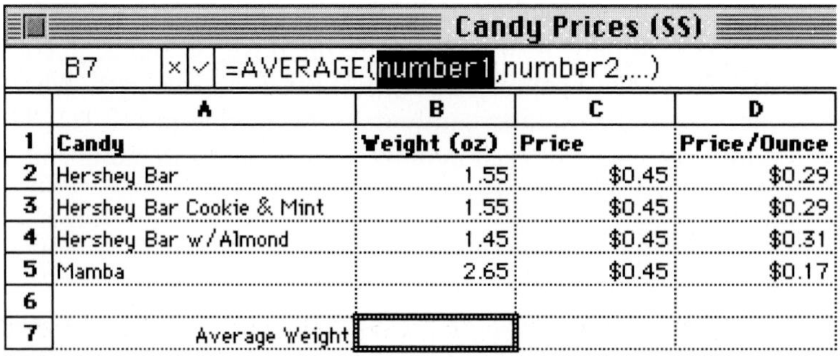

Pasting the Function

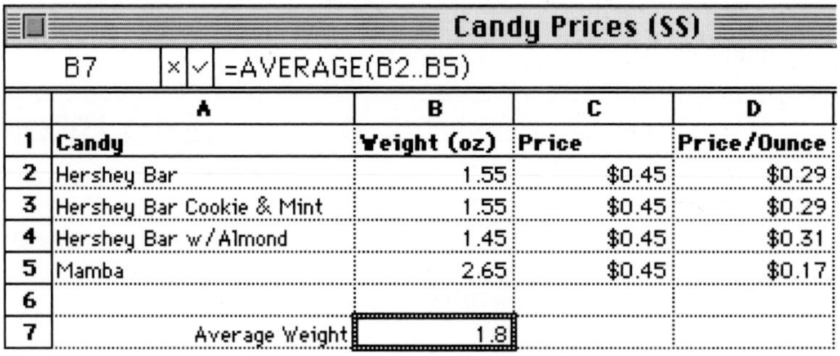

Formula with Cell References

3. Select the **Average** function and then click **OK** to paste it into the cell. The function is displayed in the Entry bar and must be modified to work.

The **Average** function requires a set of values consisting of either a series of numbers (96, 97, 78, 63, etc.), a series of cells (C1, C2, C3, etc.), or a range of cells (C1 . . C5). In most cases, you will want to enter a range of cells, since you are calculating the average of a column rather than listing each individual cell.

To calculate the average weight of our candy we will enter a range of cells for values. Since we want the average of cells B2, B3, B4, and B5, we can enter the range.

4. The range is entered by specifying the first cell and the last cell. Before entering the range, select the data inside the parentheses () and press **Delete**.

5. Type the range as B2..B5 (type two periods between the two values).

6. An alternative to typing the range is to click on the appropriate cells. Start by clicking the cursor between the two parentheses in the function and then click in cell B2 and drag to cell B5.

7. Click the checkmark or press **Return** to accept the function.

The average is displayed in cell B7 of our spreadsheet (see Figure 8-12).

CREATING CHARTS

Charts and graphs provide a visual means for representing numbers from data students enter into a spreadsheet. Students can create a bar chart illustrating the frequency count of their data to discover patterns and relationships. Similarly, a math student can graph a linear equation and observe the relationship between the variables as each changes. A teacher or student can create an interactive display between a graph and a spreadsheet so the user can immediately observe the effects

Power Tip ▲▲▲   *Protecting Data*

Students have a long history of changing software both by accident and as a challenge. Consider the time you might spend creating our sample candy prices spreadsheet by entering the names of 20 to 30 types of candy and creating the formulas to determine the price per ounce for each. Then, five minutes into the lesson, one of your students deletes the column of candy names and saves the file before you can leap to the aid of your spreadsheet. The only safe procedure is to keep several backup copies of your spreadsheet at home, in the principal's office, your safety deposit box, and under the sink; you can make it more difficult for the adventuresome student to ruin your file!

Let's examine how we can protect our candy prices spreadsheet. The column of candy names and the price/ounce columns are the only ones with data that we have entered. Most spreadsheets will allow us to lock the data so that it cannot be changed. In ClarisWorks we can select the cells in column A that have data and then select **Lock Cells** from the **Options** menu. We did not select every cell in the column as we wanted students to have the capability of adding additional items at the end of our list. Once the cells are locked, the student cannot change the information without unlocking the cells.

of changing variables. Let's examine how to create a chart using our candy prices spreadsheet.

In ClarisWorks, the rows and columns to graph must be contiguous. We created our spreadsheet (see Figure 8-13) so that the type of candy bar and the price per ounce columns were next to each other. If you want to create a chart with cells that are in columns that are not next to each other, you will need to copy and paste the cells. However, you will also need to revise any calculations you have made to correct the references.

Figure 8-13   Arranging Spreadsheet Columns

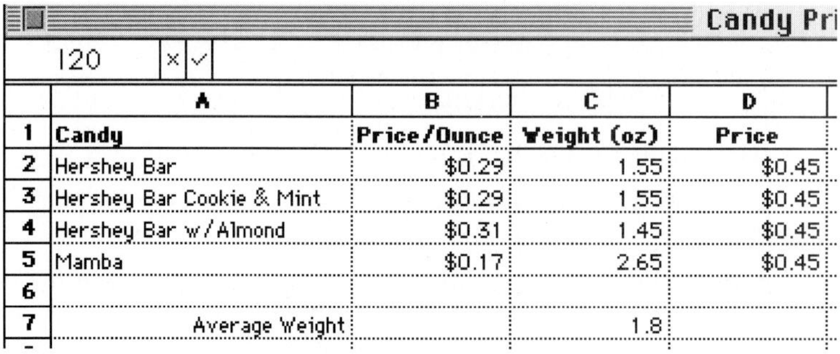

	A	B	C	D
		Price/Ounce	Weight (oz)	Price
1	Candy			
2	Hershey Bar	$0.29	1.55	$0.45
3	Hershey Bar Cookie & Mint	$0.29	1.55	$0.45
4	Hershey Bar w/Almond	$0.31	1.45	$0.45
5	Mamba	$0.17	2.65	$0.45
6				
7	Average Weight		1.8	

To create a graph of the price per ounce for each candy bar in ClarisWorks, select the rows with data in columns A and B. After selecting the cells, select **Make Chart** (⌘ then **M**) from the **Options** menu to display the **Chart Options** dialog (see Figure 8-14). There are 12 types of charts available to graph the data. There are also options for creating color, horizontal (e.g., the bars on a bar graph go across rather than up), shadow, and 3-dimensional charts. If you are printing to

Figure 8-14   Selecting the Chart Options Dialog

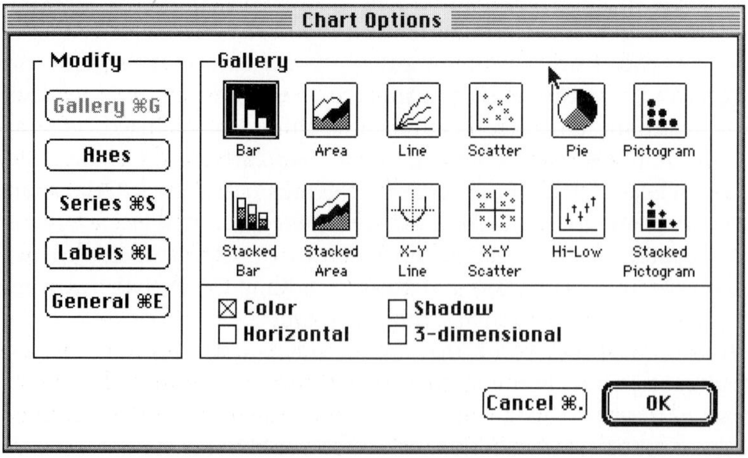

a noncolor printer, you may find that black and white charts produce the best results.

Next we need to label each of the axes. Click on **Axes** to display the **Axes** pane (see Figure 8-15). The Y axis is selected by default and you can enter the label in the Axis label field. The Y axis label for the candy price chart is Price/Ounce. Click **X** axis and enter the label, Candy. We can also change the display of the data by entering minimum, maximum, step size, and log amounts for the chart.

Figure 8-15   Labeling the Graph Axes

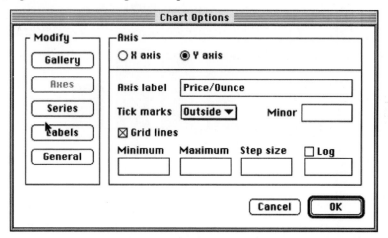

When graphing three or more columns of data, you can enter information on each series (column) by clicking **Series** in the **Chart Options** dialog. The **Labels** pane provides a means to enter and place an overall label to the chart and adjust the position of the legend. The **General** pane allows you to change the range (e.g., columns) to include in the chart. Once you have selected and entered the information, click **OK** to create the chart (see Figure 8-16).

If you are planning to use the chart in another document (e.g., word processing or drawing), then you should drag it to the appropriate size while in the spreadsheet document. If the tools are not showing, select **Show Tools** from the **View** menu. To change the color or shading of the chart, click on a square in the legend and then select a new color or shading from the palette. You can also change the text by clicking the text and the selecting **Font, Style, Color,** or **Size** from the **Format** menu. The chart can also be copied and pasted into a draw document. To make changes to the text or chart, ungroup the elements and then make the changes (see Chapter 10). After making the changes, select everything on the chart and group it to keep the parts together.

Now that you have a basic understanding of how to use a spreadsheet, let's examine how to integrate this tool into your lesson. The next section of this chapter describes how to develop an integrated spreadsheet lesson using the iNtegrating Technology for inQuiry (NTeQ) model.

Figure 8-16   Displaying a Spreadsheet Chart

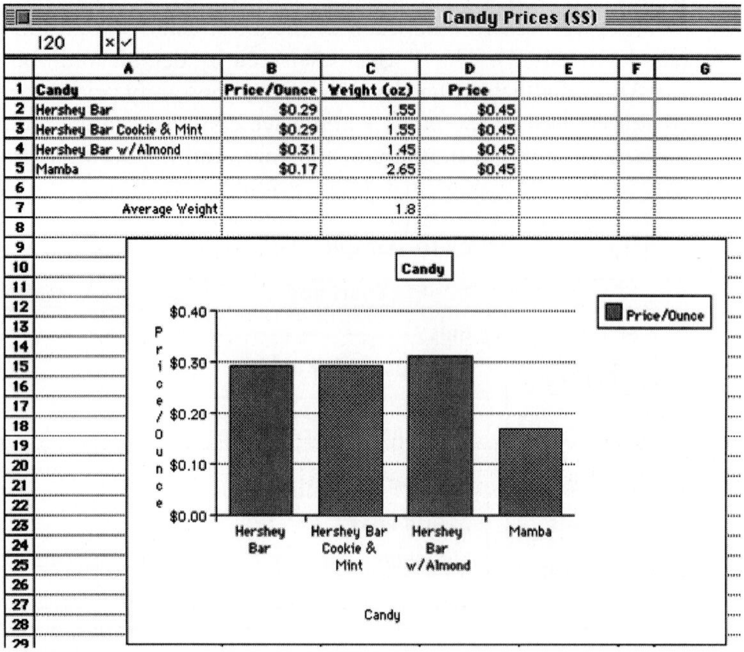

DESIGNING AN INTEGRATED LESSON WITH A SPREADSHEET

The first step in integrating a spreadsheet activity into a lesson is to identify the lesson's objectives. If there is a match between the objective(s) and the functions of a spreadsheet, then you can plan to integrate the spreadsheet activity into the lesson. If there is not a match between the objectives and the spreadsheet's functions then you should consider another strategy rather than the spreadsheet. For example, we observed a teacher recently who had the class enter data about classical music composers, their compositions, and the style of music into three columns of a spreadsheet. She then wanted the class to sort the items by composer and then later by style of music. When one of the students attempted to sort the list, only one column was selected. As a result only that column was sorted; thus, the links were lost with the composer. A database would have been a more appropriate tool for this activity. Think carefully to select the best tool for the task. This selection should reflect the tasks you want the students to perform and the cognitive skills you want them to master. Let's examine the relationship between the functions of a spreadsheet and instructional objectives.

MATCHING THE OBJECTIVE TO COMPUTER FUNCTIONS

We can categorize the functions of a spreadsheet into three broad categories: manipulation of numbers, creation of charts and graphs, and discrimination and interpretation. The first, manipulation of numbers, includes the capabilities to add, subtract, multiply, divide, sum, sort, convert, and find the highest and lowest numbers, to name a few. Spreadsheets can do a number of mathematical calculations ranging from simple addition to geometric calculations to financial calculations. The second grouping of functions is the creation of charts and graphs. Once students have entered their data, they can create a variety of charts and graphs to display the data visually. The third category is discrimination and interpretation, which includes inferring, discriminating, interpreting, and generalizing. Students can analyze the results of a sort, selection, calculation, or chart to make inferences, predictions, generalizations or to interpret the data to make a decision.

There is a very close relationship between objectives and functions. Both are verbs (e.g., sort, add) and both are observable actions. For example, an objective might state that the learner will determine the average number of people in the five largest cities of a state. One of the functions of a spreadsheet (actually, a built-in function) is the capability of averaging a row or column of numbers. Thus, there is a match between the objective and a spreadsheet function. Similarly, an objective in a psychology class studying experimental methods might require students to interpret the results of a taste test using a bar chart. Again, there is a match between the objective, interpret, and the charting function of a spreadsheet. Some objectives related to spreadsheet functions are listed in Table 8-1. Although this is not a complete list, it provides several examples related to manipulation of numbers (e.g., alter, convert, combine), charting and graphing (e.g., chart, graph), and discrimination and

Table 8-1 Objectives and Functions of a Spreadsheet

LEARNING TASK	SPREADSHEET FUNCTION
Add, Divide, Multiply, Subtract, Sum, Average, Calculate	Enter a formula to calculate the temperature range on the hottest and coldest days of the year.
Alter, Change, Vary	Determine the effect on profit if the fixed price increases.
Analyze, Chart, Graph	Determine which city had the greatest rainfall in June.
Compare, Contrast, Differentiate, Discriminate, Relate, Assess	Compare the voting record of young voters in a rural and an urban environment.
Deduce, Infer, Generalize, Estimate, Predict, Formulate	How much will the force on a billboard increase if the wind increases from 12 mph to 20 mph?
Interpret, Interpolate, Extend	Which region of the country has the most rain per year?
Solve, Determine	Based on the per capita income for the surrounding counties, which would be the best for a mid-value car dealership?

interpretation of numbers (assess, discriminate, differentiate, infer). (See Appendix A for a more complete listing of objectives and tool functions.)

Once you have specified the objectives for the lesson and found a match between your objectives and an appropriate computer tool, you are ready to design the lesson. Let's examine how to design a lesson using a spreadsheet as a tool.

IDENTIFYING THE PROBLEM

After you have specified your objectives, the next step in designing the lesson is to specify a problem for the students to solve or investigate. Individual units of instruction might have only one problem, for example, what agricultural products could we grow in this area if the effects of global warming were to raise our average temperature by 10 degrees? Other units might require the learner to solve several smaller problems that have a narrower focus. For example, you might pose the problem of identifying voting precincts in the city or county that students could use to accurately predict the presidential election. Or they could determine on which planet they would weigh the most and on which planet they would weigh the least. Once a problem statement is developed, identify alternative ways of stating the problem.

Problem statements should focus on issues students feel are relevant and worthy of solving (see Table 8-2). The problem context should be anchored in a realistic setting that has meaning for the students and motivates them (Cognition and Technology Group at Vanderbilt, 1990). For example, a math unit or a psychology unit on experimental methods might focus on frequency distributions and measures of central tendency. One approach is to define a problem in the context of a scientist

Table 8-2 Sample Problem Statements

OBJECTIVE	PROBLEM TO SOLVE
Students explain the relationship between supply and demand curves.	What would be the effect on the demand for gasoline if the price dropped by 25¢ per gallon?
	What would be the effect on the price of gasoline if everyone decided to purchase an extra tank of gasoline a week?
Students calculate the volume of a cylinder.	Your company is introducing a new type of soup in a 10 1/2 oz. can. To gain recognition, what are the dimensions you could use to create different can sizes to hold the soup?
Students explain the dew point.	Using recent weather data, determine what days are most likely to have dew, frost, or fog.

collecting data in a lab. A more realistic setting would cast the student as a researcher hired by the local grocery store to conduct a taste test of five new brands of crackers. Although both contexts allow for developing a data collection strategy, the grocery store context provides a realistic setting that students could use to collect data in their school.

DATA MANIPULATION

Once you have identified the problem, you need to identify the data the students will use to solve the problem. Will they collect all or part of the data or use data you provide? If the students are collecting the data, you will need to plan for the collection process. For example, if they are doing an experiment, they will need equipment and materials. If the students are working on designing a new can for their soup, they will need at least one appropriately sized can to calculate the needed volume, or you will need to provide the volume data. Similarly, if the students are searching for information on a CD or the Internet, you will need to develop guidelines to help their search. If you are providing the data, you will need to organize the data and either prepare handouts or files with data. Giving careful consideration to the data the students will use can help solve problems as the students work on the unit.

RESULTS PRESENTATION

After the students have solved the problem, they will need to present their work and solution (see Chapter 11). Their results can take the form of numeric answers on the spreadsheet or a chart or graph generated by the spreadsheet application. For most reports, the students may want to include either parts of the spreadsheet or the graphs in their written report. You will need to determine some basic guidelines and expectations for the report before the students start the lesson. For example, will they make a slide show, multimedia presentation, a poster presentation, a written report, or some combination of these?

MULTIDIMENSIONAL ACTIVITIES

The next step of the NTeQ lesson design is to plan the various instructional activities that will engage the learner and lead to mastery of the objectives. A number of carefully planned activities that support the objectives are needed to successfully integrate the lesson. The following paragraphs describe four types of strategies you need to plan before the instruction. These activities include those while using the computer, prior to using the computer, after using the computer, and supporting activities.

PLANNING: ACTIVITIES WHILE USING THE COMPUTER.
What will the students do when they work at the computer? For example, if they are entering information, will they use a template you have created or will they create their own? If they are doing calculations, will they use your formulas or must they create their own? You can create spreadsheet templates that include the formulas and the students need only

It is helpful for students to work collaboratively on a spreadsheet.

enter their data. Students can also use a spreadsheet template that already has the data; they add the formulas and calculations to answer questions and solve problems. Another alternative is to allow the students to create the complete spreadsheet using data they have gathered and then create the necessary calculations. For example, the designing a soup can problem might have students in a lower grade enter various heights and radii to calculate the volume while a high school class might create the formula for the calculation. Proper planning for the computer activities will help you determine the materials and instructions that you must provide for efficient computer time. If the students are unfamiliar with the computer task, you may need to develop a step-by-step instruction sheet for creating and using a spreadsheet (see Chapter 3).

PLANNING: ACTIVITIES PRIOR TO USING THE COMPUTER.

As you plan the lesson, consider how you can make each students' time at the computer efficient and effective. For example, if students are searching a CD-ROM or the Internet for information, they could generate a list of key words or terms to use *before* they start searching. Similarly, if students are entering data they have collected from observations, experiments, or other research, they can organize the data before they have an opportunity to enter the data. Thus, if students must enter their own formula for calculating the volume of a can, they should have instructions to determine the formula *prior* to using the computer. If they must also create the spreadsheet, they can plan for the labels, columns, rows, etc. Careful planning of these activities will help students have adequate access to the limited computers to complete their work. When planning these activities, you may need to complete each step of the process yourself to identify what the students must do. Working through these steps can help you identify organizational and planning activities that are not readily apparent.

PLANNING: ACTIVITIES AFTER USING THE COMPUTER.

Once the students have manipulated their data in a spreadsheet, what should they do with the information? As a teacher, you may need to help them interpret the data or charts so that they can solve the problem. Guidance for exploring the spreadsheet data or charts can take different forms. For example, if your chemistry class has entered data from a series of experiments, you might prepare a Think Sheet (Chapter 3) with questions that will focus the students' attention on the salient points. In their quest to find an appropriately sized can, you might have them create models from construction paper and collect data from others as to which can is most appealing. They might also determine which can appears to hold the most and why. As each group works through their analysis and interpretation, you can facilitate their efforts by asking questions and modeling the behaviors you are teaching. Once the students understand the process for analyzing and interpreting the data, they will need less and less direction from you.

PLANNING: SUPPORTING ACTIVITIES.

The last set of learning activities to plan are the additional activities that support the achievement of the objectives. Students are engaged in these activities when they are not working on computer-related tasks. We can group these activities into four categories. First, students can review prior learning and pursue areas of interest related to already learned ideas. Second, students can do additional readings or research on the current topic or they can pursue related topics of interest. Third, students can explore enrichment activities that further enhance their learning or develop their critical thinking skills. Fourth, students can complete additional reading and exercises to improve their comprehension of the topic.

Review activities are designed to help students prepare for the current lesson and may not be needed by every student. Review activities can include reading either old or new materials, completing a tutorial, or working practice problems. For example, students working on the can design problem might practice some problems on calculating the area of circle prior to working on the formula for calculating the volume of a cylinder. Similarly, younger students might measure the amount of sand in various shaped cans (of the same volume) to understand volume and how differently shaped objects can hold the same amount.

The second type of supporting activity is for all students; however, you can adapt your classroom environment to provide different forms of delivery. Students *might* have the choice of completing additional readings, participating in an experiment, watching a videotape, or listening to an audiotape to gain the same information. The activities can also be on different but related topics that support the objectives. Students can then strengthen their various learning skills rather than rely on only their favorite form of learning.

If you want to promote transfer of the students' knowledge, you can provide additional practice activities that illustrate how they can apply their knowledge to different problems. For example, students might extend their calculation of a cylinder's volume to calculating the optimum shape of a barrel that will be transported on a truck. They must consider the size of the trailer and the maximum height they can stack the barrels (or containers) so the trailer will pass safely under overpasses.

The last type of supporting activity is enrichment that is available to all students once they have demonstrated mastery of the skills and knowledge for the unit. These activities broaden students' understanding beyond the content of the unit. A student completing the can design example might do additional reading on advertising while another explores the process of making cans, either in print, from a CD-ROM, or on the Internet. Another student might study the recycling of cans and develop an interest in alternative forms of packaging.

As you design the multidimensional activities for a unit, keep in mind that they should support the objectives for the unit. You should avoid creating "busy work." If you plan to use a unit in the future, you can add one or two additional activities each year—consider some of the ideas students generate for additional learning.

At The Classroom's Doorstep
▲▲▲

Questions Teachers Ask

My students are having trouble using a spreadsheet. What can I do? One approach is to prepare a template complete with instructions. For example, you can include the instructions and spreadsheet in a single draw document (see Chapter 10). The spreadsheet frame might include only a few rows and columns with necessary instructions.

My students have a tendency to lose, modify, or erase the formulas that I include. Is there any way to keep them from modifying my spreadsheet? There are two solutions. First, you can save your spreadsheet as a stationary file. When they try to open it, ClarisWorks will open an exact copy of your original spreadsheet. Second, you can select the cells with your data and formulas and lock them in ClarisWorks. Students will not be able to change the cell. If you are creating a spreadsheet frame in a draw document (see Chapter 10), you can also lock the spreadsheet frame to keep students from moving it about the document.

How can I tell if my students are old enough to use a spreadsheet? We have seen first graders use a spreadsheet to enter data and copy calculations. Younger students often need more hands-on directions, as do many inexperienced learners. A spreadsheet provides a virtual playground for the inquisitive student who is interested in discovering mathematical concepts and relationships. As a teacher, you must keep in mind both the students' developmental readiness and their computer skills.

NTeQ Lesson Plan
▲▲▲

Figure 8-17   NTeQ Lesson Plan

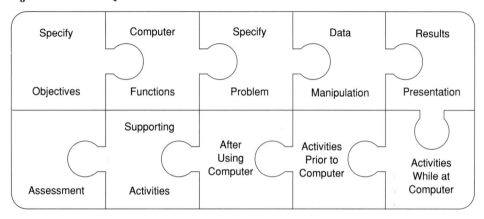

Lesson Title: Candy Money
▲▲▲

Subject Area: Math   Grade Level: 5–8

Learning Objective
By the end of this lesson, students will calculate price per ounce/gram to determine the best buy on a selection of candy.

Computer Functions
Spreadsheets will be used to calculate price per ounce/gram and total amount spent.
Word processing will be used to write a letter to the principal.

Specify Problem
The principal of your school has received a donation of $500 to purchase candy treats for all the students in your school (625 students). Your class has been assigned the task of finding the best buy on candy. The problem is: "What is the best way to spend $500 to buy candy for 625 students—keeping in mind that students need to receive about the same amount of candy, but a variety of candy will be needed to satisfy different tastes?"

Data Manipulation
  • Students will use a spreadsheet to calculate the price per ounce/gram of each candy and calculate total amount spent for several combinations of candy.

- Students will use word processing to edit and revise a letter to the principal that proposes how to spend the candy money.

RESULTS PRESENTATION

The final product will be a word processed letter that contains graphs supporting the final decision on how to spend the candy money.

MULTIDIMENSIONAL ACTIVITIES

Small groups of students complete the following activities.

ACTIVITIES PRIOR TO COMPUTER

- Decide on a plan of action for solving the problem.
- Collect the candy information (i. e., name of candy, number of ounces/grams, price).
- Determine how to set up the spreadsheet (i.e., column and row names, formulas for calculating the price per ounce/grams and for calculating the total cost of different configurations of candy).
- Draft a copy of a letter to the principal that proposes how to spend the money.

ACTIVITIES WHILE AT COMPUTER

Computer tasks are divided among group members:

- Create spreadsheet columns and rows.
- Enter formulas.
- Enter candy data.
- Manipulate candy data to determine which combination of candy provides approximately equal portions with the greatest amount of variety.
- Create a graph that effectively depicts the final candy selection.
- Enter and revise the letter to the principal, being sure to include a graph that depicts the final selection.

AFTER USING COMPUTER

- Answer the Think Sheet items:
  1. List the supporting reasons for the final candy selection.
  2. Which candy would you choose if the principal would have wanted each student to receive the same candy? Please explain why.
  3. What was the most difficult aspect of this lesson?
- As a large group, have the reporters from each group share their findings. Facilitate a summary and review session with the whole class by discussing the Think Sheet responses. During the discussion, clarify any misconceptions that arise and reemphasize the key learning objective.

SUPPORTING ACTIVITIES

- Create a list of guidelines for eating healthy, emphasizing that candy is a treat to be enjoyed occasionally.
- Create a chart of the selected candies that compares the nutritional values of each.

EVALUATION

Create a rubric for assessing the following:

Spreadsheet

- Columns and rows named appropriately.
- Data entered accurately.
- Formulas are accurate.
- Manipulation of data is evident.

Graph

- Depicts the final candy selection.
- Displays information in easy-to-read manner.
- Appropriate graph is used.

Principal letter

- Supporting arguments are reasonable.
- Format is appropriate.
- Letter is free of errors.

LESSON BYTES FOR SPREADSHEETS

▲▲▲

Following are different spreadsheets that students could create to manipulate data. A variety of problem statements can be derived from each spreadsheet.

PLOTTING DATA

▲ Growth of bacteria under different conditions (light, heat, moisture).

▲ Number of paragraphs read.

▲ Height of a Ping-Pong ball bounce when dropped from different heights.

▲ Plant growth in different soils.

▲ Number of students with specific genetic traits (attached ear lobes, eye color, tongue curling).

▲ Length of jumps for plastic frogs.

▲ Number of seeds by weight and circumference of pumpkins.

▲ Heart rate by minutes of exercise.

CALCULATING AND/OR PREDICTING

▲ Calculate distance (shortest route to a vacation spot, distance walked to and from school in one month, amount of fuel needed to complete a three-planet tour, miles traveled by migrating animals).

▲ Predict election results based on number of voters per precinct who voted in the previous election.

▲ Calculate pounds of paper recycled and number of trees saved in a community environmental project. Predict how many trees would be saved by the year 2000 if the recycling project continued.

▲ Calculate the price per square inch for round pizzas to see who has the best pizza prices.

▲ Calculate the volume of different containers (cereal boxes, soup cans, pickle jars).

▲ Calculate the average height and arm span of class members.

▲ Calculate the miles-per-gallon for vehicles holding different numbers of occupants to predict impact on natural resources.

▲ Compare the amount of money students spend on cafeteria lunches with what they would spend at a fast food restaurant.

REFERENCES
▲▲▲

Adams, F. G. & Kroch, E. (1989). The computer in the teaching of macroeconomics. *Journal of Economic Education, 20,* 269–280.

Cognition and Technology Group at Vanderbilt. (1990). Anchored instruction and its relationship to situated cognition. *Educational Researcher, 19,* 2–10.

Mercer, J. O. (1993). Some surprising probabilities from Bingo. *Mathematics Teacher, 86,* 726–731.

Niess, M. L. (1992). Math: Winds of change. *Computing Teacher, 19,* 32–35.

North Carolina State Department of Public Instruction. (1992). *Voteline: A project for integrating computer databases, spreadsheets, and telecomputing into high school social studies instruction.* ERIC Document ED350243.

Salomon, G. (1993). On the nature of pedagogic computer tools. The case of the writing partner. In S. P. LaJoie & S. J. Derry (Eds.), *Computers as cognitive tools.* Hillsdale, NJ: Lawrence Erlbaum Associates.

Smith, L. M. & Smith, L. C. (1988). Teaching macroeconomics with microcomputer spreadsheets. *Journal of Economic Education, 19,* 363–382.

Timmons, T. (1991). A numerical and graphical approach to Taylor polynomials using an electronic spreadsheet. *Primis, I,* 95–102.

Verderber, N. L. (1992). Tin cans revisited. *Mathematics Teacher, 85,* 346–349.

Walsh, T. P. (1996). Exploring difference equations with technology. *Learning and Leading with Technology, 24,* 28–32.

CHAPTER 9
Databases

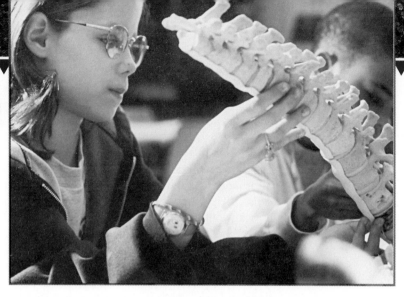

▶ Introduction

Students are normally required to learn about U. S. presidents both in elementary school and high school. Teachers use a variety of activities to help students learn this information. These activities typically include memorizing the names and years of service for each president, writing a booklet with a description of each president, answering questions on worksheets, or creating a poster display of a favorite president. As a result, most people can probably state who our presidents were and when they served, but is that the most critical information to know about our nation's leadership?

Rather than having students memorize the names and the years of service, or create a booklet or poster, the students can create a presidential database that will help them achieve a greater depth of understanding about our nation's leaders. The database could include personal information such as date of birth, birthplace, height, religion, interests, political party, marital status, number of children, age at election, occupation prior to presidency, number of terms, age at death, and cause of death. The database could also contain other details such as important presidential accomplishments and world events during the term(s). Students will benefit from the research required to complete the database as well as from conducting searches to determine patterns and trends in the presidential information. For example, students could determine if patterns exist between religion or birthplace and political party. Or they can find out if major accomplishments during a presidency are related to past occupations (i.e., past military service associated with a major war) or other world events.

▶ Computer Skills Used in This Chapter
Create database fields
Enter data into fields
Sort data
Create reports

▶ Key Topics
Databases in the Classroom
  Ease of Use
  Engagement in Critical Thinking
  Common Tool
Examining Databases
  Basic Components
  Defining Fields
  Entering Information
  Creating New Layouts
  Reports
Designing an Integrated Lesson Using Databases
  Specifying the Instructional Objective
  Matching the Objective to Computer
    Functions
  Specifying a Problem for Students to Solve
  Data Manipulation
  Results Presentation
  Multidimensional Activities

In this chapter, we will look at how students can use databases to critically examine information in new and meaningful ways to solve problems, answer questions, and conduct investigations that lead to a greater depth of understanding.

DATABASES IN THE CLASSROOM
▲▲▲

Databases are an easy and efficient means of storing, organizing, and manipulating information or data. Databases can be integrated into numerous lesson plans because their functions emulate many learning objectives that focus on developing critical thinking skills. When students create a database, they are actively engaged in reading, analyzing, categorizing, organizing, and paraphrasing. When students use databases, they are able to manipulate information to solve problems, answer questions, and conduct investigations that promote meaningful learning. If students are placed into groups to solve problems, they can collaboratively generate predictions and ask "what if" questions that lead to additional database queries as they search for solutions. As a result, students are able to critically examine bodies of information to detect trends and commonalties. The database skills that students acquire in school will be used throughout their lives because databases are used for information management throughout our society. This section will discuss the following areas related to databases in the classroom.

EASE OF USE

The database software that comes with most integrated packages such as Claris-Works or Microsoft Works is easy to learn and use. The database format helps students set up the database structure by requesting the needed information. As information is entered into the computer, it is automatically kept with similar information. For example, all of the information about George Washington stays in his record and all of the information about Bill Clinton stays in his record, no matter how many different ways the information is organized or sorted. Database information is also very flexible, because new information can easily be added to or deleted from the records. When students are ready to examine the information they have entered, they can create reports that show anywhere from just one type to all the information in the record. Therefore, students can quickly and easily answer questions as they occur, for example, "Are there commonalties between presidents who served in World War I and those who served in World War II?"

Even primary grade students can create a simple database and do sorting, matches, and searches to find the answers to problems. For example, Betty Lindhardt has her students use a database to solve the following problems: "What is the most common type of fall leaf in our area?" and "What differences are there in the sizes of our fall leaves?" This lesson could begin with students collecting leaves while taking a "Fall Walk." After the leaves are collected, students return to the classroom and use a field guide to identify the specific leaf names. They also record the following information for each leaf: color, type of leaf (simple or compound), and the measurement of both the widest part of the leaf and the leaf stem. The students enter the descriptive information about each leaf into a database (see Figure 9-1). They then sort the information in a variety of ways to answer the questions posed at the beginning of the lesson.

Figure 9-1   Leaf Database

Leaf Database

Name of Leaf	Oak
Type of Leaf	Compound
Color	Orange
Width (inches)	8
Stem (inches)	1.5

Name of Leaf	Elm
Type of Leaf	Compound
Color	Yellow-Orange
Width (inches)	5
Stem (inches)	2

Name of Leaf	Sycamore
Type of Leaf	Compound
Color	Redish Orange
Width (inches)	7
Stem (inches)	2.5

Fran's Diary

▲▲▲

Our school is located in an area where there is a lot of growth, and we get many students new to the school system. I moved many times as a child and remember how traumatic going to a new school can be. I want my students to make a new friend in the classroom before the end of the first day. I begin working on this goal before the first day of school by creating a "Getting to Know You" database template on one of the computers in the classroom. Many parents bring their children to the school before the first day, so I have the new students, with the help of a former student and/or parent, enter data about themselves into the database.

I keep this database and have any new students who come in the first morning add their data. I then put the database on the server in the computer lab and reserve a time to take my class to the computer lab sometime during the first day of school. That morning we begin a unit on friendship and brainstorm to list those things that make a person a friend—leading them to the idea that friends usually have similar interests, likes, dislikes, etc. I then ask them to write a short para-

Continued

graph that describes their idea of a "perfect friend." After they have written their paragraphs, I ask them if the computer could help them find their "perfect friend," and if so, how? I tell them that I know where there are some computers in the school that can help them find a new friend. I take the class to the computer lab and reintroduce them to the "Getting to Know You" database. I demonstrate how to do simple sorts to find all the students who like the same thing.

I then put the students in pairs and have them each complete a "Getting to Know You" activity sheet (see Figure 9-2). By the time they have finished sorting the data and completed the activity sheet, they will have found some classmates that have similar likes. I collect the activity sheets and we return to the classroom. While they are involved in other activities, I use information from

Figure 9-2   Getting to Know You Activity Sheet

Getting to Know You

Name_____ Date_____

Complete the sentences in each box with your favorite. Then open the "Getting To Know You" database. Use the sort function to find classmates that have the same favorites as you. Write their names in the boxes below.

My favorite color is_____ .	My favorite subject is_____ .
My favorite sport is_____ .	My favorite food is_____ .
My favorite holiday is_____ .	My favorite game is_____ .
My favorite pet is_____ .	My favorite snack is_____ .

Look at the names in the boxes. Does anyone have many of the same favorites as you? Write that person's name. _____

the activity sheet to pair the students. Later in the day, these pairs work to-gether to introduce each other to the class.

I have found this to be a very good activity. The students are introduced to a database and learn how to sort and analyze data in a fun and meaningful way. They are introduced to the idea that the computer is more than a word proces-sor or a game machine. They learn that the computer is a tool that can help them solve problems. In addition, the students have found others in the classroom that have similar likes, and the beginnings of friendships have been formed.

ENGAGEMENT IN CRITICAL THINKING

The entire process of creating and using a database involves students in a number of critical or higher-order thinking activities (Resnick & Klopfer, 1987). To create a database, students must carefully define what information is needed to answer questions, solve problems, or conduct investigations. The database provides stu-dents with an excellent means of examining the collected information because of its sorting and searching capabilities. Databases allow students to sort information in either an alphabetical or numerical manner; thus, patterns emerge as similar items are grouped or as values change.

Let's look at an example of middle school students solving the problem "How is the lifestyle of teenagers in Europe different from the lifestyle of teenagers in the United States?" The students might begin the lesson by determining underlying factors in the lifestyle of teenagers that can be compared. These factors would be the basis for de-signing the database. Some of these factors might include types of housing, subjects studied in school, favorite school lunch, and favorite activity (see Figure 9-3).

Figure 9-3   Teenagers Database

Name	Country	Age	Type of Home	Favorite Activity	Favorite Lunch	Math	Science	Lang. Arts
Pierre	France	14	Apartment	Soccer	Hamburger	Algebra	Biology	French
Hilda	Germany	14	Single Family Home	Ice Skating	Pizza	Algebra	Chemistry	German
José	Mexico	14	Multiple Family Home	Soccer	Enchiladas	General	Physical	Spanish
Elizabeth	England	13	Condo	Chess	Lamb Stew	Geometry	Physical	English
Shiji	China	13	High Rise Apartment	Computers	Squid	Algebra	Chemistry	Chinese & English
Francis	Canada	14	Single Family Home	Baseball	Pizza	Algebra	Biology	French
Jonathan	Israel	14	Single Family Home	Computers	Hamburger	Algebra 2	Chemistry	English

Teen Database (DB)

Records: 30 Unsorted

Students could gather the information by sending a survey via e-mail to students across the United States and in Europe. Once the surveys are returned, students would need to critically analyze each response to determine if it is valid or really answers the question. After the information is verified, students enter it into the database. Critical thinking skills are required again as students begin to generate reports of the database information. Each report focuses on answering some aspect of the problem introduced at the beginning of the lesson. Students may begin by creating general descriptions of teenage lifestyles from each location. This information could be followed by observations of similarities and differences and explanations as to why the differences occur. The explanations would probably require the students to conduct further research to determine the impact of things such as political influences, culture, and geographic resources. Students can expand the database to include this new information.

Common Tool

Databases are commonly used for the management and retrieval of the majority of information in our society (medical records, social security records, inventories, military records, etc.). This is due to the fact that databases efficiently and effectively store information and make it possible to retrieve just the information that is needed at the time. Using databases in the classroom will prepare students to understand the basic structure of databases and how to use the stored information in a meaningful way.

Examining Databases
▲▲▲

Database applications are used to store, manipulate, and retrieve information. The following section discusses the basic components of a database, how to define fields and enter information, and how to create new layouts and reports.

Basic Components

A computer database electronically stores sets of related information in *data files*. Within a data file, there are individual *records* that all contain similar types of information stored in *fields* (see Figure 9-4). The fields typically contain either text or numerical data; however, in some database applications the fields can also contain pictures, dates, and times. Once the fields have been defined and the information has been entered for each record, queries or computer searches can be conducted to answer particular questions. For example, in a database of the 50 states in America the fields might include: the state name, flower, bird, population, and average yearly rainfall. Once students had a complete database of information about the states, they could answer a variety of questions. Which states, if any, have the same state bird or flower? What are the five most populated states? Which three states could you live in if you wanted very low humidity and a small population?

Figure 9-4   Basic Components

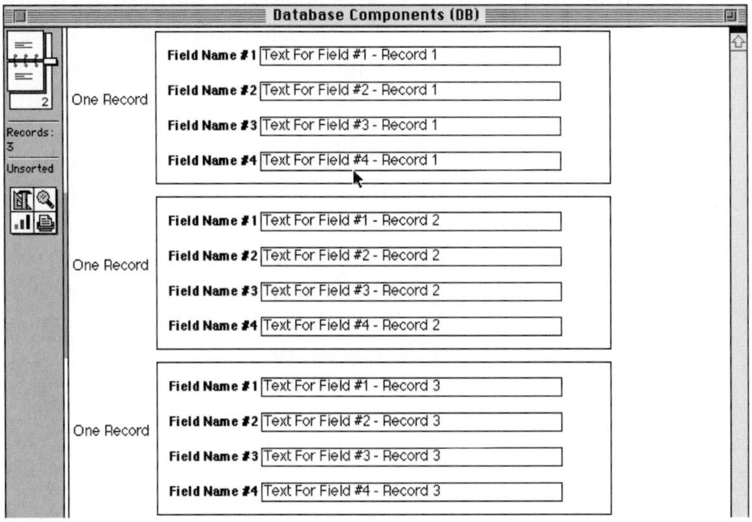

DEFINING FIELDS

The first step in creating a database is to define the fields of information that will be stored in each record. This can be done by carefully describing the problem to solve and identifying the information needed to solve the problem. It is helpful to involve students in this process because it increases their understanding of the purpose and meaning of each field. Another benefit is that students gain a sense of ownership of the database when they help define the fields. The following example demonstrates one way to have students participate in defining the fields of a database. Imagine a fourth grade class with the following problem to solve: "Why are some dinosaurs much bigger than other dinosaurs?" The teacher writes "Dinosaur Name" on the board, then tells the students, "If we are going to use a database to solve our problem, we need to know the name of each dinosaur. What other information about dinosaurs is needed to solve the problem?" The students will probably suggest things such as how tall they were, how much they weighed, where they lived, what they ate, who their enemies were, how long they lived, and during what time period they lived. After a list is generated, the teacher leads a discussion about each field and the information it would contain to determine if the field is needed to help solve the problem. This discussion would focus on two primary considerations for defining fields:

- Fields need to be limited to one type of data or information.
- Vocabulary for each field needs to be predetermined.

FIELDS NEED TO BE LIMITED TO ONE TYPE OF DATA OR INFORMATION. It is important to limit each field to one type of data or information because it makes the database more useful. For example, if one of the fields in the dinosaur database was

"Dinosaur Size," a student might enter, "12 ft. tall by 15 ft. long." The data would be more useful if it were entered in two fields: "Dinosaur Height" and "Dinosaur Length." This enables students to compare dinosaurs by either height or length. It is also useful to choose field names that are concise and easily understood, such as "Diet" rather than "What the Dinosaurs Ate."

VOCABULARY FOR EACH FIELD NEEDS TO BE PREDETERMINED.

Once the fields are determined, the specific vocabulary for each field needs to be established. This helps to avoid student use of a variety of descriptive terms within each field. For example, if the height information for four dinosaurs was entered without guidelines, the data entries might resemble what is seen in the following "Without Guidelines" column. However, if guidelines such as "height will be entered as numbers and the numbers represent feet" are used, the data are entered in a consistent manner, as seen in the "With Guidelines" column. When data are entered with specific, predetermined vocabulary, they can more accurately be sorted or matched with other information, as seen in the "Tallest to Shortest" column.

WITHOUT GUIDELINES		WITH GUIDELINES		TALLEST TO SHORTEST	
Dinosaur 1	8 ft	Dinosaur 1	8	Dinosaur 2	12
Dinosaur 2	12 feet	Dinosaur 2	12	Dinosaur 3	10
Dinosaur 3	ten feet tall	Dinosaur 3	10	Dinosaur 1	8
Dinosaur 4	7.5'	Dinosaur 4	7.5	Dinosaur 4	7.5

One way to assure that data are entered accurately is to use predefined lists displayed in pop-up menus within the fields (see Figure 9-5). In the database of teenagers seen earlier, a predefined list is used for the type of housing. Use of the

Figure 9-5   Predefined lists

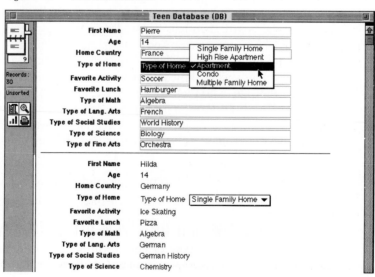

predefined list helps eliminate possible typing errors, or the use of similar but inexact words that hinder searching and sorting capabilities (e.g., entering "Apt.," "apart.," or "apartment").

ENTERING INFORMATION

After the fields are defined, the database is ready for information to be entered. The information for each field is typically classified as one of the following: text, numbers, dates, times, and sometimes graphics. When using dates or times, most software can automatically enter the date or time the record was created. When the information being entered is names, definitions, descriptions, etc., it is considered text. The entries are classified as numbers only when totals or averages are going to be calculated from the entries, not when the entries are numbers such as dates, times, or phone numbers.

To enter information into a field, use the Tab key or the mouse to position the cursor within the field. Once the cursor is in the proper field, either type in the information or select it from a predefined list, if the field has one. Information in the predefined list is selected by using either the arrow key to move to the desired selection and then pressing enter, or using the mouse to double click it. The information within each field can be changed by using word processing functions such as delete, copy, paste, bold, and underline (see Chapter 7). After the information has been entered into a field, use the Tab key or the mouse to move to the next field. Again, it is very important to use consistent terms and to check spelling to aid in conducting accurate queries.

Power Tip ▲▲▲   *Using Real Data from the "Net"*

The Internet contains vast amounts of information that is constantly being updated—a true advantage over print materials. This current information can be placed into databases created by your students. The instructions for getting information from the Internet are listed as follows. We will use statistics from the National Football League as our example.

1. Search the web for the information to be placed in a database. The information should be in a list format with columns and rows, even though lines may not be dividing the data. For our example, we did a search for NFL, then selected statistics for the Dallas Cowboys.

2. Retrieve the data. This can be done in two ways:

   a. use the **Save As** command from the **File** menu. Save the text as "text only," then open it in a word processing application;

   b. use the mouse to highlight the information to be placed in the database, then copy and paste it into a word processing document.

3. Once the information is in a word processing application, replace the space between each different type of information with a tab space. This can be done by highlighting the space then pushing the Tab key (see Figure 9-6).

continued

Figure 9-6   Text File of Dallas Cowboy Information

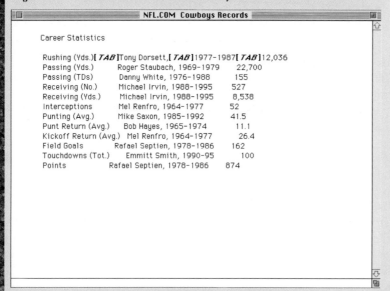

```
                    NFL.COM  Cowboys Records

    Career Statistics

    Rushing (Yds.)[ TAB ]Tony Dorsett,[ TAB ]1977-1987[ TAB ]12,036
    Passing (Yds.)      Roger Staubach, 1969-1979     22,700
    Passing (TDs)       Danny White, 1976-1988        155
    Receiving (No.)     Michael Irvin, 1988-1995      527
    Receiving (Yds.)    Michael Irvin, 1988-1995      8,538
    Interceptions       Mel Renfro, 1964-1977         52
    Punting (Avg.)      Mike Saxon, 1985-1992         41.5
    Punt Return (Avg.)  Bob Hayes, 1965-1974          11.1
    Kickoff Return (Avg.)  Mel Renfro, 1964-1977      26.4
    Field Goals         Rafael Septien, 1978-1986     162
    Touchdowns (Tot.)   Emmitt Smith, 1990-95         100
    Points              Rafael Septien, 1978-1986     874
```

4. Open a database program and create fields for each of your sets of information. For the NFL data, we created fields for: Type, Name, Year, and Yards. Place the fields in the same order as the information is set up in the word processing document.

Figure 9-7   Dallas Cowboy Database

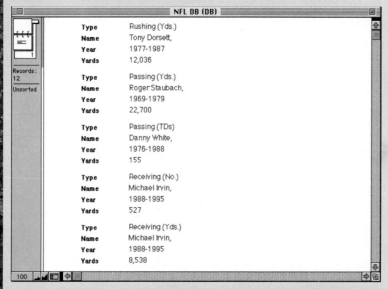

```
                         NFL DB (DB)

                  Type    Rushing (Yds.)
                  Name    Tony Dorsett,
                  Year    1977-1987
                  Yards   12,036
    Records:
    12            Type    Passing (Yds.)
    Unsorted      Name    Roger Staubach,
                  Year    1969-1979
                  Yards   22,700

                  Type    Passing (TDs)
                  Name    Danny White,
                  Year    1976-1988
                  Yards   155

                  Type    Receiving (No.)
                  Name    Michael Irvin,
                  Year    1988-1995
                  Yards   527

                  Type    Receiving (Yds.)
                  Name    Michael Irvin,
                  Year    1988-1995
                  Yards   8,538
```

5. Return to your word processed information and highlight just the information that will be placed in the database. Copy the information, then open the database that has been created.

6. In the database, make sure the cursor is not in any of the fields. In ClarisWorks this is done by pushing the Enter key. When the cursor is not in any fields, select the paste command and the information will automatically be placed into the fields. It will create a record for each set of data (see Figure 9-7).

CREATING NEW LAYOUTS

Most databases have two default layouts. One is a standard layout that presents all information from each field in an individual record in a scrolling list. The other is a list layout that lists the data fields for each record in a table format (see Figures 9-8 and 9-9).

Figure 9-8   Standard Layout

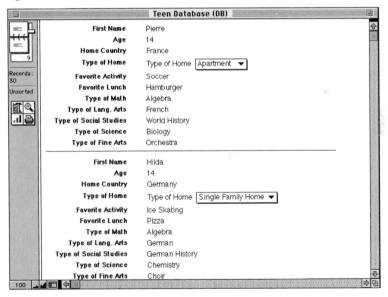

Customized layouts can be created for most databases. To do this, select **Layout** from the **Layout** menu. When in the layout mode, the field names and fields become objects that can be resized and/or moved to any location. A field must be selected, or clicked on with the mouse, before it can be moved or resized. The selected field becomes highlighted, which means a box with "resizing handles" at each corner is placed around it. The selected field can be changed in the following ways: drag it to a new location, make it smaller or larger by dragging one of the

Figure 9-9   List Layout

First Name	Age	Home Countr	Type of Home		Favorite Act	Favorite Lun	Type of Matl	Type of La
Pierre	14	France	Apartment	▼	Soccer	Hamburger	Algebra	French
Hilda	14	Germany	Single Fam...	▼	Ice Skating	Pizza	Algebra	German
José	14	Mexico	Multiple Fa...	▼	Soccer	Enchiladas	General	Spanish
Elizabeth	13	England	Condo	▼	Chess	Lamb Stew	Geometry	English
Shiji	13	China	High Rise A...	▼	Computers	Squid	Algebra	Chinese &
Francis	14	Canada	Single Fam...	▼	Baseball	Pizza	Algebra	French
Jonathan	14	Israel	Single Fam...	▼	Computers	Hamburger	Algebra 2	English
Francis	14	Canada	Single Fam...	▼	Baseball	Pizza	Algebra	French£

Teen Database (DB)
Records: 30   Unsorted   100

corner handles, delete it, or change the text by selecting a different font, size, style, or color. The layout mode also allows the user to add graphics such as clip art, lines, borders, or colors (see Figure 9-10).

Figure 9-10   Customized Layout

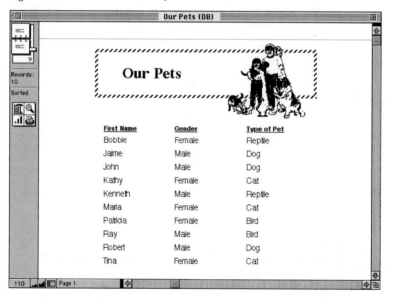

Reports

After creating the database and entering the information, there are a variety of ways to examine the data. Students can create reports that include data from a single field to data from all of the fields. The data in the reports can be sorted or matched to specific criteria. Students can also customize the layout for each report or use one of the default layouts, such as the **List** layout.

The **Sort** function in a database allows the information in fields to be arranged in either an ascending or descending manner. A student working with the differences between American and European teenagers could sort the list of favorite activities in an ascending list that would start at the beginning of the alphabet. For example, all the students who listed Bike Riding as their favorite activity would be listed together. This reinforces how critical it is to use a common language when entering data. If someone entered Riding Bikes, it would not be grouped with the other bike riders. A field that contains numerical data sorted in ascending order starts with the smaller digits, and data sorted in descending order begins with the larger digits. For example, the chart with dinosaur heights mentioned earlier had data in the last column sorted in a descending order from tallest to shortest.

Specific searches also can be conducted to find answers to questions. If students want to know how many presidents served two or more terms they can match records with the following formula: Terms>="2." Some of the more common matching computations include: = (EQUAL); > (GREATER THAN); < (LESS THAN); AND; and NOT.

DESIGNING AN INTEGRATED LESSON USING DATABASES

▲▲▲

There are four primary steps involved in designing lessons that integrate the use of a computer database: defining the lesson objective(s), matching the objective to database functions, creating a problem to solve, and planning the multidimensional activities. The steps are similar to any lesson development procedure; however the use of a database or other computer application changes the learning environment.

SPECIFYING THE INSTRUCTIONAL OBJECTIVE

Teachers are often given specific objectives and standards that their students are required to achieve during an academic year. As teachers use these objectives to plan their curriculum, they also have to plan ways to integrate technology into their lesson plans. This can be done by evaluating each objective to determine if the use of computers will enhance student learning. To determine if databases can help students achieve the lesson objective, it is necessary to understand the functions of the database as they relate to how a person learns.

MATCHING THE OOBJECTIVE TO COMPUTER FUNCTIONS

The functions of a database can be compared to how a person processes information. Obviously, a computer can process the information much faster and more accurately. This efficient processing allows the learner to concentrate on learning rather than on physically organizing sets of information. Samples of the types of processes or functions that database software can perform are listed in Table 9-1.

To determine if a database can be effectively integrated into a lesson, examine the lesson objectives to see if any of the database functions align with the objective. As seen in the table, some will have a direct correlation because the functions are similar to many objectives. In other instances, the teacher may want to modify an objective that only requires simple rote recall to one that requires the students to

Table 9-1 Functions of a Database

LEARNING TASK	DATABASE FUNCTION
Arrange	Arrange states by year of entry into the Union.
Assemble, Produce	Assemble information about your community.
Choose, Select, Categorize	Categorize a list of animals by their eating habits.
Classify, Identify, Isolate, List,	List 19th century artists by type of work.
Collect, Gather	Collect daily observations of a crystal formation.
Combine, Match, Sequence	Match agricultural products with region where they are grown.
Compare, Contrast, Differentiate, Discriminate, Relate	Compare male and female reading preferences.
Report	Report differences in types of environmental protection laws by country.
Solve, Determine	Determine which state has a low cost of living and low crime rate.
Synthesize	Synthesize a list of foods by common elements.

engage in more critical thinking. This modification can often be accomplished through integrating the use of databases or other computer applications.

SPECIFYING A PROBLEM FOR STUDENTS TO SOLVE

Once the lesson objectives are identified, and the use of a database is considered appropriate, the next step involves creating a problem for the students to solve. The problem should be structured in such a way that students will achieve the objective by solving the problem. Coming up with meaningful problems for students to solve often takes practice and creative thinking on the teacher's part. It is sometimes helpful for a small group of teachers or students to brainstorm ideas of problems. Some examples of objectives and the related problems are listed in Table 9-2.

Notice that each problem requires students to accomplish the listed objective. The problem, however, embeds the objective in a "fun," more relevant manner than merely reading about the topic, filling in a worksheet, then memorizing the information to answer questions on a test. As the problem is being developed, it is important to make it as relevant to the students as possible by keeping the problem "real-world" (Bransford, Sherwood, Hasselbring, Kinzer, & Williams, 1990). This can be accomplished by letting students gather "real data" from surveys they create or experiments they conduct. In the examples mentioned earlier, the elementary grade students collected their own leaves, and the teenagers actually surveyed students living in other countries to determine how their lives varied from teenagers living in the United States.

DATA MANIPULATION

After the problem has been specified, the data manipulation can be planned. With a database, there are two primary ways to manipulate the data: sorting and matching. The type of data manipulation selected is determined by the types of answers

Table 9-2 Objectives and Related Problems to Solve

OBJECTIVE	PROBLEM TO SOLVE
Students will identify precipitation patterns in the United States.	Which states could you live in if you had a breathing condition that required a very low amount of humidity? Where would your company find the best market for a grass that needs very little water?
Students will list the main types of artwork created by American Indians in the 1800s.	Our class has been asked to make a display of Native American art from the 1800s. What supplies will we need to make a sample of the major types of artwork?
Students will classify plant leaves as simple or compound.	How many ways can you divide the leaves you have collected into two groups?

needed to solve the problem. When appropriate, involve the students in determining how to manipulate the data in order to reach a solution.

When a list of information is sorted, similar items are grouped together, thus enhancing student ability to identify patterns and trends within the information. For example, students could use the information in the presidential database to answer

Student pairs can help each other enter data into a database.

the question "Do presidents who have previous military experience tend to focus more on national security issues than on education or health related issues?" Students would answer this question by creating a new layout that included the following fields: presidents' names, past employment, and major presidential accomplishments. The students could sort the list by type of accomplishments. This sort would allow an analysis of whether or not those who served in the military were more involved in military-related accomplishments such as a war or enlarging the military forces during their term(s). When numerical data are sorted, the sorted information can depict groups of similar items as well as show trends found within information. Examples of trends include more money spent on business subsidies than on education, less rainfall in the southwest region of a state, or more fat grams eaten by American teenagers than by European teenagers.

A problem may need to have specific fields of information matched with other fields in order to determine a solution. When this is the situation, the selection criteria are specified and then information in the database is matched to the criteria. Examples of these criteria include American cities with populations larger than 500,000; endangered species with fewer than 1,000 animals remaining; or buildings that have more than five shapes used in their construction.

Results Presentation

After the data manipulation plans are determined, a means of presenting the database results and problem solution can be selected (see Chapter 11). As noted earlier, data reports can be presented in any type of layout desired because all of the information can be moved or reformatted, and graphics or draw elements can be added to the final presentation. The type of data layout should be determined by the type of final product the students will be creating. If the final product is a report, the data should be kept in a format similar to the report format, i.e., same font and borders. If the students are going to create a display, the data can be presented with color backgrounds and graphics that relate to the data. When the final product is going to be a hypermedia stack, the results need to be presented in smaller groups because the screen size can only accommodate limited amounts of information.

Multidimensional Activities

Students engaged in a problem-based learning situation have multiple opportunities to participate in a variety of activities. These activities encompass many dimensions.

- How will the students be grouped (individually, in small groups, whole class)?
- What instructional format will be used (traditional lecture or student-centered)?
- What resources are needed (Internet, reference books, student-collected data)?
- What content areas are included (math, language arts, social studies, etc.)?

To assure that these activities are engaging and effective, always incorporate generative learning strategies into the lesson (refer to Chapter 3). These strategies help students process information to a greater depth, and students understand more. One way of incorporating generative strategies is through the use of the Think Sheet as described in Chapter 3.

When planning the activities for a lesson that integrates the use of a database, it is helpful to divide the activities into two different categories. The first category includes computer-related activities, or those activities done before the computer, at the computer, and after the computer. The second category of activities are the supporting activities or those that do not involve any aspect of computer use yet support the overall achievement of the lesson objective(s).

Please note that the following steps are for planning the lesson rather than for implementing the lesson. Therefore, the "Activities While Using the Computer" are given before the "Activities Prior to Using the Computer." Once the computer activities are planned, the activities needed to prepare the students for computer use can be planned.

PLANNING: ACTIVITIES WHILE USING THE COMPUTER.

At this point in the lesson, the objectives have been identified, the problem statement has been formulated, the objectives have been related to the functions of a computer, and the data manipulation has been determined. The next step is to define the actual activities the students will be engaged in at the computers.

One of the best ways to plan for student use of a computer database is for the teacher to actually develop a sample of what the students would generate during the lesson. This task involves deciding which fields are needed in the database, actually collecting some data from the resources the students will use, entering the information into the fields, and generating sample reports required to reach a solution. This database can serve as a prototype when showing the students how to build their databases. When students become more familiar with the database structure, they can begin to design their own databases. The student databases may not have exactly the same fields or layouts as the teacher prototype. In addition, the students may possibly reach different solutions than what the teacher expected, yet their engagement with the information will still help them achieve the lesson objectives (Resnick & Klopfer, 1987).

Once a workable prototype of the database is developed, the teacher needs to decide how to group the students at the computer. Will individual students go to the computer and complete various activities, or is it more beneficial to have students working collaboratively? In developing a database, it is sometimes helpful to have two students involved in creating and entering the data into the fields. With students paired at the computer, one student can enter the data, and one can read the information to enter. When students are manipulating the data in an effort to answer questions, small groups of students gathered at the computer are often beneficial. Group members can all make predictions, suggest new ways to organize the information, and describe what they think the various results mean. The synergism created from these small group activities can increase the amount of meaningful learning that takes place.

To promote equity among student opportunities, the number of computer tasks needs to be estimated and divided among the students. This strategy gives all students opportunities for keyboarding and other computer experiences. The student groups may need to be monitored to assure that the more computer literate student does not do the majority of the computer work because it easier than letting the less proficient member struggle through the required steps.

PLANNING: ACTIVITIES PRIOR TO USING THE COMPUTER.

After the computer activities are planned, the next step is to determine what students need to do as preparation for their computer time. These preparations can include both whole class activities and small group activities depending on the instructional approach used. In some instances, the students may determine the fields without using any resources. For example, high school students could probably figure out the major fields to include in a database of American presidents without looking at an encyclopedia or textbook. However, students creating a database of Native American art may need some resources to help determine how the artwork can best be described and, therefore, what fields will be needed.

If students are going to be sharing database files, it is important that all groups have the *same* database fields and configure their data in the same manner. However, if students are approaching the instructional problem from a small group perspective, then the needs for consistent fields and data are not as important. After the fields are identified, either as a whole class or as small groups, students can either use the computer and create the fields to determine if they are workable, or they can begin gathering data to enter in the identified fields.

As students progress through their research and data entry, they may realize that the database would be more functional if it were modified by adding new fields, deleting existing fields, or adding predefined pop-up menus to fields. This process of identifying database fields involves the students in the generative learning strategies of organization and categorization. The research needed to find the required information for each field engages the students in reading, analyzing, categorizing, organizing, and paraphrasing activities (Jonassen, 1988). If computer resources are available, the research also helps develop student computer search skills, either on CD-ROMs or the Internet.

When students first start using databases, develop a sheet for students to record the information that will be entered into the database (see Figure 9-11). As students become more proficient using a database, they can develop their own means of recording the collected information.

PLANNING: ACTIVITIES AFTER USING THE COMPUTER.

When students have entered the information into the database fields and have conducted their data queries, they may want to print out the reports and review them away from the computer. As the reports are analyzed, students may generate new questions that require further queries to be run on the data. This may be a time when the group goes back and forth between their group area and their assigned computer. This is also a time when the group decides how to report their findings.

It is a good idea to have students participate in some kind of culminating activity that requires them to reflect on the learning that has occurred. This culminating activity can involve writing a group report that includes reports printed out from

Figure 9-11 Database Record Sheet

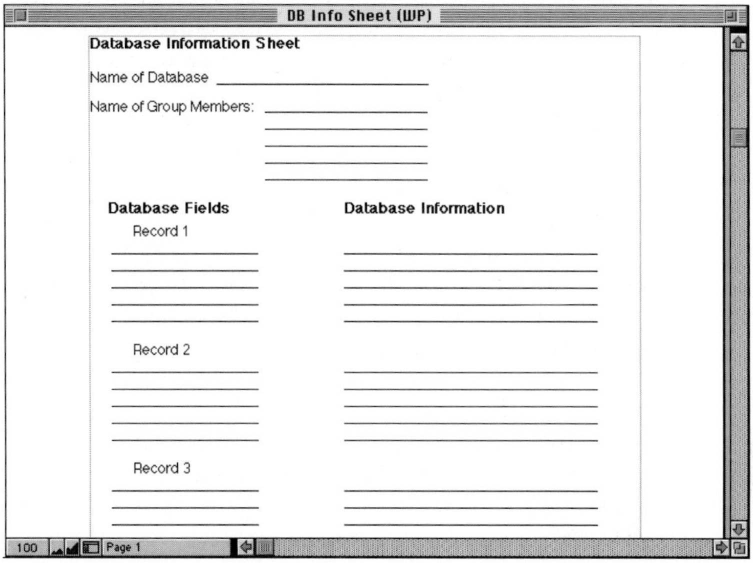
DB Info Sheet (WP)

Database Information Sheet

Name of Database ______________________

Name of Group Members: ______________________

Database Fields | **Database Information**

Record 1

Record 2

Record 3

100 Page 1

the database or reports created from placing database results into a spreadsheet and generating graphs of the results. Or students could create a multimedia presentation in a program similar to HyperStudio (see Chapter 11). Again, all of these activities actively engage the students in multiple generative learning strategies.

PLANNING: SUPPORTING ACTIVITIES. When planning a lesson that integrates student use of computer databases, remember that there are four main types of activities: review of prior learning, required research/reading, additional practice, and enrichment activities.

The activities used for reviewing prior learning may not be needed by all the students. These activities may consist of completing a reading assignment, working through a designated section of a tutorial, or completing some practice problems. Students working on the teenager database may need to review their geography skills to understand where the different students in their database live. This could be done by creating a center that includes a CD-ROM describing different locations around the world or by having a World Atlas available.

The next type of supporting activity requires students to complete specific reading assignments or conduct related research. These activities are directly related to the achievement of the objective, but they do not require the use of a computer. For example, the students working with the presidential database might read about the requirements for election as president of the United States. The elementary students who created the leaf database may need to watch a videotape about the role of leaves. The students conducting the survey of teenagers may need to first study about how to conduct a survey. These supporting activities should build the knowledge base required to solve the given problem.

Students collecting data to be placed in a database.

Another type of supporting activity provides students with additional practice. Such activities might involve students in keeping a journal about the processes they are involved in during the lesson. For example, the students taking the "Fall Walk" could create a "Scientist Log" where they write entries similar to the following: Why I am going on the Fall Walk; What I am going to collect; Where I found each leaf; and What I did with each leaf. They could also make leaf rubbings of plants around their homes and then classify each leaf as simple or compound. The students with the teenage database could write a series of predictions about what types of responses they think they will receive from students living in the different countries. Student groups could discuss their predictions and share them with the class. As the results of the surveys are tallied, the class could compare their predictions with what actually occurred and discuss possible reasons for the differences. An activity that would provide additional practice for the high school students who built the presidential database could involve constructing various displays that depict presidential patterns. As an example, they could create a seven foot wall chart showing the heights of all the presidents. Or, on a map of the United States, students could add the names of presidents and their political parties to the states in which they were born.

The final type of activities to plan for are enrichment activities. These activities build on the lesson objective but go beyond them. These enrichment activities involve students in creative and "what if" thinking. The high school students could write a paper describing what they think would have happened if Abraham Lincoln had served his full term. The younger students might create a story about why green leaves turn into autumn colors. The middle school students could imagine that they are one of the students in another county and write an entry to a diary. These activities can also involve students in community awareness activities, such as students creating a community monument, giving a special gift to a member of the community, or donating their time to a worthy cause. The young students may help clean up a local park that has lots of trees. Students may send a package of special "United States Stuff" to a teenage student living in China.

The important thing to remember when planning supporting activities is to avoid "busy work." Assess each activity to determine what the students are actually learning. If generative learning strategies are used for each activity, whether or not it is computer related, the students will be engaged in a meaningful manner.

At The Classroom's Doorstep
▲▲▲
Questions Teachers Ask

Will it really be beneficial for my students to spend the extra time it takes to build a database that is only used for a couple of lessons? Building a database can be very beneficial for students because it requires a great deal of information processing. However, you probably do not want to use a database for every lesson. If your lesson objectives involve a rich set of information, then the use of a database will extend the processing abilities of the students and promote active engagement with the information (Derry, 1990).

Creating and using a database seems to be a pretty complicated process. How can younger students do this? Students should be able to read before they create and use a database. You can start young students with very simple databases that only have two or three fields. You may want to begin with a database that you have created. You can even have all the fields as Pop-up Menus so the students do not have to enter any words. An easy way to start would be with a birthday database to familiarize your students with a monthly calendar. Students could enter their name, date of birth, and then select their birth month from a Pop-up Menu.

NTeQ Lesson Plan
▲▲▲
Figure 9-12   NTeQ Database Lesson

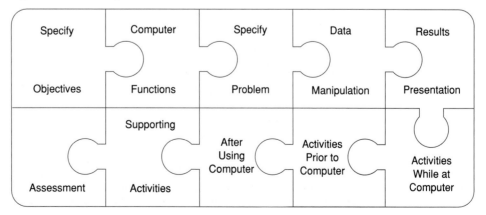

LESSON TITLE: OUR FALL LEAVES

SUBJECT AREA: Science   GRADE LEVEL: 2–3

LEARNING OBJECTIVE
By the end of this lesson, the students will classify leaves as simple or complex.

COMPUTER FUNCTIONS
Database will be used to organize information collected about the fall leaves. Word processing will be used to write a final report about the fall leaves.

SPECIFY PROBLEM
"What is the most common leaf shape in our playground?"

DATA MANIPULATION
- Students will use a database to examine descriptive information about the leaves they collect (name of leaf, color, type, etc.).
- Students will use word processing to edit and revise a report describing how they determined the most common shape of leaf found on the playground.

RESULTS PRESENTATION
The final product will be a word processed report describing the fall leaves on the playground.

MULTIDIMENSIONAL ACTIVITIES

ACTIVITIES PRIOR TO COMPUTER
- Students break into small groups.
- Student groups decide how they will collect leaves and how they will record their observations of each leaf.
- Students go outside and collect leaves.
- Students return to class and begin recording observations of each leaf on "Leaf Data Sheet" (color, size, edge patterns, type, etc.).
- Students plan computer tasks:
  - define fields for database
  - choose common words for data entry (e.g., Leaf edge = smooth or jagged; not smooth and wavy)
  - how data will be sorted
  - what database reports will be printed
  - what will be included in word processed report
- Students write a draft of the final report.

ACTIVITIES WHILE AT COMPUTER

Computer tasks are divided among group members:

- create database fields
- enter data—each student enters their data
- sort data—each student does a different sort
- print results—each student prints results from their sort
- each student enters a portion of the final report

AFTER USING COMPUTER

- Answer the Think Sheet questions:
    1. What is the most common shape of fall leaf in our playground?
    2. What differences are there in the sizes of our fall leaves?
    3. What differences are there in the colors of our fall leaves?
- As a large group, have the reporter from each group share their findings. Discuss the characteristics of a simple and compound leaf. Facilitate a summary and review session with the whole class by discussing the Think Sheet responses. During the discussion, clarify any misconceptions that arise and reemphasize the key learning objective.

SUPPORTING ACTIVITIES

- Make leaf rubbing of both a simple leaf and a complex leaf.
- View videotape on fall leaves.

EVALUATION

Create a rubric for assessing the following:

Database

- Fields named appropriately.
- Data entered accurately.
- Sorts are accurate.
- Printed reports contain appropriate information.

Report

- Meaningful problem solution is presented.
- Information is clear and easy to understand.
- Information is accurate.
- Format is appropriate.
- Letter is free of errors.

LESSON BYTES FOR DATABASES
▲▲▲

The following list contains suggestions for databases that can be created by students. Numerous problem statements can be generated from each database.

▲ U.S. Presidents

▲ Authors and their works

▲ Artists and their works

▲ Weather patterns

▲ Observation data (plants, rocks, clouds, people wearing seat belts, smokers, number of cars passing through an intersection)

▲ U.S. cities or states

▲ Endangered species

▲ Active volcanoes

▲ Food groups

▲ Classification (shapes, parts of speech, animal and plant groups)

▲ Major events of specified time periods

▲ Character portraits from stories

▲ Survey information (political views, food recycling habits, genetic traits)

▲ Planets

▲ Periodic table

▲ Wars

▲ Scientists or mathematicians

▲ Current or past government representatives

▲ Careers

▲ Colleges and universities

▲ Historical landmarks

RESOURCES
▲▲▲

Database Tutorials

Fields, N., Wetzel, K., & Painter, S. (1997). *Microsoft Works 4.0 for the Macintosh—A workbook for educators*. ISTE Publications, Eugene, OR, ISBN 1-56484-126-X.

Rathje, L., Heyerly, J., & Schenck, B. (1996). *ClarisWorks for students* (4th ed.). HRS Publications, Eugene, OR, ISBN 0-9644314-3-2.

Wiebe, J. H., Moreton, J. M., & Slovacek, S. P. (1996). *Works for Windows for educators*. Franklin, Beedle & Associates, Wilsonville, OR, ISBN 0-938661-74-4.

Yoder, S. & Moursand, D. (1995). *Introduction to ClarisWorks 4.0—A tool for personal productivity* (Mac or Windows). ISTE Publications, Eugene, OR, ISBN 1-56484-086-7.

Databases in the Classroom

Ryba, K. & Anderson, B. (1993). *Learning with computers: Effective teaching strategies*. ISTE Publications, Eugene, OR, ISBN 0-924667-64-8.

Smith, I., Yoder, S., & Thomas, R. (1997). *Classroom activities with ClarisWorks 4.0*. ISTE Publications, Eugene, OR, ISBN 1-56484-099-9.

REFERENCES
▲▲▲

Bransford, J. D., Sherwood, R. D., Hasselbring, T. S., Kinzer, C. K., & Williams, S. M. (1990). Anchored instruction: Why we need it and how technology can help. In D. Nix & R. J. Spiro (Eds.), *Cognition, education, and multimedia: Exploring ideas in high technology* (pp. 115–142). Hillsdale, NJ: Erlbaum.

Derry, S. J. (1990). *Flexible cognitive tools for problem solving instruction.* Paper presented at the annual meeting of the American Educational Research Association, Boston, April 16–20.

Jonassen, D. H. (1988). Integrating learning strategies into courseware to facilitate deeper processing. In D. H. Jonassen (Ed.), *Instructional design for microcomputer courseware.* Hillsdale, NJ: Erlbaum.

Resnick, L. B. & Klopfer, L. E. (1987). Toward the thinking curriculum: An overview. In L. B. Resnick & L. E. Klopfer (Eds.), *Toward the thinking curriculum: Current cognitive research.* Alexandria, VA: ASCD.

CHAPTER 10
Drawing

▶ Introduction

About the only value we ever found in tests as grade school students was the "privilege" of drawing on the backside of the test when we finished our work. Prior to the introduction of computers in the classroom, teachers seldom allowed students to create drawings for communication outside of art class. Teachers tended to divide learning between the visual world and verbal world. Twenty years ago, it was almost unheard of for a student to include a picture in a report. Today, more and more students download images from the Internet and CD-ROM encyclopedias to include in their reports. Although we doubt that there has been an exponential growth in the number of pictures available, it is easier for students to gain access to pictures. For example, a student could copy a picture from a book on a copy machine and include it in a report rather than draw a copy by hand. Similarly, students could copy and paste electronic images from the Internet and CD-ROMs into their documents. In this chapter, we examine how students can manipulate picture data with a computer.

▶ Computer Skills Used in This Chapter

Manipulating the mouse to create objects
Selecting and dragging objects
Opening and saving files
Cutting and pasting

▶ Key Topics

Using Pictures and Graphics for Instruction
Painting and Drawing Documents
    Objects versus Pixels
    Making the Choice
Drawing Objects
    Drawing Tools
    Manipulating Objects
Painting the Screen
    Painting Tools
    Transforming Objects
Integrating Drawing and Painting into a Lesson
    Map Reading
    Creating Graphics and Computer
       Manipulatives

Using Pictures and Graphics for Instruction

▲▲▲

There is considerable research on the value of using pictures in instructional materials (e.g., Bradens, 1996). The research on student-generated pictures, however, is rather limited (Rieber, 1995). Some research suggests student drawings are helpful for elaboration (e.g., generative learning) and cognitive maps (Jonassen, 1988). Also of interest to teachers is the area of visual literacy (http://www.emporia.edu/S/www/slim/resource/IVLA/IVLA.htm) that promotes the use of visuals for learning. Cassidy and Knowlton (1983) have questioned the use of the term "literacy" to describe this area of research, since visual imagery is not a language. While we agree with Knowlton that the term "visual literacy" is inappropriate, we believe that this concept provides teachers with excellent examples of the use of visuals in instruction.

There are ample examples of how teachers have used student drawings as part of their instructional plans. For example, Guthrie and Su (1992) reported success in teaching students to draw based on their observations. Similarly, Kleiman and Zweig (1995) had students analyze architecture from around the world using geometry concepts. Students then designed a house using both two- and three-dimensional drawings. There are also reports of students writing and illustrating their own books (Stuhlmann & Taylor, 1996) and using drawings to develop vocabulary (Bazeli & Olle, 1995). After reviewing the research on visualization, Rieber (1995) concluded that there is evidence that students should use the design tools (e.g., computer applications as well as paper and pencil) for problem visualization.

In this chapter we will focus on how students can use their drawings and graphics for generative learning and as a tool for solving problems. Let's start by examining the drawing and painting tools.

Painting and Drawing Documents

▲▲▲

Beginners might view paint and draw documents as the same because both are used to create visual images and text on the screen. There are several differences between the two documents, though, and these differences will help us choose which one to use. Let's compare the two.

Objects versus Pixels

One of the major differences between paint and draw documents is how they draw on the computer screen. Let's consider a drawing of a spotted leopard. We would probably start by drawing an outline of the leopard. Then, we add spots to the leopard. We could use either a drawing or paint document in ClarisWorks to draw the leopard—the computer and ClarisWorks will follow our instructions exactly. The application, though, will store the information differently, and that is the source of the difference between the two documents.

As we drag the cursor over a *pixel* (a scientific name for an off and on switch the size of a small dot on the computer screen) to draw our leopard, the computer turns the pixel on so that it is black or the color we selected. Think of your computer screen as a grid of 640×480 pixels that we can turn on or off with the cursor. The computer remembers which pixels are on and which pixels are off using a map of the screen grid. A paint program treats a word you have typed the same as

Allow time for students to do sketches of their draw documents before going to the computer.

a circle—both are described as pixels that are on (e.g., black) that part of the map. When you save your file, the computer writes this map with the on and off position of each pixel to the disk. When you open the file, the computer reads the map and turns the pixels on or off to recreate your illustration. It is somewhat like playing chess or checkers with someone at a distance. You tell them where you moved and they make an appropriate mark on their map or board. When they send you information about their move, you update your map. If your dog or cat knocks the board off the table, you can recreate the layout by tracing the moves. A paint document, then, is a map of the computer screen with an indication of which pixels are on and which are off. Paint documents are often referred to as bit-mapped graphics because they are a map of the computer screen.

In comparison to a paint program, a draw program is a mathematical wonder. A draw program also "paints" the screen like a paint program. However, a draw program creates objects such as lines, squares, circles, and text that are described by mathematical equations which literally draw the object. For example, a draw program might describe a circle as having an origin at grid location 200,145 on the screen with a radius of 78. The drawing program uses a formula to draw the circle. Thus, each object drawn is stored as a mathematical formula or function rather than as one map of the screen. Draw programs will save information for each object to disk when you save the file and then use this information to redraw each object when the file is opened. Thus, a paint document sees the whole painting space as a single map with off and on switches. A draw document uses a mathematical formula to keep track of every object—its location on the screen, its size, etc.

MAKING THE CHOICE

Selecting a draw or paint document depends on your objective. Table 10-1 describes the advantages and disadvantages of each.

Table 10-1 Comparison of Draw and Paint Capabilities

TASK	DRAW	PAINT
Drawing circles, squares, lines, etc.	Easy to do with the tools.	Easy to do with the tools.
Moving an object such as a circle.	Click on the object and drag it to the new location.	Difficult to select if it overlaps with other part of the drawing.
Resizing an object such as a circle.	Select the object and drag a handle to the correct size.	Can resize, but image is often distorted with jagged edges or lines.
Selecting part of an object.	Cannot do, must select whole object.	Can select and move any part of the image.
Changing parts of the drawing or an object.	Cannot change the parts of a circle.	Can use various tools to change individual *pixels* of the drawing.
Layering objects.	Can easily layer objects and change them.	Can layer objects, but cannot move individual layers once they are layered.
Overlap objects with transparent mode (when top object filled with a color).	Cannot do.	Can make objects opaque, transparent, or tinted.

Selecting the type of document to use is based on what you want to do and your level of skill. For example, if you want to create an illustration such as a still life, then you will probably want to use a paint document. If you are creating a layout for a poster that uses objects and text, then you would probably select a draw document. Some tasks such as editing a picture taken with a digital camera are best accomplished in a painting program. We have found that individuals who have well-developed drawing or painting skills are very adept at using a paint document. Lacking such a skill, we prefer to use draw documents that allow us as much freedom as possible to correct our mistakes!

DRAWING OBJECTS
▲▲▲

There are a lot of similarities between the drawing and painting tools in Claris-Works (as well as in many other applications such as Photoshop, Canvas, and Illustrator). Let's examine the tools for the drawing document first.

DRAWING TOOLS

We can divide the drawing tools into four groups (see Figure 10-1). The first group draws individual lines. The second group draws geometric figures. The third group changes the thickness of lines or adds color or shading. The fourth group consists of the frame tools. The applications of these tools are explained in Tables 10-2 through 10-5.

Figure 10-2 (on page 211) illustrates the six pen and color tool palettes. These palettes are tear-off menus you can drag off the tool section to create a palette that floats above your work (see Figure 10-3 on page 212).

Figure 10-1 Drawing Tools

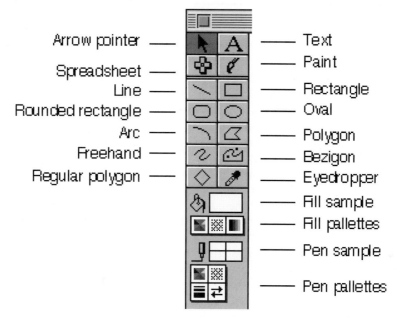

Arrow pointer ——   —— Text
Spreadsheet ——   —— Paint
Line ——   —— Rectangle
Rounded rectangle ——   —— Oval
Arc ——   —— Polygon
Freehand ——   —— Bezigon
Regular polygon ——   —— Eyedropper
—— Fill sample
—— Fill pallettes
—— Pen sample
—— Pen pallettes

Table 10-2 Line Drawing Tools

TOOL	FUNCTION
Line	This tool draws straight lines at any angle. Holding down the shift key while drawing constrains the line to 90° or 45°.
Arc	This tool draws arcs. If you select a fill color, the arc tool produces a pie-shaped wedge. Holding down the shift key while drawing flips the shape of the arc 180°.
Freehand tool	This tool draws any shape of line or object. It works like a pencil on a sheet paper.
Bezigon	This tool draws Bezier curves and angles. Drag the general shape of the curve and the tool will produce a smooth curve.

Table 10-3 Geometric Figure Tools

TOOL	FUNCTION
Rectangle	This tool draws a rectangle with square corners. Holding down the shift key while drawing produces a square.
Rounded rectangle	This tool draws a rectangle with rounded corners. Holding down the shift key while drawing produces a square with rounded corners.
Polygon tool	This tool draws polygons with different sides. To set the number of sides, click the tool and then select **Polygon Sides** from the **Options** menu. (In a paint document or frame, double-click the polygon tool in the toolbar.) Enter the number of sides in the dialog box and click **OK**.
Oval	This tool draws an oval. Holding down the shift key while drawing produces a circle.

Table 10-4 Pen and Color Tools

TOOL	FUNCTION
Fill color palette	If an object is selected, it is filled with the selected color. New objects are filled with the selected color. To draw an object with no fill or color, select either white from the color palette or transparent from the patterns palette.
Fill pattern palette	Fills the selected object with a pattern selected from the palette. New objects are filled with the selected pattern as they are drawn. Selecting the icon in the top left corner of the palette (see Figure 10-3) will make the object's center transparent. You can also select a pattern for an object that has color fill to create interesting effects.
Fill gradient palette	Gradients are used like color to fill an object. You *cannot* add a pattern or color to the gradient.
Pen color	You can change the color of a line or the border of an object by selecting a color from the **Pen Color Palette.** New lines and object borders are drawn in the selected color.
Pen pattern palette	The pen pattern palette is used to change the pattern of a line or object border. Selecting one of the patterns is useful for creating a gray line that will print on a black and white printer.
Pen width palette	You can draw lines in different widths or change the width of a selected line with the pen width palette. To change a line's width, select the line and then select a new width. New lines are drawn in the selected width.
Arrowhead palette	The arrowhead palette is used to change lines to arrows by adding arrowheads to either or both ends of the line. To remove an arrowhead(s), select **Plain Line** from the palette.
Eye dropper	The eye dropper tool allows you to select the color of an object (including the border and fill). Select the eye dropper tool and then click on the object. The color(s) are selected and any new object will be drawn with the combination.

The function of the tools are explained in Table 10-4 and Table 10-5 describes the three frame tools available in a draw document.

MANIPULATING OBJECTS

Each item you draw or paste into a draw document is an object. The tool tables describe how you can also change the line size, pattern, and color of the objects. In this section, we will describe how you can manipulate, group, size, and duplicate these objects.

SELECTING AND DESELECTING OBJECTS. To change the color, pattern, size, or placement of an object, you must select it. An object is selected by clicking it. If you have an object without a solid center (see Figure 10-4), you will need to click on the line or border. Once an object is selected, handles appear at the edges. When you want to select more than one object at a time, click on the first object and then hold down the shift key as you click each additional object. To move the selected objects as one, click and drag on one of the selected objects.

Table 10-5 Frame Tools

TOOL	FUNCTION
Text	Text frames are created so that you can add text to a drawing. Select the text frame tool, click on the drawing, and start typing. Once you have finished entering the text, select the arrow pointer and move the text to the desired location. You can also adjust the width of the field by dragging the handles. Text fields can be transparent or filled with a color. You can also add a border by selecting the field and then selecting a color from the pen color palette.
Spreadsheet	The spreadsheet frame creates a spreadsheet in the draw document. Select the tool and drag the appropriate number of columns and rows. You can select a fill color for the cells, or make it transparent and drag it over another object. To move the spreadsheet object, select the arrow pointer to select and drag it.
Paint	The paint frame allows you to combine both paint images and draw objects in the same document. You can create a paint frame and then paste or draw a paint image. Selecting the arrow point allows you to drag the paint frame like a drawing object so that you can place it anywhere on the draw document. Paint frames are useful for displaying scanned or digital images in a draw document.

Figure 10-2   Pen and Color Tool Palettes

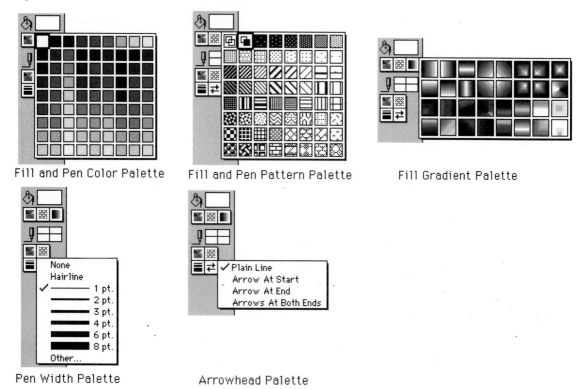

Fill and Pen Color Palette   Fill and Pen Pattern Palette   Fill Gradient Palette

Pen Width Palette   Arrowhead Palette

Figure 10-3   Filled and Transparent Objects

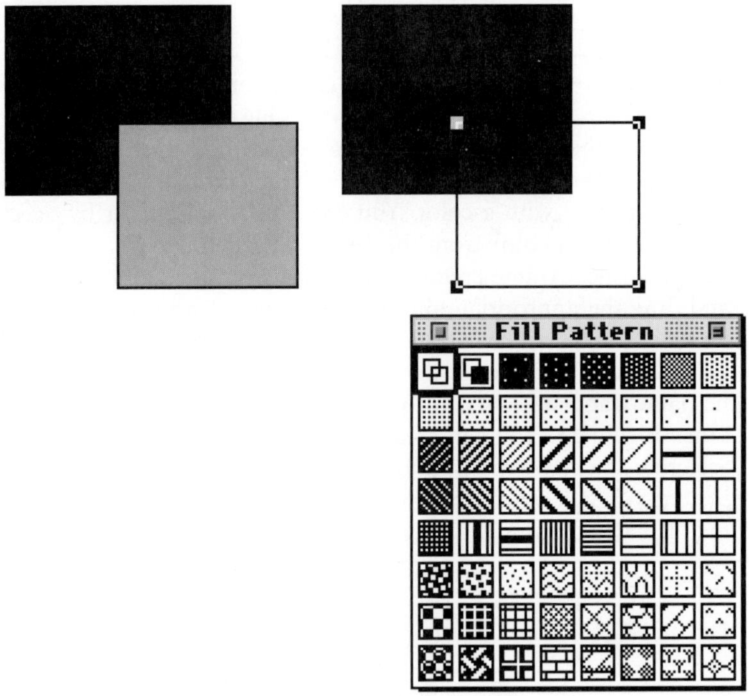

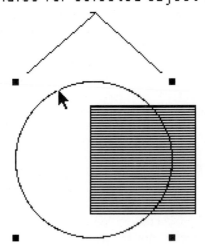

Figure 10-4   Selecting Objects

Handles for selected object (circle)

Power Tip ▲▲▲   *Autogrid*

As you move objects about the screen you may find that they have a mind of their own. Claris-Works has a feature named Autogrid that causes objects to snap in place on an imaginary grid. If you use the arrow keys to move an item, it will jump about 8 pixels. You can turn the autogrid on or off by selecting the **Autogrid** item from the **Options** menu.

To deselect a single object that is selected, click on another object or on the background of the picture. If you have selected several objects and want to deselect one of them, click it while holding the shift key down.

Figure 10-5   Layering Objects

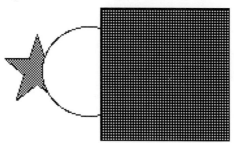

ARRANGING OBJECTS. As you draw objects, they are placed on different layers, with the newest object placed in the top layer. For example, in Figure 10-5 we drew the star first, then the circle, and finally the square. If we overlap the objects, the last drawn is in the top or frontmost layer. Unfortunately, we want the star on top inside the circle, which we want inside the square. To complete the drawing, we select the star and then select **Move to Front** from the **Arrange** menu (see Figure 10-6 —Before). The star is now in the top layer. Next, we need to move the circle forward so that it is in the layer between the star and the square. We select the circle and select **Move Forward** from the **Arrange** menu (see Figure 10-6—After). We can also move objects to the back or backward by selecting the object or objects and the appropriate item from the **Arrange** menu.

Now we want to arrange the objects so that they are centered over one another to create our design. We start by selecting the star and then holding down the shift key to select the circle and square. Next, we select the **Align Objects** from the **Arrange** menu and ClarisWorks displays the **Align Objects** dialog box (see Figure 10-7). Since we want to center the three objects, we selected **Align Centers** for both **Top to Bottom** and **Left to Right.**

By selecting the **Align Centers** option for both orientations, our three objects are perfectly aligned on top of one another (see Figure 10-8). Selecting only a radio

Figure 10-6   Arranging Objects in Layers

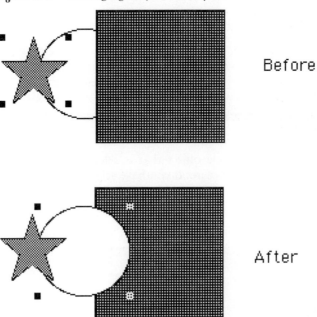

Before

After

Figure 10-7   Aligning Objects

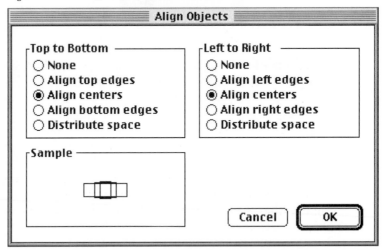

button (the small circle left of the option) in the **Top to Bottom** results in the objects aligning left to right at either the top, center, or bottom. Similarly, selecting only an option from the **Left to Right** orientation results in the objects aligned in a vertical column on their left, center, or right edges.

Object alignment is particularly useful if you are making a poster or display. For example, in Figure 10-9 we aligned our star bullets on their left sides and the text

Figure 10-8   Aligning Objects on their Centers

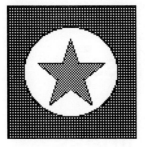

Figure 10-9   Aligning Left Side of Objects

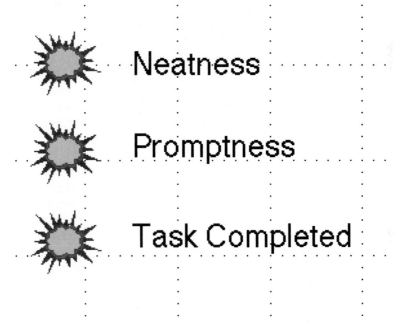

objects on their left sides. We can also select a bullet and word on a single line and align their centers from Top to Bottom so that they are aligned in a single row. Using the **Alignment** dialog box is faster, easier, and more accurate than dragging the objects along one of the grid lines.

GROUPING OBJECTS.   Now that we have the bullets and words aligned, we want to "fix" each row so that it does not change as we work on the poster. We can group any number of objects so they behave as one object. We can move them, change their color, or change their pattern by selecting the group. To group two or more objects, select them and then select **Group** from the **Arrange** menu. Notice in Figure 10-10 that the top row shows both items selected. The bottom row has already been grouped and has handles on the edges of the grouped object rather than on

Figure 10-10   Grouping Objects

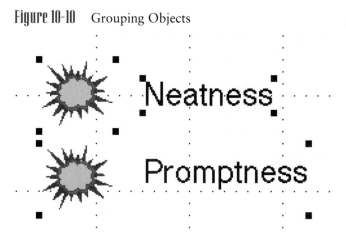

the individual objects. You can ungroup a group object by selecting it and selecting **Ungroup** from the **Arrange** menu.

One last step that we can complete with our poster is a final alignment. We want to align these three rows on their left sides and create an equal amount of space between each. First, we select all three objects. Second, we select **Align Objects** from the **Arrange** menu. Third, we select **Distribute space** from the **Top to Bottom** orientation. Distribute space will divide the space between the top and bottom objects and equally distribute each object (or row in our poster). Fourth, we selected **Align left edges** from the **Left to Right** orientations to align the three objects on the left side. The result is an evenly spaced display that lines up on the left side.

LOCKING OBJECTS.   If you are creating draw documents that you do not want your students to change, you can lock an object or frame. To lock an item or items, select them and then choose **Lock** from the **Arrange** menu. You can unlock the item by selecting it and then selecting **Unlock** from the **Arrange** menu.

If you lock an object, a student cannot move it or change the color or pattern. If you lock a spreadsheet, paint, or text frame in a draw document, the student can make changes in the frame, but they cannot move it. Thus, if you want to create a Think Sheet or worksheet for students to complete on the computer, you can lock it once you have it designed. Students can make changes to individual frames, but they cannot change draw objects or move any item!

RESIZING OBJECTS.   There are many times when an object, clip art, or frame is either too small or too large. We can resize an object by dragging a handle to make it smaller or larger; however, dragging produces varying results with frames. A more accurate method is to select the object and then select **Scale by Percent** from the **Arrange** menu. You can scale either the horizontal, vertical, or both size using different percentages (see Figure 10-11). If you want an equal resizing, enter the same percentage for both sides.

Figure 10-11   Scaling an Object

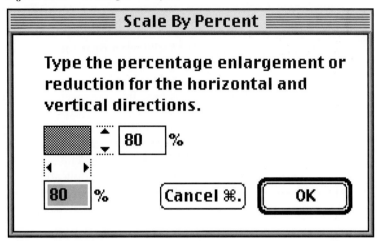

ROTATING OBJECTS.   The last object manipulation we will describe is rotating and flipping an object. Figure 10-12 shows the variations for rotating and flipping objects from the **Arrange** menu. If you select **Free Rotate,** the cursor changes to a crosshair. You use the crosshair to drag an object's handle in order to rotate direction and number of degrees.

Figure 10-12   Rotating an Object

DRAWING FILE FORMATS.   There are a number of file formats for picture and image files. For example, ClarisWorks will save a draw document in a special ClarisWorks file format while Photoshop, Illustrator, and Canvas use special file formats for their documents. There are also a number of "generic" file formats that different drawing applications can open. Table 10-6 lists four common file formats that ClarisWorks 4.0 and 5.0 can open or import.

Table 10-6 Picture File Formats

FILE FORMAT	APPLICATION
PICT	A common Macintosh format for saving drawing (object) files. This format is often used for clip art and for exchanging documents between applications.
GIF or GIFF	This format is used for many web pictures that can be viewed with a browser such as Netscape.
TIFF	A common DOS and Windows format for pictures. This format is also found on some clip art CDs.
EPS	A format commonly used for clip art. Can also be imported or opened by many drawing applications.

PAINTING
▲▲▲

Paint documents are similar to using water colors on paper; once the brush touches the surface of the paper, you can only erase the "brush" stroke. Those of us with little artistic capabilities often find that drawing-type applications are much easier, especially if we limit our work to geometrically shaped objects! We tend to use paint documents to work with screen shots (e.g., a picture taken of the computer screen) and digital photographs. Let's start by examining the tools we can use to create and manipulate a paint document.

PAINTING TOOLS

Figure 10-13 shows the tools available in a paint document. Notice that the first seven rows of tools are the same as those in the Draw document, as are the fill and line palettes. They produce the same type of object or line, but you cannot move the object as you did in the draw document. For example, if we were to draw the same illustration as in Figure 10-8 in a paint document, we could not select each object or layer and move them as easily. Once we move the circle inside the square, the circle replaces the pixels beneath it and the circle and square are joined. Clicking on the circle no longer selects it. Let's examine the new tools added for a paint document. We have divided the tools into two groups: selection tools (Table 10-7) and drawing tools (Table 10-8).

Once you have selected part of the image you can drag it by moving the pointer over the image and clicking, or you can use the arrow keys. To move an object one pixel at a time with the arrow keys, select **Turn Autogrid Off** from the **Options** menu.

TRANSFORMING OBJECTS

One advantage to working with a paint document is the ability to modify an image using the features from the **Transform** menu. In Figure 10-16, we created each of the words as separate images. Next, we filled each letter with gradient. Then, we selected each word and chose **Perspective** from the **Transform** menu. By dragging the handles, we created a distorted word. The **Transform** menu provides a number of options to manipulate a paint image.

Figure 10-13 Painting Tools

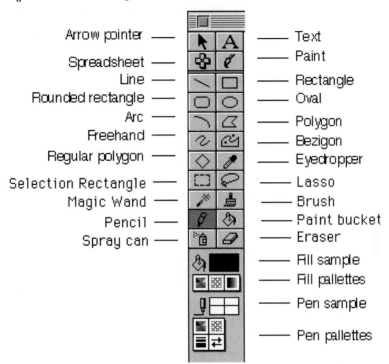

Arrow pointer — ■ — Text
Spreadsheet — ■ — Paint
Line — ■ — Rectangle
Rounded rectangle — ■ — Oval
Arc — ■ — Polygon
Freehand — ■ — Bezigon
Regular polygon — ■ — Eyedropper
Selection Rectangle — ■ — Lasso
Magic Wand — ■ — Brush
Pencil — ■ — Paint bucket
Spray can — ■ — Eraser
— Fill sample
— Fill pallettes
— Pen sample
— Pen pallettes

Table 10-7 Paint Selection Tools

Tool	Application
Selection rectangle	Use this tool to select a rectangular area by dragging the rectangle over the image area. To select just the outline of an image such as a circle, hold down the command key (⌘) as you drag the rectangle.
Lasso	This tool is used to select irregular shapes without the surrounding white space.
Magic wand	Click and drag the magic wand over a single or multiple colors to select *all* image areas with the color. For example, if you drag the wand across a white area, it will select the whole image if you have a large white area in the document!

Table 10-8 Paint Drawing Tools

TOOL	APPLICATIONS
Brush	Use this tool to draw a line using the current color and pattern. If you double-click the paint brush tool, ClarisWorks will display the **Brush Shape** dialog box (see Figure 10-14) and you can change the shape and size of the brush tool.
Pencil	The pencil tool works much like the brush tool except it is used to create fine lines. If you double-click the tool it will enlarge the size of the drawing by 800% (fat bits) so you can click and change individual bits creating the picture (see Figure 10-15). Double-click the pencil tool to return to normal size.
Paint bucket	The paint bucket is used to fill an enclosed area with the current fill color and pattern or gradient. If the fill does not work as expected, select **Undo Paint** from the **Edit** menu.
Spray can	Use the spray can to paint an area much like you would with a real can of spray paint. If you double-click the spray can tool you can edit the type of pattern. The image is in the fill color selected.
Eraser	The eraser will remove the pixels from the screen as you drag it over them. Double-clicking the eraser tool will erase the whole painting.

Figure 10-14   Changing the Brush Shape

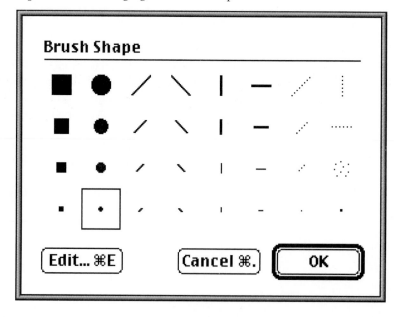

Figure 10-15   Editing Image Bits

Figure 10-16   Manipulating a Paint Image

NewS Notes

Fran's Diary

Drawing and painting on the computer screen is fun for students. They pick up these skills quickly and are never afraid to experiment. When we are in the paint application, they know that they have an eraser and if they double click on the eraser icon, the whole screen is cleared and is ready for them to begin again! They are great teachers, too. In fact, I only have to show a few students something new. They have no problem showing each other drawing and painting "tricks" and are eager to share what they have learned. I've even learned a few things from them!

I try to coordinate the drawing or painting activity with a curriculum area and lesson being taught in the classroom. The students made patchwork quilts after they had read the story, "The Patchwork Quilt" in their reading books. I showed them some examples of patchwork quilts from books and some real quilts. They used the drawing application to make their patchwork quilts. The grid lines became their quilt templates. They drew squares and then filled them with colors and textures. We printed their patchwork quilts in color. These computer-generated quilts made a great display for Open House.

The students wrote reports about Indian cultures after they had studied the Anasazi Indians in social studies. They used the program "Storybook Weaver" to write these reports. The program has pieces of clip art that can be incorporated into a written report or story. The activity taught them the basics of using clip art. They learned how to move, delete, and duplicate pieces of clip art. Unfortunately, I could not print these reports as they were very color intensive, but I did put them on disks and the students were able to share them in the classroom.

The students created an electronic classroom zoo when they studied animals in science. Each student chose an animal. They had to do some research using the CD-ROM encyclopedias and the Internet to find some basic facts about their animals. We used the program, "HyperStudio" to create this electronic zoo. Students created cards with a painting of their animals and some basic facts about those animals. The students drew large rectangles for the cages and then painted their animals in them. Then they used the line tool to create the bars of the cages. They made signs for the animals' names and basic facts by creating text boxes. The students shared this HyperStudio stack with their parents during Open House.

The students also created "GeoPets" when they studied geometric shapes in math. They used the shape tools and the polygon tool to create imaginary animals. These animals were made by putting various geometric shapes together. They also created text boxes for the animals' names. They used the word processing application to write the directions for the care and feeding of this pet. The GeoPets were printed in color and made a very colorful hall-way display!

The only problem that I have with students using the drawing and painting applications is that I cannot print everything that they do. Our paper and ink budget is insufficient for the amount of work that is done on the computer in our classroom. As a result, I have to make decisions about what can or cannot be printed. Sometimes, I have the students print their drawings in black and then color them with markers, crayons, or colored pencils. Although it is not the same as printing their drawings in color, it does give them something that they can take home and share with their parents. I also try to find other ways their art can be shared with others, such as creating ClarisWorks slide shows and HyperStudio stacks.

Integrating Drawing and Painting into a Lesson

Student use and generation of graphics for learning is often limited to embellishing a report. Although it is unlikely that you would create an integrated lesson based on a draw or paint application as you might for a database or spreadsheet, there are ways that students can manipulate data with a graphics application. In this section, we will describe examples of how students can manipulate data with graphic programs as *part* of a larger integrated lesson.

Map Reading

Maps are an important part of social studies and science classes and offer several opportunities for manipulating data. Let's examine how to manipulate data in a social studies and science lesson using maps.

In the early grades, students often learn how to read a map, plot a route, and calculate distances. You can find maps on CD-ROMs, and several web sites on the Internet will generate custom maps of most any neighborhood in the United States. Check these out:

www.mapblast.com

www.MapsOnUs.com

www.bigbook.com

Each student or teams of students can generate and download a map or maps for the area around their school or other location. (Note: Most of these maps are copy-righted, which will require you to follow their guidelines for educational use.) These maps provide details of the streets and a scale. You can pose several problems, such as how far is it from your home to school, or what is the distance from your home to two of your friends' homes and then to school (see Chapter 14 for information on personalizing this type of problem). Students can plot the distance on a printed map, or draw the route with a line tool over the map in a draw application (see Figure 10-17). In this figure, we had students create a dotted line by selecting a line pattern so that we could distinguish the route from the streets. They then measured the printed map with a ruler, or converted their route in the draw program to a straight line(s) and measured with a ruler on the screen (see Figure 10-18). To extend this lesson, students could use a spreadsheet to calculate how far they walk to and from school in a week, month, or grading period (a great source of data for the typical parent's whine of "When I was child I walked . . ."!).

Figure 10-17   Creating a Route to School

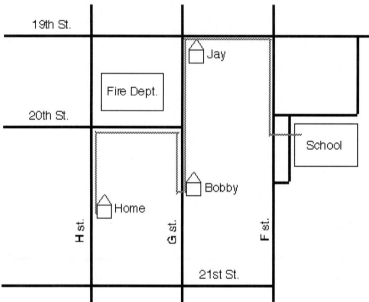

Figure 10-18   Determining the Distance of the Route

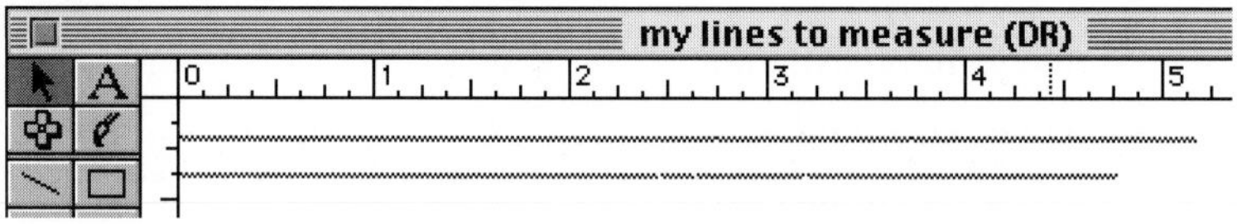

Another method of manipulating graphic data is to have students create a map and add the appropriate cartographic symbols for schools, fire and police, religious institutions, etc. They can draw the map from scratch, use a map you have created, or download a map from the Internet. They can also create weather maps to plot weather patterns and make predictions of the local weather using data from www.weather.com. Another idea is to have students use maps to plot different types of trees, plants, and animals (e.g., birds and insects) as a means of providing other data for a spreadsheet or database. They can also analyze why certain plants or animals grow or live in a specific area.

CREATING GRAPHICS AND COMPUTER MANIPULATIVES

Over the years, we have seen a number of kits produced for educational purposes as well as manipulatives for teaching mathematics. One perennial problem with kits such as those used in a chemistry class is that the parts students use to create molecules seem to disappear, making it impossible to construct the molecules. One alternative to using manipulatives is having students either draw or construct images using a stationary file that provides the pieces available in a kit. For example, you could provide students with a chemistry kit that includes the molecules and bonds they can use to create a molecule (see Figure 10-19). When they have created the molecule, they can group the objects and rotate the molecule to view it from different perspectives.

Figure 10-19   Manipulating Molecules

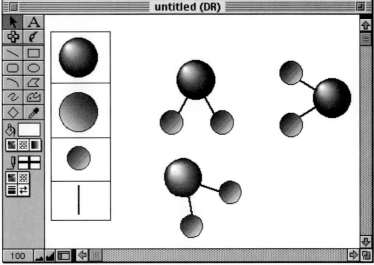

Students can also use clip art or create their own drawings to document their observations or to apply principles they have learned. For example, students could create a new insect or plant that is beneficial to the home or schoolyard. They could then prepare a written description of their design and describe how it would be beneficial. The emphasis in this type of lesson is not on the drawing but on applying principles (e.g., the type of defense or chewing mechanism in an insect) to create a unique design.

Draw documents can also be done collaboratively.

At the Classroom's Doorstep
▲▲▲
Questions Teachers Ask

Isn't it a waste of time to have students create drawings at the computer? There is no simple answer to this question. If the drawing exercise is part of your objectives for the unit, then it should support the required learning experiences. If you are developing a lesson with the iNtegrating Technology for inQuiry (NTeQ) model, the drawing activity should focus on manipulating graphic data either through creating information (e.g., documenting an observation or creating a new plant), making predictions (e.g., weather forecasting), or learning a new skill (e.g., calculating distances on a map), to name a few.

What does the research say about the use of graphics? Several of the studies mentioned at the beginning of this chapter have found support for using graphics for teaching, and that the graphics support the learning of related text material (e.g., Levie & Lentz, 1982). The research on student-generated or manipulated graphic information does not appear to exist. Bradens (1996), for example, does not mention student creation of graphics in his review of visual literacy.

REFERENCES
▲▲▲

Bazeli, M. J. & Olle, R. E. (1995). Using visuals to develop reading vocabulary. (ERIC Document Reproduction Service No. ED 391 519).

Bradens, R. (1996). Visual literacy. In D. J. Jonassen (Ed.), *Handbook of research for educational communications and technology*. New York: Macmillan Library Reference USA.

Cassidy, M. F. & Knowlton, J. Q. (1983). Visual literacy: A failed metaphor? *Educational Communications and Technology Journal, 32,* 107–125.

Guthrie, P. J. & Su, C. (1992). The significance of young children's visual skills in graphic depiction of spatial representation: Testimony from two drawing researchers. (ERIC Document Reproduction Service No. ED 354 994).

Jonassen, D. J. (1988). Integrating learning strategies into courseware to facilitate deeper processing. In D. J. Jonassen (Ed.), *Instructional designs for microcomputer courseware*. Hillsdale, NJ: Lawrence Erlbaum Associates, Inc.

Kleiman, G. & Zweig, K. (1995). Designing spaces: Visualizing, planning, and building. Seeing and thinking mathematically in the middle grades. (ERIC Document Reproduction Service No. ED 381 369).

Levie, H. & Lentz, R. (1982). Effects of text illustrations: a review of the research. *Educational Technology and Communication Journal, 26,* 25–36.

Rieber, L. P. (1995). A historical review of visualization in human cognition. *Educational Technology, Research, and Development, 43,* 46–56.

Stuhlmann, J. & Taylor, H. (1996). *Whole language strategies for integrating technology into language arts*. Paper presented at the National Educational Computing Consortium, Minneapolis, MN.

CHAPTER 11
Publishing Tools

▶ Introduction

One process that computers have made much easier is publishing, both on paper or in an electronic format. Anyone who has a computer can publish a paper, newsletter, newspaper, book, web page or CD-ROM. Publications such as newspapers and books that we have always viewed as printed on paper are now published on a web site or sent to readers via e-mail. Twenty years ago we might have viewed the information explosion as limited to a finite supply of paper and ink. Today the information explosion is limited only by electronic storage capacity which seems to grow at an even faster rate than the information! Although we do not want to clutter the world with trivial information, we do believe that students of all ages can produce knowledge that is both of interest and helpful to others. For example, we recently attended a conference where an astronomy teacher described how scientists from around the country have commented on his students' astronomy papers published on the school's web page. Now that your students have solved the problem, it is appropriate for them to publish their results to share with their classmates, other students, parents, and maybe the rest of the world.

▶ Computer Skills Used in This Chapter

Various functions (e.g., bold, italics, columns) of a word processor
Create graphics or use clip art
Cut and paste graphics
Create a HyperStudio stack
Create a web page and place it on a server

▶ Key Topics

WHY PUBLISH?
▲▲▲

If your students have completed an integrated computer lesson, they have learned new content, solved problems, and may have discovered new relationships between ideas that you had not anticipated. The final step in an integrated lesson is for each student or team to publish their results. This publishing process can help students synthesize ideas as they work through their data and determine what they want to tell others (Brookes, 1988; Corbine, 1995; Johannessen & Kahn, 1991). The process of writing or elaborating on ideas can help students discover ideas and relationships (Corbin, 1995) from their data analysis. Students can also respond to provocative questions from the teacher and their peers, which helps focus their writing and improve their understanding of the content (Brookes, 1988).

If you are using portfolios to collect a longitudinal record of your students' progress, a published report adds another dimension to portfolio assessment. Middle and high school teachers as well as elementary teachers in departmentalized (e.g., different teachers for different subjects) schools can use the publishing step as a cross-disciplinary project that integrates English classes (e.g., writing across the curriculum) with the other disciplines. The spreadsheet and database components of integrated software such as ClarisWorks and Microsoft Works (or stand alone applications) provide opportunities to enter and manipulate data and generate charts to show results. The word processing component or application allows the learners to synthesize and report what each has learned from the data manipulations. The following sections of this chapter illustrate how to create reports, books and newsletters, slide shows and presentations, and web pages.

CREATING REPORTS
▲▲▲

There are a variety of formats for students to develop including book reports, science reports, and short stories, to name a few. The basics of using a word processor to create these reports were described in Chapter 7. Once the report is written, the author can use various techniques to communicate the ideas in the report by improving the organization and aesthetics. Let's examine how we can publish reports to improve the communication between the author and the reader.

BASIC LAYOUT

Layout refers to how the report looks on the page and includes the margins, the font, and text styles. The margins determine where the text will print on the page. Pages with a margin that is too narrow or with too little white space appear cramped and may dissuade some readers. Fonts are used to create emphasis and to communicate a feeling about the report. Some fonts (e.g., Helvetica) are perceived as strong, while fonts such as Times are seen as congenial (Morrison, 1986). Text styles, such as **bold face** or *italics,* are a way to cue the reader about the structure of the text.

MARGINS.   Word processors have a default page that is used each time you create a new document. For your own personal computer, you might want to customize these settings to fit your needs. Classroom and lab computers, however, should all use the same default page. Students can then change the margins on their individual documents to suit their needs. If you or the students plan to bind the reports, you may need additional space on the left or top margin. Here is how to change the margins of a document.

In ClarisWorks, use the following steps.

1. Select **Document** from the **Format** menu. ClarisWorks will display a Document dialog (see Figure 11-1).

Figure 11-1   Document Margins

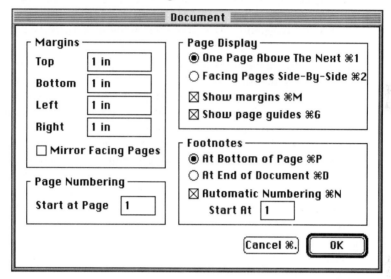

The default setting for margins in ClarisWorks is inches. You can change these settings to centimeters, millimeters, picas, or points by selecting **Rulers** from the **Format** menu. Once you have made the change, the margins will change to the same measurement setting as your text ruler. In Microsoft Word, select **Options** from the **Tools** menu and click on the **General** tab. At the bottom of the page, there is a pop-up menu that allows you to change the unit of measurement.

Why would you want to change the measurement unit? If your students are producing a newsletter or newspaper, you might select picas as the unit of measurement as it is the term used by printers and newspaper. The measurements do not change the way the word processor works, as this change is the same as having students measure their heights with a meter stick as opposed to a yard stick. This option allows you to create a realistic environment such as a newspaper office by using the same types of measurements.

Power Tip ▲▲▲   *Changing Rulers*

2. To change a margin setting, select the margin (e.g., **Top, Left,** etc.) and highlight the text. Then, enter the new setting.

3. When you have made your changes, click **OK.**

These measurements will affect *only* the current document. Any new documents will use the default settings in ClarisWorks (1 inch for word processing documents). You can easily create a special template for your students so that all of the documents will have the same margins. After you have set the margins, select **Save As** from the **File** menu. In ClarisWorks, click **Stationary** and then give the file a name. In Microsoft Word, select **Stationary** from the pop-up menu. When students double-click your stationary file, a new document is created using the settings from your file. Since your "template" file is a stationary file, the students cannot save their work over your file, at least not without a great deal of effort!

FONTS. Most computers arrive with fewer than a dozen different fonts. We have found computers that still have only three or four fonts, and we have found computers that have a hundred or more fonts (yes, one of us is guilty!). You can download fonts from the Internet, you can purchase CD-ROMs with fonts, and you can also receive free CD-ROMs with fonts when you purchase certain magazines and books. Our advice, however, is to keep only a few fonts on your computer. If you look at a book or magazine, you will find that only two or three fonts are used throughout the entire document. Good designs typically use only one or two fonts rather than a ransom note approach!

How can your students select an appropriate font for a report or newsletter? First, on a Macintosh, avoid fonts that are names of cities like Geneva or New York. These fonts are specifically designed to work on the screen and were not meant for printed documents. For all but graphic design classes, we suggest that you have your students select only *one* common font for a report such as Helvetica, Times, Palatino, or New Century School Book. Selecting a font installed on all of your computers makes it easy for students to work on different computers. One font, however, does not mean their report will look plain. The secret is to use many variations. They can use different sizes of type for headings. They can use bold, italics, shadows, or outlines for emphasis. By using one font with many variations as opposed to multiple fonts, the students can produce a more professional-looking document while avoiding the ransom note, disorganized look.

STYLES. Styles are predetermined formatting selections that students can apply to their documents. For example, if your class is creating a book consisting of a chapter from each of four groups, then you might want each chapter to have a consistent look. That is, the chapter heading might be 36 point Times and centered while the body of the report is 12 point Times. Headings in the chapters might be 14 point Times in bold. You can add these styles to your template or stationary document so that the students can produce similar looking documents. Similarly, you can create a template for research papers. Students can then gain experience in using consistent styles for their papers that follow a published style guide (e.g., *MLA Style Guide*). Let's examine how to create styles.

Use the following steps to create a new style in ClarisWorks.

1. Select the **Show Styles** item from the **View** menu. ClarisWorks will display a stylesheet of all existing styles (see Figure 11-2).

Figure 11-2 Using the ClarisWorks Stylesheet

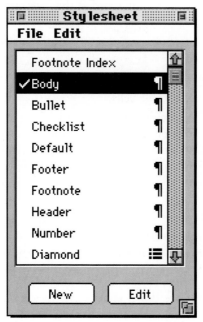

2. To create a new style, click **New** at the bottom of the stylesheet. ClarisWorks will display the **New Style** Dialog (see Figure 11-3).

Figure 11-3 ClarisWorks New Style Dialog for Creating a New Style

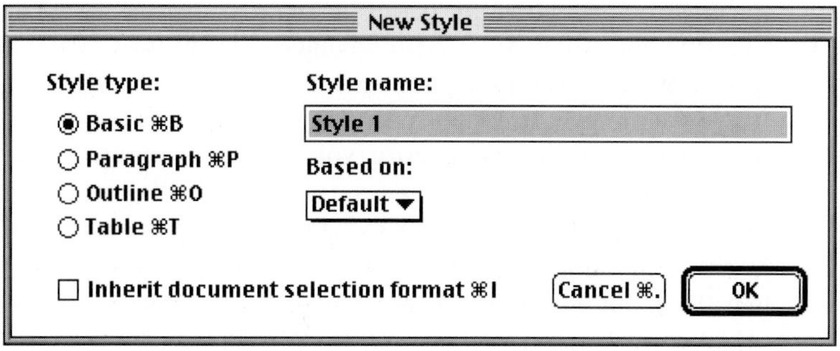

3. Now, enter a name for the style you are going to create. Try to find a descriptive name such as "Chapter Title" so that your students will know which style to use. Also, we have found that adding a letter such as **R** at the beginning of the style name (for **R**esearch paper) will cause all of your new styles to be grouped together and easier to find.

4. Next, you must choose a style type. The following is an explanation of the four style types.

   Basic: Style changes only the word(s) that are selected (e.g., use to bold a word).

   Paragraph: This style changes the style of the whole paragraph (e.g., indent).

   Outline: Use this style to format an outline.

   Table: Use to format table cells.

5. The **Based on** pop-up menu allows you to create a new style based on a style you have already defined or on a default style for the word processor. For example, the Default style might use 12 point Helvetica. If you are creating a style to bold a word, then the font of the selected word will change to Helvetica 12 point bold when you apply the style. If you want to change *just* the style to bold and leave the original font, then select **None** from the pop-up menu.

6. Click **OK.** Notice that your cursor changes to an arrow with an S. You can select the **Text, Style,** and **Size** for the style. If you are creating a paragraph font, you can also choose the alignment (e.g., **Center**), fonts, and ruler changes. Select each option as though you were changing a text selection. When you are done, click **Done** in the Stylesheet to create the style.

To change the style of a character or words with a Basic style, select the character or words. Then, click on the style name in the Stylesheet. ClarisWorks will apply the style. If you want to use a paragraph style, click the cursor in the paragraph. Next, select the style from the pop-up menu on the ruler or from the Stylesheet. ClarisWorks will change the style of the paragraph based on the previously determined font and formatting decisions.

Styles provide a way to produce consistent documents that are very useful if you are creating a single book based on reports or projects created by different groups. Creating and using styles is an advanced feature of ClarisWorks that could be confusing for less experienced computer users. While styles can make the task of formatting a document much easier, they may introduce an additional complexity that frustrates some users. Therefore, you may want to introduce your students to styles by using only one or two choices, for example, Report Title and Section Headings. You can add additional styles as students become more familiar with using styles. Students can help decide which other elements of the report would be easier to format if a designated style were created.

RULES

Rules are thin lines used to separate text. Books often have a rule near the top of the page to separate the chapter heading or page number from the text. Newspapers use rules to separate stories or quotes in a story or to highlight a table. Students can use rules to add flair to their written documents. Here is how to create a graphic rule in a ClarisWorks word processing document (see Figure 11-4).

1. If the tools are not displayed on the left side of your window, select **Show Tools** from the **View** menu.

2. Select the **Line** tool and draw a line in the approximate location and to the size you want.

Figure 11-4   Creating a Rule in ClarisWorks

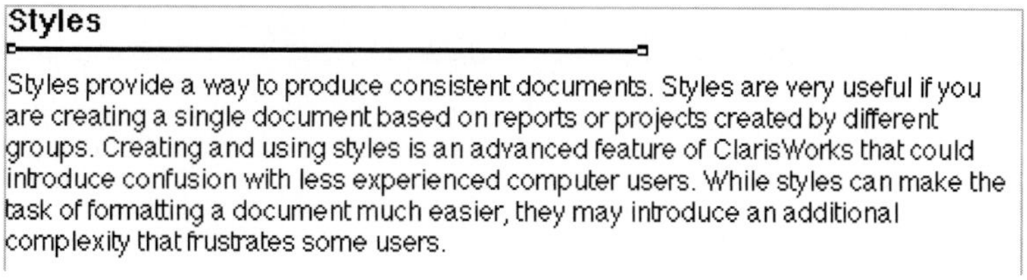

> **Styles**
>
> ────────────────────────────
>
> Styles provide a way to produce consistent documents. Styles are very useful if you are creating a single document based on reports or projects created by different groups. Creating and using styles is an advanced feature of ClarisWorks that could introduce confusion with less experienced computer users. While styles can make the task of formatting a document much easier, they may introduce an additional complexity that frustrates some users.

3. Change to the arrow pointer tool and select the line.

4. Choose **Cut** from the **Edit** menu.

5. Click on the **Text** tool. Now, click on your text where you want to place the rule.

6. Choose **Paste** from the **Edit** menu to paste the rule.

If you do not complete Steps 3–6 and add or delete some text, the rule will not move with the text (see Figure 11-5). When you paste the rule (or any graphic) it will maintain its position as the text moves.

Figure 11-5   Example of a Misplaced Rule

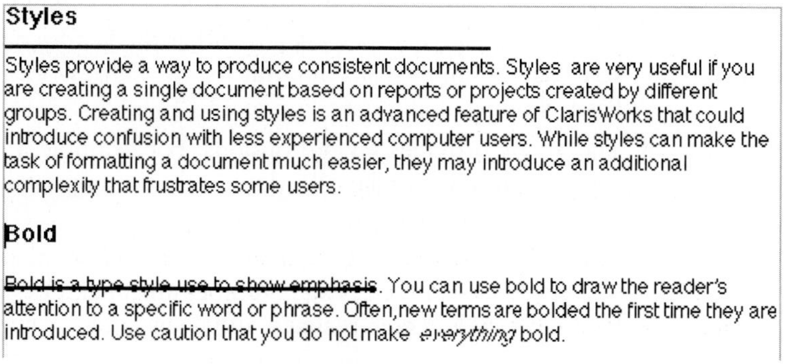

> **Styles**
>
> ────────────────────────────
>
> Styles provide a way to produce consistent documents. Styles are very useful if you are creating a single document based on reports or projects created by different groups. Creating and using styles is an advanced feature of ClarisWorks that could introduce confusion with less experienced computer users. While styles can make the task of formatting a document much easier, they may introduce an additional complexity that frustrates some users.
>
> **Bold**
>
> ~~Bold is a type style use to show emphasis~~. You can use bold to draw the reader's attention to a specific word or phrase. Often, new terms are bolded the first time they are introduced. Use caution that you do not make *everything* bold.

HEADERS AND FOOTERS

Headers and footers are used to place the same information at the top and bottom of every page in a document. They are particularly useful when assembling a portfolio or a document with contributions from several students. Students can use headers and footers to identify individual contributions or sections and to add page numbers to each page. The following steps describe how to create a single header or footer in a ClarisWorks document.

1. Using the **Format** menu, select **Insert Header** or **Insert Footer.** ClarisWorks creates a header (see Figure 11-6) or footer on each page.

Figure 11-6   Blank Header

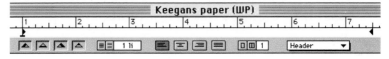

Character Analysis Sheet

by Keegan Morrison

Atticus Finch has multiple character traits such as: kind, cheerful, optimistic,

2. Click in the header or footer area and type the information you want to appear on each page. Headers usually include information such as the title of the paper or name of the section. For a book of students' work, the header might include the name of the student or group's work. The footer is typically used to display only the page number. You can also create tabs; left, center, or right justify; and use different styles and fonts for the text in the header and footer. The header and footer text is often a smaller size than the body of the document—you might want to use 9 or 10 point text in the header and footer.

3. To insert a page number, click in either the header or footer. Then select **Insert Page Number** from the **Edit** menu. ClarisWorks will display the **Insert Page Number** dialog (see Figure 11-7).

4. The dialog provides several options. For example, if you select **Page Number** and click **OK,** ClarisWorks inserts the page number, which prints automatically on each page.

5. If you want to show the page number and total pages in the document (e.g., 6–12), then select **Page Number** and click **OK.** The current page number is inserted. Enter a space and then either a hyphen or word such as "of" (e.g., 6 of 12). Select **Insert Page#** again from the **Edit** menu. Click on

Figure 11-7   Inserting a Page Number
in the Header or Footer

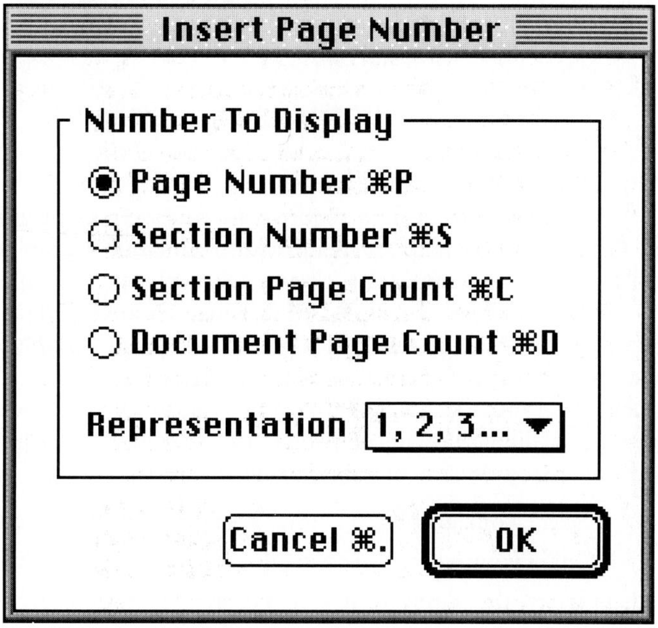

```
╔══════════════════════════════════════╗
║ ▦▦▦▦▦   Insert Page Number   ▦▦▦▦▦ ║
║ ┌──────────────────────────────────┐ ║
║ │ ┌─ Number To Display ──────────┐ │ ║
║ │ │ ◉ Page Number ⌘P             │ │ ║
║ │ │ ○ Section Number ⌘S          │ │ ║
║ │ │ ○ Section Page Count ⌘C      │ │ ║
║ │ │ ○ Document Page Count ⌘D     │ │ ║
║ │ │                              │ │ ║
║ │ │ Representation [ 1, 2, 3... ▼]│ │ ║
║ │ └──────────────────────────────┘ │ ║
║ │                                  │ ║
║ │   [ Cancel ⌘. ]    (( OK ))      │ ║
║ └──────────────────────────────────┘ ║
╚══════════════════════════════════════╝
```

Document Page Count and then click **OK**. The total number of pages in the document are inserted.

To create a more attractive header, you can underscore the full header. You can enter a carriage return on the first blank line of the footer and underline the blank line to create the same effect. Adding an extra line after a header or before a footer will separate them from the text, creating a polished look.

INSERTING A RULE IN A HEADER.   Putting a rule in a header takes a couple of extra steps. The following steps illustrate how to accomplish this task (See Figure 11-8).

Figure 11-8   Inserting a Rule in the Header

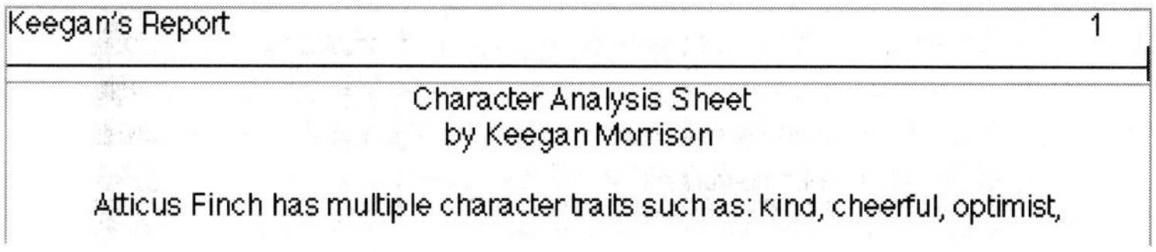

```
┌─────────────────────────────────────────────────────────┐
│ Keegan's Report                                       1   │
│═══════════════════════════════════════════════════════════│
│                                                           │
│                 Character Analysis Sheet                  │
│                    by Keegan Morrison                     │
│                                                           │
│ Atticus Finch has multiple character traits such as: kind, cheerful, optimist, │
└─────────────────────────────────────────────────────────┘
```

1. Press the Return key after the last word or number in the header. This action adds a new line to the header.

2. Use the drawing tools to draw your rule in the header. Rules can vary from a single line to two lines of either the same or contrasting thickness.

3. Select the line and select **Cut** from the **Edit** menu.

4. Type a couple of letters on the second line.

5. Click in front of the letters you typed.

6. Select **Paste** from the edit menu.

7. Delete the extra characters you added to the second line to place your rule.

USING PICTURES AND GRAPHICS

The final aspect of creating a report is to add pictures or graphics to illustrate the text. Often students (and teachers) want to include a graphic with their report. A graphic can illustrate an idea such as a cell nucleus or a graph of the results entered in a spreadsheet. A graphic could also just serve as a decoration for the report. Most word processing and desktop publishing applications allow the user to include graphics with the text. Students can use graphics that they have created with a draw program (Chapter 10), digital pictures, scanned pictures, and clip art in their reports. The following steps illustrate how to place a picture in a ClarisWorks word processing document using frames.

1. Select your graphic by either creating it or opening the graphic file.

2. Open your word processing document (the cursor will change to an arrow).

3. Select the **Paint** tool (see Figure 11-9) and draw a rectangle slightly larger than the graphic to create a paint frame. The exact position and

Figure 11-9   Drawing a Frame for a Picture

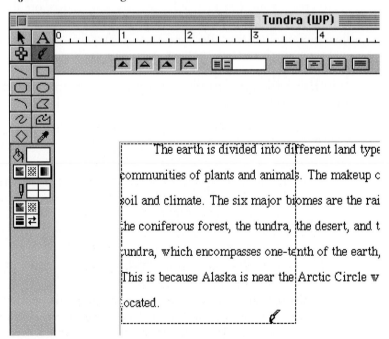

size of the rectangle are not critical since you can resize and move it later.

4. Select your graphic document so that it is the front window.

5. Select the graphic or the part of the graphic you want to include in the report. You can select it by clicking on the graphic or by using the selection rectangle tool or the lasso.

6. Copy the graphic to the clipboard by selecting **Copy** from the **Edit** menu (⌘C).

7. Select the word processing document so that it is the front window.

8. Select **Paste** from the **Edit** menu (⌘P) to paste graphic. The graphic will appear in the rectangle or Frame you created (see Figure 11-10).

Figure 11-10   Pasting into a Frame

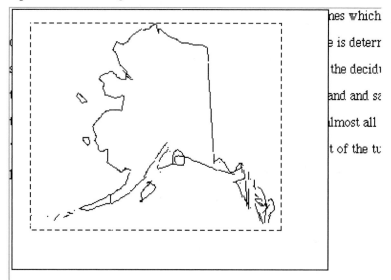

9. You can position the graphic in the frame by clicking on it and dragging it. If the graphic is not selected (e.g., the "marching ants" rectangle), then use the selection rectangle to select it.

10. Once the graphic is positioned, you can click on the frame (see Figure 11-11) and resize the frame. Note that the cursor changes to an arrow when it passes over the border of the rectangle.

11. The next step is adjusting the text wrap for the graphic. Click on the graphic frame to select it (see Figure 11-12).

12. Select **Text Wrap** from the **Options** menu. ClarisWorks will display the **Text Wrap** dialog. You can select one of the three options for wrapping the text around the paint frame. **None** prints the text behind the picture frame as shown in Figure 11-10. **Regular** wraps the text around the frame's rectangle, which is the most common type of text wrapping. The

Figure 11-11   Positioning a Paint Frame

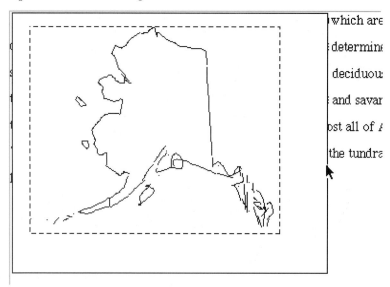

Figure 11-12   Adjusting Text Wrap for a Graphic

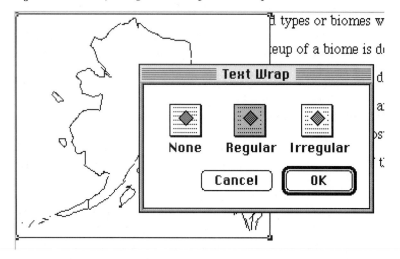

Irregular option wraps the text around the shape of a drawn object. Click **OK** to apply the text wrap to the selected frame. You can always change it by repeating these steps.

These procedures for using styles, headers and footers, and graphics can give your student reports a professional appearance. One problem we have observed with desktop publishing is that there is more emphasis on the desktop publishing aspect of the report than on the actual research and writing aspects. We are reminded of an old computer phrase, GIGO—garbage in results in garbage out. In other words, a pleasing appearance will not improve the information in a poorly written and researched report.

Books and Newsletters

▲▲▲

Sometimes your students may want to do something more than *just* create a report. A book or newsletter might provide a more appropriate method for them to disseminate their new knowledge. For example, a class that has created a number of reports on animals might prepare a book for a lower grade. If a class has completed a project identifying plants in a park or school, the group might want to create a book for the library or the park commission. Similarly, the class might want to prepare a newsletter describing their activities. This section describes the tools students can use to create books and newsletters.

Fran's Diary

What I really like about using computers in the classroom is that they allow my students to publish their work in a variety of formats. Students are limited only by their imaginations as to what they can publish in the classroom.

We study communities in our social studies curriculum. One of our thematic units is the study of our own community. We spend four weeks learning all about our community and its history. As a culminating event, we take a walking field trip to visit the town square, post office, police station, fire station, and several of the historic buildings. The students always enjoy this field trip. They especially like to see things such as the mail carriers sorting the mail before putting it on the mail trucks, the police dispatcher's desk where the 911 calls are answered, the inside of a police car, the rescue fire truck, etc. In the past, the students returned to school and wrote and word processed paragraphs about something that they had seen on the field trip.

One year, the students decided to write a book about their community. They wanted to take what they had experienced and learned on the field trip and add to it. The field trip was not the culminating activity that year, but rather the beginning activity for a book publishing project.

The students wanted to learn even more about the community. So, we invited some community business and civic leaders to come into our classroom to tell us about our community: its past, present, and future.

We learned a lot and we wanted to pass this knowledge on. Since many of us were new to the community and had recently experienced a move, we thought it would be a good idea to write a book about the community. This book would be written specifically for children, and it would portray the community from a child's perspective. The students hoped that this book might introduce children moving into the area to our community and convey the message that our community was a great place for kids to live!

Continued

The students were divided into groups of four. Each group was given a historic place, school, or community building to research. They had to draw the building, research its history, and interview people associated with it. This activity was completed after school and on Saturday mornings. After collecting their information, the students worked in their groups to write a page about their assigned building. These pages were word processed and the drawings were scanned to made up the body of the book. We added another section because we had learned so much interesting information! We created a "photograph" section—Looking at Our Community Through Our Eyes. Each student drew a picture of something or somewhere special in the community and wrote a caption to go under the picture. We scanned these drawings and each student hand-wrote the caption.

I helped them put everything together and printed a copy of the book. They were so excited! They all wanted the book. I felt like each student had to have a book. They had worked so hard. I didn't know what I was going to do. My prayers were answered! A local business had heard about our project and volunteered to print copies of our books. In fact, they were going to print a 1,000 copies so that the Chamber of Commerce could put them in the packets that are sent to people wanting information about the community.

The company that printed our books invited us to their printing facility. They had a complete graphic arts department and printing press. We visited the graphic arts department and the director put the computer disk that had the student's book on it into his big screened computer and showed the students how he could manipulate their drawings and text. There were a lot of oohs and ahhs! He then took us into the printing shop and showed us the equipment. As we stood watching the printing press, the pages of our book began to come off the press. I will never forget the looks on the students' faces. It was so exciting! We also got to watch the books go through the machine that folded and stapled the pages together.

The students got to take their books home that night. Not only did they get a book published, but they also got a once-in-a-lifetime experience. They got to see a project develop from the conception of an idea to the finished product. They also learned a lot about their community and developed a sense of community pride. Best of all, they were able to give a little of themselves back to the community by writing this book.

Books

Many of the techniques used to prepare a report are applicable to creating a book. There are three additional considerations for a book. First, you must allow a larger left margin for binding the book. Second, you must plan for a table of contents. Third, you need to print the book to create facing pages.

BOOK MARGINS. Extra space is needed on the left margin for binding the book, either with staples or other types of fasteners. The following steps describe how to adjust the margins.

1. Select the **Document** item from the **Format** menu in ClarisWorks to view the **Document** dialog (see Figure 11-13).

Figure 11-13   Document Dialog for Setting Margins

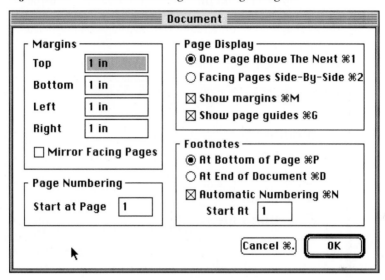

2. Enter the width of the left margin. This amount should allow the reader to easily read the information that appears near the left or inner margin of the book. We have found that 1.5 inches is adequate for most books.

3. Click **OK**.

TABLE OF CONTENTS. The table of contents provides a listing of the major sections or chapters of your book (See Figure 11-14). Your students may want to study the tables of contents from a variety of books to find a style they wish to use.

Figure 11-14   A Table of Contents

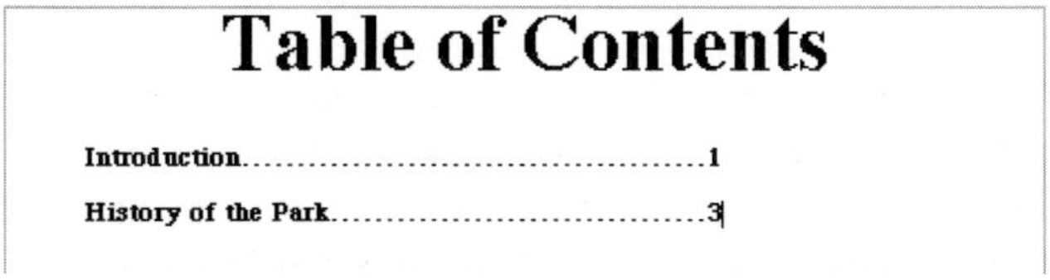

The following steps describe how to create a table of contents such as that in Figure 11-14.

1. Identify the major sections of the book and the beginning page number of each section.
2. Create a new word processing document.
3. Set a left tab at 1.5 inches by dragging the tab to the ruler. Set a right tab at 5.5 inches.
4. Double-click on the tab set at 5.5 inches to display the **Tab** dialog (see Figure 11-15).

Figure 11-15   Setting the Fill Option with the Tab Dialog

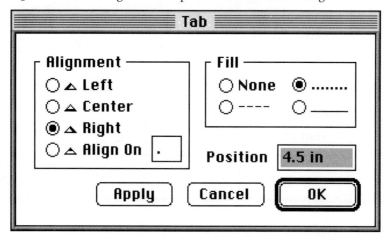

5. Select one of the **Fill** options to create the line from the chapter or section name to the page number. We selected the . . . . . . option for the table of contents in Figure 11-14.
6. Click **OK** when you are finished.

FACING PAGES. When creating a book, you will print on both sides of the paper (or at least copy on the front and back if you are making multiple copies). Thus, if you were to open the book to page 4, which might be on the left side (see Figure 11-16), then page five would be on the right side. The left margin on page 4 would be on the *outside* of the book, while the left margin for page 5 would be on the *inside* near the binding. When printing a book, the larger margin should always be nearest the binding edge.

Most word processors and desktop publishing tools have a way to adjust the pages so the "left" margin prints in the correct position—closest to the binding. Here is how to select this feature in ClarisWorks.

Figure 11-16   An Illustration of Mirror Margins

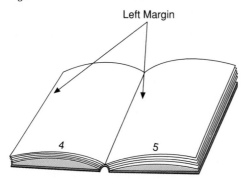

1. Select the **Document** item from the **Format** menu in ClarisWorks to view the **Document** dialog (see Figure 11-13).
2. Select **Mirror Facing Pages.**
3. Click **OK.**

The margins of facing pages will mirror one another when they are printed, making it easy to assemble a book with the wider margin on the binding side.

NEWSLETTERS

Another alternative for students to use when publishing the results of their work is a newsletter. They can use newsletters as a means of publishing their work as it progresses, or as the final product of their work (see Figure 11-17). Most word

Figure 11-17   An Example Student Newsletter

Project News

Lincoln Elementary's Fifth Grade Team Reports

Tree Mapping Team	Plant Identification Team
We are making a map of all the trees at the school. We draw a picture of each tree on our map. The picture is what a bird sees when flying. One of us prints the name of the tree in the picture using the computer. We glue the name on the picture.	Our team is naming all the plants at the school. A woman from a nursery came to school this week. She helped us use a book to find the plant names. We found many types of bushes.
Next week, we will color each of the trees. We need to select colors for the	We are going to name the different types of flowers. Some flowers only bloom one time. Other flowers bloom every year.

Power Tip ▲▲▲   *Clean Printing*

If you are planning to make copies of your book, we suggest that you print on only one side of the paper. Printing on both sides causes the image to show through the paper, creating a ghost or smudge image on the copy. By printing on only one side of the paper, you can copy the pages front to back to create a nice-looking book.

processors can create multiple columns of text and even present templates for creating newsletters. The following steps describe the process for creating the newsletter in Figure 11-17.

1. Create a new word processing document in ClarisWorks. (You can also create a newsletter in a draw document using linked frames. This approach, however, requires a skilled user.)

2. Enter the text for your banner or heading that will extend across the columns. We chose 72 point type for the project news title and 14 point for the secondary header. Add an extra return after the last line of the banner.

3. Highlight the text and center it. You can also experiment with different layouts for your banner.

4. Draw two horizontal lines with the line tool and align them.

5. Click below the double lines to place your cursor below the banner.

6. Select **Section** from the **Format** menu to display the **Section** dialog (see Figure 11-18). Select **New Line** from the **Start Section** pop-up menu. Each

Figure 11-18   Section Dialog

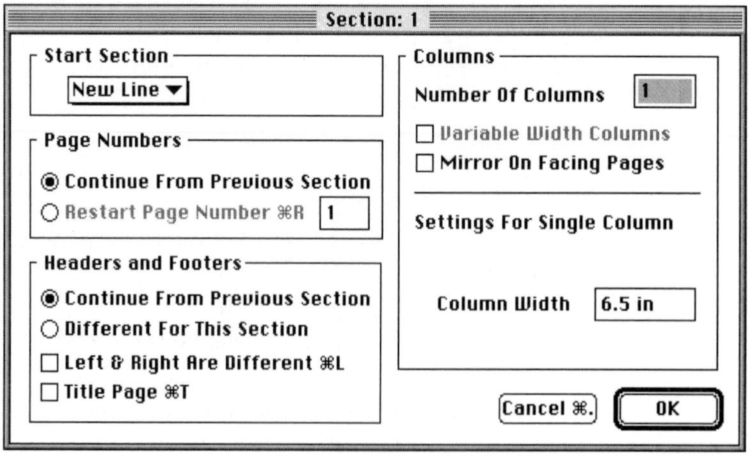

time you insert a section break, the new section will start on a new line rather than a new page.

7. With cursor below the banner, select **Insert Section Break** from the **Format** menu. ClarisWorks will create a new section and draw a gray horizontal line to indicate a new section (see Figure 11-19).

Figure 11-19 Creating Columns

Column Icon

8. Now, click the **Column** icon to create two columns (see Figure 11-19). ClarisWorks will display gray lines to indicate the margins of each column. If you want to create a 3 column format, we recommend switching to a landscape (horizontal) layout (select **Page Setup** from the **File** menu) to create a column of adequate width.

9. To start typing, click in the left-most column (or at the end of your text if you have already entered information). As you type, the information will fill one column and then automatically go to the next column.

10. To stop entering information in one column and then switch to another, select **Insert Column Break** from the **Format** menu. ClarisWorks will automatically move your cursor to the next column.

11. If you want to create a break between sections or change the number or size of the columns, select **Insert Section Break** from the **Format** menu. ClarisWorks will create a new section. You can change the size of the columns or the number of columns in the new section without affecting other sections.

12. If you want to use graphics, create a paint frame and then paste the graphic into the frame. You can then move the frame and wrap the text around the frame.

13. You can also add headers and footers to your newsletter to add page numbers or other information such as the publication date.

MULTIMEDIA PRESENTATIONS
▲▲▲

Sometimes printed materials are not suitable for presentation of student results even when printed with a color printer. An alternative to printed communication is a multimedia presentation that can incorporate sound, graphics, animation, video, and text. Students can create these presentations as electronic slide shows or hypermedia stacks. Although multimedia presentations provide a number of "bells and whistles," consider the reason for developing such presentations. We have often encountered teachers who simply teach their students how to develop a multimedia presentation for the sole purpose of creating the presentation. We encourage you to consider the purpose of the assignment and develop a clear rationale for including such a project. In the following section, we will describe how to create an electronic slide show with ClarisWorks and a hypermedia presentation using HyperStudio to present the students' inquiry results.

Students should complete two tasks before creating an electronic slide show or hypermedia stack: (1) plan the structure and (2) create a storyboard. When planning the structure of the project, the students need to address the following:

Who is the intended audience?

What is the project topic?

What information will this project share?

What is the actual purpose or goal of this project?

Next, students need to create a storyboard of the project. Storyboards are sketches of each card in the stack. Students can draw storyboards on a piece of notebook paper, divide the paper into four sections, or use notecards. Drawing only one card per page makes it very easy to reorder the cards. Careful planning prior to going to the computer results in less student frustration and more meaningful presentations (McBride and Luntz, 1996).

ELECTRONIC SLIDE SHOWS

There are several applications for creating electronic slide shows. Some, including PowerPoint™, are designed specifically for creating electronic presentations. Drawing programs such as ClarisWorks and Canvas™ have a slide function. One advantage to using PowerPoint is the ability to print handouts and lectures notes.

You can use ClarisWorks to create a slide show from all but the communications module. The draw module offers the most flexibility for creating a slide show since you can easily position the text, graphics, or any other element on the page. The following paragraphs describe how to create a slide show using a draw document.

1. Create a new document in ClarisWorks.

2. Select **Document** from the **Format** menu and ClarisWorks will display the **Document** dialog for draw documents (See Figure 11-20). Keeping only one page across makes it easier to organize and sequence your slide show.

3. Enter the number of slides in your slides show in the **Pages Down** edit field. We usually add at least two additional slides so that we have a blank

Figure 11-20   Setting the Number of Pages in a Draw Document

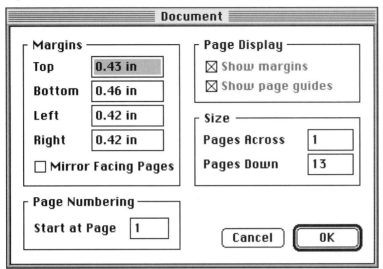

one at the beginning and end of the presentation. You can change the number of pages at any time.

4. Select **Page View** from the **View** menu to display the margins of each page. This view will allow you to see each page of the draw document.

5. Select **Edit Master Page** from the **Options** menu. The master page is a template that we can use to place the same graphic or logo in exactly the same

Determining the type of final product should be a group decision.

position on each page. We can also use it to align our text on each page so that it does not jump from one slide to another.

Before we create the page, consider the color of the text and the color of the background. The default text color is black. If you want to use a lighter color, such as white or yellow, for your text, you will need to add a color "background" to your master page. To add this background, draw a rectangle that fills the master page. Select a color for the background that will provide enough contrast to make your text legible. The other objects of your master page are drawn on this background.

6. Figure 11-21 shows our master page. We placed our logo in the top right corner. The two sets of lines are used to align our text. Text is placed next

Figure 11-21   Creating a Master Page

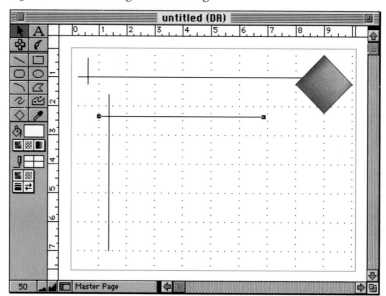

to the horizontal and vertical line so that it is in the same position for *every* slide. There is only one horizontal line in the lower pair which is used to place the first item. All other text is placed against the vertical line and then spaced at an appropriate distance vertically. If we were using bullets on these items, we could add another vertical line to indicate where to place the bullets.

7. After you have created your master page, select **Master Page** from the **Options** menu to return to the drawing pages. Notice that when you return to the drawing pages, you cannot select or move the objects on the master page.

8. We like to keep the first slide and last slide blank so that the audience is not trying to read our first and last slide when we start and quit the slide show. To start on the second page, scroll down until it is in view.

9. You can now add text and graphics to the page (see Chapter 10). Using the same font and size for each level of information creates a pleasing and easy-to-follow presentation. You can also create a spreadsheet on a slide by selecting the **Spreadsheet** tool and "drawing" a spreadsheet.

10. To add a QuickTime movie to your slide show, click on the slide where you want to place the movie. Select **Insert** from **File** menu and select the movie. You can drag the movie to an appropriate location on your slide just as you do text and other objects. To play the movie, click on the movie badge (the film icon). Then click the play arrow on the movie controls.

11. When you complete your slides, you can remove the template items from the master page. Figure 11-22 shows a sample slide after the template was removed from the master page.

Figure 11-22   Sample Slide from a ClarisWorks Slide Show

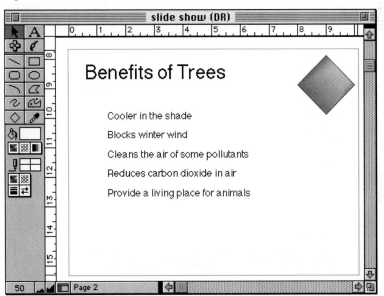

The next step is to display the slide show either as part of a presentation or as a self-running display. If you are planning to make a presentation, you should make sure that the computer you will use has the same version (or later) of Claris-Works that you used to create your slide show. Here is how to present a slide show.

1. Start by opening your slide show document. Then, select **Slide Show** from the **View** menu. ClarisWorks will display the **Slide Show** dialog (see Figure 11-23).

2. You can make adjustments in the presentation order by dragging the slides in the **Order** list. For example, if you discover that you need another slide

Figure 11-23 Presenting a Slide Show

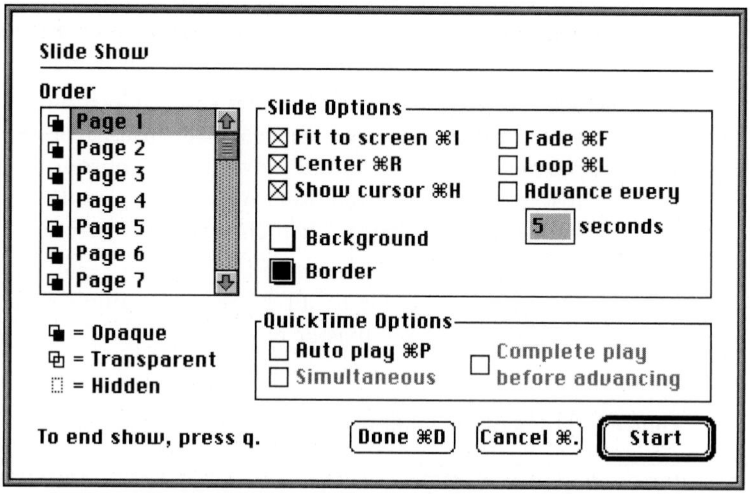

after slide 3, you can add it to the end of your list and then change the sequence in this dialog.

3. The **Fit to screen** will reduce large slides to fit the screen of the computer. **Center** will center your slide in the horizontal and vertical center of the screen. If you want to see the cursor and use it as a pointer, select the **Show cursor** option.

4. The **Background** and **Border** pop-up menus allow you to select a color background that is displayed behind your text. (If you added your own color background on the master slide, you can leave it white). The border color will fill the border around the slide. You can select the same color as the background or a contrasting color.

5. Selecting **Fade** will fade each slide in and out. Although this feature has its appeal, it can be very tiresome and add time to your slide show. If you want a slide show to run unattended, you can select the **Loop** and **Advance every** options. Enter a time in seconds for displaying each slide.

Power Tip ▲▲▲   *Hiding the Slide Show Dialog*

If you are presenting in front of a group, you may not want to display the Slide Show dialog. Here is how to avoid this step. When you finish creating your slide show, select **Slide Show** from the **View** menu and set your options. Then, click **Done** rather than **Start**. When you want to show your slide show, hold down the Option key when you select **Slide Show** from the **View** menu. ClarisWorks will bypass the dialog and automatically start your slide show using the options you set.

6. If you have a self-running slide show with a QuickTime movie, select **Auto play** and **Complete play** before advancing. When a slide with a movie is displayed, the movie will play automatically and the slide will not advance until the movie is done.

7. To show your slide show, click **Start.** If you do not want to show the slides now, but want to save your settings, then click **Done.**

HYPERMEDIA PRESENTATIONS

HyperStudio is an easy to use tool for creating hypermedia and multimedia presentations. Hypermedia and hypertext allow students to navigate through the content in different ways and explore the information based on their needs. A hypermedia unit incorporating sound, graphics, animations, and/or digital video is referred to as multimedia. Multimedia units provide students with unique ways of communicating their ideas via the computer. An advantage of hypermedia and multimedia over an electronic slide show is that the user can select the sequence rather than following a set sequence of slides. There is also a HyperStudio player you can install on any computer to run your stacks. In addition, you can also publish your stacks on your web site. The following steps describe how to create a HyperStudio stack.

1. After launching HyperStudio, select **New Stack** from the **File** menu. HyperStudio asks if you want to use the same size card and number of colors. For most stacks you can click **Yes.**

2. Programmers call the first card or screen a splash screen. It is used to identify the topic and author of the stack. For this splash screen, create one field for the title and one field for the author's name. Select **Add Text Object** from the **Objects** menu and HyperStudio will create a rectangular edit field that you can drag and resize. Repeat this step to create the second field.

3. When the text object is sized and positioned, click the cursor outside of the text object to place it. The **Text Appearance** dialog will then appear (see Figure 11-24).

Figure 11-24   Setting Text Options in the Text Appearance Dialog

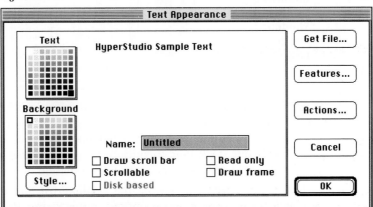

Power Tip ▲▲▲   *Dressing Up Stacks*

Are you tired of black and white cards in your stack? There are two ways you can dress up your stacks.

First, you can select **Erase Background** from the **Edit** menu and select a color for the card. Any new cards will have the same color background.

Second, you can paste a picture onto the card or use the paint tools to create a colorful (or subtle) background. To make a new card with the same background, select **Group Card** from the **Ready Made Cards** hierarchical menu under **Edit**.

4. Since our title and name are only one or two lines long, we do not want to draw the scroll bar, have scrollable text, or draw the frame. You can also select a color for the text and color for the space inside the text object from the two color palettes. Click **Style** to set the text style for this field in the **Text Style** dialog (see Figure 11-25). Hint: Fields that the user

Figure 11-25   Setting the Text Style

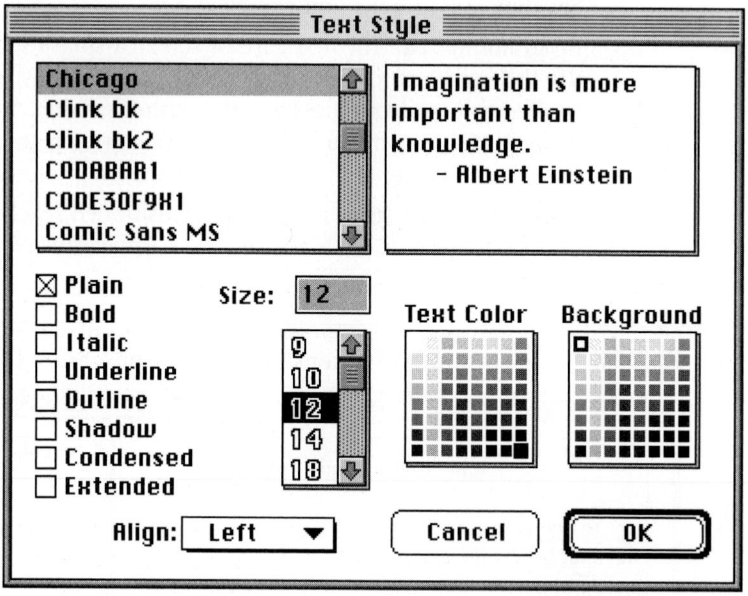

does not change typically do not have a frame around them. You can make your stack user friendly by consistently using a frame only around fields in which users are to enter information.

5. You can select a font from the scrolling list and the size and style (e.g., bold, italic, etc.) from the options in this dialog. If you are planning to run

the stack on other computers, you will want to select a font that is likely to be installed on the other computers (e.g., Chicago, Monaco, Helvetica, Times, etc.). Click **OK** when you have made your selections. When you return to the **Text Appear** dialog, click **OK.**

6. The cursor is placed in the text object and you can enter your text. If you need to resize the object, select the **Editing** tool (arrow) and resize or move the text object. You can also change this field to a read only object which keeps the casual users from making changes. Double-click the object to display the **Text Appearance** dialog and select **Read only.** The text object is locked and you can only make changes by unselecting **Read only.**

7. Next you need to create a button the user can click to move to the second card. To create a button, select **Add a button** from the **Object** menu and you will see the **Button Appearance** dialog (See Figure 11-26).

Figure 11-26   Setting the Button Features

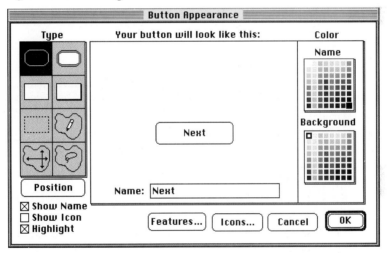

8. Enter the name of the button, **Next,** into the name field. If you have selected **Show Name,** then the name is displayed in the button object. Selecting **Highlight** will cause the button to flash when clicked to provide the user with feedback that the mouse click was noticed.

9. If you want to include an icon with the button (and maybe no name), click **Icons** and select an icon from the list. Click **OK** when you are done. You can now drag and resize the button. Click outside the button object when you are done to see the **Actions** dialog (see Figure 11-27).

10. You can select a **Place to Go** (such as the next card) and/or a **Things to Do** for the button actions. Select **Next card** for this button and the **Transitions** dialog is displayed. Selected the default of **Fastest** transition at the fastest speed (see Figure 11-28). You can also select one of the transitions for a different appearance.

Figure 11-27   Creating Button Actions

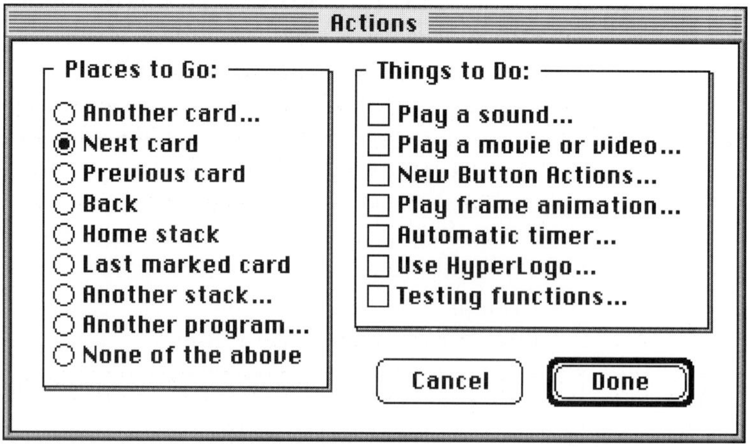

Actions

Places to Go:
- ○ Another card...
- ● Next card
- ○ Previous card
- ○ Back
- ○ Home stack
- ○ Last marked card
- ○ Another stack...
- ○ Another program...
- ○ None of the above

Things to Do:
- ☐ Play a sound...
- ☐ Play a movie or video...
- ☐ New Button Actions...
- ☐ Play frame animation...
- ☐ Automatic timer...
- ☐ Use HyperLogo...
- ☐ Testing functions...

[Cancel]   [Done]

Figure 11-28   Selecting a Transition

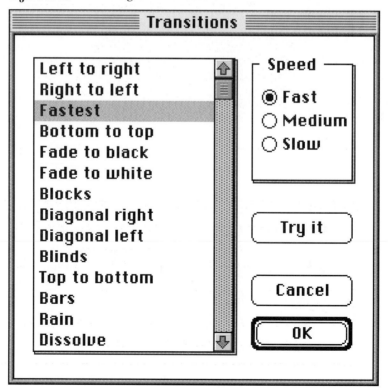

Transitions

Left to right
Right to left
Fastest
Bottom to top
Fade to black
Fade to white
Blocks
Diagonal right
Diagonal left
Blinds
Top to bottom
Bars
Rain
Dissolve

Speed
- ● Fast
- ○ Medium
- ○ Slow

[Try it]

[Cancel]

[OK]

11. Select **New Card** from the edit menu to create a new card. Now, select **Previous Card** from the **Move** menu and test the button by clicking **Next.** You should move to the new card you just created.

12. In our sample stack we want to use a picture of the food pyramid downloaded from the USDA web site (www.nalusda.gov/fnic/Fpyr/pyramid.html). You can open the picture with ClarisWorks and resize it to fit the card. Next, copy it to the clipboard and paste it onto your card (see Figure 11-29a). You can also use clip art by copying and pasting it onto individual cards.

Figure 11-29   Pasting a Picture to a Stack

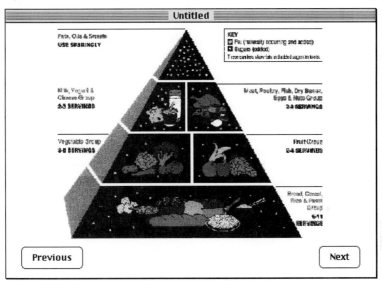

(a)

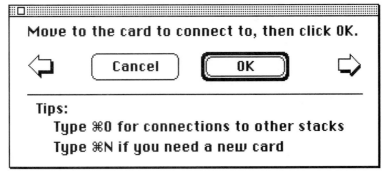

(b)

Power Tip ▲▲▲   *HyperStudio Cards*

The HyperStudio Tutorial (p. 72) suggests a maximum of about 20 cards per stack. We encourage our students to create a maximum of about 16 cards. With only 16 cards, they can then add one or two cards to the stack to correct any problems. After 16 cards, the students start a new stack and link the last card from the first stack to the second stack. We have also seen larger stacks that approach 1 megabyte or more of disk space. The advantage of the smaller stack is easier backup and fewer lost cards if there is a problem with your disk or stack.

---

13. The next step is to create links from the pictures of the food groups in the pyramid to cards with more detail about each group. Select **Add a button** from the **Object** menu and you will see the **Button Appearance** dialog (see Figure 11-26). You are going to create an invisible button by making one of the blocks of the pyramid a button. The four options for creating invisible buttons appear at the bottom under **Type** on the left of the dialog. You can use the marquee to select an area, a pencil, or the lasso, or you can select an expanding area (the one with double arrows), which you click inside the object to create a button. For the pyramid, select either the lasso or pencil button, click to position, and then drag around the fruit block of the pyramid. When you complete a loop, a dialog will ask you to either try again or accept the area selected. When you click **OK,** you will see the **Actions** dialog (see Figure 11-27). You can then click **Another card,** which will display a window to select a card (see Figure 11-29b).

14. Click the left or right arrows to navigate to the appropriate card (or create a new card or open a different stack). When you see the card, click **OK** to create the link. This feature allows you to create hyperlinks so the user can navigate various paths rather than follow a set sequence. Eventually, we will add links from each of the pyramid blocks, creating the hyperlinks. Each student can then explore the links in a sequence of their choosing.

15. Save your stack before quitting. It is always a good idea to save the stack after you create each card.

Electronic slide shows and multimedia programs provide a variety of ways for students to present their research. They can use these publication tools to make presentations to their class, other classes, parents, or as self-running programs at an open house.

CREATING WEB PAGES

Printed materials and multimedia presentations reach a relatively small audience and are typically limited to times the student or author is available to present the information. The World Wide Web offers the advantage of making student research available to others beyond the classroom (see Chapter 13). Software applications such as Netscape Navigator Gold™, Claris Home Page™, and Adobe PageMill™ make web page creation as easy as writing a report with a word processor. Students can create web pages to present the results of their research that others with web access can link to and read. A search of the web will produce many K–12 school sites that publish materials on specific themes (e.g., astronomy, mammals, comets, ecology, etc.) and add to the sites each year with new materials produced by new students. Sites that contain unique information such as information on ancient mathematicians or scientists researching AIDS can provide valuable information to not only other students but to other web surfers.

WEB PAGE TERMINOLOGY

Web pages are created using special tags that tell the browser how to display the text, graphics, animations, movies, and other features. These tags are referred to as HyperText Markup Language or, more commonly, HTML. Fortunately, you can design a web page without knowing this language by using one of the applications described in the previous paragraph. A basic understanding of the features of HTML, however, can help you better design your web page. Let's examine some of the features related to text, tables, graphics, color, and links.

TEXT. There are several options for displaying text on a web page. You can select the size of the font and styles such as bold and italic (see Figure 11-30), however,

Figure 11-30   Text for a Web Page

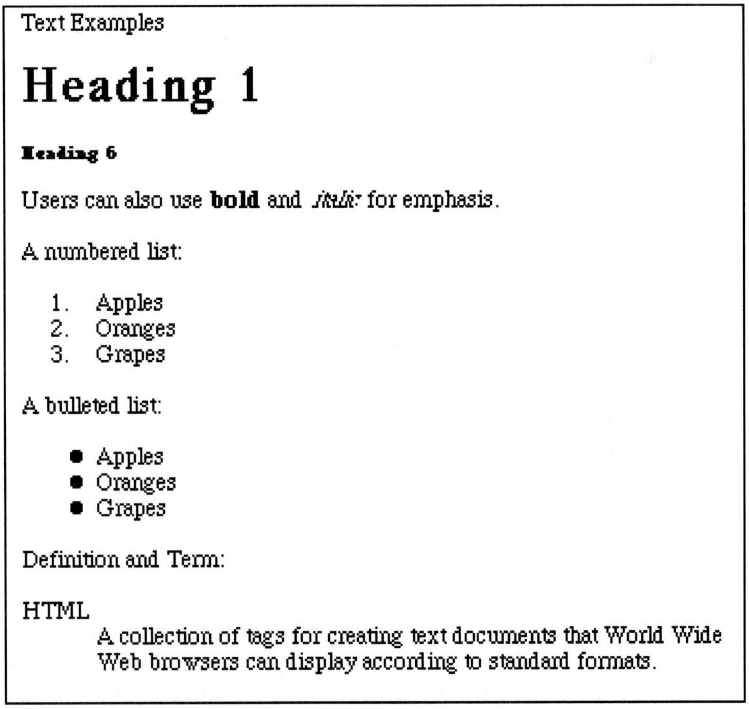

Text Examples

Heading 1

Heading 6

Users can also use **bold** and *italic* for emphasis.

A numbered list:

1. Apples
2. Oranges
3. Grapes

A bulleted list:

- Apples
- Oranges
- Grapes

Definition and Term:

HTML
    A collection of tags for creating text documents that World Wide
    Web browsers can display according to standard formats.

you should not specify a font (e.g., Times or Helvetica) with the current HTML standards (3.0). If you specify a specific font and the user does not have access to the font, then the browser may not display the page as you intended. Even worse, the browser might crash! There are also six different preset heading levels you can select when creating a web page. Heading 1 is the largest and heading 6 is the smallest. These headings are used much like the headings in desktop publishing— to indicate different sections of the content. You can also use different colors for your text and links but, remember, most links are in blue prior to accessing them and then turn to purple once you have followed the link.

There are several ways of formatting different types of text. For example, if you have a list of items, you can use either a bulleted or numbered list. Most browsers will format these lists by identifying them and adding a number or bullet before each item. If you need to create a glossary or dictionary of terms, you can use the HTML term and definition tags to create a unique layout.

TABLES. If you need to display information in a row and column format, you can create a table to align the data. Each cell of a table can hold text and/or a graphic (see Figure 11-31). You can also adjust the width of the table border from no border to a very thick border.

Figure 11-31   A Table from a Web Page

Group	Example
Fats, Oils, & Sweets	Cake
Milk, Yogurt, & Cheese	Skim milk
Meat, Poultry, Fist, Dry Beans, Eggs, & Nut Group	Omelet
Vegetable Group	Carrot
Fruit Group	Apple
Bread, Cereal, Rice, & Pasta Group	Brown rice

GRAPHICS. You can use a clip art, digital or scanned photos, your own drawings, and rules in a web document. Clip art and pictures that you draw are typically saved as GIF files, while photographs are saved as JPEG files that allow for more colors. Some web page creation applications such as Claris Home Page and Netscape Navigator Gold allow you to paste a picture into a web document and the application automatically converts it to a GIF file. Another "graphic" that is part of the HTML tag is a rule that is used much like a rule in desktop publishing (see Figure 11-32). Remember, the use of graphics in your web pages can slow down the loading of the page and cause some users to skip your site.

Figure 11-32   A GIF Image and Rule on a Web Page

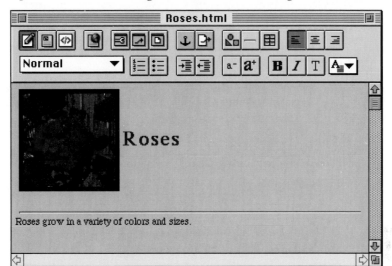

COLOR.   Web page documents allow you to specify the color of the background (the part of the window where the text is printed), color of the text, and the color of links. While different colored backgrounds and text may look very appealing on your monitor, they may appear unreadable on another computer monitor due to the way the computer displays the selected colors. Most experienced web masters test their color schemes on several different computers and monitors to make sure all the information is readable. We have found that simple color schemes with plenty of contrast between the background color and the text are easily read on most computers.

LINKS.   The greatest feature of web pages is the ability to link a word or graphic on your page to another page either on your server on another server halfway around the world. This process of linking documents is another example of hypertext—the ability to jump from one idea to another with a click of a mouse. A link is created by providing a Uniform Resource Locator (URL) or File Transfer Protocol (FTP) address (see Chapters 12 and 13) to another page (URL) or file (FTP).

Many books and web resources can guide you in designing a web site and web pages (see Resources at the end of this chapter). Good web pages and sites are user friendly—they are designed for the person reading the page and not the person *creating* the page. We recall one web master who had designed several pages that our students could not read in the lab. When informed of this problem, the designers simply stated that the pages were readable on their computers. Rather than reading a poorly designed page, our students found another site with the same information. If you want web surfers to visit your site and return to it many times, then focus on making your pages user friendly.

CREATING A WEB PAGE

Claris Home Page, Adobe PageMill, and Netscape Navigator Gold have many similar features for designing a web page. All three allow you to "draw" the page as you want it to appear. The following steps describe how to create a web page using Claris Home Page.

1. When you start Home Page, it will create a blank web page document. Select **Document Options** from the **Edit** menu to display the **Options** dialog (see Figure 11-33).

Figure 11-33   Setting the Web Document Options

```
╔══════════════════════════════════════════════════════════════╗
║                     Untitled.html Options                      ║
║  ┌─ Basic      ▼ ────────────────────────────────────────┐   ║
║  │                                                          │   ║
║  │        Text: ▓   Normal Link: ▓    Active Link: ▓        │   ║
║  │  Background: ░   Visited Link: ▓                         │   ║
║  │                                                          │   ║
║  │  Background Image:  [ Set... ]  [ None ]                 │   ║
║  │  ┌────────────────────────────────────────┐  ┌──────┐  │   ║
║  │  │                                        │  │      │  │   ║
║  │  └────────────────────────────────────────┘  └──────┘  │   ║
║  │                                                          │   ║
║  │       Document Title: │Fruit│                           │   ║
║  └──────────────────────────────────────────────────────────┘  ║
║                                                                ║
║  [?]  [ Use Defaults ]              [ Cancel ]  [[ OK ]]        ║
╚══════════════════════════════════════════════════════════════╝
```

2. The name entered in the **Document Title** field will appear in the window bar of the document when it is viewed with a browser. Clicking on one of the color options for text, background, or links displays the color picker so that you can specify a color. You can also select a background image to fill the window instead of a color. When you have made your selections, click **OK.** You can always make changes later by displaying this dialog.

3. The first object on this page will be a picture of a rose taken with a digital camera. The image was saved as a JPEG file in the same folder as the web pages you will create. To include the picture on the web page, select **Image** from the **Insert** menu and select the image from the list of files.

4. Next, add a title next to the image. Click once on the image to select it and then select **Show Object Editor** from the **Window** menu to display the object editor (see Figure 11-34).

5. There are five options for aligning text with the image (see Figure 11-34). Select **Middle** so that the text and image are aligned on their horizontal centers.

Figure 11-34   Setting the Text Alignment with the Object Editor

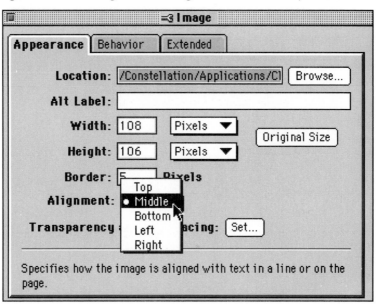

6. Now type the word **Rose**, which will appear beside the image. Next, select the word Rose and choose **Heading 1** from the pop-up menu (see Figure 11-35). The word Rose will change to a larger font in bold. Press **Return** after the word Rose to move to the next line.

7. Click on the **Rule** icon to insert a rule on the next line (see Figure 11-36).

Figure 11-35   Selecting a Heading

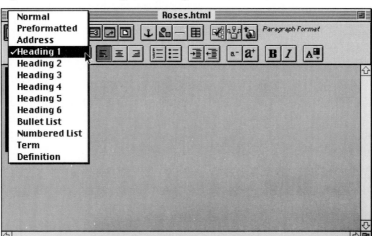

Figure 11-36   Inserting a Rule

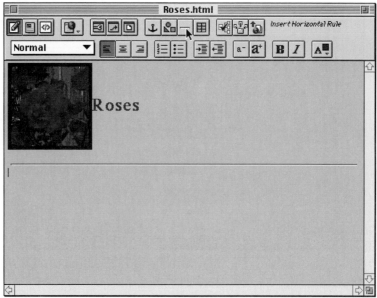

8. You can now enter text, another graphic, or a table to finish the document. After entering the text, you can enter links. For example, we have a picture of a yellow rose that we want to link to the word "color."

9. To create a link to another web document, select the word(s) or image. Next, select **Link to URL** from the **Insert** menu. Home Page will display the **Link** dialog (see Figure 11-37). Since the web document we want is on our hard drive, we can click **Browse Files** and find the file. If it were on another server, we could type or paste the URL into the field. Once the URL is entered, the selected word will change to the color of a link (usually blue), and it will automatically be underlined.

10. Once you have finished the page, you can save it. For compatibility with all systems, you should choose a filename that is 8 characters or less and end with .html or .htm. We named our file rose.html.

To make your pages accessible to others, you will need to move them to your web server. Depending upon your setup, you can either drag the files to the web server or you can use an FTP program to transfer the files.

DESIGN CONSIDERATIONS

A poorly designed web page can prove useless to its author and frustrating to users who choose to visit the site. Before spending time creating a web page, take the time to consider some basics of design: goal of the page, the content, graphics, and layout (Snyder, 1996).

Figure 11-37   Using the Links Dialog

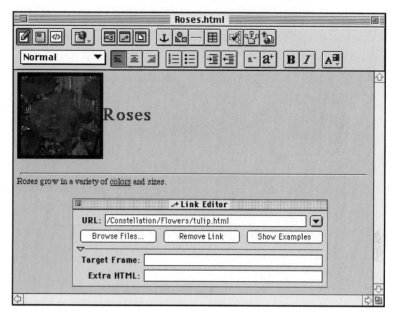

GOAL. Why are your students going to publish? What do you want the web page to accomplish? How does it tie in with your objectives for the project? These are all important questions to consider before students create their own web pages. Once you or your students have clearly and specifically articulated the goal, make sure the design supports the goal. For example, a page designed solely to provide educational information will look much different from a page designed to be interactive.

CONTENT. *Nothing* is more frustrating than surfing through a series of links only to find the final link that says, "Under Construction!" Content is everything on the net. Be sure that your site has something to say, say it, and leave overused options such as counters, guest books, and feedback buttons to other sites (unless these options support your goals).

GRAPHICS. Learn to be conservative in your use of graphics. They can often be distracting to readers, and they require a lot of memory which makes it time-consuming for users trying to link to your page. We have often stopped a connection to a link because it was taking too long to download. If you want users to stay connected, make graphics useful.

LAYOUT. Help users locate information quickly on your web page by giving an overview up front. Many teachers create wonderfully extensive sets of web pages, but lose those readers who just don't have the time to leisurely browse through web pages. A table of contents, an introductory paragraph, or a mini-search engine built

Production of a quality final product takes time and careful planning.

into the top of the page will help users find what they want fast. Also, make the title succinct and as descriptive as possible. This will also help when your page comes up as a hit in a search engine. Users can determine quickly whether they want to visit your site or not.

At The Classroom's Doorstep
▲▲▲
Questions Teachers Ask

What is the value of letting students publish their results? Publishing results is a strategy to help the students synthesize what they have learned by solving a problem. The answer to the problem might be very simple such as the "I would weigh more on Jupiter than the earth." Students probably learned more than where they would weigh the most. They gained an understanding of gravity and our solar system as well as related concepts such as revolution, rotation, and day and night. The publishing strategy provides a means for them to go beyond the answer to the question and elaborate on their findings and observations.

Will anyone read my students' publications? To paraphrase a famous line, if they write, others will read. There are four potential audiences for your students' publications. First is their classmates who might use the publications for learning or reference information. Second is students in lower level grades who can use the materials for learning or reference. Third is parents who could benefit from the research from such projects as the cost per square inch of pizza that might be published in either a classroom or school newsletter. Fourth is anyone who surfs the web, visits the class web page, and reads the materials.

Should I encourage my students to produce multimedia projects since other teachers are doing it in their classes? The answer depends upon both your objective and your students' objective. If you have an objective that specifies the development of multimedia materials, then such a project is appropriate. For example, if you are teaching a high school speech class, it may be appropriate for your students to develop an electronic slide show as part of one or all of their speeches. If a hypertext document with links best communicates the information the students have generated, then a HyperStudio stack may be appropriate. Requiring students to create multimedia materials because the software is on the computer is as logical as requiring first graders to learn the history of computers before they learn keyboarding skills. The learning tasks should have a purpose and support the achievement of an objective.

NTeQ Model
▲▲▲

Publishing can be part of the results presentation step in most lesson plans (see Figure 11-38).

Figure 11-38   NTeQ Model

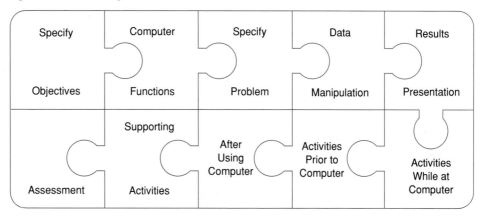

Jump Start

Since publishing can be a part of most lessons developed with the NTeQ model, we will describe some examples of how other lessons have incorporated publishing.

Books for Younger Students. A by-product of your students' research might be a book for younger students. For example, students who have researched animals might create an alphabet book for younger students that includes an animal for each letter and a brief description of the animal they created from their research. Similarly, students in a science class might create a series of science experiments for younger students based on class projects or science fair projects. Students can also create multimedia presentations for their classmates and lower level grades to share their results.

REPORTS FOR PARENTS. One theme for a classroom might be to produce a *Consumer Reports* style magazine during the year to report the results of their product testing. Students can conduct research incorporating math and science principles and report the results in their special bulletins or magazine. One example mentioned is calculating the cost of a square inch of pizza which uses the calculation of the areas of rectangles and circles. Other projects might include the evaluation of paper towels, price per ounce of selected types and sizes of laundry detergent, capacity of trash bags, and effectiveness of dish washing liquids. Students who have conducted surveys or studies such as the number of individuals wearing seat belts or the varieties of trees in a park might submit their reports to appropriate government agencies.

WEB PUBLISHING. Students can also publish their work on the school's web site. A visit to K–12 web sites will reveal a number of approaches to publishing student projects. Some schools publish a mixture of papers related to different grade levels and a variety of topics. Other schools focus on a specific theme for their papers. One secret to increasing the visibility and number of visitors to a web site is to provide information on related topics. For example, The University School of Nashville (http://www.university-sch.davidson.k12.tn.us/astronom) publishes student (grades 9–12) research papers and experiments in astronomy. Focusing on one theme or related themes allows students to both benefit and build on the work of other students, creating an additional advantage to the publishing activity.

RESOURCES
▲▲▲

HTML Style manuals:
http://info.med.yale.edu/caim/manual/contents.html
http://heasarc.gsfc.nasa.gov/0/docs/heasarc/Style_Guide/styleguide.html
http://www.sun.com/styleguide/

http://www.utoronto.ca/webdocs/HTMLdocs/NewHTML/intro.html
Tutorials:
http://www.ncsa.uiuc.edu/General/Internet/WWW/HTMLPrimer.html

Advanced HTML information:
http://webreference.com/html/
http://www.Stars.com/

REFERENCES
▲▲▲

Brookes, G. (1988). Exploring the world through reading and writing. *Language Arts, 65,* 245–253.

Corbine, M. (1995). The effective use of student journal writing. *ERIC Digest,* Bloomington, IN:ERIC/REC [ED378 587].

Johannessen, L. R. & Kahn, E. A. (1991). Writing across the curriculum. Paper presented at the Teachers' Institute, Summit, IL.

McBride, K. H. & Luntz, E. D. (1996). *Help, I have HyperStudio® . . . now what do I do?* Glendora, CA: McB Media.

Morrison, G. R. (1986). An investigation of the communicability of the emotional connotation of type. *Educational Communications and Technology Journal, 34* (4), 235–244.

Roger Wagner Publishing, Inc. (1995). *HyperStudio: Software for a Mediacentric World Tutorial.* El Cajon, CA: Roger Wagner Publishing, Inc.

Snyder, J. (1996). Good, bad and ugly pages. *Internet World* (April), 26–27.

CHAPTER 12

The Internet in the Classroom

▶ Introduction

The Internet—the greatest innovation in information technology since Johann Gutenberg's moveable type or a technological fad soon to go the way of opaque projectors and ditto machines? What started as a mechanism for a group of university researchers to communicate with one another now impacts information access world-wide. As of mid-1997, over 30 million people use the Net and these numbers increase dramatically every month (Georgia Institute of Technology, 1997).

Opponents and proponents are still arguing over issues of access, rights, and security, but the benefits and uses of the Internet for education are growing. Owston (1997) shows convincing evidence that the Internet can make education more attainable by more people, promote improved and new types of learning, and do both while containing the costs of education. Thousands of schools across the U.S. now have on-line access. The ConnecTen Project (Tennessee Department of Education, 1997) recently reached its goal of connecting every public school in the state to the Internet. This access project is just one example of hundreds now popping up around the country.

Gaining access to any technology is only the first step. Teacher training in Internet use and curriculum integration must occur hand-in-hand with the purchase of hardware and access if it is to be used successfully in schools (Siegel, 1995). Research has demonstrated repeatedly that teacher training is one of the most important (yet often neglected) aspects of technology implementation. This chapter provides some of the basics necessary to begin integrating the Internet into your curriculum.

▶ Computer Skills Used in This Chapter

E-mail
World Wide Web
FTPs
Gopher
Listservs
Newsgroups
Chat groups (IRC, MOOs, chat rooms)

▶ Key Topics

Internet Components
  The World Wide Web
  FTPs
  Gophers
  E-mail
  Listservs
  Newsgroups
  Chat Forums
Integrating the Internet into the Curriculum
The Internet as an Information Source
  Curriculum Guides for Teachers
  Information for Students
  Downloading Files
  Copyright Issues
The Internet for Collaboration
  Connecting with the Community
  Connecting with Other Schools
  Connecting with Experts
  Connecting with the World at Large
The Internet for Publishing
  School Web Pages
  Student Publications

Here are three main educational uses for the Internet. It serves as (1) a source of information, (2) a place for collaboration, and (3) a place to publish. Let's get acquainted with each of the components of the Internet. If you are already familiar with the Net, skip this section and move on to the final section called Integrating Internet into the Curriculum.

INTERNET COMPONENTS
▲▲▲

What exactly is the Internet and how does it differ from the World Wide Web? Think of the Internet as "the mother of networks." Linking computers together with a telephone line is known as a network. The Internet is the largest network, and all single computers and smaller networks can connect to it. In Figure 12-1, we see that the Internet encompasses many components including the World Wide Web (WWW), e-mail, File Transfer Protocols (FTPs), gophers, listservs, newsgroups, and chat forums.

Notice that the WWW overlaps with the other Internet components. This overlap occurs because of the recent development of "web browsers"—web viewing software that handles access to multiple Internet components. Just a few years ago, you needed separate software to access each Internet component separately; it was not very user friendly. As web viewing software becomes even more savvy, we will continue to see a blurring of the boundaries of various Internet components and functions.

THE WORLD WIDE WEB
▲▲▲

The World Wide Web (WWW) began as a means for a group of scientists to "converse" with one another. It has now developed into the largest public forum for disseminating all kinds of information. Web sites currently number in the millions, so it is easy to see why the WWW has become the number one source for the latest information on almost any topic.

Figure 12-1   The Internet

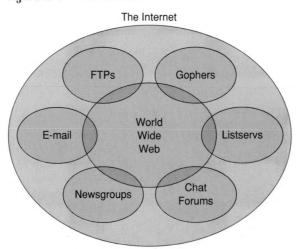

Figure 12-2   WWW Page

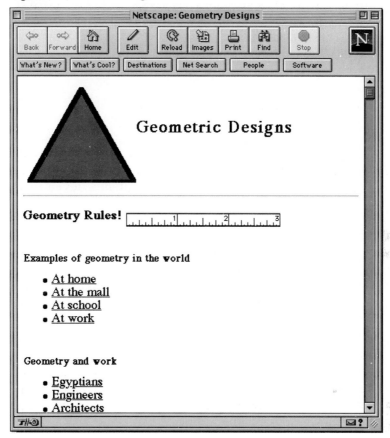

Courtesy of Gary Morrison.

The WWW consists of graphics-based pages (see Figure 12-2) containing colored "links" that allow you to jump from one page to another with one click. Many pages contain sound bites, video clips, or live images, and some have interactive capabilities. Web sites offer exciting educational opportunities for teachers and students. Let's examine some of the terms often associated with the WWW (see Figure 12-3).

BROWSERS.   The web is accessed with software known as a browser. Netscape and Microsoft Internet Explorer are two of the most popular browsers. Let's take a look at the tool bar on Netscape to see how a browser operates (see Figure 12-4).

Clicking on the **Back** button takes you to the previous web pages you accessed, one page at a time. Similarly, **Forward** works in the same manner, taking you forward along a path you've been traveling. The **Home** button takes you to the first page that loads up each time you start the browser. The Home site is usually defaulted to go to the browser's home page unless you change the default location. **Edit** is used to perform editing functions when developing your own web sites in

Figure 12-3   WWW Terminology

TERM	DEFINITION
Browser	Software that enables viewing of web pages and launches applications. Examples include Netscape and Microsoft Explorer.
Download	Transfering files from another computer to your computer.
Upload	Transfering files from your computer to another computer.
URL (uniform resource locator)	An address of a web site. These addresses begin with prefixes such as http, ftp, gopher, or telnet. For example, http://www.xyz.com.
HTTP (hypertext transfer protocol)	A URL prefix that indicates an address of a web page.
Link	A colored text or graphic you click on to jump to another page.
HTML (hypertext markup language)	The language used to create web pages; recent web authoring programs are WSYWIG (what you see is what you get), so it's unnecessary to learn HTML for most web publishing purposes.
Search engines	Tools that allow you to search for information on the web (see Chapter 13).
Plug-ins	Small applications downloaded to your computer that allow you to view special effects on the web.
FAQ (frequently asked questions)	Many web sites contain an FAQ link. It's an easy way to get an overview of what the site has to offer.

Figure 12-4   Netscape Tool Bar

Netscape. Clicking **Reload** refreshes the current page you're on. This is often help-ful when you are looking at video clips that update every 30 seconds, for example. The **Images** button allows you the option of turning off the ability to download graphics on web pages. This option is helpful if you are in a hurry or using a modem for your Internet connection. When you click **Print,** the browser will dis-play the printer dialog. **Find** lets you conduct a search for specific words on a given web page. Searching a single page is helpful if the site is long and you want to get directly to a specific part. **Stop** is definitely one of the most useful buttons on the

Power Tip ▲▲▲   *Locating Plug-Ins*

The following URLs offer up-to-date lists of all recent plug-ins and a little information about each. BrowserWatch illustrates what the plug-in looks like in action.

Real TV Links
http://www.realtv1.com/tools. html

B&B's Download Plug-Ins
http://www.bbp. com/plugins.html
BrowserWatch Plug
http://browser.watch. lworld.com/plug-In.html

tool bar. You can click Stop during a search or download and the browser will quit downloading or searching at that moment. This feature is most useful when your computer seems to get stuck trying to find a location, or you decide you don't want to wait for an entire page to download.

PLUG-INS. Plug-ins are small applications that you download to your computer to view special effects on web sites. You can watch and hear a video interview, interact in three dimensions, or take advantage of special color effects. Some of the most popular plug-ins include Shockwave, RealAudio, and QuickTime. Once you have taken the time to download a plug-in to view a particular web site, you need only download it again when there is an update.

FTPs

File Transfer Protocol (FTP) refers to the process of downloading a file to your computer. Downloading copies a file from the memory of one computer to the memory of another. Some files that are often accessed via FTP include journal articles, software, books, and song lyrics. As a teacher, you can see the potential value of FTP. For example, if you are trying to locate information for parents about the use of whole language, you can access an article on-line and print it out to share with them. Several years ago, the only way to FTP was to use a special software, such as Turbo Gopher. However, most current web browsers now access sites designated as FTP and download the files. In fact, many users are often unaware that web links they click on are actually FTP sites. See Chapter 13 for search tools that assist in locating FTP sites.

GOPHERS

Before the advent of web browsers, gophers were used to locate information over computer networks. The name "gopher" referred to the notion of a rodent navigating its way through a series of tunnels. Gophers, which look much like a collection of folders (see Figure 12-5), are an older way of organizing and presenting files over the Internet. However, many ERIC (Educational Resources Information Center) files are still organized with gophers, so educators should be familiar with their format. As with FTPs, gopher menus can be accessed using web browsers.

Figure 12-5   Gopher Menu

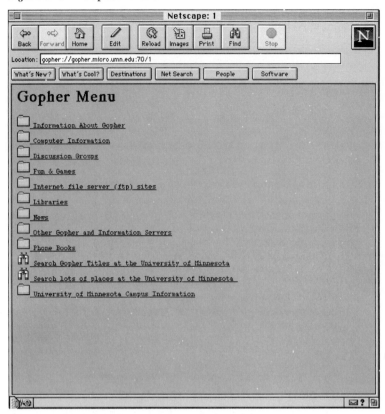

Source: University of Minnesota. Used by permission.

E-MAIL

Most computer users are now familiar with the concept of electronic mail (e-mail). E-mail software allows users to send messages electronically through phone lines from their computer to another computer. Again, most popular web browsers have the ability of sending and receiving e-mail. Most users, however, prefer to use a dedicated application such as Eudora or Emailer to send and receive their e-mail. To send a message using e-mail, you must have an e-mail account. These can be obtained through Internet Service Providers (ISPs) such as those offered by AT&T, Sprint, your local telephone or cable TV company, or through educational institutions.

Once you have configured your e-mail application of choice, locate the "New Message" feature and begin typing your message. Figure 12-6 shows an example of an e-mail message written using Eudora.

E-mail messages consist of four main parts:

1. The e-mail address of the person(s) to whom the message is being sent.

2. The subject of the message (while this can be left blank, it's better to put in a two or three word subject).

Figure 12-6   E-mail Message Using Eudora

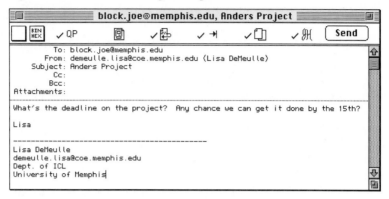

3. The body of the message.

4. The signature (optional depending on how you want yourself identified to the reader).

E-MAIL ADDRESSES.   E-mail addresses are easy to differentiate from web addresses (URLs) because they always include an "at" sign, @, in the address. A typical address might look like:

> block.joe@memphis.edu

The first part of the address (block.joe) is known as the *username*. It may or may not contain a period. This part of the address lets a server know the specific person who is to receive the message. The second half of the address (memphis.edu) is known as the *domain name*. The domain name indicates which network is to receive the message. In this case, a user known as Joe Block would be receiving a message through the server located at an educational institution in Memphis. We know it is an educational institution because of the suffix ".edu." Other common suffixes include .com (commercial), .gov (government), .mil (military), .org (nonprofit organization), and .net (ISP). To locate a user's e-mail address, try the Lookup directory described in Chapter 13.

SUBJECT OF MESSAGE.   Include a one to three word description of the content of your message. Often these are left blank. However, this can be a mistake, especially if the person to whom you're sending the message isn't familiar with you. Many people subscribe to listservs and as a result receive numerous e-mail messages. If a subject title is missing, they might assume it is a message from the listserv and delete it without ever having read it.

BODY OF MESSAGE.   The body of the message is typed in the large window. The beauty of e-mail is that is can be short and sweet without being socially inappropriate. In fact, unless you are writing to your mother, most readers of e-mail prefer short, concise messages. Be aware that typing in all capital letters is equivalent to shouting.

Power Tip ▲▲▲   *Replying to E-mail*

When replying to e-mail, it often makes sense to include a portion of the original message you received. Readers are often irritated by other users who copy the *entire* message when a single line or two is all that is needed. In Emailer, for example, highlight the text you want to copy to the new message and then click Reply. The message is automatically pasted into your new e-mail message with a leading character such as ">". For example, if we quoted the first line of this tip it would appear as follows in the reply message:

>When replying to e-mail, it often makes sense to include a portion of the
>original message you received.

The greater than sign (>) signals the reader that the line or lines are a quote from a previous message.

THE SIGNATURE. The final part of an e-mail message is the signature. You can enter a signature each time a message is sent, or the e-mail application can do it automatically by setting your preferences. Although it may not make a difference on personal e-mail, for work related messages always include:

Your name:	Joe Block
Your place of employment:	Dept. of Instruction & Curriculum
	The University of Memphis
Reply address:	block.joe@memphis.edu

The following steps describe how to add your signature automatically to all e-mail messages when using Emailer.

1. Select **Signatures** from the **Setup** menu.

2. Select your account from the **Signature** list and double-click the name.

3. Emailer will display an edit field where you can enter your signature. That signature will be automatically appended to all your e-mail messages. You can add an extra return at the top of your signature to separate it from your message.

LISTSERVS

A listserv provides a forum for a group of people to exchange e-mail about a particular topic. Listservs are social, educational, or informational in nature. Lists are open (available to the general public) or closed (open only to specific members). There are lists specifically for teachers and lists available only to students.

All participation in lists is handled via e-mail, although it is possible to find and subscribe to lists over the web. See Chapter 13 for references on where to locate a list that might interest you.

SUBSCRIBING/UNSUBSCRIBING TO A LIST. Technically, a *listserv* is a computer server that handles the functions of running a list. The *list* is the members who comprise the discussion group. The listserv has an e-mail address that is different from the

Figure 12-7   Subscribing to a List

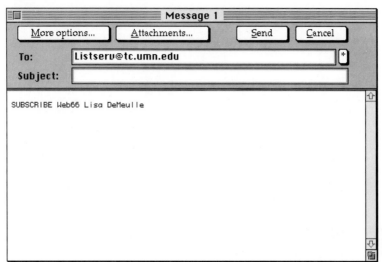

address used to send messages to group members. You only subscribe to a list once. Subscribe to a list by sending an e-mail to the listserver.

For example, Figure 12-7 provides an example of how to subscribe to the list Web66, a list for K–12 educators using the web in the classroom.

Note that, in the **TO:** window, the message is being sent to the listserv. Most listserv addresses use this format to distinguish the *listserv address* from the *list address*. Leave the subject heading blank. In the body of the message type the word "subscribe," along with the name of the list and your name, as in the example. If your subscription is successful, the listserv will send you an automated message giving details of how to communicate on the list. Be sure to print or save this e-mail for future reference. The procedure for unsubscribing is the same as this, but change the word "subscribe" to "unsubscribe."

SENDING MESSAGES TO THE LIST.   Once you have subscribed to a list, you are ready to participate. Begin your participation by lurking (reading without participating) to get a feel for the nature of the group. Once you are ready to participate, send messages to other participants using the *list* e-mail address. Do not use the *listserv* address to send messages to specific people on the list.

For example, to send messages to the members of Web66, use the address:

WEB66@TC.UMN.EDU

NEWSGROUPS

Newsgroups also provide a forum for exchanging ideas on a multitude of topics. However, they differ from lists in that messages sent using e-mail are posted to an electronic bulletin board rather than received via e-mail (see Figure 12-8). These

Figure 12-8   Example of a Newsgroup

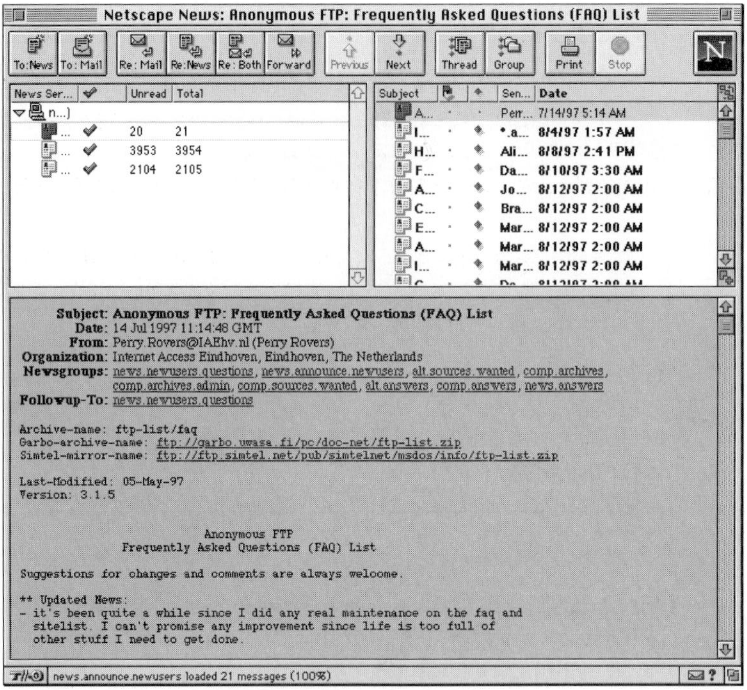

Courtesy of Netscape Communications Corporation.

bulletin boards are accessible only through the web or by using a newsgroup software program such as InterNews. One of the most popular newsgroups for educators is K–12.chat.teacher. Newsgroups are also becoming popular for kids, although these may or may not be appropriate for your classroom. Again, see Chapter 13 for information on where to find newsgroups of interest to you.

CHAT FORUMS

Chat forums differ from e-mail, newsgroups, and listservs in that the "chat" or talk occurs in real-time. Similar to a telephone call, chat forums provide users the opportunity to "talk" with users stationed at other computers. As text is entered on one screen, it simultaneously appears on other users' screens, and they can immediately respond in a conversation format. There are several different means of chatting using the Internet. Some of the more popular forms include IRC (Internet Relay Chat), Telnet-based chat (such as MUDs and MOOs), web-based chat, chat plug-ins, and CU-See Me (Bremser, 1997).

INTERNET RELAY CHAT.   IRC is a text-based chat model and probably the least popular form of communication for educators. Access to IRC requires a free program that you may have received as part of your initial software package. Use of IRC re-

Power Tip ▲▲▲   *Internet Relay Chat*

See http://www.kei.com/irc.html for access to a good IRC FAQ. Once you have loaded an IRC "client" on your computer, begin by opening an active window, type **/list** for a list of channels (conversation groups), and try **/help** when you need a list of commands.

quires some time and exploration to become familiar with various commands and modes of operation, but for those more technologically sophisticated, it offers customization capabilities that users might find handy.

TELNET-BASED CHAT. Telnet allows you to directly log on to another computer or server. Access to Telnet is usually provided by your ISP. Using Telnet, you are able to participate in chat forums such as MOOs (Multiple user dimension Object Oriented).

We feel that Telnet is slightly more user-friendly than IRC for communication, and the MOO forums offer the extra advantage of creating a three-dimensional world through text. Users can move "north, south, east, and west" and can go to different rooms or locations such as a train station that then transports them to another city. MOOs can be social, academic, and theme-based, and several MOOs cater to teachers and students.

WEB-BASED CHAT. Web-based chat is among the newer and most exciting forms of real-time conversation on the Internet. It's easier to use and access than Telnet or IRC because it is available over the web, but at this point its use is limited in education. A nice example of web-based chat for students is Homework Heaven where students can get help with homework in different content areas by "chatting" with homework experts. Using software such as WebBoard, WebCT, or Web in a Box, educators are now creating on-line sites for chatting and posting messages around a given topic. Teachers can put syllabi, assignments, and tests for students to access at the same location. To see an example of WebBoard used in teacher education, go

Power Tip ▲▲▲   *MOOs*

Locating MOOs
http://www.yahoo.com
http://www.pitt.edu/~jrgst7/MOOcentral.
   html#header1
http://www4.ncsu.edu/~asdamick/www/moo.
   html

Using MOOs
Begin by finding a MOO of interest, log on, and follow the preprogrammed set of directions for navigating and participating on the MOO. If you are interested in teaching your students to use MOOs, there is a specially designed MOO just for that purpose. See Diversity University MOO at telnet://moo.du.org :8888

to http://www.coe.memphis.edu/ and click on *On-line WebBoard Conferences*. We are convinced, though, that it won't be long before web-based chat develops to serve additional useful purposes in education.

CHAT PLUGS-INS. Chat plug-ins are gaining in popularity. A popular one used by teachers is Global Chat at http://arachnid.qdeck.com/chat/schedule.html. It's free and easy to use, especially for those who don't have access to IRC or Telnet.

CU-SEE ME. CU-See Me is a video software program that allows users to see each other as they talk. Each user must have the program loaded on their hard drive as well as a small camera attached to their computer. Students in different parts of the country and the world are able to hook up and see one another as they communicate, and more than two groups can participate at once. Get more information at http://www.gsn.org/.

INTEGRATING THE INTERNET INTO THE CURRICULUM

▲▲▲

In the recent past, only teachers who were techno-wizards would have considered integrating the Internet into their curriculum. Now, as schools and classrooms gain access to the Information Superhighway, the next step after becoming acquainted with the various components of the Net is to use it effectively as a part of the learning process. There are several ways teachers can begin using the Internet in their instruction.

1. Obtain ready-to-use Internet curriculum materials.
2. Rework existing lesson plans to incorporate aspects of the Internet.
3. Develop Internet curriculum materials from scratch.

As more teachers gain access to the Internet, many companies are offering lesson plans and strategies for using the Internet as a part of instruction. While these materials may not be specific to your grade level or particular topic, they offer an excellent starting place for the novice Internet user. You can adapt many of the lesson plans to your particular context. You will find Internet lesson plans in several places—published books, curriculum guides, columns in teacher's journals such as *Instructor* and on-line. *Classroom Connect* specializes in Internet curriculum.

As you expand your use of the Internet and its potential use in your classroom, we'd like to offer some helpful hints for reworking some of your existing lesson plans. First, there are particular types of lessons that lend themselves to incorporating the Internet (Classroom Connect, 1997):

- comparing and classifying
- inducing/deducing
- analyzing errors
- abstraction
- analyzing perspectives

Power Tip ▲▲▲   *Internet Curriculum Materials*

Check the following resources to get ready-to-use Internet curriculum materials.

JOURNALS

MultiMedia Schools

Classroom Connect

Electronic Learning, The Magazine for Technology & School Change

http://www.scholastic.com/public/EL/EL.html

BOOKS

The Online Classroom, (Cotton, 1997)

NetLearning: Why Teachers Use the Internet, (Serim & Koch, 1996)

The Internet Kids Yellow Pages, (Polly, 1996)

Teaching Social Studies with the Internet, (Classroom Connect, 1997)

Teaching Grades K–12 with the Internet, (Classroom Connect, 1997)

Internet Curriculum Planning System, (Classroom Connect, 1997)

ON-LINE

Kidlink	gopher://kids.ccit.duq.edu
NASA K–12	gopher://quest.arc.nasa.gov
SchoolNet	gopher://schoolnet.carleton.ca
Scholastic Net	gopher://scholastic.com
Teachnet.Com	http://www.teachnet.com/lesson.html
World School	http://www.bell-atl.com/wschool/
The Faculty Lounge	http://www.naples.net/media/wsfp/lounge.htm
Classroom Connect	http://www.classroom.net/classroom/default1.html

- information gathering
- team building

The Internet is an excellent tool for locating the latest news not yet published elsewhere (such as voting results, weather information, or economic information), information from a personal perspective (such as parent or expert opinions about childcare issues), governmental data, and specialized information (Serim & Koch, 1996). However, do not count on the Internet to offer much help when you need information fast on a general topic. You are better off checking the encyclopedia.

Second, start small and continue integrating the Internet slowly into your teaching. Do not expect to include the Internet in every lesson or to revamp your curriculum overnight. The process of learning to rework curriculum to incorporate technology may continue over several years. Starting with one unit, search for on-line resources that you might incorporate as a part of the lesson. As you gain skills, have your students use the Internet for gathering their own information, to communicate with experts in subject areas, or to develop your own Internet project.

Once you and your students are involved in the Internet, it does not take long before you're ready to develop your own materials and projects. Examples include units developed from the ground up, a collaborative on-line project, or an on-line student publication. Before attempting any new venture on the Net, spend some time familiarizing yourself with the medium to avoid pitfalls.

In the following section, we describe three ways for teachers to think about the Internet as a potential part of their curriculum: (1) as a source of information, (2) as a means of collaboration and communication, and (3) as a place to publish.

The Internet as an Information Source

Many users would consider the greatest strength of the Internet to be the amount and types of information available at the touch of a mouse button. This information can influence a teacher's thinking about a given topic, provide a handout for a class, or serve as a source of data for students. The possibilities for using this information are limitless.

Mike Morrison is a middle school teacher of science and mathematics. Although his school has no direct access to the Internet, he was intrigued with the medium and decided to explore a way to integrate the Net into his curriculum. He began by participating in a newsgroup for K–12 teachers, k12.chat.teacher, at home in the evening. Through the bulletin board, he heard about an on-line project called "Fantasy Hoops" that was just getting started. Fantasy Hoops was a competition among classrooms wherein students chose NBA basketball players to create their own fantasy team. Each players' stats would be posted for the week, which Mike then downloaded from home to take back to the classroom. He then taught statistical concepts such as mean, medium, mode, and scatterplots using the basketball players' statistics. His students were very motivated and engaged in the project and learned statistics in a real and authentic way. Due to the response of his students, and the meaningful learning that occurred in his classroom, Mike was encouraged to continue integrating the Net into his curriculum. The following section describes some additional ways that the Internet can serve as an informational database for teachers and students.

Curriculum Guides for Teachers

One of the easiest ways for teachers to incorporate the Internet into their curriculum is to create *curriculum resource guides*. These guides can include things such as reference materials, class handouts, maps and charts, or lists of web sites appropriate to your topic. Curriculum resource guides can either be centered around particular content area subjects or by Internet tools. Do what makes the most sense for your curriculum.

For example, let's say you would like to start a resource guide for science or perhaps a specific topic in science such as plant anatomy. Obtain a binder with tab dividers or use an accordion folder. Next, decide how to categorize the information you collect. Will you categorize by unit topics such as types of plants, ani-

Students gathering information for their Internet search.

mals, weather, and the food chain? Or will you divide it up by Internet tools such
as web sites, listservs, e-mail, and newsgroups? Once you have decided upon the
organization, start searching for information appropriate to your topic. At a minimum, keep a list of appropriate URLs with a short description of what the site has
to offer. It's also helpful to print a copy off the web site itself (or newsgroup posting, etc.), and include it in your binder. For future reference, always make sure to
put the URL on each printed piece. Make your curriculum resource guides available to students or other teachers. Kathy Roemer, director of an early childhood
education center, made an Internet resource guide of important information for
parents. Some of her categories included local resources for parents, information
on developmentally appropriate practice, and nutrition. Keep adding to your curriculum guides over the years. It's also helpful to create an index for the binder and
each section to give the user a quick overview of the contents.

Information for Students

Once you have explored different aspects of the Internet, you are ready to get your
students involved in the fun. What kind of information is available over the Net?
Almost anything you can imagine! Students can collect factual, geographical, and
historical information, personal opinions on any topic, currency conversion tables,
travel information, photographs, paintings, video clips, and sound bites. The list
goes on and on.

Because the amount of information available on the Internet is truly overwhelming, you need to establish limits or guidelines as to the manner in which students can locate information. With younger children, it might be appropriate to
bookmark one or two sites to visit for a specific purpose (see Chapter 13). For

older students with more access or exposure to the Internet, you might offer guide-lines such as time constraints for Internet use, a specific list of web sites they can visit, or a particular listserv you will allow them to join.

DOWNLOADING FILES

There are several ways to download or obtain information off the Internet. Users can print a copy of the web page, copy and paste text, save graphics, or download files to their hard drive. Printing a copy of the web page is done the same as in word processing programs. Choose **Print item** from the **File** menu.

COPYING AND PASTING TEXT. Similar to copying and pasting text in a word pro-cessing program, users can copy and paste text from most Internet applications to other applications such as word processing programs or spreadsheets. To do so, highlight the text you wish to copy and choose the **Copy** item from the **Edit** menu. The text is then saved to the clipboard until you are ready to paste it into another document.

SAVING GRAPHICS. The web has wonderful graphics for teachers and students to use. Angela Settles, an inner-city second grade teacher, downloaded professional photographs of African-American children and had them enlarged to portrait size. She used these to create a "Photo Gallery" in her classroom, which she tied into a social studies unit she was conducting on Black Awareness. To save a graphic from the web, place the mouse pointer on top of the graphic, click and hold the mouse button. A menu, such as the one in Figure 12-9, appears offering you the option to **Save this image as . . . .**

By choosing this option, you are presented with a dialogue box that lets you save the graphic to your hard drive in the same manner as you would save any file. It only takes a few seconds to save a graphic. You can then open the graphic with

---

Power Tip ▲▲▲

To locate just about anything you'd like to download, including browsers, plug-ins, com-munication tools, page creation tools, applica-tions, multimedia, patches, and software, go to one of several software sites:

http://www.download.com
http://www.shareware.com
http://www.pccomputing.com

Many files are downloaded as a compressed or "stuffed" file. Your computer automatically

Downloading and Unstuffing

unstuffs the file if you have a small software program located on your hard drive that per-forms this function. StuffIt Expander is a com-monly used program for this purpose on Mac-intosh. See:

http://www.aladdinsys.com/consumer/
    expander2.html
http://www.covis.nwu.edu/tech-support/
    expander.html

Figure 12-9   Saving a Graphic

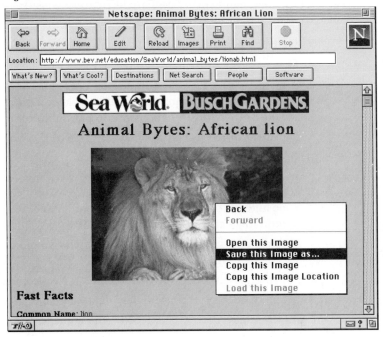

Courtesy of Sea World Orlando.

your browser or one of several graphics applications. Most graphic files are saved in a GIF file format that some graphic applications cannot open. However, you can open it on your browser and then copy and paste the image into another application such as a word processor. As an alternative, you can select **Copy this image** and then paste it into most documents.

DOWNLOADING FILES.   To download a file, open the browser, locate the file of your choice, and click on the link. Instead of seeing a new page as you would when linking to a new web site, your computer begins downloading the file to your desktop or download folder. Your computer automatically converts the file into a useable format if you have installed the proper software.

COPYRIGHT ISSUES

As with any medium that is public domain, copyright of Internet material is an issue. Copyright protects an author's work from being stolen by someone else or being used in a way that the author is uncomfortable with, such as using a graphic in curriculum materials. All information published on the Internet is technically copyrighted, even though the copyright may not be visible with the work. So, what can be copied off the Internet freely? What needs permission of the author?

The law allows for "fair use" of copyrighted material (Crawford, 1993). Educational uses and newsworthy uses are likely to be considered fair use. Factors considered in fair use include the following.

1. The purpose and character of the use, including profit.
2. The character of the copyrighted work.
3. How much of the work is used: not more than one copy per student; 250 words or less of a poem; a complete article or 2,500 words or less; excerpts of 500–1000 words; one illustration per publication.
4. The effect of the use on the market value of the work.

The following guidelines also apply to classroom use.

1. The copies may be used for only one course in the school.
2. Same author copies may not exceed more than one article or two excerpts, or more than three from a collection of works.
3. Multiple copying for one course is limited to a maximum of nine instances during the term.
4. Copying may not be used to substitute for collections of works.
5. You may not copy "consumable" materials such as workbooks.
6. Students may not be charged for the copied material, other than photocopying costs.

Therefore, it is permissible to download and/or use the materials below as long as you address the above constraints.

- shareware (as long as you pay the shareware fee if you continue using the application after the demonstration time period)
- icons and/or graphics specifically offered for downloading
- other files, such as a 1,500-word article, or a 200-word song lyric
- a graphic copied only for use in a class report
- Each copy should include a notice of copyright.

The following would be examples of copyright infringement:

- Placing another person's graphic or photograph on your web page.
- Copying text and including it in curriculum materials from which you or others gain profit.
- Copying icons not specifically created to be shared publicly.

To obtain permission to reproduce copyrighted material, contact the author (easy to do as most authors give e-mail addresses on their web pages) indicating how the material will be used, what credit they would like to be given, and what payment they would like, if any. Getting a signature should avoid problems with future legal actions (see Crawford, 1993, for further guidance).

INTERNET FOR COLLABORATION

▲▲▲

One of the greatest strengths of the Net is its ability to extend learning beyond the four walls of a classroom and get students involved in collaborative efforts. Teachers and students can get connected with their community, other schools, experts, and people and sites around the world. Through these collaborations, students become more aware of the global nature of information and discover the importance of connecting with others in the pursuit of knowledge.

CONNECTING WITH THE COMMUNITY

To connect yourself and your students with the local community, consider how different Internet tools can help. For example, does the mayor have an e-mail address? Is there a local newsgroup for your city? What types of information do local businesses provide over the web? What types of information or services can your school offer to the community through a school web site? The more you explore local Internet resources, the more your thinking will be stimulated about how to connect with the community through cyberspace.

PARTNERS IN BUSINESS. Many schools now work in partnership, or have been adopted by local businesses. The Internet can provide wonderful support for these partnerships through web sites. Students' work, photos, and letters can be posted to the web site. Students and employees might choose to exchange questions and answers via e-mail. Or students can conduct inquiry projects about their local business partners.

COMMUNITY PROJECT SUPPORT. Students at Highland Middle School decided they wanted to participate in a local recycling project. In order to garner community support, they put out notices over the Internet asking for neighbors and parents to bring their recyclables to the school. They posted to a local area newsgroup and posted a notice on the school's web page. Parents and neighbors got involved by the hundreds, and students were able to see that their efforts made a difference in the community. Log on to Hamilton Elementary School's web page (http://www.memphis-schools.k12.tn.us/schools/hamilton.es/home.htm) in Memphis, Tennessee, to see another example of how schools can reach out to the community over the web.

LOCAL SOURCES OF INFORMATION. You can help students become aware of their greater community by tracking local sources of information available over the Internet. For example, are there web pages for the police and fire departments? Can students e-mail local school board members? Do the local colleges and universities have web sites? Each of these local informational sources can be integrated into units that teachers teach every day.

CONNECTING WITH OTHER SCHOOLS

Students get *excited* when they have the opportunity to connect with students from other schools. Whether they are collaborating for the purposes of knowing more about each other's geographical location, for sharing student work, to learn more about a specific culture, or to participate in a larger on-line project, getting connected with other kids is fun for teachers and students alike. If you are hesitant to start a collaboration with another school, start by communicating one-on-one with a teacher who might be posting in a newsgroup. Once you get a sense of one another, you might find a possibility for some type of on-line collaboration.

If you have a project in mind and would like to find another teacher who's interested in working with you, try the following suggestions.

1. Determine whether you want a local or long-distance collaboration. If local check the school district's web site. Most larger districts now have web pages and often include a section for teachers wanting to collaborate.

2. If you are seeking a long-distance collaboration, determine the grade level and geographic location and post a message on a K–12 bulletin board.

3. Check publications such as *Classroom Connect*. They have a section devoted to teachers seeking collaborative partners.

TIPS FOR ON-LINE PROJECTS. There are a variety of on-line projects that lend themselves to classrooms. These include competitions, on-line conferences and correspondence, information gathering, and interactive writing. With on-line projects, students can extend their learning beyond the four walls of the classroom. They begin to develop an appreciation for the opinions of others and become connected to the larger global community.

After spending a while participating in on-line projects, think about developing one of your own! Here are some suggestions for making your project successful (Classroom Connect, 1997; Serim & Koch, 1996).

Power Tip ▲▲▲   *Finding On-Line Collaborators*

WEB SITES

Global SchoolNet Foundation, http://www.gsn.org

Scholastic Center, http://scholastic.com:2005

Classroom Connect, http://www.classroom.net/classroom/default1.html

NEWSGROUPS

alt.education.distance

alt.education.Email-project

k12.chat.teacher

misc.education

MAILING LISTS

Kidsphere, subscribe to kidsphere-request@vms.cis.pitt.edu

Middle-L, subscribe to listserv@listserv.net

1. Be specific about the goals of your project. What do you want to accomplish?

2. Plan your design to include specific tasks and outcomes that support your goals. Assign responsibilities appropriately. Older students may be able to handle much of technological aspects of project management.

3. Create a timeline that includes a beginning and ending date. Consider the flow of the school year calendar.

4. Locate your participants several weeks before the beginning date—do it too early and people will drop out, too late and you may not find enough participants. Post notices on K–12 listservs with calls for participation. Be explicit about the project goals, tasks, deadlines, grade levels, etc.

5. Keep in touch with participants!! They need to be updated during the project as well as thanked and informed of the results at the conclusion. Encourage them to share the results with their school and larger community.

CONNECTING WITH EXPERTS

Add spice to your lessons by letting your students contact experts on given topics. These connections can be a one-time event, or they can grow into on an on-going collaboration. Reference the list of experts below for given content areas, or find your own "expert" on a given topic. For example, if you're studying animals in a second grade classroom, find a veterinarian or zookeeper who might be willing to correspond via e-mail with your students. These contacts only require an e-mail program, so even if your school isn't yet wired to the Net, compose a query as a classroom and then send the message from your home. Reconsider who counts as an expert. Look beyond professionals and Ph.D.s, and don't forget to include people who have first hand experience with the subject matter. For example, if you're studying the Civil Rights Movement, check with the Civil Rights Museum in Memphis, Tennessee, to locate an "expert" who may have been present the day Martin Luther King Jr. was assassinated.

Power Tip ▲▲▲   *Project Addresses*

Try some of these URLs to find a project of interest to your class:

K-12 Net
www.vivanet.com/freenet/k12Net/channels.html

NASA's Internet in the Classroom
quest.arc.nasa.gov/interactive.html

IECC-Projects
http://www.stolaf.edu/network/iecc/iecc-projects.html

Global SchoolNet Foundation
http://www.gsn.org

Academy One
http://www.nptn.org/cyber.serv/AOneP/academy_one/project-index.html

Teacher assisting students with an Internet publication.

CONNECTING WITH THE WORLD AT LARGE

With the recent widespread use of the Internet, we have truly become a global community. The opportunity to connect with the world at large has never been greater than before. Here are some examples of teachers and students reaching out:

- Maya Quest (http://www.mecc.com/mayaquest.html) is a continuing journey that involves students communicating via the web and e-mail with a team of five explorers as they bicycle through Mesoamerica over a six week period. Over 1 million students have helped guide the team as they investigate the ancient Mayan civilization. This year's emphasis is on discovering lost Mayan cities.

- Global SchoolNet (http://www.gsn.org/kid/sa/index.html) offers a Student Ambassadors Program where students have the chance to explore ways the Internet can improve the learning environment, learn about other cultures around the world, and share work through on-line publishing and video conferencing. Students ages 6–18 years are eligible to participate.

- One of the authors of this book sought teacher keypals for a graduate class she teaches on Internet integration. After posting a call for participation in several K–12 newsgroups, she received over 40 responses from teachers around the world, including Australia, Germany, Canada, England, and the

Bahamas. Needless to say, her students were enthusiastic about having a key-pal from another part of the world and were motivated to keep up the correspondence.

THE INTERNET FOR PUBLISHING
▲▲▲

Why and what do teachers and students publish on the web? We now see thousands of examples of school and classroom home pages, lesson plans, and other student-driven projects. These projects include student-authored books and stories, surveys with students collecting the data, interactive quizzes designed for other students, and newsletters on specific topics. We are just beginning to understand the larger educational potential of web publishing. In Chapter 11 we discussed the mechanisms by which you can publish on the Web. In this section we look at some examples of how teachers have integrated web publishing in the curriculum.

SCHOOL WEB PAGES

Becky Birdsong, a first grade teacher at Ross Elementary School (http://206.23.148.16/SCS/elementary/Ross/default.html) in Memphis, Tennessee, decided to develop web pages for her school (see Figure 12-10).

Here she describes the process she went through to achieve a set of school web pages.

I began by looking at many home pages on the Internet. I studied size and style of writing, layout of information and kind of information displayed. I discovered many features were possible, but I wasn't quite sure how to do the same thing. I played and learned . . . and gained ideas from readings. I decided I wanted to include pictures of our school, administration, and faculty. I had to design my layout. I wanted a main page with four linking sections: administration, staff, special programs, and PTA. I felt these were the important aspects to cover about our school. I tried to keep color and design uniform throughout the home page. I wanted it to be easy to read and not too "busy" as I have seen on many pages. Everything seemed to flow together as I continued to work.

Figure 12-10 Ross Elementary School Web Page

Courtesy of Ross Elementary School.

Note the types of links Becky found important to her school. You should be willing to adjust your school web pages to support the greater context of your school and community. As time has gone on, Becky continues to learn and continuously update her school's pages.

> I have already revised the home page two times, and realize that this will be an ongoing project with frequent revisions. I want to include a calendar of our school year with special events. I also want to include a student section where student work can be included.

STUDENT PUBLICATIONS

As teachers become more comfortable with the Internet, many get involved in publishing and many more take the next step to consider how their students can connect with others through web publishing. Just to give you an idea of what's possible when it comes to students publishing their own work on the web, look at some of these real life examples that we've come across.

- Many kids are getting involved in publishing newspapers and magazines. *Children's Express* (http://www.ce.org/) is a news service produced by kids on the

Power Tip ▲▲▲   *School Web Pages*

For examples of other school and classroom web pages:

Classroom Web

http://www.classroom.net/classweb/

Web 66 International School Director

http://web66.coled.umn.edu/schools.html

For tips on web page design considerations:

HTML Crash Course for Educators

http://k12.cnidr.org:90/htmlintro.html

A Beginner's Guide to HTML

http://www.ncsa.uiuc.edu/General/Internet/WWW/HTMLPrimer.html

issues that affect their lives. They also run opinion polls. *Midlink Magazine* (http://longwood.cs.ucf.edu:80/~MidLink/) is an electronic journal produced by middle school students. *Middlezine* (http://www.gsn.org/kid/kc/resources. html) is an on-line magazine created by eighth grade students at Hudson Middle School filled with student writings on fiction, poetry, opinions, and news.

• Consider working with your students to create information sites for other students. For example, Kathy Heller, a nationally recognized teacher of mathematics works at College Station Elementary School. She worked with her fourth grade students to create "The Moldy Oldies Collection" (http://www. ualr.edu/~klheller/moldy.html) web site (See Figure 12–11). Groups of students were required to research an ancient mathematician, write a report, and draw a portrait of the mathematician. These reports and pictures were put on-line. As a continuation of the project, the students created an interactive mathematics survey for kids which Kathy then put on-line.

• Mrs. Freeman's third grade class at Willow Accelerated Elementary School got involved in a real-world problem solving activity by exploring what hands-on community resources were available to families. After discovering a lack of resources, they decided to get in touch with local experts and the mayor. They conducted Internet surveys to brainstorm ideas for developing these family resources. After much input from the community over the Internet, the class proposed the idea of a children's museum. To learn more about their project, visit their web site at http://www.pekin.net/pekin108/willow/index.html.

Once you've decided to have your students publish on the web, involve them in all aspects of the process. Work together to outline the goals of the page. Let them

Figure 12-11   Moldy Oldies

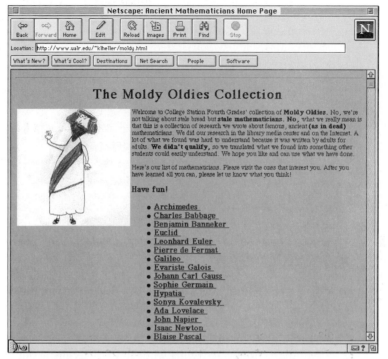

Source: College Station Elementary School. Used by permission.

serve in the roles of information gatherers, graphics collectors and scanners, page designers, layout artists, copywriters, etc. Have one group start by finding sample web pages they believe to be eye catching. Depending on the age level of the group, they may be able to handle much of the web publishing aspects themselves.

FRAN'S DIARY
▲▲▲

When I was introduced to the World Wide Web, I fell in love with it. It was so exciting to think that with a few simple commands, I could surf the world! I entered a Cybersurfari contest and spent many hours on the World Wide Web searching for hidden treasures. I would get up early in the morning and drink my cup of coffee at the computer as I surfed. I had so much fun and it was so interesting that I hated to have to stop. I'd go to school and think about all the places that I had visited. I could see how the World Wide Web could be integrated into the curriculum and wished that I had access at school. As soon as I would get home from school, I'd turn on my computer and try to surf while I cooked dinner. I became obsessed! The more places that I visited in my search for treasures, the more excited I became. Luckily for my family, the contest only lasted two weeks.

I had a wonderful time participating in the Cybersurfari contest and surfing the World Wide Web. I got far more from this experience than I ever expected. I was introduced to a new and powerful tool.

I was also taking a class at this time that dealt with using the Internet in Education, and I was required to do a final project. I could see the potential of using the Internet in the classroom and I wanted to share what I had found. I decided to write an Internet activity book for children for my final project. I wanted this book to be something that could be used by teachers and parents to introduce children to the World Wide Web in a safe environment. I wanted to be able to take children to the web sites that I had found and give them something to do that would allow them to use the information found at that web site. This book became a children's Internet ABC activity book.

I made some copies of the book and sent them home over Winter Break with some students and teachers that had Internet access. I wanted to get some feedback about the web sites and activities from a student's, parent's, and teacher's point of view. I got very positive reviews. Unfortunately, I was not able to use these books that year in my classroom, as I did not have access to the Internet at my school. I put them on my shelf and hoped that I would be able to use them someday.

Having an Internet connection in my classroom became number one on my wish list! After the Winter Break my principal asked me if I would be interested in writing a grant proposal for the State of Tennessee's ConnecTEN Project. If we received this grant, our school would become connected to the Internet that spring. Of course I said yes! I wrote the grant proposal and our school was chosen to become one of the ConnecTEN Schools.

We were connected to the Internet in March. Our project for this grant was to create a virtual field trip that would be exchanged with a partner class in East Tennessee. We decided that our virtual field trip would be a visit to our town's historic square and railroad display.

In preparation for this project, the students researched information about trains using library and Internet resources. They invited resource people into our classroom to share the history of our town square and information about trains. The students e-mailed information about their community back and forth with their partner class.

Students went on a field trip to the town square and railroad display. They took the digital and video cameras with them and took photos and videos of the old log cabin, the Civil War monument, the gazebo, the town square clock, the historic buildings that surround the square, and the insides of the different

Continued

railroad cars. They even recorded the sound of the town square clock striking and playing "Amazing Grace" and a train coming through town.

The students took all the information, photos, videos, and sounds they collected on their field trip back to school and created a virtual field trip. Their virtual field trip began as they walked out of the school to a waiting bus, continued as they walked around the Historic Town Square and through the Railroad Display, and ended as the they got off of the bus and walked back into the school building. They used Hyperstudio to create this virtual field trip.

They exchanged their field trip with their partner class. Their HyperStudio stack was compressed and sent as a Eudora Mail attachment through the Internet. It was a very exciting process. It was amazing to the students that they could send their HyperStudio stack from our school to another school across the state in such a short amount of time!

This was a great learning experience for the students. They learned to use a very powerful communication tool. They began to understand that through e-mail communication they could not only make new friends, but also share their community with another class without ever having to leave their classroom.

As you can see, my experiences with the Internet built slowly, one upon another. I have encountered many frustrations along the way, but the benefits my students receive almost always outweigh the negatives.

At the Classroom's Doorstep
▲▲▲
Questions Teachers Ask

I'm totally unfamiliar with the Internet and feel intimidated about using it with my students. Where should I start? Start slowly. Skip the on-line projects for now. Rather, begin by browsing the Web. Locate information that can help inform lessons you are currently teaching. Keep a record of the sites you visit. Or, get involved by reading some of the postings on the K–12 newsgroups. You don't have to respond until you feel comfortable. Finally, you may be inspired by checking web sites specifically developed for teachers, such as the *Classroom Connect Resource Station* at http://www.classroom.net/classroom/edulinks.html. By taking small steps, you will gain the confidence to keep going further.

My school only has one computer with Internet capability, and it's located in the library. How can I get my students involved when they have so little time available for surfing? Check Chapter 6 for tips on classroom management when integrating technology. Also, recall the case of Mike Morrison earlier in the chapter. He was able to involve his whole class in an on-line project by serving as a go-between. You might consider teaming up with teachers in other subject areas to keep students focused on one major project at a time. For example, if you teach science, team up with the math teacher to team teach a unit on gathering and plotting weather data.

I'm concerned about publishing students' photographs and/or work on the Internet. Do I need parental permission? Most school districts have now set policies regarding usage of the Internet. Some require parents to sign permission slips, others do not allow the publishing of photographs, and some publish photos but leave off the student's name. Find out the school and district policy.

Plug-ins seem confusing and a waste of time. Why would I want to use them with my students? Some teachers question the value or benefit of plug-ins, especially considering the time that might be involved to download a site using a plug-in. For example, to download a totally 3D interactive site on Stonehenge (http://www.superscape.com/intel/shenge.htm) can take up to twelve minutes, but the value of being able to "walk" through Stonehenge may be worth it to some educators. The initial installation of plug-ins can be handled in one or two afternoons after school. You may save class time by downloading time-consuming sites during recess, before school starts, or during transition times.

LESSON BYTES

- To study severe weather, post a notice to Kidsphere asking for personal accounts of those who have experienced severe weather such as a hurricane or tornado. Read the stories as a class and create a "Severe Weather Sites Map" that shows the location of each e-mail received (Serim & Koch, 1996).

- Integrate math and social studies by having students participate in a "Dream Vacation." Assign groups to a continent and assign a budget. Students must plan airfare, hotel, and food costs, and calculate currency exchange rates. They also have to plan the sights they want to visit, they have to know the language and customs of people, and they have to know what to expect in terms of weather. Have them present their findings in a multimedia tour created with information and graphics downloaded from the Internet (Serim & Koch, 1996).

- Set up an "Internet News Bureau" where students can work in groups to track the latest local, national, and international news on-line, and then report the findings by creating an on-line classroom newspaper. They can also do a weekly news broadcast over the school's P.A. system (Cotton, 1997).

INTERNET RESOURCES
▲▲▲

TEACHER RESOURCES

Classroom Connect	http://www.classroom.net/classroom/ default1.html
Web66: A K12 WWW Project	http://web66.coled.umn.edu/
WCGU: The Faculty Lounge	http://www.naples.net/media/wsfp/lounge.htm
EdWeb	http://edweb.gsn.org/
Scholastic	http://place.scholastic.com/index.htm
Intel Teachers' Corner	http://www.intel.com/intel/educate/

| Teacher Talk | http://www.mightymedia.com/talk/working.htm |
| The Family Center | http://www.ok.bc.ca/TEN/family/family.html |

STUDENT RESOURCES

Yahooligans	http://www.yahooligans.com
CyberKids	http://www.CyberKids.com
Kid's Web	http://www.npac.syr.edu/textbook/kidsweb
Writers' Corner	http://www.mv.com/Writers-Corner/Homepage.html
Homework Heaven	http://www.homeworkheaven.com

LANGUAGE ARTS

Human Language Page	http://www.willamette.edu/~tjones/Language-Page.html
Emily Dickinson	http://www.planet.net/pkrisxle/emily/dickinson.html
Children's Story Books Online	http://www.magickeys.com/books/

SCIENCE

Electronic Zoo	http://netvet.wustl.edu
Monarch Watch	http://monarch.bio.ukans.edu/
Sea World Teacher Guides	http://www.bev.net/education/SeaWorld
VolcanoWorld	http://volcano.und.nodak.edu
U.S. Geological Survey	http://info.er.usgs.gov
EarthViewer	http://www.fourmilab.ch/earthview/vplanet.html
Periodic Table of Elements	http://mwanal.lanl.gov/CST/imagemap/periodic/periodic.html
NASA's Spacelink	http://spacelink.msfc.nasa.gov/
Science Learning Network	http://sln.fi.edu/tfi/sln/sln.html
Views of the Solar System	http://bang.lanl.gov/solarsys
Weather Underground	http://groundhog.sprl.umich.edu/
Marine Mammal List	http://elpc54136.lboro.ac.uk/links.html

MATH

MegaMath	http://www.c3.lanl.gov/mega-math
Math Forum	http://forum.swarthmore.edu/
Houghton Mifflin's Math Center	http://www.hmco.com/hmco/school/math/

SOCIAL STUDIES

Virtual Tourist II	http://city.net/regions/
Guide to the U.S. Congress	http://policy.net/capweb/congress.html
CIA World Fact Book	http://www.odci.gov/cia/publications/pubs.html
The White House	http://www.whitehouse.gov
Library of Congress	http://lcweb.loc.gov
Smithsonian	http://www.si.edu
World War II on the Web	http://www.bunt.com
K–12 History on the Internet	http://www.xs4all.nl/
Politics Now	http://www.politicsnow.com/

Current World News	http://www.yahoo.com/headlines/international
Santa Claus On-line	http://www.santaclausonline.com/santapages/main/html
ARTS	
WebMuseum	http://sunsite.unc.edu/louvre/
World Art Treasures	http://sgwww.epfl.ch/BERGER/

REFERENCES
▲▲▲

Arntson, L. J., Berkemeyer, K., Halliwell, J., Neuburger, L. (1997). *Learning the Internet.* New York: DDC Publishing, Inc.

Bremser, W. (1997). Cutting through the chatter. *The Net,* 36–46.

Classroom Connect. (1997). *The Internet curriculum planning system.* Lancaster, PA: Author.

Cook, J. (1992). Negotiating the curriculum: Programming for learning. In Boomer, G., Lester, N., Onore, L., & Cook, J. (Eds). *Negotiating the curriculum.* London: The Falmer Press.

Cotton, E. (1997). *The online classroom: Teaching with the Internet.* Bloomington, IN: EDINFO Press.

Crawford, T. (1993). *Legal guide for the visual artist.* New York: Allworth Press.

Georgia Institute of Technology. (1997). *GVU's 7th WWW User Survey.* [On-line]. Available: http://www.gvu.gatech.edu/user_surveys

Jensen, C. (1997). *Internet lesson plans for teachers.* St. Claire Shores, MI: Brighter Paths.

Owston, R. D. (1997). The WWW: A technology to enhance teaching and learning? *Educational Researcher, 26*(2), 27–33.

Polly, J.A. (1996). *The internet kids yellow pages.* New York: Osborne McGraw-Hill.

Serim, F. & Koch, M. (1996). *NetLearning: Why teachers use the internet.* Sebastapol, CA: Songline Studios, Inc.

Siegel, J. (1995). The state of teacher training. *Electronic Learning,* 43–53.

Tennessee Dept. of Education. (1997). *Connect Tennessee students.* [On-line]. Available: http://www.state.tn.us/education/mpartner.htm

CHAPTER 13
Searching for Information

▶ Introduction

Once students engaged in inquiry-based learning identify the problem, the next step is to locate the appropriate data to answer the problem. This data, or information, can be provided by the teacher, generated by the students, or located in the library, on the Internet, or on CD-ROM.

Whether it is the teacher or students locating the required information, these searches can become confusing and time-consuming unless users have the necessary skills to determine where and how to search. A major goal in the inquiry process is the development of a productive and time-efficient search approach. In this chapter we focus the use of Internet technology as a search tool. We offer a four-step process to assist students and teachers in their search endeavors.

1. Determine information needs.

2. Develop a search strategy.

3. Document the search approach.

4. Assess the quality of retrieved information.

To help you understand what this process might look like in today's classroom, throughout this chapter we'll follow Tameka, a fourth grader, as she leads her collaborative team through a search process.

▶ Computer Skills Used in This Chapter

Various Internet tools (e-mail, listservs, newsgroups, World Wide Web, etc.)
Search engines and other search tools

▶ Key Topics

SCENARIO: FOURTH GRADE COLLABORATIVE SCIENCE PROJECT
▲▲▲

After consulting the curriculum guide for appropriate objectives, Ms. Schultz asked Tameka, Sherilyn, and Joe to brainstorm what they already knew about our solar system and what they would like to know more about. After much discussion, Tameka's team discussed their interests, and with Ms. Schultz's approval they chose to explore the problem of How does our solar system work? The team decided to work together to determine their information needs and develop a search strategy. They split up to gather the needed information and then regrouped to share results and present their report.

DETERMINING INFORMATION NEEDS
▲▲▲

Once the information needed to solve the problem is determined, students and teachers can develop a search strategy that fits their needs. For example, if students need to know the interest rates currently offered by local banks, the Internet may not be the best choice because local banks may not have a web page. The ability to locate resources and gather data is influenced by several factors.

FACTORS INFLUENCING DATA COLLECTION

There are four primary factors influencing data collection to consider prior to deciding on the types of resources required to solve the particular problem or area of inquiry. The first factor is who will locate the information, the students or teacher. The second consideration is how much time can be allotted for the search. The next factor to consider is whether or not the lesson will have minimum information requirements that the students must fulfill as part of the project. And finally, the last factor is what form the final report must take. Planning for data collection can be simplified with the use of a form (see Figure 13-1).

WHO LOCATES INFORMATION?   When planning an inquiry project, the teacher must decide if she or the students will locate the resources. This decision is influenced by

Figure 13-1   Planning for Data Collection

PLANNING FORM FOR DATA COLLECTION
_____

Team: _____

Topic: _____

Who: _____ Students _____ Teacher _____ Both

Time: _____

FORM OF REPORT: _____

_____ Multimedia   _____ Video and/or Sound Clips

_____ Oral Report

_____ Paper   _____ Still Photos or Graphics

_____ Drama

the amount of time the teacher is able to allocate, the objectives of the lesson, and the age of the students. In many instances, it might be easier and more appropriate for a teacher to locate the information ahead of time and then provide it to the students. For example, it may make more sense for a teacher to provide students with newspaper clippings showing local interest rates rather than having the students conduct a web search for the information. Alternatively, if a main objective of a lesson is to locate the latest information about the space program it would be appropriate to give students several days to conduct an extensive search via e-mail by contacting experts at NASA.

TIME ALLOCATED TO STUDENTS FOR SEARCHING.   If students have three weeks to complete a project, they are able to access more time-consuming sources of information (such as listservs which involve sending and receiving e-mail messages). However, if students have only 30 minutes on the Internet to gather information, they have to be very selective in their information gathering.

MINIMUM INFORMATION REQUIREMENTS.   Are there minimum information requirements that all students must fulfill to complete their projects? Does everyone have to include information from the World Wide Web or a CD-ROM encyclopedia or from a minimum number of sources? This decision is based on the objectives the teacher is trying to accomplish in the lesson. For example, a teacher may have recently introduced her students to listservs. She now wants to reinforce their use by requiring students to use them to access information from other users.

FORM OF FINAL REPORT.   What form will the final report take? Will it be a research paper, a multimedia presentation, an oral report, or a dramatization? The final form often influences the type of information accessed. Multimedia presentations often lend themselves to incorporating additional types of information such as sound or film clips. In contrast, a written report is limited to still graphics and a narrative.

Once these data collection issues are considered, teachers and students are then ready to determine the type of information they need to solve their problem.

INFORMATION NECESSARY TO SOLVE PROBLEM

What information is needed to solve the problem? It is this point in the search process that students should be provided with maximum opportunity for ownership. Because there are always multiple ways to answer any question, students should be able to brainstorm a variety of informational sources to answer their specific question. It is here that students begin to "own" the project. Because these sources of information are based on students' own interests and ideas, students become more vested in accomplishing the project goal (Cook, 1992). Just as students can be inspired by work they have helped create, they can become apathetic toward teacher-generated projects. So what role does the teacher play? As we discussed in Chapters 3 and 9, the teacher still has a critical role in ensuring that students stay

The Internet provides students with current, real-world information.

on track with their generated ideas and that teacher suggestions help students meet the objective(s) of the project.

TAMEKA'S TEAM. Given the objectives she is required to cover, Ms. Schultz has provided each team with very specific guidelines to follow in creating their reports. She has asked each to use only the CD-ROM encyclopedia, the World Wide Web, e-mail, or the library for gathering information. They can present the final report as either an oral or multimedia presentation. She has allocated 50 minutes per day for two weeks for each team to work on their inquiry and presentation. With these guidelines, Tameka's team can now focus on what specific information they would like to gather to answer their question on How does the solar system work? With their limited knowledge of the solar system, they are able to determine that they would like to know more about:

- the names of all the planets and moons in our solar system
- the relationship of our solar system to the galaxy
- the rotation schedules of the planets
- the latest information about "Planet X," a hypothesized tenth planet

Tameka met with Ms. Schultz to share her team's ideas, and Ms. Schultz has given her approval to move ahead on the project. They have also decided to present their findings using a multimedia presentation.

Developing a Search Strategy

▲▲▲

Now, how do you or your students go about gathering the information to solve the problem in a systematic way? In the next section, we outline how to use search plans to keep searches focused and students on task. We also discuss the variety of Internet search tools and their strengths and weaknesses.

Fran's Diary

▲▲▲

I learned a lot about searching on the Internet when my class did a special project on trains. This project involved pairs of students researching different aspects of trains, everything from the kinds of cars on a freight train to monorails and subways. This information was used to create a train display that was put up in the school hallway. The purpose of this display was to share what they had learned about trains with the other students in the school. As we worked on this project, I discovered some strategies that were helpful, as well as some of the problems that can occur when using the Internet in the classroom.

One of the first things that I learned is that you have to have a search plan before the project begins. When I introduced this project, I had the students list those things that they knew about trains and what they would like to learn about trains. I used this information to make a list of potential topics based on what they wanted to learn about trains. Each pair of students picked a topic from this list after they had done some preliminary research on trains. As a class, they brainstormed to list the places that they could find information about trains. This list included library books, CD-ROM encyclopedias, the Internet, people, the railroad display in our community, and train lines.

I spent the next few days gathering resource materials. I checked out all of the age-appropriate books about trains that I could find from the school and public libraries. I borrowed extra CD-ROM encyclopedias from the other technology teachers. I got on the Internet and did some searches based on their project topics. I soon found that the amount of information about trains was overwhelming and that I would need some way to limit their searches. I also felt uncomfortable letting them freely search the Internet since they were young and inexperienced. I solved these two problems by creating a set of train bookmarks and limiting their search engine to Yahooligans, a search engine designed specifically for children.

Once I had gathered the resources, they began their research. We only had one computer in the school that had Internet access and it was located in the

Continued

conference room next to the library. There was no way that I could take 24 students in that small room with one computer and keep them under control. I realized that I would only be able to take a small group at a time. I made a special arrangement with the teachers on my grade level to use our teaching assistant for an hour a day for one week. I set up a rotation schedule and she watched a group of students in the classroom as I took the other group to the conference room. The students that were in the classroom rotated between the library resources and the CD-ROM encyclopedias. I had to take more students to the conference room than I could handle with just one computer. I solved this problem by rolling in carts of bound encyclopedias from the library. The students that were not on the Internet sat at the conference table and used the encyclopedias while they waited for their turn.

We had to work on this project in the afternoon after lunch because our teaching assistant was also responsible for lunchroom duty. This happened to be a very busy time on the Internet and we had to redial many times to make a connection. Our record was one hundred redials! The students would get very impatient as they were used to the immediate action that happens when they play video games. I took pieces of candy in my pocket. They would make predictions as to how many times it would take them to redial to make a connection. The student that got the closest would get a piece of candy. This seemed to keep them occupied. The only problem was that they sometimes got excited and disturbed the library next door!

They would also get impatient when they were downloading pictures. I wasn't able to solve that problem, but I learned later that there is software that can download the pages of a web site and save it to a disk. This disk can be used at any time and it simulates the actual Netscape program. Unless the students knew, they would not be able to tell it from actually being on the World Wide Web via Netscape. The problem of the time that it takes to download a picture would be solved. This disk could also be used on multiple computers if the teacher wanted all of the students to search the same web site.

Although we encountered some problems, the project was very successful. We created a fantastic wall display with twelve different projects and photos that showed the students working on this project from the beginning to end. You could feel the excitement of the learning that took place during this project just by looking at the students' faces in these photos!

SEARCH PLANS

An effective strategy to keep a search systematic is the use of a search plan (Serim & Koch, 1996). Search plans keep students focused on their specific information needs and appropriate data sources and can also serve as a means of accountability.

TAMEKA'S TEAM. As mentioned earlier, Ms. Schultz limited the options available to Tameka's team by outlining the data sources in the following search plan (see

Figure 13-2   Search Plan for Tameka's Team

DATA SOURCES				
INFORMATION NEEDED	**CD-ROM ENCYCLOPEDIA**	**WORLD WIDE WEB**	**E-MAIL**	**LIBRARY BOOKS**
Names and pictures of planets and moons (Tameka)	X	X		
Relationship between solar system and galaxy (Sharilyn & Tameka)	X			X
Rotation schedule of planets (Joe & Sharilyn)	X			X
Latest information about Planet X (Joe)		X	X	

Figure 13-2). These included CD-ROM encyclopedias, the World Wide Web, e-mail, and library references. After Tameka's team filled in the left column, they discussed which data sources would be most appropriate for each piece of information needed.

At this point, the team met with Ms. Schultz to defend their rationale for each data source. They reasoned that pictures and basic factual information would be easily obtained on CD-ROM and the World Wide Web, and they could download color pictures from each of these sources to include as part of their multimedia report. They felt that encyclopedias and library books would give more in-depth information regarding rotation schedules and the relationship of the solar system to the galaxy. Because they wanted the most recent information about Planet X, they decided to use the World Wide Web and also contact a NASA expert via e-mail, something they had done on a prior science project. Ms. Schultz was pleased with their rationale. At this point, the team divided up responsibility for collecting the information and was ready to move to the next step: deciding which search tools were most appropriate for their needs.

CHOOSING AN INTERNET SEARCH TOOL

The amount of information available over the Internet is mind boggling. At the end of 1996, it was predicted that over 150 million web pages were publicly available (Conte, 1996; Venditto, 1996). Although many web developers are working toward creating one ultimate search tool (as we are now seeing in the form of metasearch tools), teachers and students still need to be familiar with a variety of search tools for their information needs. Figure 13-3 outlines the most popular Internet search tools, where to locate them on the Net, and some of their strengths and weaknesses.

Figure 13-3   Internet Search Tools

Internet Search Tool	Name and Location	Strengths/Weaknesses
Directories search by topic to locate information.	*Yahoo!* www.yahoo.com	Largest and most popular directory.
	Magellan magellan.mckinley.com	Four star rating system; ability to narrow search by number of stars, mature content, or popular sites.
	Yahooligans! www.yahooligans.com	Directory developed specially for kids.
Search Engines search by key words to locate information.	*AltaVista* altavista.digital.com	Results extremely comprehensive, can be overwhelming.
	Excite www.excite.com	Chooses popular sites; hard to pinpoint specific information.
	Lycos www.lycos.com	Very comprehensive results based on popularity.
	Infoseek guide.infoseek.com	Locates selective, relevant sites; good search parameters.
	HotBot www.hotbot.com	Quick, comprehensive results; excellent search parameters that are user friendly.
	Web Crawler www.webcrawler.com	Quick, current searches; display limited to titles only.
E-mail Directories search for E-mail addresses by person's name and location.	*Four11 Directory* www.four11.com	Free; 10 million e-mail addresses; able to register.
	Lookup www.lookup.com/ lookup/search.html	Lookup is designed to search the Four 11 directory, and does so more efficiently than Four 11's own search engine.
Newsgroups search tools search by topic to locate postings, date, newsgroup, and author.	*Deja News* www.dejanews.com	Best search options; powerful.

Adapted from Conte (1996).

Figure 13-3   *(continued)*

	Sift sift.stanford.edu	Free; articles filtered by topics and listed on a single web page.
Listservs search tools search by topic to locate postings, date, listserv and author.	*Liszt* www.liszt.com	Listservs updated weekly, some search parameters offered.
Software search tools search by type or title of software to locate free software.	*Shareware.Com* www.shareware.com	Free; over 175,000 files of software.
FTPs search tools by filename to search locate documents.	*FTP Search* ftpsearch.ntnu.no/ftpsearch	Good search options; searches only file name; over 3,000 sites.
	Snoopie www.snoopie.com	Fast, but can only search on one name.
Metasearch engines search several databases by topic to locate information.	*Savvy Search* cage.cs.colostate.edu:1969	Searches five databases at once; eliminates duplicates; superior metasearch tool.
	All-In-One Search www.albany.net/allinone	Offers over 200 search forms on one web site; each search performed individually.
	Internet Sleuth www.isleuth.com	Largest collection of over 900 searchable databases; excellent for locating specific information.
	Search.Co www.search.com	Offers a directory, specialty searches, whole list A-Z.

DIRECTORIES.   Similar to the Yellow Pages, web directories offer a hierarchical listing of web pages by topic and subtopics (see Figure 13-4).

Yahoo!, Magellan, Pointcom, Excite, and Yahooligans! are all examples of directories. Using a directory as a search tool has specific advantages. First, because information is arranged in a hierarchy by topic, it is an easy to way to browse what type of information might be available about a certain topic without having to know keywords or selected terms. Second, the listings provided in a directory are selective. Many directories screen submissions for quality and popularity. Yahoo! is by far the largest and most popular directory, but Magellan offers the advantage of

Figure 13-4   Yahoo! Directory

Courtesy of Netscape Communications Corporation.

rating many of its sites using a four star system. Yahooligans! is a directory made especially for kids.

SEARCH ENGINES.
By far, the most popular search tools for the majority of web users are search engines such as Lycos, AltaVista, Excite, HotBot, Web Crawler and Infoseek. Search engines differ from directories in that web pages aren't arranged in categories that users can browse. Rather, users type in a key word or words they wish to conduct a search on, and the search engine returns with links to web pages that contain that word in the title or document itself. Figure 13-5 shows a screenshot of Lycos (http://www.lycos.com).

Search engines vary greatly in their strengths and weaknesses. Some engines, such as AltaVista and Lycos, are very popular because they offer extremely comprehensive results and often include references to FTPs and listservs in addition to web pages. However, this comprehensiveness can be overwhelming for those wanting very specific information. Note in Figure 13–6 that the words "solar system planets picture" have been typed in the search box. After clicking on the **Search**

Figure 13-5   Lycos Search Engine

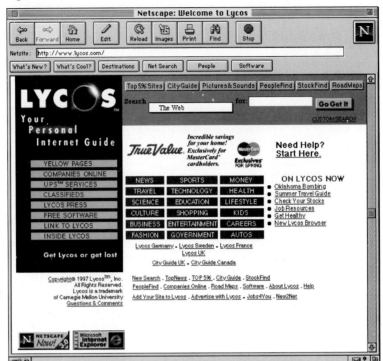

Courtesy of Netscape Communications Corporation.

button, Lycos will retrieve all links that include any of these words in the title or in the document itself. We used the **custom search** feature in Lycos to conduct a search on the keywords listed.

Note that results were returned listing 34,355 references! Some search engines, such as Infoseek, offer search parameters (discussed later in this chapter) that let users be more selective in their searching. In Figure 13-7 we used Infoseek's parameters of double quotes (" ") to search for a specific term, and a plus (+) sign to indicate that these words must be included in the results. Note that we were able to narrow our results down to 205 links—a much more manageable number than 34,355!

The greatest mistake that users can make is sticking with one search engine to meet all their search needs. Results vary greatly, and it is generally worth the user's time to explore at least two engines when searching for web information. For a detailed description of the most popular search engines and their specific search options, see Arntson et al. (1997).

E-MAIL DIRECTORIES.   Looking for a long-lost friend, relative, or expert in a specific content area? Use the e-mail directories to locate a specific person's e-mail address. All you need to begin is a person's name. Knowing the city, state, country, or company helps narrow the results. Four11 is an e-mail directory with over 10 million

Figure 13-6   Lycos Results

Courtesy of Netscape Communications Corporation.

Figure 13-7   Infoseek Search Results

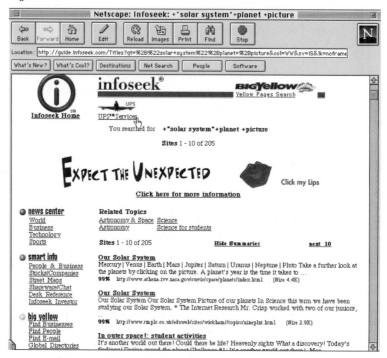

Courtesy of Netscape Communications Corporation.

Figure 13-8   Four11 Directory

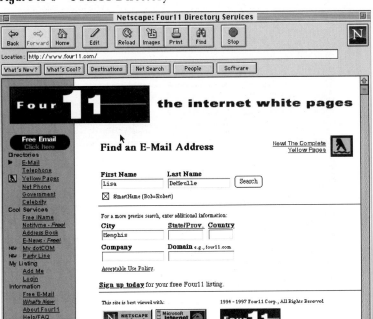

Courtesy of Netscape Communications Corporation.

e-mail addresses. To use these directories, simply type in as much information as you have available about the person you're trying to locate (see Figure 13-8).

Lookup is a search tool designed to search the Four11 directory, and it does so more efficiently than Four11's own search engine! When one of the authors did a search on her e-mail address using Lookup, she received results in the format shown in Figure 13-9.

Lookup was able to locate one additional address that was not available when she checked the Four11 search engine. As more teachers and students wish to consult with "experts" in content areas via e-mail, familiarity with these directories will be an asset.

NEWSGROUP AND LISTSERV DIRECTORIES.   Many users of newsgroups are unaware that there are search tools to help them locate postings and newsgroups in their areas of interest. Deja News offers several outstanding features (see Figure 13-10 for the results of a Deja News search on the Civil Rights Movement). First, it archives all articles from all newsgroups. This is a distinct advantage because most newsgroups clear their postings every few days. For example, if students were studying the Civil Rights Movement, they might be surprised that Deja News offers over 1,200 postings on the topic. Second, when searching by a topic, users are provided with a list of postings, dates, the newsgroup each posting appeared in, and the author, all in hyperlink format. Third, if you're searching for newsgroups

Figure 13-9   Lookup Results

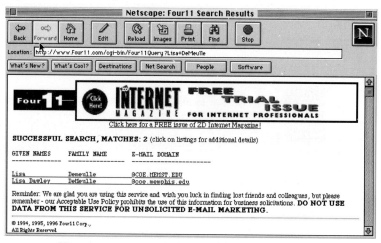

Courtesy of Netscape Communications Corporation.

Figure 13-10   Deja News Results

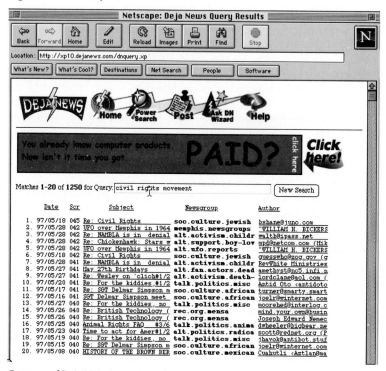

Courtesy of Deja News.

Figure 13-11   Liszt

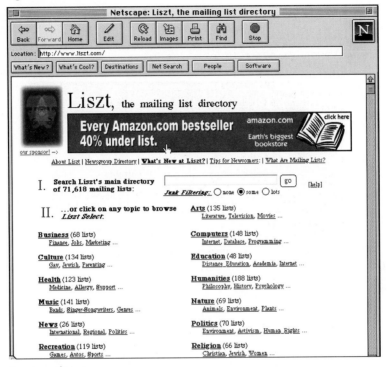

Courtesy of Liszt.

that discuss the topic you're interested in, Deja News offers an additional search tool to do so.

Using Liszt, users can search for listservs by browsing hierarchical categories or by typing in search terms (see Figure 13-11). Although many educators are hesitant to allow their students access to lists, many lists are moderated and can be quite supportive of the curriculum. For example, the ADSCARRY list follows Jill and David Scarry as they travel through Europe, Asia, and Africa. The list is moderated by a class in California, and Jill and David respond to student queries via the list.

SOFTWARE/FTP DIRECTORIES.
Although most students won't be searching for software as a part of an inquiry project, there are times when these searches come in handy. For example, students may wish to publish their work in the form of a web page. They can search for an HTML editor, download it to their home computer and work from there. Shareware.Com offers over 175,000 files of free software (see Figure 13-12).

FTPs are files such as scholarly writings, mailing lists, song lyrics, images, lesson plans, articles, and games. FTP Search offers a host of search options and has over 3,000 sites that it updates weekly. However, a limitation of FTP search engines is

Figure 13-12 Shareware.Com

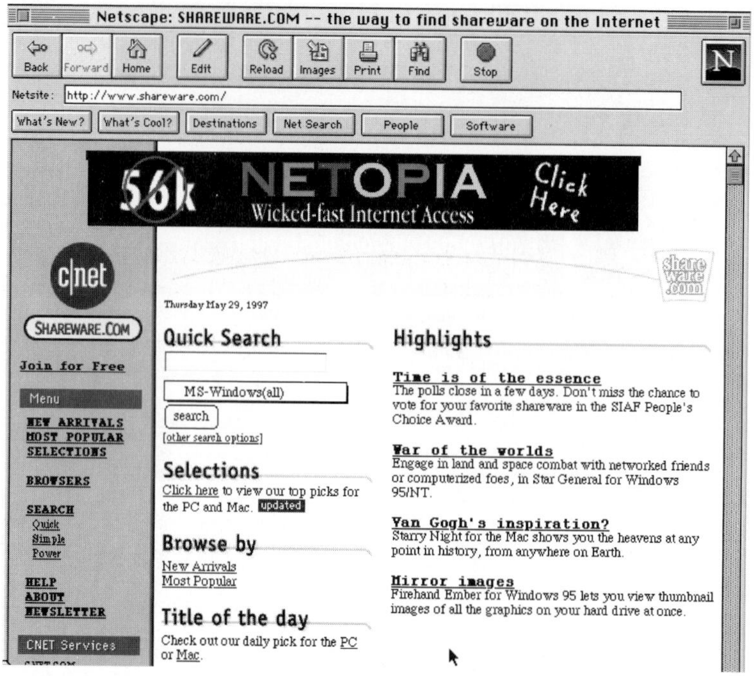

Reprinted with permission from CNET, Inc. Copyright 1995–8, www.cnet.com

that they usually search on the file name only. The major search engines mentioned earlier now include links to FTPs in their results.

METASEARCHES. Metasearch tools allow the user to query multiple databases. This ability is extremely helpful and timesaving when one is interested in getting comprehensive results. SavvySearch can search up to five databases at one time, combining results on one page and eliminating duplicate responses. It also customizes a search plan for you, offering suggestions on which search engines are most useful given your search needs. All-in-One Search offers over 200 search forms at one site, but each query must be entered individually. The Internet Sleuth offers over 900 searchable databases and lets users search up to six search engines at once (see Figure 13-13). It excels in locating specialized information. Examples of its specialized databases include Civil War photos, Alice Cooper lyrics, and an e-mail directory of anthropologists.

TAMEKA'S TEAM. Tameka and her teammates are now ready to determine which search tools are most appropriate for their project by matching their information needs with the capabilities of search tools. After some discussion, they decide to use Internet Sleuth to search for pictures of the planets and moons. Although the comprehensive results might prove a little time-consuming, they feel they have enough time to accomplish their goal and still get the best quality photos. They'll also use

Figure 13-13   The Internet Sleuth

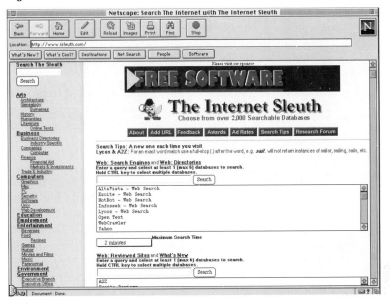

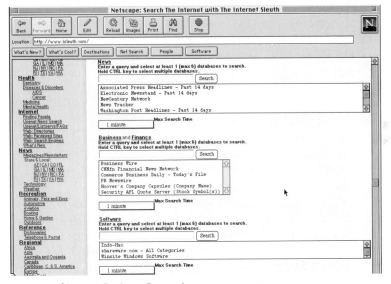

Courtesy of Internet Business Connection.

Internet Sleuth to locate information about Planet X, a specialized topic. In order to locate their NASA expert's e-mail address, they have decided to try the Lookup directory. The rest of their information needs can be met through CD-ROM or library books. Once this decision is made, they record their databases in their search log (see Figure 13-14 in the following section).

CONDUCTING AND DOCUMENTING THE SEARCH

▲▲▲

Documenting a search can be important for several reasons. First, a documented search provides an excellent means of keeping track of the search strings used. This becomes valuable when a search is proving unfruitful and the teacher needs to step in and help identify possible overlooked search terms or databases. A record of the search also gives the student a written record that can later be returned to for reference on future projects. Finally, a documented search provides the teacher with a means of assessing the extent of the student's search. These logs can then be included as part of a larger portfolio when it comes time to assess the project.

SEARCH LOGS

A search log not only serves as an excellent means for documenting a search, but it helps students learn how to search thoroughly and systematically. Search logs should be constructed to meet the needs of the student population. For example, a search log for a second grade class might only include the headings "Where I Searched," "What I Looked For," and "What I Found." At the high school level, search logs can be made more complex, given the objectives of the lesson. Students might be required to list some or all of the following in their logs:

- date of search
- reference, database or index
- location or URL

Students discuss and review Internet resources.

Figure 13-14   Tameka's Search Log

Date of Search	Reference or Database	Location	Search Terms	Results
11/9	CD-ROM		solar system	moon photos
11/9	Internet Sleuth	www.isleuth.com	solar system pictures Planet X	saved as bookmark for reference
11/10	WWW - Nine Planets Multi-media Tour	seds.lpl.arizona.edu/ nineplanets/nineplanets/ nineplanets.html		planet photos, sound clips, sun and sun spots
11/11	Four11	www.four11.com	Dr. Gary Anderson	ganderson@nasa.gov

Adapted from Wehmeyer (1996).

- dates covered
- search commands/terms
- results

TAMEKA'S TEAM. Take a look at Tameka's search log (Figure 13-14) to get an idea of what a search log might look like for her type of project.

SEARCH TERMS

In a library, most materials are arranged according their subject. These subjects are broad and usually determined by the Library of Congress. However, most Internet search tools provide more information by accepting both subject and keyword searches (Serim & Koch, 1996). That is, you enter a keyword(s) or a subject you are interested in knowing more about, and results are returned by subject and by sites which contain the keyword in the title and contents of a document. This result makes keyword searches challenging because they must be refined to locate the specific type of information you are trying to find. For example, let's say you were trying to locate information about a new computer virus call VRAD. If you searched just using the term "virus," you would receive links to sites containing information about cold viruses, bacteria, etc., in addition to sites about computer viruses. Instead, make your search as specific as possible. Search specifically for "VRAD virus," or "computer viruses." You are much more likely to save yourself time and frustration.

OPERATORS. Another way to increase the success of your search is to become familiar with "operators." Boolean operators such as "and" and "not," and grouping operators such as double quotes and parentheses, allow you to refine your search even further (see Figure 13-15).

Figure 13-15   Operators and Their Functions

BOOLEAN OPERATORS

AND   The results of the search must include all words joined by the AND operator. For example, a search for *classroom* AND *management* AND *techniques* will only retrieve those documents containing all of the three words.

OR   The results of the search will contain at least one of the words joined by OR, but not necessarily both. For example, a search for *food* OR *nutrition* will contain documents that contain either the word *food* or *nutrition*.

NOT   The results must not contain any word that follows the NOT operator. For example, *virus* NOT *cold* will return documents which contain the word *virus* but not *cold*.

NEAR   The results must contain the words joined by the NEAR operator within a specified number of words, most typically ten.

GROUPING OPERATORS

Double quotes " "   The results must contain the words contained within the quotes exactly as written. For example, *"solar system"* will return only documents containing that phrase in that order, not documents with just the words *"solar"* or *"system."*

Parentheses ( )   Parentheses can be used to define the order in which Boolean operators are read. Any terms in parentheses are given first priority in the search. For example, *(planets OR moons) AND pictures* will return results containing either the words *planets* and *pictures,* or *moons* and *pictures.*

Not all search tools accept operators and only experience with multiple search tools will teach you which operators can be used with which search tool. Some search engines, such as Lycos, have developed their own operators. For example, instead of NOT, they use a minus (–) sign. A dollar sign ($) extends the search string. For example, entering *teach$* will obtain results such as "teaching" and "teacher." The moral of the story is to spend the time learning the operators used with each particular search tool. Most search tools offer a "search tips" or "custom search" link that explains the search parameters applicable to that particular tool.

UNSUCCESSFUL SEARCHES

So you've followed the tips mentioned so far and your search is still unsuccessful. You are either receiving Error messages or hits resulting in zero. What now?

Power Tip ▲▲▲   *Printing URLs on Your Web Pages*

Save yourself and others valuable time! For future reference, *always* note the URL (uniform resource locator), or web address at the top of any printed web pages. A nice option in Netscape Navigator handles this task for you.

Choose **Page Setup** under **File**

Under **"Right Header"** change **None** to **Location**

Click **OK**

This option prints the URL as a right header. Customize the option to your needs; choose the left, right, or middle header or footer.

1. Look for spelling errors in your search string, especially if it's long.

2. Many search tools are case sensitive. Therefore, check capitalization and leave it off unless it's a name, city, or other word that is always capitalized.

3. Make sure the spacing between the words is correct.

4. Try another search tool. Remember, by limiting yourself to one or two search tools, you greatly limit your findings.

5. Finally, try alternative search terms. Instead of looking solely for *solar system,* try *planets, space exploration,* or *stars.* These alternatives are where the power of the search plan comes into play. For those who have been faithfully documenting their search terms, the teacher can often provide alternative terms that the students may not have considered.

ASSESSING THE QUALITY OF RETRIEVED INFORMATION
▲▲▲
Given the unique nature of information available over the Internet, it is imperative that students become critical and discriminating in assessing the quality of retrieved information. Because the web is available to almost anyone with access to a computer, students and teachers must assess the quality and trustworthiness of the information they have accessed. But how is this task accomplished? Begin with some basic steps:

1. Who is the author of the web page? Is it an individual, an institution, an organization?

2. Ask yourself what their motives are for publishing this information on the Web. Teach yourself and your students to seek out experts on the topic. Larger organizations are usually more reliable sources of information in most cases. For example, Tameka's team looked at NASA's web pages to get information on the solar system. Most users would presume that this information would have more reliability and accuracy than web pages published by a classroom of fifth graders doing a science report. However, there are exceptions to this rule. For example, a person living in Honolulu could give more detailed and current weather information about their city over a listserv than could be obtained by going to a national weather service web page.

Power Tip ▲▲▲   *Organizing Bookmarks*

Both you and your students will come across many valuable web sites on the Internet that you will want for future reference. You can save these sites as bookmarks, and begin to organize them in a way that makes sense for your curriculum. For example, an elementary teacher may organize his bookmarks by content area, i.e., science, math, language arts. The secondary or thematic teacher might organize her bookmarks by topic area, i.e., the polar region, ancient explorers, or Victorian times. Following are steps to save and organize web pages as bookmarks in Netscape Navigator™ Gold:
TO SAVE:

   Go to desired web page

Choose **Add bookmark** from the **Bookmarks** menu.

Each web site will be saved by title name under the Bookmarks heading.
TO ORGANIZE:

Choose **Bookmarks** from the Window menu.

You should see a display of your saved web titles.

Choose **Insert Folder** under **Item**

Enter name of new folder

Click **OK**

To add bookmarks to your folders, click and drag sites into the new folders.

---

3. Has the author put a lot of time into providing extensive links to other valuable pages? If so, this makes it a valuable site to save as a bookmark because it provides "jumping off" points to other links of interest. This saves time.

4. Is there an e-mail address provided so you can contact the author or organization for more information? Giving an e-mail address lends credibility.

AT THE CLASSROOM'S DOORSTEP
▲▲▲

QUESTIONS TEACHERS ASK

Do I need to "teach" search strategies directly or should I integrate searching as part of a content lesson? You should do both, although the amount of time spent on teaching search strategies should be limited to what is required to meet your objectives. Begin slowly by having students look for information using a specific search engine on the Web or by locating an e-mail address with the Lookup directory. As students become more knowledgeable about the peculiarities of different search tools, they are better able to discern what tools they require for their search. In most cases, searching for information is integrated as part of the overall inquiry project.

The process outlined in this chapter seems time-consuming. Are my students required to do each of these steps every time they need information? No, it depends on the extent of the project. For larger projects, go through all the steps, integrating the search log into the assessment process. For one shot information needs, draw on pieces of the process that meet your needs. The process outlined in this chapter is for your information as the teacher. Remember, your students will only become search savvy by having teachers who are knowledgeable themselves.

REFERENCES
▲▲▲

Arntson, L. J., Berkemeyer, K., Halliwell, J., & Neuburger, L. (1997). *Learning the Internet.* New York: DDC Publishing, Inc.

Conte, R. (1996). Guiding lights. *Internet World,* May, 41–44.

Cook, J. (1992). Negotiating the curriculum: Programming for learning. In Boomer, G., Lester, N., Onore, L., & Cook, J. (Eds.). *Negotiating the curriculum.* London: The Falmer Press.

Cotton, E. (1997). *The online classroom: Teaching with the Internet.* Bloomington, IN: EDINFO Press.

Jensen, C. (1997). *Internet lesson plans for teachers.* St. Claire Shores, MI: Brighter Paths.

Serim, F. & Koch, M. (1996). *NetLearning: Why teachers use the internet.* Sebastapol, CA: Songline Studios, Inc.

Venditto, G. (1996). Search engine showdown. *Internet World,* June, 79–86.

Wehmeyer, L. B. (1996). Teaching online search techniques your students can use. *Syllabus,* September, 52–56.

CHAPTER 14
Instructional Materials

▶ Introduction

During the "purple era" of American education, teachers were faced with the almost daily challenge of creating worksheets (ditto sheets) using a rather messy spirit duplicator that churned out one potent-smelling, blue-inked sheet with each crank. The worksheets were made from a ditto master that was created with a typewriter or handwritten by the teacher. The only way to correct mistakes on the masters was to scrape the "ink" off the back of the master with a razor blade, then reprint or retype. The process was ongoing because the ditto masters had to be remade when all the ink was dissolved. Today, with a computer and copier, teachers can easily produce and modify a variety of instructional materials that incorporate elaborate graphics and carefully designed text layouts.

In the first 13 chapters of this book, we have focused on how to integrate computers into the curriculum with an emphasis on how students can use the computer as a tool. We now want to shift our focus to how teachers can use computers as a productivity tool for teaching.

▶ Computer Skills Used in This Chapter

Database creation and manipulation
Word processing
Audiotape production
Mail merge
Creation of graphics

▶ Key Topics

Computer-Generated Teaching Materials
Multimedia Presentations
Creating Audio-Tutorial Materials
Personalized Worksheets
Classroom Printed Materials
Educational Software
Types of Educational Software
Software Evaluation

Computer-Generated Teaching Materials

▲▲▲

You can use a computer in a variety of ways to create materials for teaching and for individualized instruction. In this section, we will explore these ways. Our discussion will focus on slide shows, audio-tutorial materials, personalized worksheets, computer-based instruction tutorials, and classroom materials.

Multimedia Presentations

Multimedia presentations or computer slide shows are the modern day replacement for overhead transparencies. We are typically limited to the number or type of overhead transparencies we can prepare by the cost of the materials and the limitations of the copying process (e.g., solid blacks and shades of gray do not reproduce well). A multimedia presentation is only limited by the disk space available either on your hard drive, a removable cartridge, or a floppy disk.

Multimedia presentations serve two purposes. First, the act of creating the presentation can help you plan and organize your information. Preparing the outline and individual slides can help you sequence and develop examples to illustrate your content. As you prepare your slides, you can "view" them from the students' point of view, changing the sequence and adding new slides as needed. This can help you enhance your "lecture" through the process of creating the presentation (Frye, 1975).

Second, drawing tools and clip art make it easier for you to visually enhance your message. That is, how can you create a picture that accurately communicates

Teachers can incorporate charts and graphs into their multimedia presentations.

Figure 14-1 Slide with Graphic Illustration

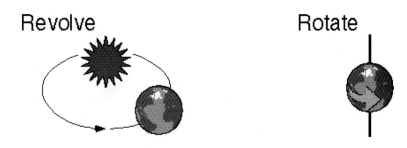

an abstract idea to your students? For example, how could we teach the concepts "revolve" and "rotate" as part of a science presentation on the solar system? We want to be more creative than many multimedia presentations that would simply slide the word "revolve" across the screen and then slide the word "rotate" across the screen. If we can create an accurate graphic, we can help the learner comprehend the concepts and understand the difference between revolve and rotate by providing them with a concrete image (see Figure 14-1).

As you design a presentation, consider what to include and exclude on each slide. Too many multimedia presentations are little more than an outline or script. While the slides in a presentation *do not* need to include every word that you plan to speak, they should provide a *brief* outline of the key points. We have found that single words or short phrases work best. With too much information on the slide, students feel obligated to copy the information word-for-word and fail to listen carefully to what we have to say. The best presentations are those that incorporate a few words with relevant graphics (see Figure 14-2). The resulting slide is not only visually more appealing, but it provides a concrete referent for your ideas.

You can make your presentation user friendly and professional if it has a consistent look. For example, in a textbook the first page of each chapter is designed consistently with the chapter number and chapter title in the same typeface and in the same location. The headings in the chapters all use consistent formatting as do the headers and page numbers. You can create the same appearance in multimedia presentations by using the master page in ClarisWorks (see Figure 11-21) or the Master Slide in PowerPoint. Using this template, you can place titles, text, and graphics consistently on all slides. When each slide has a similar appearance, users quickly learn how to read the slide. For example, they know that the slide's title is in the top left corner, a logo or icon appears to the right of the title, and the key words are listed below the title. The consistency helps readers concentrate on the information, not the format. Steps for creating a slide show in ClarisWorks are described in Chapter 11.

Figure 14-2 Slide with Graphic

Technology Type III

✓ Create the integrated system

✓ Consider the teacher, the student, and the instruction

✓ Build a system that is in harmony

CREATING AUDIO-TUTORIAL MATERIALS

One problem teachers must address when using models such as the iNtegrating Technology for inQuiry (NTeQ) model is providing scaffolding, or individualized instruction to address different student needs. Often, individual students need to have the same instruction but at different times. Although there are a variety of methods, we have found one based on the Audio-Tutorial method (Postelthwait, Novak, & Murray, 1972) applicable to a variety of grade levels. Postelthwait developed the audio-tutorial method while teaching a college-level botany course. This approach involves a number of features including labs, group meetings, and individualized materials. In an open-ended learning environment, the audio-tutorial presentations are useful. Traditionally, these presentations have consisted of a booklet, an audiotape, and possibly some lab materials (e.g., plant specimens).

Postelthwait created his tapes by visualizing a student sitting next to him as he explained the materials. He told the student when to turn the page. If the student was to write something, perform a calculation, or examine a specimen, then he directed the student to pause or turn off the tape player. A short (14–20 second) music piece was recorded to let the student know where to pause the tape and also as a signal that nothing was missing from the tape.

Teachers can create the traditional audio-tutorial materials using a word processor or graphics application to create the booklet, or they can substitute a multimedia presentation for the booklet. Although it is possible to capture the audio on a computer, most verbal presentations will take a great amount of disk space. Thus, we suggest that you still use an audiotape for the verbal presentation.

CREATING AN AUDIO-TUTORIAL PRESENTATION. Start the production of your presentation by creating the booklet or slide show. Gather any manipulatives, objects,

Figure 14-3   Preventing Erasure of an Audiotape

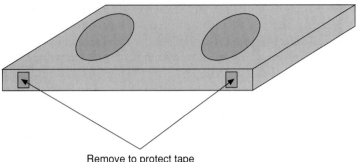

Remove to protect tape

specimens, equipment, or materials the students will need. You can store these items in a small bin that students can use during the lesson. Print a copy of the booklet or slide show (you may want to use black-and-white for a slide show to decrease the printing time). As you create each segment, make notes on the paper about what you want to say. Now, practice your presentation with the materials. To keep the presentation fresh, practice only once or twice—an audio-tutorial lesson should not sound like a professional presentation. Next, make a recording of your presentation as you work through the booklet or slide show. Remember to talk slowly and give the student directions such as turning a page or examining an object. "Notice the number of legs on the spider. How many are there?" If you make a mistake, continue with the tape as if the tape is a conversation, not a lecture. If you want the student to pause or stop the tape to complete a task, give the student directions to pause and then record 10–15 seconds of music before you start talking again. This music serves as a cue to stop the tape as well as a filler. When the student starts the tape again, he or she will hear the music and know that no information was skipped.

When you finish your recording, check the tape to make sure both your voice and music were recorded clearly. To prevent students from accidentally erasing the tape, you can break off the tab on the rear corner of the tape (see Figure 14-3). If you need to record over the tape, place clear tape over the opening.

STUDENT USE OF AN AUDIO-TUTORIAL LESSON. Students can use the audio-tutorial lessons at a learning center, a computer, or at their desks. If you are using print materials, you need to determine whether you want the students to write in the booklet or on separate sheets of paper. When students are ready for a lesson, they can select the appropriate bin and a tape player. The bin can hold a disk (if there is a slide show), booklet, extra paper, and any other materials or equipment. If students are using headphones, you can purchase adapters that allow several students to connect to the same recorder at one time. These audio-tutorial units can provide students with introductory, remedial, and advanced materials on a variety of topics that they can use at any time.

PERSONALIZED WORKSHEETS

If you have ever observed a teenager opening a piece of junk mail that has "The Mitchell family of Bedford, Indiana, is a guaranteed winner of $1,000,000," then you understand the effect of seeing one's name and other personal information in print. We can adapt this advertising strategy to the classroom to create personalized math worksheets for each student (Dorsey-Davis, Ross, & Morrison, 1991; Ross & Anand, 1987). Personalized worksheets usually include the student's name and personal information (e.g., names of friends, favorite candy, pet's names, etc.). Personalized problems provide a meaningful context by using familiar items (e.g., friends, food, etc.) that make the problems easier to understand (Ross & Anand, 1987).

CREATING PERSONALIZED WORKSHEETS.   These worksheets are created with a process called "mail merge." You can use the mail merge feature of Microsoft's Word or ClarisWorks to create personalized worksheets. We have found that ClarisWorks is the easiest tool to use because you can create a database of student characteristics to merge with a word processing document. The following paragraphs describe how to create a personalized worksheet for each student in your class.

After you have identified the math skills (or other content area skills) that you want to teach, you will need to construct the problems. You may find it easier to adapt existing story problems or exercises by modifying them with personal information. Once you have developed your problems, you can create either a questionnaire or database the students can use to enter their own personal information (see Figure 14-4). If your students are skilled at using a database, they can enter their own data directly into the database.

The database should have a field for each type of information you need for the problems. Putting the data into different fields allows you to create additional problems using the same data (see Figure 14-5). See Chapter 9 for instructions on creating a database in ClarisWorks.

Figure 14-5   Database Fields for Personalized Data

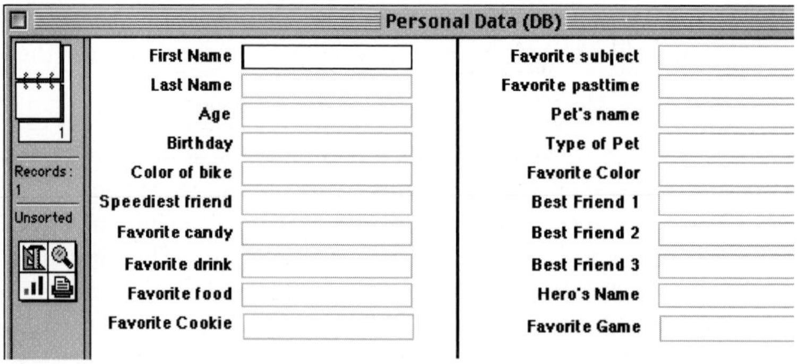

With a completed database, you can create individualized worksheets. The following instructions describe how to create a mail merge word processing document.

1. Create a new word processing document.

2. Select **Mail Merge** from the **File** menu. ClarisWorks will ask you to locate the database you want to use for the mail merge. ClarisWorks will display the **Print Merge** palette (see Figure 14-6). You are now ready to start typing.

3. We started by creating a title and adding the student's name in the title (see Figure 14-5). First, type the title for the worksheet and then press **Return** once or twice. To add the students' name, select **First Name** in the Field Names list. Now, click **Insert Field**. The field variable (<<First Name>>) is inserted into your word processing document at the current cursor position. Press the space bar to add a space and insert the last name field. You can select both field variables and change the font, style, and size for printing.

Figure 14-4   Student Questionnaire

All About YOU!

What is your first name? _____
What is your last name? _____
How old are you? _____
When is your birthday? _____
What color is your bike (if you have one)? _____
Who is your speediest friend? _____
What is your favorite:

       candy? _____
       drink? _____
       food? _____
       subject? _____
       pastime? _____
       color? _____
       game? _____

What is your pet's name (if you have one)? _____
What kind of pet is it? _____
Who are your three best friends?

       1. _____
       2. _____
       3. _____

Who is your hero? _____

Figure 14-6   Print Merge Palette

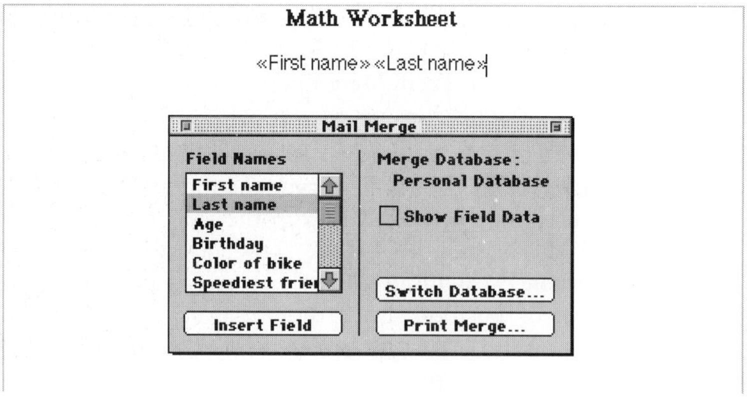

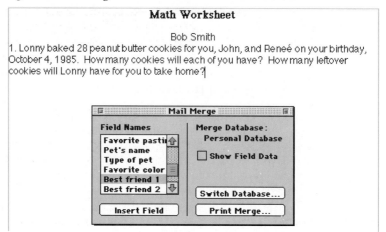

4. Next, we skipped a couple of lines and started typing our first problem. Note how we inserted the fields from our database into the problem statement (see Figure 14-7). If we select **Show Field Data,** we can see how the problem will look when it is printed.

Figure 14-7   Merged Data for Personalized Problem

5. We can also add information to one of our merged fields. For example, in Problem 2 we want to reference John's (Best friend 2) mother. All we need to do is add an apostrophe and s after the **Best Friend 2** Field variable (see Figure 14-8).

6. To print, click **Print Merge** on the **Print Merge** palette. Click **Print** in the **Print** dialog and ClarisWorks will print a worksheet for each student. You can also print select pages by entering in a starting record number and an ending record number. Another way to print selected records is to use the **Match** or **Find** function and then hide the **Unselected** or **Selected** records. Only the visible records will print (see Chapter 9).

Figure 14-8 Customizing the Field Variables

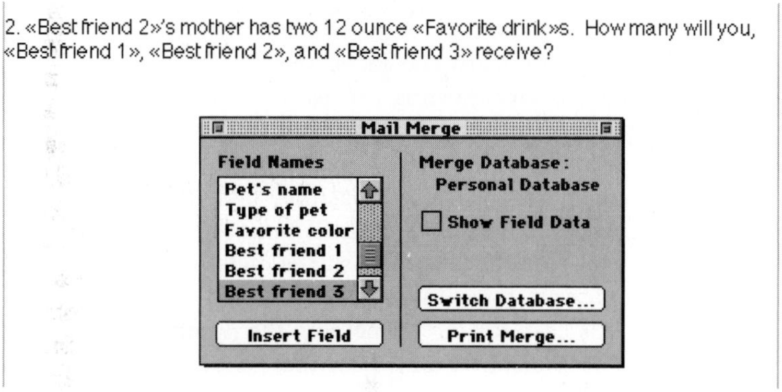

2. «Best friend 2»'s mother has two 12 ounce «Favorite drink»s. How many will you, «Best friend 1», «Best friend 2», and «Best friend 3» receive?

```
┌─────────────── Mail Merge ───────────────┐
│                                           │
│  Field Names          Merge Database:     │
│  ┌─────────────┐      Personal Database   │
│  │ Pet's name  │⬆                         │
│  │ Type of pet │      ☐ Show Field Data   │
│  │ Favorite color│                        │
│  │ Best friend 1│                         │
│  │ Best friend 2│                         │
│  │ Best friend 3│⬇     ┌─────────────────┐│
│  └─────────────┘      │ Switch Database...││
│                       └─────────────────┘│
│  ┌─────────────┐      ┌─────────────────┐│
│  │ Insert Field │     │  Print Merge... ││
│  └─────────────┘      └─────────────────┘│
└───────────────────────────────────────────┘
```

Properly designed personalized worksheets can provide concrete, real-world problems for individual students. Including personal information can also enhance student motivation. Personalized worksheets are useful for the NTeQ model activities prior to using the computer, after using the computer, and for supporting activities.

FRAN'S DIARY
▲▲▲

What I like about having a computer in my classroom is that I can create worksheets and learning materials that are customized to the curriculum and the group of students that I am working with. I can remember the days of dealing with the purple ditto and the frustrations of trying to create the quality worksheet. I always had purple ink on my hands! I also remember the black-line masters. I didn't have to deal with the purple ink, but many times these weren't quite what I needed. With the computer, I can easily adapt worksheets to meet the needs of individual students and have been able to create quality learning materials inexpensively.

I teach third grade and learning the multiplication facts is one of the highlights of that year. I am able to use all applications of ClarisWorks to create management tools, computerized tests, worksheets, games, learning aids, and contests to help make learning the multiplication facts a fun and painless process for both teacher and student.

I begin by using the spreadsheet application to create individual record sheets to help me track student progress and help students to track their individual progress. Unfortunately learning the multiplication facts requires

Continued

memorization. I use the drawing application to make sets of flash cards that can be run off and given to students to help them with this task.

As students learn the facts, they must be assessed. The students progress through this fact-learning process at various rates. I use the spreadsheet application to create a computerized test for each fact family. I put these tests in the student folder on the hard drive. The students take each test as they are ready and receive instant feedback as they take the test. I use the slide show application to make whole class quizzes. I put the slide show on the big screen TV and set it at various speeds to flash the facts on the screen one fact at a time. The students write their answers on a record sheet. As they progress through the facts, it is easy for me to increase the number of facts and lower the response time. The students can also use these slide shows individually at a computer to practice the facts at any time.

I use the drawing and painting applications to create multiplication fact variations of children's board games and games such as War, Slap Jack, and Go Fish. The students have access to these games and can play them when they have some down time during the day or when the weather keeps them inside at recess.

I use the database application to create a class database: Things That Come in 2s, 3s, 4s, etc. This becomes a class contest. As the students learn a fact family, I ask them to look for things in their environment that come in that family. For example, when they study the 3s fact family they might find such things as triplets, tricycle, trio, etc. As the students find these items, they enter their name, the item's name, and the fact family into the database. Each item can only be entered one time. It is amazing how hard they work to find these things! A sort can be done weekly to find the student who has found the most items. This student is given a multiplication facts ruler. This database is used later to make student-created word problems and multiplication fact books.

I use the drawing application to make tokens that I give to the students during the multiplication facts unit. These tokens are given to the students for everything from participation in activities, to bringing back homework assignments, to improvement points on quizzes, to helping a classmate. The students collect these tokens, and to celebrate their accomplishments at the end of the unit, I have a class auction. The parents donate small items and candy. The students use their tokens to bid on the items. They have a great time and everyone gets something!

I also use a drill and practice MECC software program called Speedway Math. I put a speedway track on the bulletin board. Each student designs a race car. At the beginning of the week, the students put their race cars on the starting line. The students compete individually as I set the number and difficulty of the problems for each student, based on ability. They use this program as many times as they want during the week and move their car one space for each time they use the program. Their short-term goal is to get to the finish line by the end of the week. Their ultimate goal is to make it to the Hall of Fame, which shows that they have mastered all of the multiplication facts. This is a great motivator to get the students to practice the facts.

CLASSROOM PRINTED MATERIALS

Drawing and word processing applications are useful tools for creating a variety of classroom materials. For example, you can use these applications to create flash cards and a variety of student handouts. Let's examine how to create printed materials for the classroom.

FLASH CARDS. We do not encourage (or even like) rote learning. We realize though, that there are some facts (or declarative knowledge) that students must learn. For example, students in chemistry are expected to recall a chemical formula (e.g., CO_2 is carbon dioxide). Similarly, students studying a foreign language must learn individual words and phrases. A computer drill-and-practice application provides an efficient flash card exercise. Access to a computer, however, is not always possible. Teacher-created flash cards provide an easy alternative to computerized drills. The following steps describe how to create customized flash cards. You can print these cards on standard paper or you can use a heavier weight paper (e.g., 110 lb. paper) that will increase the durability of the cards.

1. Create a layout for the flash cards. You can use a landscape layout to create two or four flash cards per sheet of paper (see Figure 14-9).

Figure 14-9 Flash Card Layout (front)

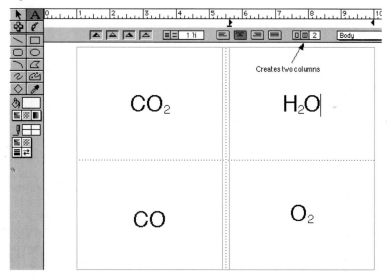

2. To create two or more cards per sheet of paper, select two columns (see Figure 14-9). We then divided the vertical columns in half by using the line tool to create a total of four cards per sheet of paper.

3. Use the **Return** key to space the word, phrase, or number on the card. You can select a large type (e.g., 36, 48, 72 point) so students can read the type from a distance. After you finish entering the information for the left side of the card, select **Insert Column Break** from the **Format** menu.

Your cursor should jump to the right column. Create a new page for each group of cards.

4. After you enter the front of the cards, you can create the back of the cards. We used the same layout (see Figure 14-10) for the back. If you are using standard paper, you might want to use a 10 or 12 point font size so that the answers do not show through the paper.

Figure 14-10   Flash Card Layout (back)

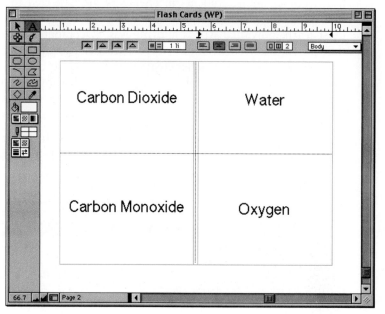

5. To print the flash cards, print only the front sides first. For example, if you have eight pages in your document, then the first four pages are the front of the cards and the last four pages are the back. Select **Print** from the **File** menu and enter **1** into the **From** field and **4** into the **To** field to print *only* the first four pages.

6. To print the back of the flash cards, place the printed cards into the tray (you will need to check your printer instructions to determine if the printed side is up or down). Select **Print** from the **File** menu and enter **5** in the **From** field. Leave the **To** field blank to print the remaining pages. (You can also print multiple copies by entering a different number in the **Copies** field.)

If you want to prolong the life of the flash cards, you can have them laminated or cover them with clear contact paper.

STUDENT HANDOUTS.   Teachers have always used a variety of student handouts to assist them with the instructional process. Some of the more typical types of hand-

Computer-generated handouts are easily enhanced with meaningful clip art.

outs include directions for assignments, information sheets, and recording sheets. Each type of handout is briefly discussed here.

Directions for assignments.

Handouts with the directions for assignments provide students with the step-by-step procedures for completing an assignment. There are two primary benefits for using a directions handout: (1) it helps the teacher clarify what students will actually do during the activity, and (2) it reduces the number of student questions about what to do.

Information sheets.

Information sheets provide students with various types of content. This can include information downloaded from the Web, information taken from several sources, or information that is rewritten for a certain grade level. Teachers can modify information downloaded from the Web by copying the information and pasting it into a word processing document. The teacher can then delete what is not going to be emphasized in a lesson, and reformat the remaining information to make it more readable. The reformatting can include changing the style or size of the font, changing the line spacing and changing the margins. Teachers who

teach younger children can also rewrite the information so it is more easily understood by their students. As teachers create information handouts, they may want to
combine information from several sources into one handout. This might include information from the Web, an encyclopedia, or a book. It is important to cite the references for each source.

Recording sheets. The recording sheets can be used for recording what students
write in their own words and to record information from experiments, surveys,
books, or the Web. Another form of recording sheet is a storyboard that is used to
plan each page in a slide show or each card in a HyperStudio Stack. An example
of a storyboard is seen in Figure 14-11. Mindy Morris combined a directions sheet
with a recording sheet for her lesson on Monarch butterflies. An example of this
sheet is seen in Figure 14-12.

When creating handouts with the computer, the following guidelines will help
make the handouts more useful. Also refer to Chapter 11 for more suggestions.

1. Use clear, easy to understand language.

2. Place information into a numbered or bulleted list when possible.

3. Leave lots of white space.

4. Use graphics for clarification of content as well as for motivation and fun.

5. Leave ample room for student responses.

6. Provide lines for student responses (see Power Tip on page 340).

Figure 14-11   Sample Storyboard

Figure 14-12   Monarch Butterflies Handout

Metamorphosis of a Monarch Butterfly

Name _____

Directions:
Complete the sequence below by writing what happens for event 2, 3, and 4.

EVENT 1 . . . A Monarch butterfly lays an egg

EVENT 2 . . .

EVENT 3 . . .

EVENT 4 . . .

Now use the information you just wrote to write a narrative explaining the metamorphosis process from the butterfly's point of view. Also, use facts in your narrative that you learned from the story *Monarchs*. Write your rough draft below, then use ClarisWorks to write your final copy. Send the final copy to me via email. Use the back if needed.

EDUCATIONAL SOFTWARE

In addition to teachers making their own instructional materials with the aid of a computer, numerous educational software packages are also readily available. In fact, there is an overabundance of these computer-based resources. For this reason, teachers need to know how to determine the instructional value of educational software.

TYPES OF EDUCATIONAL SOFTWARE

Educational software presents the student with content and/or activities focused on increasing a particular type of knowledge or skill. There are four main types of educational software:

Drill and Practice—provides student with practice and feedback of information that has been previously taught in another session.

Power Tip ▲▲▲

Using Tabs to Create Lines

Follow these steps to create lines for student responses:

1. Open a word processing document.
2. Enter the introductory material
3. Determine where the lines will be placed.
4. From the **Format** menu, select **Rulers**.
5. In the **Rulers** dialog box, select **Text** as the **Ruler Type**.

6. Use the mouse to select and drag the right justified tab marker to the place on the ruler that you want your line to end. For example, if the right margin is set at 7 inches, you would place your tab close to 7 inches (see Figure 14-13).

Figure 14-13   Tab Markers

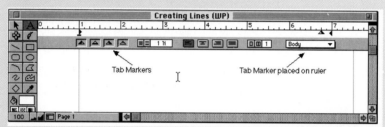

7. After the tab marker is placed on the ruler, double click the marker to open the Tab dialog box (see Figure 14-14). Notice that the **Alignment** is **Right** and set for **6.75** inches. For the **Fill**, select the solid line, then click **OK**.

8. Make sure the cursor is in the place where you want the line to begin, then press the **Tab** key and a line will automatically be filled-in from the beginning of the cursor to 6.75 inches.

Figure 14-14   Tab Dialog Box

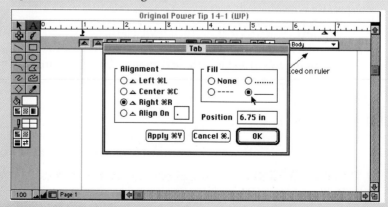

continued

9. If you want more than one line for a response, press **Return** and then press the **Tab** key again. This time the line will go from the left margin to 6.75 inches. For example, if this were a recording sheet for student responses, the line could begin at the end of this sentence and extend one more line:

_____

_____

10. You can also choose the other types of fill for a different look. Below are the three types of fill:

Dashes - - - - - - - - - - - - - - -

Dots . . . .

Solid _____

Tutorials—present students with new information and provide practice and feedback.

Learning Games—most provide drill-and-practice of previously learned material, although some teach new information. The difference between games and drill-and-practice is the competitive and motivational nature of the software.

Simulations—present simulated, real-world situations in which students engage in problem-solving and decision-making processes.

SOFTWARE EVALUATION

There are two things you need to know to be able to determine the educational value of software: the criteria for judging the software effectiveness and how to find or conduct software reviews and evaluations.

SOFTWARE EVALUATION CRITERIA.
Four types of evaluation criteria for educational software are consistently found (Gill, Dick, Reiser, & Zahner, 1992; Hannafin, & Peck 1988; Hubbard, 1992; Rickenberg, 1996):

* accuracy
* effective instructional strategies
    * learner control of various program features (sound, pace, sequence, etc.)
    * variety of appropriate feedback
    * maintains student interest
* meets instructional objectives
* ease of use
    * technical quality
    * precise and consistent directions

SOFTWARE REVIEWS.
Reviews of educational software can be found at a variety of locations on the Web. These reviews are conducted by professional reviewers, teachers, parents, children, university faculty, and graduate students (Gill et al.,

1992; Rickenberg, 1996). A listing of some of these review sites is seen in Figure 14-15.

CONDUCTING A SOFTWARE EVALUATION.   Software evaluations can provide some background information about the effectiveness of a piece of educational software. However, for teachers to be confident that the software will meet the needs of their

Figure 14-15   Software Review Sites

SMARTKID EDUCATIONAL SOFTWARE REVIEWS
Educational software for home, family, parents, and schools; great reviews of CD-ROMs, books, toys, and Internet sites.
http://www.smartkid.com/default.htm

AskERIC INFOGUIDE
AskERIC InfoGuide. Education Software.
http://ericir.syr.edu/cgibin/markup_infoguides/Alphabetical_List_of_InfoGuides/Education_Software-5.96

GET THERE FROM HERE (TEACHERS RESOURCES)
[Teachers' Staffroom] [Students Only] [P&C Centre] Subjects. Teachers. Net Pals. Fun. Organizations. Vendors. Hot Sites. Sites. News. Search. Reviews.
http://www.schoolpc.acp.com.au/sites/teachers

EXCELLENT EDUCATION REFERENCES AND TUTORIALS
Excellent Education References and Tutorials. Tutorials. Map tutorial. The National Atlas on SchoolNet Teaching Module—Fundamentals of Cartography.
http://www.kaleidoscapes.com/1educate.html

EDUCATIONAL SOFTWARE—INTERNET RESOURCES FROM THE MINING COMPANY
Educational Software reviews.
http://edsoftware.miningco.com/msub1.htm

SUPERKIDS EDUCATIONAL SOFTWARE REVIEW
SuperKids Educational Software Review provides reviews of children's software by parents, teachers, and kids.
http://www.superkids.com/aweb/pages/text.html

SOFTWARE REVIEWS AND EVALUATIONS
The Summit County Instructional Software Preview Center. Software Reviews and Evaluations.
http://www.summit.k12.oh.us/site/tech/preview/review.htm

SCHOOL HOUSE
Welcome to the School House! Educational software reviews, feature articles, cartoons, cool sites, downloads and more! Copyright © 1996 InfoMedia.
http://www.worldvillage.com/wv/school/html/scholalt.htm

particular students, they may want to conduct their own evaluation. This process can involve two approaches. The first involves the teacher using his or her experience and expertise to evaluate the software. A form for conducting a software evaluation is seen in Figure 14-16.

The second approach is proposed by Reiser and Dick (1990) and looks at whether or not students can actually learn from the software. This approach takes more time and teacher involvement than filling in an evaluation form. However, the benefits of collecting student performance and attitude data outweigh the effort when considering the purchase of an expensive educational software package to integrate into your curriculum. The criteria for software selection and the evaluation steps can be seen in Figure 14-17.

Figure 14-16   Software Evaluation Form

Software Evaluation Form

Title: _____

Type of Software: ❑ Drill and Practice   ❑ Tutorial   ❑ Simulation
                   ❑ Game   ❑ Other _____

Subject Area: _____

Grade Level: _____

Instructional Objectives:
_____
_____
_____
_____

Rating..

Accuracy	❑ High	❑ Medium	❑ Low
Effective instructional strategies	❑ High	❑ Medium	❑ Low
Learner control of various features	❑ High	❑ Medium	❑ Low
(sound, pace, sequence, etc.)			
Variety of appropriate feedback	❑ High	❑ Medium	❑ Low
Maintains student interest	❑ High	❑ Medium	❑ Low
Meets instructional objectives	❑ High	❑ Medium	❑ Low
Ease of use	❑ High	❑ Medium	❑ Low
Technical quality	❑ High	❑ Medium	❑ Low
Precise and consistent directions	❑ High	❑ Medium	❑ Low

Best Features _____
_____

Worst Features _____
_____

NOTES _____
_____
_____

Figure 14-17   Software Evaluation: Student Performance and Attitudes

---

CRITERIA FOR SELECTING SOFTWARE
Software that is to be evaluated with this process needs to meet the following two criteria:

1. Highly rated by commercial or educational sources
2. Has identifiable instructional objectives

EVALUATION STEPS FOR THE TEACHER

1. Review software with a form similar to the one in Figure 14-16.
2. Develop the following tests to measure attainment of instructional objectives:
   1. pretest
   2. posttest
   3. retention test
3. Develop student attitude survey that measures:
   1. enjoyment
   2. recommendation to other students
   3. description of what students thought they were supposed to learn
4. Administer pretest to whole class to identify a high, medium, and low achiever for the field-test.
5. Field test the software with the three identified students.
6. Administer the posttest and attitude survey to the three students.
7. Administer the retention test two weeks after the posttest.
8. Review the results, preferably with colleagues, and make decision.

Adapted from the Evaluating Instructional Software Model (Reiser & Dick, 1990).

AT THE CLASSROOM'S DOORSTEP
▲▲▲

QUESTIONS TEACHERS ASK

It takes me quite a bit of time to create my handouts on the computer. Is it really worth the extra time? When you first create computer documents, it does take longer than it would for you to create them by hand. Your work time is not lost, though, because your document is saved electronically. The next time you use the materials, you will probably only need minor modifications. Plus, as you work with the computer over time, you will gain speed and accuracy.

There is a lot of controversy about using educational games or drill-and-practice software, but my students really enjoy these packages. Is there a way I can use them in a more meaningful way? One of the best ways to use different educational software packages is to review the packages to determine what skills or knowledge they teach or reinforce. Once you know the educational benefits, carefully plan when and how to integrate them into your curriculum. Rather than having students arbitrarily choose packages, designate specific ones for specific lessons. Many times you may also want your students to complete just one section or lesson within a package. It is also helpful to plan pre- and post-activities to reinforce what has been learned.

References
▲▲▲

Dorsey-Davis, J. D., Ross, S. M., & Morrison, G. R. (1991). The role of rewording and context personalization in the solving of mathematical word problems. *Journal of Educational Psychology, 83*, 61–68.

Frye, H. (1975). For visual teaching aids: Why local production? *Viewpoints, 50*, 51–57.

Gill, B. J., Dick, W., Reiser, R. A., & Zahner, J. E. (1992). A new model for evaluating instructional software. *Educational Technology, 32*(3), 39–44.

Hannafin, M. J. & Peck, K. L. (1988). *The design, development, and evaluation of instructional software*. New York: Macmillan Publishing Co.

Hubbard, P. (1992). Software evaluation guide. [Online]. Available: http://www.owlnet.rice.edu/~ling417/guide.html

Postelthwait, S. N., Novak, J., Murray, H. (1972). *The audio-tutorial approach to learning*. Minneapolis: Burgess.

Reiser, R. A. & Dick, W. (1990). Evaluating instructional software. *Educational Technology Research and Development, 38*(3), 43–50.

Rickenberg, D. (1996). Software evaluation and selection page for educators. [Online]. Available: http://www.sp.utoledo.edu/~lelsie/StudF96/dricken/software.html

Ross, S. M. & Anand, P. (1987). Computer-based strategy for personalizing verbal problems in teaching mathematics. *Educational Communication and Technology Journal, 35*, 151–162.

CHAPTER 15
Computers as a Tool for Teachers

▶ Introduction

In the time of B.C.C. (before computers and calculators), teachers regularly sat at their desks absorbed in a task that tested their patience and compassion. They were adding all homework grades, test scores, and participation grades and subtracting the demerits. The reason they were "testy" was that they were doing the calculations by hand. And, about the time they had summed 43 of the 44 scores for a single student, someone would invariably interrupt them with a question such as "Do we need to spell all the words correctly?" It seemed that adding all those scores took about five weeks, which meant teachers had about one week of relief before they started the process again. Today, teachers can rapidly determine the grades of a class by using a computer. With similar agility and speed, a teacher can prepare a personalized letter to each parent detailing a student's progress (or lack thereof) on official looking paper along with a computer-printed envelop. During the past 25 years, we have heard many predictions of how computers will affect learning in the classroom. It appears, however, that the power of a computer in a teacher's hands has often been overlooked.

In the first 14 chapters of this book, we have focused on how to integrate computers into the curriculum with a focus on how students can use the computer as a tool. We now want to shift our focus to how teachers can use computers as a management productivity tool.

▶ Computer Skills Used in This Chapter

Database creation and manipulation
Word processing
Mail merge
Spreadsheet and formula creation
Creation of graphics
Printing labels
Web page creation

▶ Key Topics

Computers for Classroom Management
Electronic Gradebooks
Lesson Plans
Student Groups
Seating Charts
Communication with Parents
Mail Merge Letters
Newsletters
Web Pages
Classroom Materials
Name Tags and Folder Labels
Coupons
Certificates

COMPUTERS FOR CLASSROOM MANAGEMENT

▲▲▲

One of our first uses of computers was to create an "electronic" gradebook using a spreadsheet. This gradebook saved us hours of calculations and recalculations with a calculator, plus it enabled us to create graphs and to easily weight various grades. After we learned that computers were also a valuable tool for teachers, we found and learned of many ways a computer can improve the productivity of a teacher. In the following sections, we will describe how teachers can use computers for classroom management, communication, and creation of classroom materials.

One of the major complaints we hear from teachers in our courses is about the paperwork and management tasks required of them. Once these teachers learn how to use computer tools for classroom management, they find that they have more time to spend on their "teaching" duties. In this section, we will describe how to use computer tools to create an electronic gradebook, lesson plans, a system for managing classroom groupings, and a seating chart.

ELECTRONIC GRADEBOOKS

There are several commercial, shareware, and freeware gradebooks available to track and calculate grades. We like using a spreadsheet, however, since it is an application already found on most computers, and it allows us flexibility to design our own gradebook. Let's examine how to create a spreadsheet gradebook that can weight grades and calculate total scores.

With either a spreadsheet or gradebook software, teachers can easily keep track of student progress.

In our hypothetical gradebook, we have three homework assignments, six tests, and a final test that counts twice as much as the other tests and homework. After much negotiating with students, we agreed to drop the lowest of the six test grades (see Figure 15-1). For those of us who never really understood math after the third grade, this task might seem impossible and force us to reconsider simply adding all the scores and calculating an average. With a spreadsheet, we can complete these calculations *faster* than we can with a calculator. The following steps describe how to create the spreadsheet.

Figure 15-1   Creating the Basic Spreadsheet

A	**B**	**C**	**D**	**E**	**F**	**G**	**H**	**I**	**J**	**K**	**L**	**M**	**N**	**O**
1 Second Grading Period 1997-1998														
2														
3 Last Nam	First Name	Homework			Tests						Test	Final	Total	Grade
4		#1	#2	#3	#1	#2	#3	#4	#5	#6	Points	Test	Points	
5 Smith	Tom	8	9	6	76	78	56	87	83	90		76		
6 Jones	Beverly	9	9	9	82	88	86	96	99	100		91		
7 Fowler	Patrina	10	8	9	100	100	98	92	100	100		96		
8														

1. Start the spreadsheet by creating and labeling a column for the student name and each grade entry (see Figure 15-1). To resize several columns, select the contiguous columns and then select the **Column width** item from the **Format** menu (see left half of Figure 15-2). Enter the width of the column and click **OK**. You can also place the cursor over a single column separator and drag the column to the desired width (see right half of Figure 15-2).

Figure 15-2   Changing the Column Width

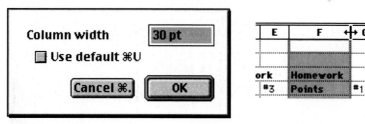

2. Next, you need to determine the total points for the six tests while dropping the lowest test score. You can create one formula to complete this task. First, calculate the total test points by adding all *six* tests. You can use a built-in function in the spreadsheet, **SUM**, to do this calculation. The test scores for Tom Smith are in columns F through K in the fifth row. To calculate the sum of the scores, the function is written as **SUM(F5..K5)**. Second, subtract the lowest test score from this sum of the six test scores. Again, you can use a built-in function, **MIN**, which identifies the lowest test score. This can then be subtracted from the sum. The function to find the minimum test score is **MIN(F5...K5)**. Finally, subtract the minimum

score from the sum of all six test scores (see Figure 15-3) to complete the formula.

Figure 15-3   Using Formulas for Calculations

		Gradebook (SS)	

L5	× ✓ =SUM(F5..K5)-MIN(F5..K5)										
	A	**B**	**C**	**D**	**E**	**F**	**G**	**H**	**I**	**J**	**K**	**L**
1	Second Grading Period 1997-1998											
2												
3	Last Nam	First Name	Homework					Tests				Test
4			#1	#2	#3	#1	#2	#3	#4	#5	#6	Points
5	Smith	Tom	8	9	6	76	78	56	87	83	90	414
6	Jones	Beverly	9	9	9	82	88	86	96	99	100	
7	Fowler	Patrina	10	8	9	100	100	98	92	100	100	

3. You can use another feature of the spreadsheet to duplicate the formula for each student. First, select all the rows in the column starting with the cell containing the formula. Second, select **Fill Down** from the **Calculate** menu and ClarisWorks will correctly copy the formula to each cell.

4. Now you are ready to calculate the total points for each student with another formula. This step involves summing the homework scores **SUM(C5..E5)**, adding the total points from the five tests (minus the lowest) which we calculated in column **L**, and multiplying the final exam (column **M**) by 2 since it counts twice as much. The formula for the **Total Points** column (column **N**) for the first student is **(SUM(C5..E5)+L5+M5*2)**. Remember, each formula must start with an equal sign (=) in the spreadsheet (see Figure 15-4).

Figure 15-4   Calculating Total Points

		Gradebook (SS)	

N5	× ✓ =(SUM(C5..E5)+L5+M5*2)												
	A	**B**	**C**	**D**	**E**	**F**	**G**	**H**	**I**	**J**	**K**	**L**	**M**	**N**	**O**
1	Second Grading Period 1997-1998														
2															
3	Last Nam	First Name	Homework					Tests				Test	Final	Total	Grade
4			#1	#2	#3	#1	#2	#3	#4	#5	#6	Points	Test	Points	
5	Smith	Tom	80	69	86	76	78	56	87	83	90	414	76	801	
6	Jones	Beverly	92	96	98	82	88	86	96	99	100	469	91	937	
7	Fowler	Patrina	100	85	99	100	100	98	92	100	100	498	96	974	

5. In the **Grade** column we can either insert a letter grade based on the points, or we can convert the points to a 100-point scale. To convert the points, you will need to divide the value in column **M** by 10 (see Figure 15-5).

Figure 15-5   Converting Total Points to a 100-Point Scale

		Gradebook (SS)	

O5	× ✓ =N5/10												
	A	**B**	**C**	**D**	**E**	**F**	**G**	**H**	**I**	**J**	**K**	**L**	**M**	**N**	**O**
1	Second Grading Period 1997-1998														
2															
3	Last Nam	First Name	Homework					Tests				Test	Final	Total	Grade
4			#1	#2	#3	#1	#2	#3	#4	#5	#6	Points	Test	Points	
5	Smith	Tom	80	69	86	76	78	56	87	83	90	414	76	801	80.1
6	Jones	Beverly	92	96	98	82	88	86	96	99	100	469	91	937	93.7
7	Fowler	Patrina	100	85	99	100	100	98	92	100	100	498	96	974	97.4

6. Last, you want to round the total points in the **Grade** column to a whole number. Select column **N**. Select **Numbers** from the **Format** menu. Click **Fixed** for the number option and enter 0 in the **Precision** field (see Figure 15-6). The spreadsheet will round the values to a whole number.

Figure 15-6 Setting the Number Format

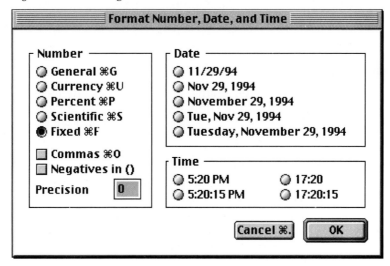

You can use functions and create formulas to do a variety of calculations in a spreadsheet gradebook. Similarly, the gradebook can be quite simple and just calculate the average of each student's homework or test scores.

Power Tip ▲▲▲ *Weighting Scores*

Some teachers like to weight the various scores so that all the scores add up to 100 points. For instance, in our example gradebook we might want the homework problems to account for 30 percent of the grade, the six tests as 40 percent of the grade, and the final test as 30 percent. You can create a formula for each of these weightings. To calculate the weighted score for the homework, you would sum the three scores, divide by 3 (to reduce to a 100-point scale), and then multiply by 30 percent. The formula is =(SUM(C3..E5)/3)*0.3. The formula for the weighted tests (after dropping the lowest) is =(SUM(F5..K5)-MIN(F5..K5))/5*0.4. The formula for weighting the final test is M5*.3. After calculating the weighted scores, you will need to add them for the total points.

Lesson Plans

Another time-consuming management task is formatting lesson plans according to guidelines from the school or school district. One approach to creating lesson plans is to use a drawing application or publishing application such as Classroom Publisher. You can create a custom format with either application, or you can use a template. The template in Figure 15-7 was created in a ClarisWorks Draw document. You can print a blank template and complete it by hand, or you can create text fields and type the information. The advantage of typing the information is that the plan is easy to modify in the future.

Student Groups

If you are using cooperative or collaborative groups in your classroom, you are probably aware of the effort required to create the groups and keep track of the group members. A database can help you with both of these tasks. For example,

Figure 15-7   Creating a Lesson Plan Template

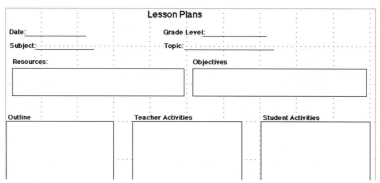

Power Tip ▲▲▲   *Using Text Frames*

If you create a template or stationery file, you can use text frames to create the appropriate sized text fields for typing your lesson information. In the draw document, select the **Text** tool and then select the **Frames Links** item from the **Options** menu. You can now drag an appropriate sized word processing frame. Select the arrow pointer from the tools and select the word processing frame. Now, select the color palette for the pen line and select black (or some other color) to frame the field. You can now save the draw document as a stationery file that will always open as a new document.

You can also create a variety of frames (text or word processing, spreadsheet, paint, draw, and graph) for students to use in a formatted document.

(Based on an article by Pavley, 1997).

Figure 15-8   Managing Student Groups

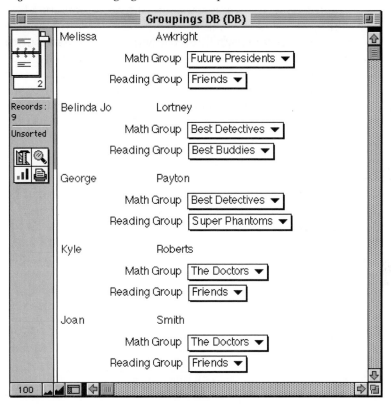

we created a database that had pop-up menus for the math and reading group fields (see Figure 15-8). After entering the students' names, we assigned each to a group. By sorting on one group, we have a listing of the students by grouping. If there is a problem in a group or we need to make a change in the group structures, we can use the database to select a different group. We can also create a variety of different report formats to print either all the groups or only members of selected groups.

Another use of this database is to add a third field for classroom responsibilities (e.g., librarian, messenger, clean up, etc.). By selecting the next item in the pop-up menu for each student, we can ensure an equitable rotation through all tasks. Another option is to add an item for each day of the week and print it on Monday morning (see Figure 15-9).

We were able to use one database for both the responsibilities and groupings. A number of report formats (see Chapter 9) were created so that only the responsibilities were displayed in the Responsibility Report, only the reading groups were displayed in the Reading Groups report, etc., to create the needed reports from one database.

Figure 15-9   Posting of Classroom Responsibilities

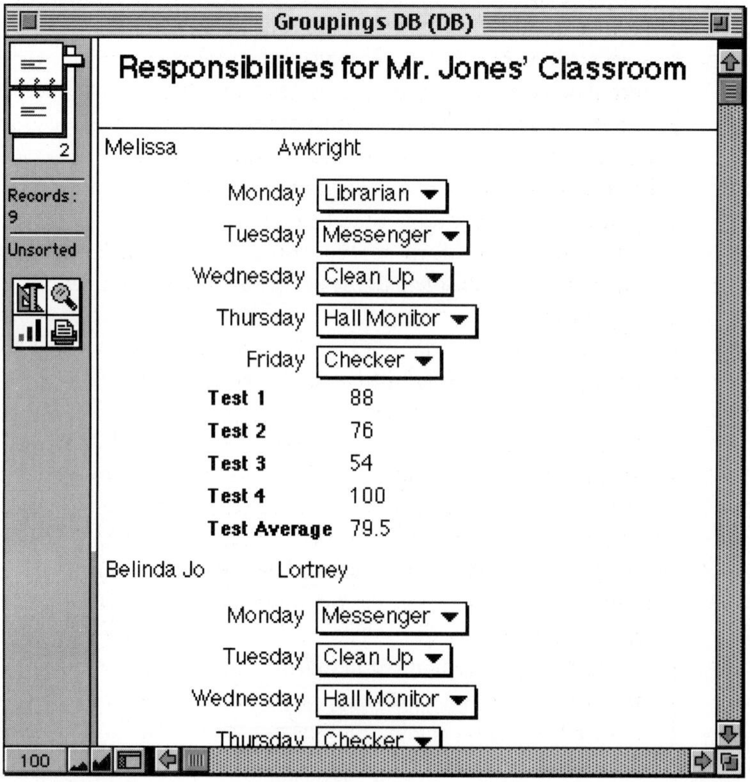

FRAN'S DIARY
▲▲▲

I couldn't exist in the classroom without my computer. I use it for all the classroom management tasks that I do on any given day. One of the first things that I do when I get a new class is to put all of the student information in a database. I use this student database in some format every day. It does take some time on the front end to create this database, but it is well worth the effort. I use this database all year for everything from creating labels to making telephone lists to writing mail merge letters informing parents of student progress to keeping anecdotal records on my students.

Another task that has been made easier by using the computer is lesson planning. I use a lesson plan template to create my lesson plans. I make this template at the beginning of the school year and block in special classes, lunch time, and recess times. What is nice about doing lesson plans on the computer is that they can be easily updated at the end of the day to reflect what has taken place that day. It is easy to move items within the lesson plan with the cut and paste functions. I don't have to worry about a substitute coming in and not knowing what to do. My lesson plans are always up-to-date. My plan book also looks neat and organized as I do not have to draw lines and arrows to indicate the changes that I might have made.

I keep my grades in an electronic gradebook. By entering my grades into an electronic gradebook as I grade papers, I always know how my students are progressing and exactly where my students stand in relation to each other. It does take a little time to enter the grades, but it makes my job easier during reporting periods. All I have to do is open my disk and record my students' grades on the grade sheet.

I also use the computer to create a variety of incentives, everything from certificates to money. One year, I created Golden Dragon statues. I used a clip art dragon and printed it on some card stock. I spray painted the dragons gold, cut them out, and attached them to wooden blocks. These became the Golden Dragons, similar to the Oscars. During the last week of school, we produced a folktale video. Each group of students was given a folktale which they had to write a script for. They also had to create the scenery, props, and costumes. Then, they performed their folktale plays in front of the video camera. We invited our parents to view this video on the last day of school. We cleaned the room and pushed the desks against the walls. We put all of the chairs in rows just like a real movie theater. We even had bags of popcorn and soft drinks for our parents. After the video, I presented Golden Dragon awards for the best actress, best actor, best girl costume . . . I had a special award for all 25 students! It was a great way to end the year. Every student was allowed to shine and everyone had fun! The parents enjoyed the video, the students had a great time performing and then watching themselves, and I was happy that I could give every student a special award. We don't always know the effect that this kind of activity has on our students. Several years after I had given the awards, I gave one of my ex-students a ride home. We talked about some of the things that she remembered about being in my class. We talked about he folktale plays and getting the Golden Dragons. She told me that she still had her Golden Dragon on her bookshelf. She said it reminded her of the great year she had in third grade.

SEATING CHARTS

Another challenge almost as great as managing the student groupings is managing the seating arrangement and learning names. A drawing program like ClarisWorks is useful for creating a seating chart (see Figure 15-10). We drew the individual chairs and arranged them on the page with the teacher desk as a reference. Once

Figure 15-10   Creating a Seating Chart

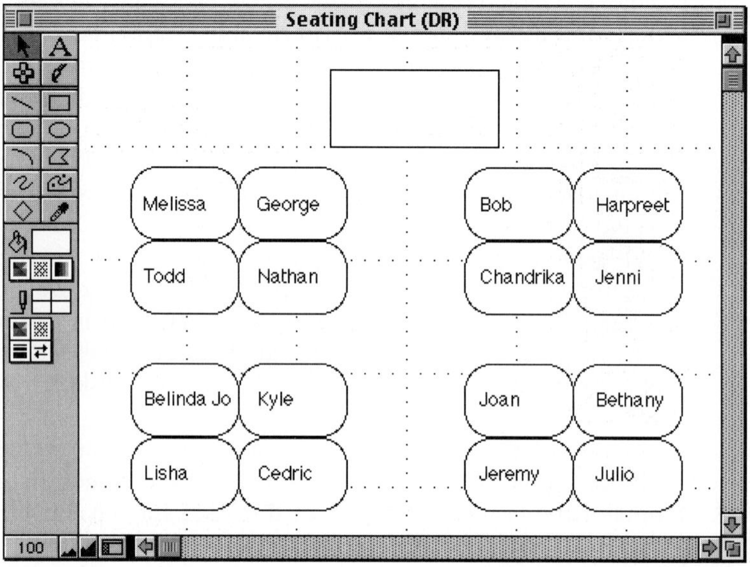

the seats were arranged, we grouped the seats and desk so they would not move. Then, each student's name was typed on the appropriate seat. We can move the names around without disturbing the seating arrangement. Of course, if we want to reorganize the room, we must ungroup the seats and move them to their new arrangement. Seating charts are particularly useful if you have a difficult time remembering student names, or have multiple classes as in the upper grades.

COMMUNICATION WITH PARENTS

Communicating with parents is an important task for the smooth operation of a classroom. As a teacher, you will need to inform them of their child's progress and events in the classroom. In this section, we will examine how you can make your communication with parents through personalized letters, newsletters, and web pages more efficient.

MAIL MERGE LETTERS

Personalized letters reporting each student's progress are helpful tools for communicating to parents. By combining the features of word processing and a database, you can create a variety of personalized letters and mailing labels for each family in your classroom. The following example illustrates how you can create three custom letters (exceptional, average, needs improvement) based on a student's progress.

1. Using the classroom database that includes the math and reading groups and the classroom responsibilities, you can create four new fields for three math tests and the average of the tests (see Figure 15-11). (We have also created fields for the parent's names and addresses in our database.)

Figure 15-11 Specifying Field Types

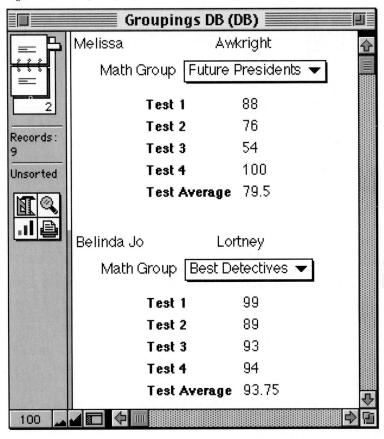

2. Notice that each of the Test fields' type is a number. If text was used as the field type, ClarisWorks could not calculate the average. The test average field type is a calculation. ClarisWorks will display the **Formula for Field** dialog (see Figure 15-12) when a calculation field is created.

3. To enter the fields for the average, delete all the example data between the parentheses (e.g., number1, number2, . . .). Next, click on **Test 1** and then type a comma. Click on each additional field name and separate each with comma. Click **OK** when all the fields are entered.

4. The average is automatically calculated as you enter or change the individual test scores.

5. The next step is to create a mail merge letter (see Chapter 14) for each of our performance groups (see Figure 15-13). You can create specific information in the letter for each group such as adding, "Please make an appointment so that we can discuss how we might improve <student's

Figure 15-12   Creating a Calculation Field

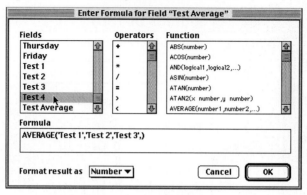

Figure 15-13   Creating the Mail Merge Letter

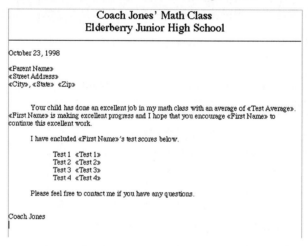

name>'s grade in math" to the "needs improvement group" for the students with the lowest average.

6. The next step is to find the records for the exceptional, average, and needs improvement letters. When you select the **Match Records** item from the **Organize** menu, ClarisWorks will display the **Formula** dialog again (see Figure 15-14). You want to select students who have an average of 90 or higher. The formula is entered as 'Test Average'>=90. When you click **OK,** only those students with an average of 90 or higher are selected. Select **Hide Unselected** from the **Organize** menu to hide all other records. By hiding the unselected records (those with an average of less than 90), you can print just the selected records.

Databases are an excellent way to keep track of students' phone numbers, addresses, and learning needs.

Figure 15-14   Entering a Match Records Formula

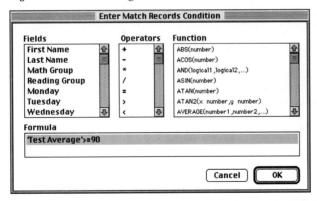

7. To print another group of students, select **Show All Records** from the **Organize** menu and enter another formula. The following formula will select the next two groups:

   AND('Test Average'<90 , 'Test Average'>=70)

   'Test Average'<70

8. Each time you change the formula, hide the unselected records and print a mail merge letter.

You can create elaborate mail merge letters by having a field that includes his/her/he/she, etc., to further personalize the letters. Similarly, you can create a basic letter that just reports the student's grades and average.

Power Tip ▲▲▲   *Tracking Student Needs*

By the end of the day, it is almost impossible to remember which student needs lunch money, who needs a new notebook, who is missing their crayons, etc. To help you remember, you can create a database of all your students. Then, create a **Checkbox** field for each item the students need (e.g., lunch money, pencils, etc.).

Students can check the box when they need a particular item.

On a given day, you can print individual reports that students can take home indicating what they are missing. When they bring the indicated items to school, they can change the database!

NEWSLETTERS

As parents, we found (and still find) the weekly newsletter essential for helping us prepare our children for each day of school. Classroom newsletters can take the form of a weekly announcement sheet or a monthly report or calendar. A drawing program such as ClarisWorks or Classroom Publisher will help you create a template for use with the newsletter. Classroom Publisher will automatically create a calendar with the appropriate dates so that you only need to fill in the information. You can also create a template (see Figure 15-15) for a weekly newsletter that alerts

Figure 15-15   Creating a Template for a Weekly Newsletter

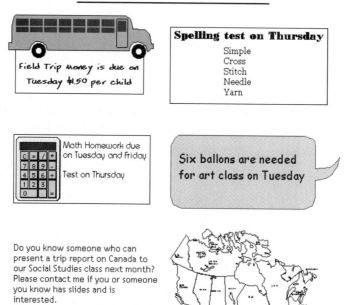

Ms. Bailey's Weekly Newsletter

Field Trip Money is due on Tuesday $1.50 per child

Spelling test on Thursday
Simple
Cross
Stitch
Needle
Yarn

Math Homework due on Tuesday and Friday
Test on Thursday

Six ballons are needed for art class on Tuesday

Do you know someone who can present a trip report on Canada to our Social Studies class next month? Please contact me if you or someone you know has slides and is interested.

parents to important events and activities. Using a consistent format will help parents easily recognize important events.

Web Pages

Another way to communicate with parents (and students) is a web page. In addition to publishing student products (see Chapter 11), you can also publish information about your classroom for parents. You can publish information that you include in your newsletter as well as homework information on your web site. If your web server administrator is cooperative, you can create a special section for parents that requires a password. We advise against publishing confidential information, however. You may want to keep some information from others such as times and places of field trips.

One limitation to using a web page instead of a newsletter is access to the Internet. You will need to provide equitable access to the classroom information for all parents. Thus, you may need to provide the information in both a printed newsletter and as a web newsletter.

Classroom Materials

▲▲▲

Although we would probably vote the electronic gradebook as the greatest time saver for teachers, using a computer to produce classroom materials is a very close second. The beginning of the school year for students is always unique, but much of it is repetitive for teachers. You can save time by creating templates and reusing old documents to accomplish many of the tasks that you must do each week, six weeks, or year. Let's examine how to create name tags and folder labels, coupons, and certificates for classroom use.

Name Tags and Folder Labels

Once you have created your database of student names for *any* purpose, you can use it to create name tags and folder labels. For example, if you are going on a field trip with young children, you can create a name tag that has emergency information for a child who manages to wander from the group. The following steps describe how to create a name tag and can also be used to create any type of label (see Chapter 9 for more details on creating custom layouts) in a database.

1. Select **New Layout** from the **Layout** menu and ClarisWorks will display the **New Layout** dialog (see Figure 15-16). Click **Labels** and select the type of label you are using from the pop-up menu. If your label is not listed in the list, select **Custom** and enter the correct sizes. Enter a name (e.g., Name Tags) and click **OK**.

2. Select **Layout** from the **Layout** menu so that you can create the appropriate layout (see Figure 15-17). You can add or delete fields from your layout, add additional text with the text tool, and add rules or graphics.

3. The trick to printing labels is to run a test print on a plain piece of paper. Then, place a sheet of labels behind the printed page and check the align-

Figure 15-16   Selecting a Label Format

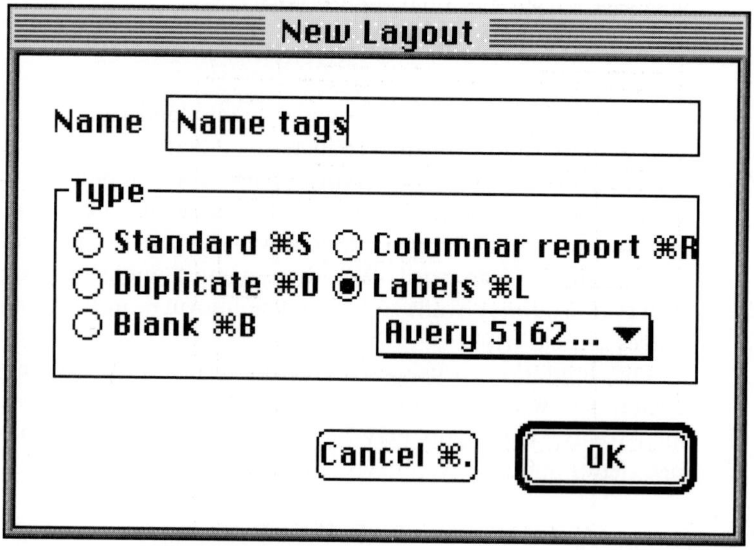

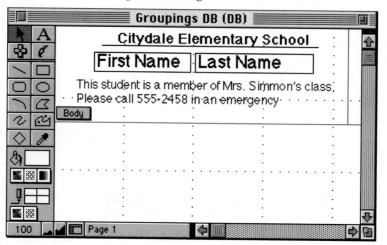

Figure 15-17   Creating a Name Tag

ment of the labels (see Figure 15-18). If they are off, make adjustments in either the label size or the document margins.

You can enhance your labels (and make them easily recognizable) by adding clip art and rules. The label layout is very similar to a draw document that allows you to add text and graphics, and to move them about within the boundaries of the label. Adding pictures to the labels can help you easily sort folders or notebooks by content area, groups, or other criteria.

Figure 15-18   Checking the Label Format

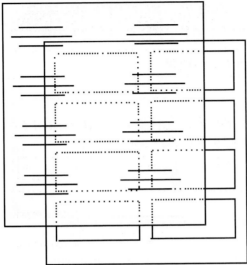

Coupons

Coupons or classroom dollars are a means of rewarding students. Students can exchange their coupons for special privileges, or use them to purchase services and goods. For example, you might create coupons that students can exchange for time to sit at the teacher's desk to do work, to be first in line, or for free reading time (see Figure 15-19). You can create coupons using a drawing program and

Figure 15-19   Creating a Coupon

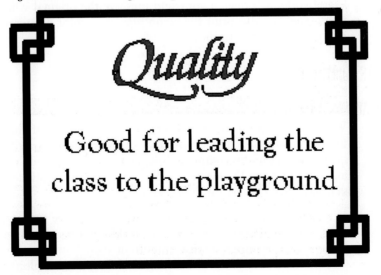

Figure 15-20   Creating a Certificate

pieces of clip art. The coupons can be printed with a color printer or on colored paper.

CERTIFICATES

Certificates are means of recognizing not only students for their achievement, but others who have contributed to your classroom. You can prepare certificates for a policeman, doctor, or pilot who visited your class as well as parents who have contributed books, materials, food, and time. You can create a certificate using clip art (see Figure 15-20), or use one of the templates provided with applications such as Classroom Publisher.

Once you have created the certificate, you can save it as a stationery file so that ClarisWorks will open a copy and preserve the original when you make modifications. You can also print the certificates on a color printer, color paper, or vellum to enhance its attractiveness.

AT THE CLASSROOM'S DOORSTEP
▲▲▲
QUESTIONS TEACHERS ASK

Where can I obtain clip art? There are many sources of clip art ranging from free to inexpensive CDs to web sites that offer clip art on specific themes. Some of the mail order computer companies often have special pricing on clip art CDs. Searching the web using the keyword "clip art" will also produce a number of web sites that have free clip art for downloading.

Is it safe to use an electronic gradebook? There are two issues to consider. First, what would happen if you lost your disk? We encourage you to keep at least one (if not more) backups of your important files. You can also print a copy of your gradebook as a backup. The danger of losing your electronic gradebook is no greater than losing your paper-based gradebook. Second, can someone make changes to my gradebook? Yes, if they have access to your computer and files. One solution to protecting your gradebook is to keep it on a floppy (or several floppies) that are kept in a secure location. A somewhat less foolproof approach is to give it a name such as "Reading Lesson Plans." If you are using ClarisWorks 5.0, you can password protect your important files to keep others from opening them.

Is it practical to put information on my web page for parents? Fifteen years ago, we might have questioned the feasibility of having students and parents watch a videotape on proper school behavior. Ten years ago, we might have questioned two student groups from two different states collaborating on a project. Each teacher will need to determine the practicality of posting information for parents on the Web. Like VCRs, computers will eventually become commonplace in the home, and use of the Web and e-mail to and from parents will be a matter of daily life. Consider the possibility that someday you might be able to arrange a video conference between your classroom and the parents' offices. Taken a step further, someday Johnny will contact his parents via video conference and explain his misbehavior or missing homework!

REFERENCES
▲▲▲

Pavley, J. (1997). How to create activities for ClarisWorks for Kids—Part one. *ClarisWorks Journal, 6,* 12–15.

► APPENDIX

LEARNING TASKS AND COMPUTER FUNCTIONS

Learning Task	Computer Function
Alter, Change, Convert, Modify, Vary	Use a spreadsheet to alter the data to produce a different graph. Convert a picture to create a different perspective, meaning, etc. Modify a sentence to create an opposite meaning.
Analyze	Use a spreadsheet to determine the smallest, largest, middle, etc. Use a database to find the most or least common characteristics. Use a spreadsheet to make a graph or chart.
Appraise	Use a graph to determine the solution to problem. Use a spreadsheet to evaluate . . .
Arrange	Use a database to arrange the states by their order of entry into the Union. Use a spreadsheet to arrange the cells from smallest to largest. Use the drawing program to arrange pictures in correct sequence.
Assemble, Produce	Produce a drawing of how you would assemble the equipment for this experiment.
Assess	Use QuickTake Camera to compare and contrast. Use word processing to write an evaluation. Use word processing to create a survey or record data on a spreadsheet or database.
Calculate	Create a formula to calculate the area of these rectangles. Determine the average weight of five pumpkins.
Choose, Select, Categorize	Use a database to sort or match records according to the common characteristics. Use the database of the presidents and select all who served two terms. Categorize the states by their electoral vote in the last three elections.
Classify, Identify, Isolate, List, Recognize	Identify the plants in the database that have . . . Use a word processor to keep a list of your new words.
Collaborate, Cooperate, Contribute	Use e-mail to collaborate with other students at a distant location. Use a word processor to share ideas and conclusions with others.
Collect, Observe, Gather	Enter your data from the observation into the database. Observe how the line changes as you change the first variable. Use the Internet to gather information and data.

Learning Task	Computer Function
Combine, Match, Tabulate, Sequence	Use a spreadsheet to determine the most preferred drink and snack from your taste test. Determine how many perennials and annuals you have observed. Sequence the states according to their joining the Union.
Compare, Contrast, Differentiate, Discriminate, Relate	Compare last year's cookies sales to this year's cookie sales. Draw two pictures to help you differentiate between rotation and revolution. Use a spreadsheet with charts to show similarities and differences. Use a database to find common/uncommon characteristics. Use word processing to communicate similarities and differences. Use draw and copy to compare geometric shapes.
Deduce, Infer, Generalize	Use a database to analyze information to support generalizations. Based on the graph of the cookie sales for the last two years, how many will this class sell this year? Based on plants with similar characteristics in the database, how would you classify this example?
Describe, Outline, Paraphrase, Reconstruct, Rephrase	Use a word processor to outline the chapter. Paraphrase the information you found in the CD-ROM encyclopedia. Based on your research, write a story to reconstruct the events leading to the railroad strike.
Design, Plan	Create a drawing showing your plan for the house of tomorrow. Use the draw program to create a safe playground. Make a map of your neighborhood.
Diagram, Draw, Graph, Illustrate, Plot	Use a spreadsheet to make a chart. Use the digital camera to illustrate safety in the classroom. Use clip art/draw program to illustrate your newsletter.
Edit, Punctuate, Write, Report	Allow students to print their first drafts and then exchange with other students to proofread. Create a worksheet. Use spell check to correct spelling errors. Type a story and have members of the group proofread, make suggestions to clarify ideas, and edit the final copy. Gather information on a given topic and write a report.
Estimate, Predict, Formulate	Use a spreadsheet to manipulate data for estimations and predictions with graphs. Use a database to sort, categorize, and support predictions. Use a database to predict the basketball scores for the teams in the NBA. On a spreadsheet, write formulas for students to multiply, subtract, add, and divide the NBA scores. Use the Internet to have the students estimate how much they would spend at three different stores.

Learning Task	Computer Function
Intepret, Interpolate, Extend	Analyze data collected on the spreadsheet and determine which planet will show your lowest and highest weight. Determine how many years it will take to arrive at a planet going a designated speed and record that on a database and spreadsheet. Then calculate your age upon arrival. Use the digital camera to take pictures of an experiment in various stages. Use the pictures and presentations in class.
Judge	Use the Grolier CD-ROM encyclopedia to review periods of history such as the World Wars and decide or judge which had the greater impact on modern life.
Judge, Evaluate	Make a judgment based on data collected from CD-ROM encyclopedias, the Internet, books, and National Geographic animal software as to which animal should be adopted as a pet. Use word processing to prepare a written report justifying your position. Use charts to make comparisons for evaluations.
Plan	Write a letter about opening your own business. Draw a floor plan in the draw program. Use a spreadsheet to plan your daily expenditures.
Solve, Determine	Use a spreadsheet to determine the classroom with the most square feet. Use a spreadsheet and database to solve word problems. Use the spell check to check spelling. Determine the mean, mode, and median scores from a basketball game. Determine which graph will best show the results.
Synthesize	Write a report using word processing, a spreadsheet, and a database.
Verify	Use a spell checker to check your spelling words. Estimate math problems and then use a spreadsheet to verify the exact answers. Use databases to verify predictions.

This chart was prepared by teachers who participated in the 1996 Project SMART summer training at the Univerity of Memphis as part of a class exercise.

▶ INDEX